Augustus

k

=

2

- 5

T

Augustus

Image and Substance

Barbara Levick

Longman
is an imprint of

Harlow, England • London • New York • Boston • San Francisco • Toronto • Sydney • Singapore • Hong Kong
Tokyo • Seoul • Taipei • New Delhi • Cape Town • Madrid • Mexico City • Amsterdam • Munich • Paris • Milan

Pearson Education Limited

Edinburgh Gate
Harlow CM20 2JE
United Kingdom
Tel: +44 (0)1279 623623
Fax: +44 (0)1279 431059
Website: www.pearsoned.co.uk

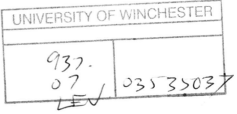

First edition published in Great Britain in 2010

© Pearson Education Limited 2010

The right of Barbara Levick to be identified as author of this work has been
asserted by her in accordance with the Copyright, Designs and Patents
Act 1988.

Pearson Education is not responsible for the content of third party internet sites.

ISBN: 978-0-582-89421-1

British Library Cataloguing in Publication Data
A CIP catalogue record for this book can be obtained from the British Library

Library of Congress Cataloging in Publication Data
Levick, Barbara.
   Augustus : image and substance / Barbara Levick. — 1st ed.
      p. cm.
   Includes bibliographical references and indexes.
   ISBN 978-0-582-89421-1 (pbk.)
   1. Augustus, Emperor of Rome, 63 B.C.–14 A.D.   2. Augustus, Emperor
of Rome, 63 B.C.–14 A.D.—Psychology.   3. Augustus, Emperor of Rome,
63 B.C.–14 A.D.—Influence.   4. Emperors—Rome—Biography.   5. Rome—
Kings and rulers—Biography.   6. Rome—History—Augustus, 30 B.C.–14 A.D.
7. Rome—Politics and government—30 B.C.–284 A.D.   8. Political leadership—
Rome—Case studies.   I. Title.
   DG279.L44 2010
   937$'$.07092—dc22

10 9 8 7 6 5 4 3 2 1
14 13 12 11 10

Typeset in 10/14 pt Galliard by 73
Printed in Malaysia, CTP-PJB

For Eileen M. Smith
A friend since our school-days
and still an admirer of Tony Blair

Contents

List of Maps and Figures

Acknowledgements

It would be a long note that set out and did justice to the various kinds of help, some involving scrutiny of part or of the whole MS, others giving access to unpublished works or papers only just out, that I have received. The notes where it is acknowledged cannot all reflect the extent of my debt. In alphabetical order I offer my warmest thanks to Karen Forsysth, Miriam Griffin, Geraldine Herbert-Brown, Olivier Hekster, Emily Hemelrijk, John Labur, Dario Mantovani, Greg Rowe, Celia Sisam, David Wardle, Anne Wilson and the late Rodney Otway. Their skill and learning are outdone only by their generosity. Years further back I became indebted successively to tutors and supervisors, such as A. J. Holladay, C. E. Stevens, C. H. V. Sutherland, E. W. Gray, and R. Syme, whose work I believe in, cherish and use. But most recently I should like to thank the staff at Pearson who have done so much for this work: in chronological order Christina Wipf Perry, Mari Shullaw, Jessica Harrison, Melanie Carter, Jenny Oates and Lynette Miller.

Barbara Levick

Publisher's Acknowledgements

We are grateful to the following for permission to reproduce copyright material:

Oxford University Press for Figure 1, from Syme, R., *The Augustan Family* (OUP, 1989) – figure originally from *The Roman Revolution* (1939); the Trustees of the British Museum for Figures 2, 4 and 7; akg-images Ltd for Figures 3, 5, 6, 8, 9, 12, 14, 15, 17, 19, 20 and 21; Bibliothèque Nationale de France, Paris for Figure 10; Bridgeman Art Library Ltd for Figures 11 and 16; Ancient Art & Architecture for Figure 13; Deutsches Archäologisches Institut for Figure 18.

The Roman Society for Map 3, from Heslin, P. J., 'Augustus, Domitian and the so-called Horologium Augusti', *Journal of Roman Studies*, 97, p. 7.

We have been unable to trace the copyright holder and publisher of *The Roman Revolution* with regards to Figure 1, and we would appreciate any information that would enable us to do so.

Abbreviations

Ancient Works and Words

A.	Aulus (*praenomen*)
App. *BC*; *Illyr.*	Appian, *Bella Civilia* (*Civil Wars*); *Illyrica* (*Illyrian Wars*)
C.	Gaius (*praenomen*)
Cic. *Att.*; *Fam.*; *Brut.*; *Ad Q. fr.*; *De Leg.*; *De Imp. Cn. Pomp.*; *Phil.*; *In Pis.*; *Pro Marc.*; *Pro Rab. Perd. Reo*; *Pro Rab. Post.*; *Pro Sest.*	Cicero, *Letters to Atticus, to his Friends, to Brutus, to his brother Quintus; On the Laws; On the imperium of Cn. Pompeius Philippics; Against Piso; For Marcellus; For Rabirius on a charge of treason; For Rabirius Postumus, For Sestius*
Cn.	Gnaeus (*praenomen*)
Cum.	*Feriale Cumanum*
D.	Decimus (*praenomen*)
Dio	Cassius Dio, *Roman History*
[*Epit. Caes*]	Anon. *Epitome of Aurelius Victor, Monograph on the Caesars*
Eus.-Jer.	Eusebius, tr. Jerome, *Chronicle*, ed. R. Helm
Fasti Amit.; *Ant.*; *Cae.*; *Cap.*; *Col.*; *Lat.*; *Maf.*; *Opp.*; *Praen.*; *Val.*; *Ven.*; *Ver.*	*Fasti Amiternini; Antiates, Caeretani; Capitolini; Colotiani; Feriarum Latinarum* (*of the Latin Festival*); *Maffeiani; Oppiani; Praenestini; Vallenses, Venusini; Verulani*
Gaius, *Inst.*	Gaius, *Institutes*
Gell.	A. Gellius, *Attic Nights*

HA	*Historia Augusta, Lives of the Caesars*
Hor., *Epist.*; *Sat.*; *Carm. Saec.*	Horace, *Epistles*; *Satires*; *Carmen Saeculare*
HS	*Sesterce(s)* (formerly = two and a half *asses*); coin and unit of currency
Jos. *AJ*; *BJ*	Josephus, *Antiquities of the Jews*; *Bellum Judaicum* (*Jewish War*)
L.	Lucius (*praenomen*)
Livy	Livy, *Ab urbe condita* (*History of Rome from its Foundation*)
Luc.	Lucian of Samosata
M.	Marcus (*praenomen*)
Macr. *Sat.*	Macrobius, *Saturnalia*
Mal.	John Malalas, *Chronicle*
Nep. *Att.*	*Cornelius Nepos*, Life of Atticus
Nic. Dam.	Nicolaus of Damascus
Ovid, *Ars Am.*, *Met.*, *Tr.*	Ovid, *Ars Amatoria* (*Art of Love*), *Metamorphoses*, *Tristia*
P.	Publius (*praenomen*)
Pan. Lat.	Latin Panegyrists
Per. Liv.	*Epitome* of Livy's *History of Rome*
Phil. *Apoll.*; *Soph.*	Philostratus, *Life of Apollonius of Tyana*; *Lives of the Sophists*
Philo, *Leg.*	Philo of Alexandria, *Legatio ad Gaium* (*Embassy to Gaius*)
Pliny *NH*	Pliny the Elder, *Natural History*
Pliny *Ep.*; *Pan.*	Pliny the Younger, *Epistulae* (*Letters*); *Panegyric on Trajan*
Plut. *Ant.*, *Brut.*, *Cic.*, *Mar.*, *Marc.*, *Mor.*	Plutarch, *Lives of Antony, Brutus, Cicero, Marius, Marcellus*; *Moralia*
Pol.	Polybius, *Histories*
Prop.	Propertius, *Elegies*
Ps.-Acro	Commentary on Horace, once taken for the work of Helenius Acro
RG	*Res Gestae Divi Augusti* (*Achievements of the Deified Augustus*)
Sen. *Contr.*	Seneca the Elder, *Controversies*

Sen. *Dial.* (*Ben.*; *Brev. Vit.*; *Clem.*; *Ira*); *Apocol.*	Seneca the Younger, *Dialogues* (*On Benefits*, *Shortness of Life*; *Mercy*, *Anger*); *Apocolocyntosis*
Ser.	Servius, commentator on Virgil
Sex.	Sextus (*praenomen*)
Suet. *Caes.*, *Aug.*, *Tib.*, *Cal.*, *Claud.*, *Nero, Galba, Otho, Vit., Vesp., Titus, Dom.*; *Gram.*; *Hor.*	Suetonius, *Lives of the Caesars* (*Julius Caesar, Augustus, Tiberius, Caligula, Claudius, Nero, Galba Otho, Vitellius, Vespasian, Titus, Domitian*); *Lives of the Teachers of Grammar and Rhetoric*; *Lives of the Poets: Horace*
Tac. *Ann.*; *Hist.*	Tacitus, *Annals*; *Histories*
T.	Titus (*praenomen*)
Ti.	Tiberius (*praenomen*)
Val. Max.	Valerius Maximus, *Memorable Deeds and Sayings*
Vell. Pat.	Velleius Paterculus, *History of Rome*
Vict. *Caes.*	Sextus Aurelius Victor, *Monograph on the Caesars*
Virg. *Ecl.*; *Georg.*; *Aen.*	Virgil, *Eclogues*; *Georgics*; *Aeneid*
Vitr.	Vitruvius, *On Architecture*
Xiph.	Xiphilinus, Epitome of Cassius Dio
Zon.	Zonaras, Epitome of Cassius Dio
Zos.	Zosimus, *Historia Nova* (*New History*)

Modern Works and Collections

AC	*L'Antiquité classique*
AÉ	*L'Année épigraphique* (Paris, 1893–)
ANRW	H. Temporini *et al.*, eds, *Aufstieg und Niedergang der römischen Welt* (Munich and New York, 1972–)
Aphrodisias	J. M. Reynolds, *Aphrodisias and Rome, Documents from the Excavation of the Theatre . . . conducted by Professor K. T. Erim together with some related Texts.* JRS Monographs 1 (London, 1982)
Ath.	*Athenaeum*
BAR	*British Archaeological Reports*
Barrington	R. J. A. Talbert, ed., *Barrington Atlas of the Greek and Roman World* (Princeton, NJ and Oxford, 2000)

BÉFAR	*Bibliothèque des Écoles françaises d'Athènes et de Rome*
BICS	*Bulletin of the Institute of Classical Studies*
BMC	R. S. Poole *et al.*, eds, *Catalogue of Greek Coins in the British Museum* (London, 1873–)
Broughton, MRR	T. R. S. Broughton, *Magistrates of the Roman Republic*. American Philological Association 15. 1–3 (3 vols, New York, 1951–86)
CA	The Classical Association
CAH	*Cambridge Ancient History* (1st edn, 13 vols, Cambridge, 1936–54; 2nd edn, 1961–)
CCG	*Cahiers du Centre Gustav-Glotz*
CÉFR	*Collection de l'École française de Rome*
CIL	Th. Mommsen *et al.*, eds, *Corpus Inscriptionum Latinarum* (Berlin, 1863–)
CJ	P. Krueger, ed., *Codex Iustinianus. Corpus Iuris Civilis* 2 (Berlin, 1877; repr. 12th edn, 1959)
CP	*Classical Philology*
CRAI	*Comptes rendus de l'Académie des inscriptions et belles-lettres*
CREBM	H. Mattingly *et al.*, eds, *Coins of the Roman Empire in the British Museum* (London, 1923–)
EJ	V. Ehrenberg and A. H. M. Jones, eds, *Documents illustrating the reigns of Augustus and Tiberius* (2nd edn, rev. D. L. Stockton, Oxford, 1976)
Fer. Dur.	R. O. Fink, A. S. Hoey and W. F. Snyder, eds, *The Feriale Duranum* (repr. from *YCS* 7, Yale, CT, 1940)
FGrH	F. Jacoby, ed., *Die Fragmente der griechischen Historiker* (4 parts, Leiden 1923–63)
Henzen, *AA*	W. Henzen, ed., *Acta Fratrum Arvalium quae supersunt* (Berlin, 1874, repr. Berlin, 1967)
IGR	R. Cagnat *et al.*, eds, *Inscriptiones Graecae ad res Romanas pertinentes* (vols 1, 3, 4, Paris, 1906–27; repr. Chicago, IL, 1975)

IK	*Inschriften griechischer Städte aus Kleinasien* (Bonn, 1972–)
ILS	H. Dessau, ed., *Inscriptiones Latinae Selectae* (3 vols, Berlin, 1892–1916, repr. 1954–55)
Inscr. Ital.	A. Degrassi, *Inscriptiones Italiae* 13: *Fasti et Elogia* (Rome, 1937, 1947, 1963)
JNG	*Jahrbücher für Numismatik und Geldgeschichte*
JÖAI	*Jahreshefte des Österreichisches archäologischen Institutes in Wien*
JRA	*Journal of Roman Archaeology*
JRS	*Journal of Roman Studies*
JS	*Journal des Savants*
Lat.	*Latomus*
LPPR	G. Rotondi, *Leges publicae Populi Romani* (Milan, 1922; repr. Hildesheim, 1962)
LSJ	H. G. Liddell and R. Scott, eds, *Greek Lexicon* (9th edn, rev. H. S. Jones, Oxford, 1940); *A Supplement*, ed. E. A. Barber (1968); *A Revised Supplement*, ed. P. G. W. Glare and A. A. Thompson (1996)
LTUR	E. M. Steinby, ed., *Lexicon Topographicum Urbis Romae* (6 vols, Rome, 1993–99)
MAAR	*Memoirs of the American Academy in Rome*
MDAI(A)(I)(R)	*Mitteilungen des Deutsches Arch. Inst.*, (*Abteilung Athen / Istanbul / Rom*)
MÉFRA	*Mélanges de l'École française de Rome* (*Antiquité*)
Mommsen, *St.*	Th. Mommsen, *Römische Staatsrecht* (3 vols, Berlin, 1³, 1887; 2³, 1886; 3³, 1887; repr. Basel, 1952)
MW	M. McCrum and A. G. Woodhead, eds, *Select Documents of the Principates of the Flavian Emperors including the Year of Revolution A.D. 68–96* (Cambridge, 1961)
OCD³	S. Hornblower and A. Spawforth, eds, *The Oxford Classical Dictionary* (3rd edn, Oxford and New York, 1996)

PCPS	*Proceedings of the Cambridge Philological Society*
PDAR	E. Nash, *Pictorial Dictionary of Ancient Rome* (New York, 1961–62; rev. edn, 1968)
PE	R. Stilgoe, ed., *The Princeton Encyclopedia of Classical Sites* (Princeton, NJ, 1976)
PIR(^{2})	E. Klebs *et al.*, eds, *Prosopographia Imperii Romani* (3 vols, Berlin, 1897–98; 2nd edn, E. Groag *et al.*, eds, Berlin–Leipzig, 1933–)
Platner-Ashby *TDR*	S. B. Platner, rev. T. Ashby, *Topographical Dictionary of Ancient Rome* (Oxford, 1926–)
P&P	*Past and Present*
PP	*La Parola del Passato*
RDGE	R. K. Sherk, *Roman Documents from the Greek East*. Senatus Consulta *and* Epistulae *to the Age of Augustus* (Baltimore, MD, 1969)
RE	G. Wissowa *et al.*, eds, *Paulys Realencyclopädie der class. Altertumswissenschaft* (Stuttgart and Munich, 1894–1980)
RÉG	*Revue des études grecques*
Rev. Phil.	*Revue de Philologie, de Littérature et d'Histoire anciennes*
Rhein. Mus.	*Rheinisches Museum für Philologie*
RIC	E. H. Mattingly *et al.*, eds, *Roman Imperial Coinage* (London, 1923–); C. H. V. Sutherland and R. A. G. Carson, I^2 (1984)
RIDA	*Revue internationale des Droits de l'Antiquité*
Riv. Fil.	*Rivista di Filologia e di Istruzione classica*
RPC	A. Burnett, J. Amandry, *et al.*, eds, *Roman Provincial Coinage* 1– (London and Paris, 1992–)
RRC	M. H. Crawford, *Roman Republican Coinage* (2 vols, Cambridge, 1974)
RS	M. H. Crawford, ed., *Roman Statutes*. Bull. of the Inst. of Class. Stud. Suppl. 64 (2 vols, London, 1996)

SCdPp	W. Eck, A. Caballos, F. Fernández, *Das Senatus consultum de Cn. Pisone patre.* Vestigia 48 (Göttingen, 1996)
SEG	J. J. E. Hondius *et al.*, eds, *Supplementum Epigraphicum Graecum* (Leiden, 1923 –)
Smallwood, *G-N*	E. M. Smallwood, *Documents Illustrating the Principates of Gaius Claudius and Nero* (Cambridge, 1967)
Smallwood, *N-H*	E. M. Smallwood, *Documents Illustrating the Principates of Nerva Trajan and Hadrian* (Cambridge, 1966)
SO	*Symbolae Osloenses*
Syme, *RP*	R. Syme, *Roman Papers*, eds, E. Badian (1–2), A. R. Birley (3–7) (7 vols, Oxford, 1979–91)
TLL	*Thesaurus Linguae Latinae. ed. auctoritate et consilio acad. quinque* (Leipzig, 1900–)
WS	*Wiener Studien*
YCS	*Yale Classical Studies*
ZPE	*Zeitschrift für Papyrologie und Epigraphik*
ZSS	*Zeitschrift der Savigny Stiftung (Romanistische Abteilung)*

Chronology

30 June	Lepidus declared *hostis*
Early July	Octavian's soldiers demand consulship for him
Mid-Aug.	March on Rome; first consulship; Lex Pedia against Caesar's murderers
Early Sept.	Octavian proceeds to Gaul against Antony and Lepidus
27 Nov.	Triumvirate legalised by Antony, Lepidus and Octavian; proscriptions;
7 Dec.	Death of Cicero
Dec.	Sex. Pompeius arrives in Sicily
42 BC, Mid-Sept.	Antony and Octavian cross Adriatic; Octavian detained at Epidamnus by illness
Late Oct., ending on 23rd	Battles at Philippi
41 BC, Jan.	L. Antonius consul; Octavian returns to Rome; Antony in East
Dec.	War over Octavian's veteran settlements
40 BC, Feb.	Defeat of L. Antonius and surrender of Perusia
Spring	Marriage of Octavian to Sex. Pompey's relative Scribonia
Summer	Lepidus departs for Africa; Antony besieges Brundisium
Early Oct.	Pact of Brundisium between Octavian and Mark Antony
Nov.	Marriage of Antony and Octavia; they winter in Athens
39 BC, Early summer	Pact of Misenum between Antony, Octavian, and Sex. Pompeius
	Birth of Octavian's daughter Julia
	Divorce of Octavian and Scribonia
38 BC, Jan.	Octavian weds Livia
38–36 BC	Octavian's war against Sex. Pompeius
37 BC	M. Agrippa's preparations against Sex. Pompeius
Early autumn	Pact of Tarentum: Triumvirate renewed for five years. Antony returns to East
36 BC, 1 July	Octavian and Lepidus attack Sex. Pompeius in Sicily; Octavian delayed by storm

Aug.	Agrippa defeats Pompeius' fleet off Mylae
3 Sept.	Agrippa defeats Pompeius off Naulochus; Pompeius leaves for East
	Lepidus attempts to take over Sicily and is deposed
Nov.	Octavian in Rome; promises return to normality
35 BC	Murder of Sex. Pompeius
35–34 BC	Octavian campaigns in Balkans
32 BC	Declaration of war on Cleopatra
31 BC, 2 Sept.	Defeat of Mark Antony and Cleopatra at Actium
30 BC, 1 and 10 Aug.	Deaths of Mark Antony and Cleopatra in Alexandria; Egypt made a province
29 BC, 13–15 Aug.	Triumphs for Actium, Egypt, Dalmatia
28–27 BC	First political settlement
27 BC, 16 Jan.	Imperator Caesar takes title Augustus
27–24 BC	Augustus in Spain
24 BC	M. Claudius Marcellus marries Augustus' daughter Julia
23 BC	Second political settlement
	Death of M. Marcellus
22–19 BC	Augustus in East
21 BC	Marriage of M. Agrippa and Julia
20–19 BC	Parthians return military standards; Armenia assigned a dependant monarch
19 BC	Third political settlement
18 BC	Agrippa given Tribunician Power. Social legislation. Revision of Senate roll
17 BC	Augustus adopts Agrippa's sons Gaius and Lucius
May–June	Secular Games
12 BC	Deaths of Agrippa and Lepidus;
6 Mar.	Augustus elected Pontifex Maximus
	Invasions of Germany begin under Nero Drusus
11 BC	Tiberius and Julia married

9 BC	Nero Drusus killed in Germany
6 BC	Tiberius Nero given Tribunician Power; retires to Rhodes
5 and 2 BC	C. and L. Caesares enter public life
2 BC, 5 Feb.	Augustus granted title 'Father of his Country' Julia exiled
1 BC–AD 4	C. Caesar in East
AD 2	Return of Tiberius from Rhodes
20 Aug.	Death of L. Caesar en route for Spain
AD 4, 21 or 22 Feb.	C. Caesar dies of wounds
26 or 27 June	Augustus adopts Tiberius and Agrippa Postumus; Tiberius given Tribunician Power
AD 6–9	Revolt in Pannonia put down by Tiberius
AD 9	Revolt in Germany. Arminius destroys P. Varus and his legions
AD 12	Germanicus Caesar consul; Tiberius given equal powers with Augustus
AD 14, 19 Aug.	Death of Augustus. Tiberius in power
14–68	Julio-Claudian Dynasty: Principates of:
14–37	Tiberius
37–41	Gaius (Caligula)
41–54	Claudius
54–68	Nero
69	'Year of the Four Emperors'
69–96	Flavian Dynasty: Reigns of
69–79	Vespasian
79–81	Titus
81–96	Domitian
96–98	Reign of Nerva
98–117	Reign of Trajan
117–38	Reign of Hadrian

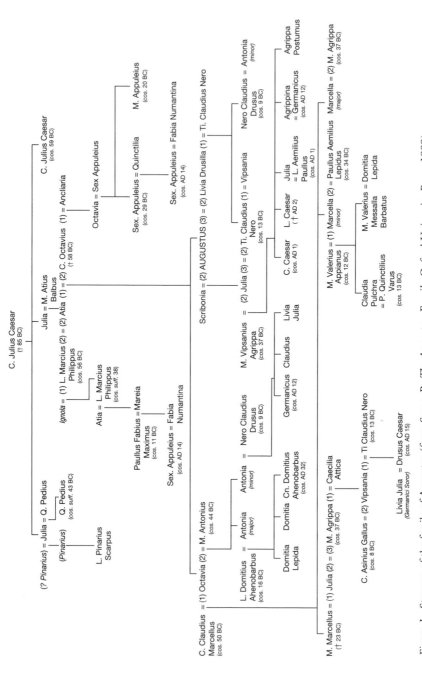

Figure 1 Stemma of the family of Augustus (from Syme, R. *The Augustan Family*, Oxford University Press, 1989)

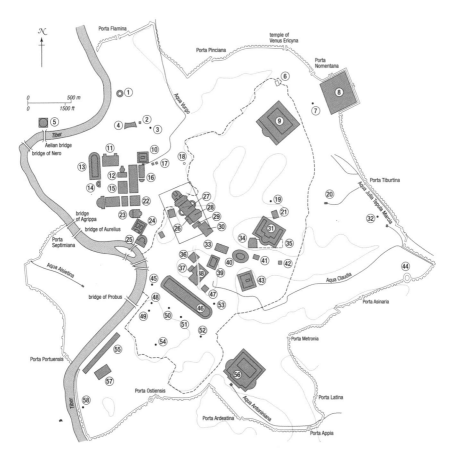

1   Ara Pacis Augustae
2   mausoleum of Augustus
3   temple of the Sun of Aurelius
4   meridian of Augustus
5   mausoleum of Hadrian
    (Castel Sant Angelo)
6   temple of Fortuna
7   field of the Praetorians
8   camp of the Praetorians
9   baths of Diocletian
10 temple of the Divine Hadrian
11 baths of Nero
12 Pantheon
13 stadium of Domitian
    (Piazza Navona)
14 odeion of Domitian
15 baths of Agrippa
16 temple of Isis
17 arch of Claudius
18 temple of Serapis
19 temple of Juno Lucina
20 arch of Gallienus

21 portico of Livia
22 Porticus Minucia Frumentaria
23 theatre and crypt of Balbus
24 portico of Octavia
25 theatre of Marcellus
26 forum of Julius Caesar
27 forum of Trajan
28 forum of Augustus
29 forum of Nerva
30 temple of Pax
31 baths of Trajan
32 Nympheum
    (temple of Minerva Medica)
33 temple of Venus and Rome
34 baths of Titus
35 site of Golden House of Nero
36 palace of Tiberius
37 temple of Apollo
38 palace of Domitian
39 temple of Elagabalus
40 Colosseum
41 Ludus Magnus

42 Mithraeum of St Clemente
43 temple of the Divine Claudius
44 Castrensian amphitheatre
45 temple of Ceres, Liber and Libera
46 Circus Maximus
47 palace of Septimius Severus
48 temple of Luna
49 temple of Minerva
50 temple of Diana
51 baths of Licinius Sura
52 temple of the Bona Dea
53 Septizodium
54 baths of Decius
55 Porticus Aemilia
56 baths of Caracalla
57 Horrea Galbana
58 Horrea Lolliana

Map 1   Map of Imperial Rome

When once a man good name gets,
He may piss the bed and say he sweats.

(Spanish proverb)

And then at one time I saw together
A falsehood and a sober truth
That as it happened started to make
For a window so as to go out.
And when they met in that place
They were stuck, the two of them,
And neither of them could get out
Because of the other, they were pressing so,
Till each of them cried aloud
'Let me go first!' 'No, you let me!
And here I will assure you,
On condition that you will do the same,
That I shall never leave you
But be your own sworn brother!
We shall mingle each with the other,
So that no man, be he never so vexed,
Shall have one of the two, but both
At once, quite against his wish,
Whether we come at morn or eve,
Whether we're shouted or softly whispered'.
So I saw false and true compounded
Flying together as one piece of news.

(G. Chaucer, *The House of Fame*, 3. 2088–109 (ed. W. W. Skeat, Vol. 3, Oxford, 1894) p. 62)

Introduction: The Enigma

The Roman Republic

Over the last five centuries before Christ the Roman Republic had developed as a militaristic and expansionist power, marked internally by strong divisions of class and rank, with factional rivalries and unstable alliances among the aristocracy that manned its Senate, provided its two equal leading magistrates, the consuls, and guided its policies.

By the middle of the second century BC strains were showing. Rivalry for power and profit intensified as the Romans acquired more overseas territories, the 'provinces' governed by senators, and fought large-scale wars against the well-organised monarchies of the East or indomitable tribesmen in the West. New men without distinguished backgrounds were struggling for position and glory, and their money helped them enter a landed aristocracy. The supply of recruits for the army began to diminish, as gruelling and long-term campaigns, notably in Spain, deterred men from leaving their farms, and it was feared that slave labour on large estates was driving out the free small farmers who were the traditional occupants and ideal soldiery.

It was attempts to remedy these problems – and to win a political advantage over rivals by finding the solutions – that led to the first violence of the late Republic, the murders at the hands of their fellow-senators of the tribunes of the *plebs* Tiberius and Gaius Gracchus in 133 and 121 BC; it was a leading priest who led the earlier attack, the incumbent consul the second. The tribunate had originally been created to defend the interests of the common people, and in 133 Tiberius was using it to divide public land among dispossessed farmers, against senatorial resistance. That favouring of the people in despite of the Senate made him a classic *popularis* tribune. He was followed by his brother Gaius, who with his political allies introduced a whole packet of measures, including renewed land distributions, colonies abroad and judicial reforms that put courts misused by the Senate into the hands of well-off non-senators (the *equites*).

The resentment caused by the deaths of the Gracchi did not fade, and measures from the Gracchan mould were put forward again in 103 and 100 BC, with the same violent outcome. The great general C. Marius, a 'new man' (*novus homo*) who had crushed the north African king Jugurtha and the German tribes who threatened Italy, was forced by senatorial pressure to put down the *popularis* politicians who had secured him his consulships and his command. Less than a decade later Rome's Italian allies, who had been a pawn in Roman party politics since the Gracchans had promised them Roman citizenship, seceded from Rome; their champion at Rome, the plebeian tribune M. Livius Drusus, had been assassinated. The 'Social War' that followed led to a civil war between Marius, who was hoping for a seventh consulship and a great command in the East, and the rising general L. Cornelius Sulla. Sulla's final victory over the Marians at the end of the 80s enabled him to take control of Rome as Dictator and re-establish a constitution controlled by the Senate, which also regained control of the jury courts. Strict rules for advancement and for iteration of office were re-enacted, and the tribunate of the plebs had its powers drastically reduced, notably in the field of legislation. The Sullan constitution left a conservative clique (*optimates*, they called themselves) dominant in the state. It also left bitter resentment both amongst Romans who had lost relatives, property and political rights, and amongst Italians battered in the Social War and not yet able to exercise the rights they had been granted. Sulla's expansion of the Senate to six hundred members from a notional three hundred, including many former *equites*, intensified competition among old members and new men who were trying to make their way to the eight praetorships that were now available and especially to the two consulships – the same number as before. Bribery, and debt, increased.

Efforts were made in the 70s to resolve these problems and to modify the Sullan constitution, but it was not until 70 BC, with the first consulship of M. Licinius Crassus and Cn. Pompeius (Pompey the Great), that the powers of the tribunes were fully restored and all the jury courts assigned a proportion of *equites*. Pompey was a gifted and unscrupulous follower of Sulla, who had threatened his way into commands against rebels in Italy and Spain. After his consulship, held with no previous magistracies and at the age of thirty-six, five years before the legal age, he took on wars against the Mediterranean pirates (67 BC) and Mithridates VI Eupator in Asia Minor (66), and was brilliantly successful against both.

Naturally Pompey was loathed by senatorial conservatives. When he returned from the East in 62 he found himself unable to provide land for his veteran soldiers or get his arrangements for the provinces ratified. He turned for help to a politician already suspect for his *popularis* connexions, which included an aunt married to Marius; C. Julius Caesar had even been accused of involvement in the conspiracy of 63 BC that is attached to the name of L. Sergius Catilina, an indebted ex-praetor who had failed to win the consulship. Caesar was a candidate for the office in 60, and needed money to secure his election. He agreed to push Pompey's measures through, and also to help Crassus secure a rebate for the tax-collectors (*publicani*) of Asia, who had over-bid in the aftermath of Pompey's victory. This loose association of the three men is known as the First Triumvirate.

Caesar's methods of passing the legislation won him even more hatred, but he escaped prosecution by having himself voted a five-year command in Gaul, extended for five more years in 55 when Pompey and Crassus were consuls again. Pompey, having helped to raise up the demonised Caesar, was persuaded with a third consulship in 52 to take charge of an increasingly unruly Rome. Something else was expected of him. Caesar's enemies tried to force him to leave his province and army in order to stand at Rome for a second consulship in 48, the first year that was legitimate under Sulla's law on the iteration of office. He did not trust them: once over the sacred boundary of Rome, the *Pomerium*, and so divested of his military command (*imperium*), he would be open to prosecution for his violence in 59. Instead he crossed the Rubicon into Italy in January 49, defeated the Senate's forces in the East, where Pompey took his stand at Pharsalus (48) – he was murdered in Egypt – and in Africa and Spain (46 and 45). He was elected to his consulship, and to a series of Dictatorships, the last made exempt from re-election by a now thoroughly compliant Senate. One-man rule was established in the Republic, but in what form? In February 44 Caesar was offered (and declined) the diadem of a monarch. He was assassinated on 15 March as the man whose unscrupulous ambitions, leading to the perpetual Dictatorship and suspicions that he intended a full monarchy and official divine status, had brought political freedom at Rome to an end. Notoriously, he had dismissed the Republic as an empty name, a thing of no substance.[1] Caesar suffered twenty-three wounds, but about sixty men were involved of the nine hundred who made up the Caesarian Senate. They included opponents he had pardoned and some of his own supporters, led by the principled Republicans M. Junius Brutus and C. Cassius Longinus.[2]

Family and youth: from Octavius to Octavian[3]

Caesar Augustus, or, more grandly, with the final *cognomen* (surname) leading, Augustus Caesar, was born on 23 September, 63 BC,[4] as an Octavius, second child of a senator who was to reach the praetorship in 61, and was given his father's *praenomen* of Gaius. The clan, which came from Velitrae (Velletri), a Volscian town, claimed an ancient history, embroidered when the Octavii were raised to patrician rank by Julius Caesar: the tale took their original membership back to the time of the kings, before 509 BC. However, this branch of the Octavii had not held the consulship, and Octavius' father was technically a 'new man', something to be held against him, as the aspersions cast in 63 BC by an aristocratic barrister on Cicero's client L. Murena show.[5] Lack of ancestry on one view could be made up for by military merit (*virtus*) and Octavius showed that during his proconsulship of Macedonia, 60–59 BC, where he defeated a Balkan tribe, the Bessi.[6] If he had passed beyond the praetorship and become a consul he would have ennobled his family, but he died. With engaging candour Augustus wrote in his *Autobiography* that he was of no higher than equestrian descent, coming from the second rank in the state.[7] By the time the *Autobiography* was written, in the 20s BC, that fact (and anything else that could be used against the family) was common property; and there was no point in passing over it, rather something to be gained in goodwill from the equestrian order.

The boy's main claim to distinction, then, was that his mother Atia was the niece of Julius Caesar. He was taken up by his great-uncle and received marks of honour similar to those he was to give his own grandsons.[8] He made his first known appearance in public when at the age of twelve he delivered a eulogy over his grandmother Julia, Caesar's younger sister, perhaps at Caesar's behest. The boy may already have been glad to emulate him: Caesar had eulogised his own aunt Julia, the wife of Marius, in 69.[9] At fifteen Octavius was co-opted into a priesthood, the prestigious pontificate, and in 47 he held the honorific post of Prefect of the City while the consuls were away at the Latin Festival. Athough he had taken no part in Caesar's African campaign, he was awarded military honours in the triumph of summer 46. By Caesar's death Octavius had been designated to the position of his deputy, Master of the Horse, in succession to M. Aemilius Lepidus, the consul of 46.[10] Caesar's last will and testament of 13 September, 45, made his great-nephew Octavius, aged almost 18, the chief heir to his fortune (see Ch. 2). That was provisional upon there being no posthumous son, and there is little to be said for the view that Caesar intended to found a dynasty, presumably of dictators. Dio's claim that both the title 'imperator' and the position of Chief Pontiff (Pontifex Maximus) were made hereditary for him are to be discounted.[11]

Writers ancient and modern refer to Octavian/Augustus in a number of ways, according to his time of life, their attitude to him, and their time of writing: by the name he took under his great-uncle's will, Caesar; or in his early years by the *cognomen* derived from his father's name, which he never used, Octavian; then there is the name conferred on him in 27 by a reverential state: Augustus (see Ch. 2). The informal title Princeps ('leading citizen'), available for any senator of distinction, had his own authorisation (he used it of himself in his *Achievements*) and came into common parlance for all the men we often refer to as 'emperors'. But it was the title of military honour, *imperator* ('commander') that gave us that word. Augustus himself used it as a forename; it was not commonly used to address or refer to him or his successors, except in military contexts. I shall use the names Octavius for the period before Caesar's death, the convenient, if demeaning, Octavian for the Triumviral period (see Ch. 1) and Augustus and Princeps from 27 BC on.[12]

Viewing Augustus

This work presents Augustus as the first Roman politician to aim right from the start at permanent sole supremacy (Ch. 1). Caesar, who has sometimes been credited with that ambition, had come to it only gradually, after he declared war on the Republic by crossing the Rubicon; Caesar's rival, Pompey the Great, had not entertained it: he reached pre-eminence at an early age and by brutal and unconstitutional means, but remained on that plateau, a leading politician and general among others, until he was manoeuvred by the optimates into confrontation with Caesar. The clarity of Octavian's purpose is revealed by his exploitation of acceptance of his great-uncle Caesar's inheritance, by his changes of name during the decade and a half that followed Caesar's death, by his conscienceless shifts of allegiance during the same period, and by the numbers of men (not counting mere pawns of soldiers) who died in the course of his rise.

Octavian kept his aim systematically in view, then, but after his victory over Antony and Cleopatra in 30 BC had to disguise it if he were to avoid his great-uncle's fate. That entailed radical twists and adjustments of policy (Ch. 2) and the development of techniques that enabled him to get his own way, often to the advantage and satisfaction of his subjects (Ch. 3). Some scholars have rebutted the idea of an 'opposition' to Augustus, but there can be no doubt that the political and social packages he offered were not acceptable to all his peers or, in its details, even to all his family (Ch. 4). After years of manipulating his image it was not difficult for Augustus to believe that his supremacy was indeed for the good of all. Of course he had his own views on current political, social and moral questions, and they could be brought out when he and his dynasty were secure and adjusted to meet the needs of Roman society at all levels (Ch. 5). How far the conception of himself that Augustus promoted was accepted and transmitted by artists and men of letters of his age is a vexed question, but it need not involve taking unwelcome decisions about their collective integrity: they were diverse individuals and they had their own power over a new autocrat (Ch. 6). As a reward for his achievements and in recognition of his relationship to the Roman People at large, Augustus featured in the calendar and eventually became a deity in Roman state religion. Much of what he had done to attain supremacy was eliminated from the record as far as it could be, perhaps even from his own mind.[13] Playing a part had become Augustus' life's work, making the mask so much the harder to remove. Yet, as time went on perspectives changed: the deified Augustus did not remain exempt from criticism from ancient writers (Ch. 7).

Personality in history

Obviously there was immeasurably more to the struggles that followed the death of Caesar and to the ensuing Augustan age than the ambitions of an individual or his coterie. 'The period of Augustus' rule encompassed not just a transformation in Rome's political system, but a new and differently constituted emphasis on "ideas, ideals, and values".'[14] Full weight must be given to empire-wide changes. Augustus, even when completely victorious and in supreme control, as he put it in his *Achievements*, had to face the problems that had led to the breakdown of the Republic in the first place: land-shortage and debt; the insubordination of generals and the alienation of the army from the state; the unsatisfied aspirations of newly enfranchised citizens. Augustus' ambitions and how he achieved them in the peace that followed his capture of Alexandria in 30 BC chimed with the desire for change. He and his subjects were in collusion.

This raises the question of the importance to be attached to any individual. It was an influential doctrine of Ronald Syme's that behind every apparent despotism lurked an oligarchy, and his work, both *The Roman Revolution* and *The Augustan Aristocracy*, published forty-seven years later, presented the Augustan age in that light. Augustus came to power as part of a transformation of the Roman ruling class, one that was to end with an oligarchy that was not *Roman* at all, but drawn from all over the Empire.[15]

More radically, even before 1914, and especially during and after the Second World War, the place of common men in history came to be acknowledged. Millions had died and governments of all colours claimed to be 'democracies'. In connexion with real political and social changes there came another shift. In France, the US and the UK, not just among Marxist historians, there was a loss of interest in individuals, biography was discredited, and historical studies focused less on politics than on economy and society, administrative machinery and the long-term view.[16] The post-war period was also one of reconstruction and the development of new institutions in Europe and its former colonies. In Germany some of the most important work on the Roman world has been on law, institutions and administration, sometimes with a tendency to legitimise the Augustan regime in all its aspects.[17]

Moreover, unlike the European tyrants, Augustus succeeded in founding a stable regime, which developed an apparatus of government that was more elaborate than anything that the West had seen. This has led in turn to more favourable assessments, such as that of W. Eck, whose original study of 1996 significantly focused on *The Age of Augustus*. There are striking exceptions: M. H. Dettenhofer's scholarly examination of 2000 deals with the career of Augustus in chronological order and finds a truly Machiavellian prince.

For ancient commentators there was no doubt of the importance of personality in history. Indeed, Roman history tended to biography, especially in the imperial age, when the whole Roman Empire was under the authority of a monarch.[18] The very fact that the responsibility of individuals for great events was taken for granted (providing easy targets for praise or blame) actually guarantees them some genuine significance.

The enigma

It was partly on account of the magnitude of Augustus' achievement, but partly because of the notorious enigma of character he poses, that the idea of writing Augustus' fictional autobiography appealed to the novelist Allan Massie.[19] Massie comes up with a remarkable conclusion:

> *How did the young man whom Sir Ronald Syme called 'the icy and blood-stained triumvir' transform himself into the apparently benign father of his country? We all know Acton's dictum: 'Power tends to corrupt and absolute power corrupts absolutely.' Augustus stands out as an exception to Acton's rule, one of the few men in history whom one may plausibly judge to have been improved by the experience of power.[20]*

The response of authors in ancient times to Octavian and the Augustan Principate will be considered later (Ch. 7), but the Roman historian Tacitus would not have accepted Massie's favourable verdict: he attributes change for the better exclusively to a later emperor, Vespasian.[21] The enigma has been familiar since antiquity. Indeed, one might almost say, with K. Galinsky, that we are dealing not so much with contradictory traditions as with the tradition of a contradiction.[22]

In modern times profound papers and volumes have examined the Augustan Principate; the danger is that the interest and intricacy of the subject matter takes it beyond criticism of its credibility: it becomes simply what is given, even fixed.[23] It was only to be expected that writers would try to resolve the problem by invoking a change of heart and direction: it was Augustus' own avowed purpose to suggest and demonstrate a sharp line of division between the two periods of his career, with the change coming when in 28–27 BC, according to his *Achievements*, he transferred power to Senate and People.[24] That development gave rise to other controversies, about the nature of the Principate itself; A. Wallace-Hadrill has provided a brief and lucid summary of two schools of thought, one 'constitutionalist', which passed from Th. Mommsen into nineteenth- and early twentieth-century English scholarship and defined the emperor by the powers conferred on him, the other, which the author characterises as 'continental', presented in the 1930s, has been enshrined since the mid-1970s in F. G. B. Millar's *The Emperor in the Roman World*: it is 'monarchical'.[25] Our concern, however, is not with the institution as it developed, but with its creator.

Augustus, as founder of a new system, has been subjected to intense scrutiny, but in spite the quantity of material available about him, even focusing on him – contemporary poetry, six books of Cassius Dio's *Roman History*, Suetonius' longest biography and innumerable other passages – he remains one of the most impenetrable personalities of the ancient world. This is not due to chance: we are not being allowed to see the real man: it was he, not his hated successor Tiberius Caesar, who was the master of dissimulation. Authors tell us of little foibles and simple human touches (see Ch. 7). But Augustus cultivated even this part of his image: he himself writes (from the years of his assured supremacy) of enjoying bread and hard grapes as he travelled in his litter. And the letters that are claimed to yield insights into his personality function for the most part at a different level from that of the political man.[26]

Modern assessments

Augustus has fared less well since antiquity, with its generally favourable verdict. Z. Yavetz finds eminent critics from Savonarola onwards: Machiavelli, Montesquieu, Voltaire and Gibbon, and there are unequivocal denunciations from the eighteenth and nineteenth centuries.[27] In recent times, distinct waves of opinion on the founder of the Principate have been shaped not only by the discovery of fresh evidence, epigraphic and papyrological, and the re-evaluation of old, literary and numismatic (see below), but by the periods in which they developed.[28] In the nineteenth century, the prime of nation-states ruled by monarchs, Augustus was well received. After the First World War his populist activities and conservative social stance chimed in well with those of the Dictators of Germany, Italy and Spain and with those in western democracies who admired men who united their nations and kept the lower classes quiet. Ancient Rome in general and Augustus in particular were natural models for Mussolini and his regime, which celebrated the bimillenary in 1938.[29] Assessments were favourable and bland, as in *Cambridge Ancient History* X (1934), although F. E. Adcock had to admit seeing Augustus deceiving himself when he compiled his public memorial, the *Achievements*.[30] But the 1930s and developments in Europe forced a change of perspective. Ronald Syme's attack on Augustus in *The Roman Revolution* was published in the year in which Britain and France declared war on Nazi Germany. The Second World War, followed by the Stalinist terror, discredited all upstart autocrats. Syme's contemporary at Oxford, C. E. Stevens, after devoting his war to the study and creation of propaganda, pithily characterised Augustus as a crook, and backed up that claim with examples, some to be restated here (Ch. 2). His concession to Augustus was that his use of ill-gotten power was better than Hitler's.[31] One difference between these two scholars lay in the attention they paid to ideology, close on the part of Stevens, while Syme has even been said to neglect it.[32]

Propaganda and ideology

It would be grossly misleading to compare Augustus out and out with any of the European autocrats. Mussolini, Stalin and Hitler at any rate were men of low class who joined mass movements with distinct ideologies, and came to lead and develop them, while Atatürk and Franco were officers imbued with the views of their order; Octavian was an aristocratic faction leader in the individual Roman style. There was no trace in his career of the modern fantasy that goes back to the Jacobins, that society can be progressively transformed by violence and the elimination of sections of it defined by wealth, class, or race. It is in methodology – mass rallies, oath-taking and self-presentation designed to win unified support from a unified citizen-body – combined with sweeteners for each class in society, that comparisons may be sought.

Something must be said about 'propaganda', 'ideology' and related words as they have been used in connexion with Octavian/Augustus, the Principate generally, and its literature and art. The first two have undergone life-threatening changes. 'Propaganda' was in vogue during and after the Second World War, not surprisingly, but came to occupy more ground than it deserved, so that it lost most of its usefulness. Associated as the word was with the section of the Vatican's organisation that was designed to propagate the Faith (De Propaganda Fide), it deals in the verbal and implies systematic campaigning. English-speaking Protestants found it suspect, and it was almost fatally injured when it was incorporated in the title of J. Goebbels' Nazi ministry of information.[33]

For a while the place of 'propaganda' was taken by the internalised 'ideology', but that too has been challenged. It is also verbal, over-systematic and self-consciously constructed. It hints at exclusion of the whole truth, however tenaciously the beliefs themselves are presented; it is even 'something shady'. Other words such as 'publicity' that have come into play have a limited use and belong to a world that knows print and the industrial revolution. They are all anachronistic. Yet there has been a comprehensive revision of attitudes towards this type of word, while even Syme in his later work became less certain of the effectiveness of imperial control.[34] Antecedent Roman attitudes, almost all conservative, did not lose their strength, and the dynasts had to negotiate with them on their own terms; this is close to A. Eich's 'representation'.[35] The reappraisals, in Lobur's words, 'place ideas and symbols at the center instead of at the margins'. On the other hand, Octavian/Augustus had machinery and operatives at his disposal that were already available to Caesar and politicians such as the tribune of 58 BC, P. Clodius Pulcher, while the turmoil of the Triumviral period created a 'vacuum of experience' that allowed for the invention of Republican 'traditions' to provide for continuity with the Principate, and ideas spread horizontally within successive peer-groups; the educated class could devise their own formulations or forms of acceptance.[36]

The modern shades of meaning even of anachronistic terms are familiar and comprehensible, and the present open state of the discussion means that these words may be used with caution, but without apology, if ever they seem appropriate to Augustan Rome and its spokesmen. In a field where terms have been so fluid, 'propaganda' itself is still legitimate for use in connexion with Roman history, notably for the stand-offs of the Triumviral years (Ch. 1), where P. Wallmann has no hesitation in deploying it; and A. M. Riggsby sensibly preserves 'propagandistic'.

Blizzards of self-interested words and images coming from all sides throughout the twentieth century have sensitised scholars to that aspect of Augustan art and literature, and it has never ceased to be stressed, although by the end of the twentieth century the favoured word had given way, as far as accounts of 'democratic' polities go, to 'spin'.[37] But that entire approach has been criticised. In his review of modern perspectives, K. Galinsky shows that Augustan writers who had been seen as mouthpieces of government were reconceived in the 1960s as presenters of subversive views. More recently still, they have been taken more subtly for purveyors of ambivalences, ambiguities and ironies, responding thereby to their times, and so carrying classical literature bravely into the postmodern era.[38]

Contemporary developments

Altogether then, in the course of the reaction a softer and less crisis-ridden view of Augustus has come into prominence than those of Syme and Stevens, more finely nuanced than before.[39] It has been brilliantly elaborated by K. Galinsky and worked out in the whole context of Augustan culture. Galinsky constructs his work on two contrasts. The first is that between *auctoritas* (personal authority: the very word is linked with the name 'Augustus'; see Ch. 2) and *potestas* (legal power), drawn by Augustus himself in his *Achievements*; Augustus did not rule through his power but by consent, by his *auctoritas* in fact.[40] The second contrast accordingly is between two kinds of leadership, the first 'transactional', which concerns itself only with the mechanical dealings of government with its subjects, the second 'transforming', a form of leadership that inspires its followers.[41] Indeed, this form needs the initiative of others, which the leader (*auctor*) guarantees and approves, so taking on a degree of responsibility. Too much attention has been paid to power, not enough to the inculcation of purpose, which can be seen in Augustus' concern with the moral transformation of Roman society. He attempted to restore the moral foundations of the *res publica* (Commonwealth) without restoring the Republic in all its transactional workings – evidently its licence. So the cities of the Empire chose to put Augustus' head on the coins they minted, guaranteeing the coins' acceptance and simultaneously reinforcing acceptance of his *auctoritas*.

This analysis is particularly effective in explaining the 'Augustanism' of literature and art, and it has much to be said for it. One of its great merits is that that it is not monolithic: it allows for complexity and for the input into the 'Augustan' age of other politicians and of independent writers. Admitting this inclusiveness in the thinking of the ruler has another advantage: it accounts for its multifariousness, even its ambiguity. Onlookers may determine for themselves what an action of Augustus or a sentence means – if it does mean one thing. In D. C. Feeney's view, what Augustus 'was' cannot be regarded as given in any context.[42]

Yet doubts arise about Galinsky's analysis. First, there is the ambiguity of the content of any 'transformation' and of the merits of a 'transforming' leader. The word was much in vogue in 2008 during the US presidential campaign and it seems to have built-in merit. But Stalin and Hitler played a part in transforming their countries (and the former is still seen by some Russians as deserving credit for it). Again, accepting Augustus' own claim in the *Achievements*, Galinsky assumes that government through *auctoritas* is necessarily good, authoritative rather than authoritarian, even when Augustus had become entrenched in his position.[43] The question then is, why did Augustus' successor Tiberius in his early days as sole ruler in AD 14 repudiate *auctoritas* in his dealings with the Senate, preferring to be known merely as the 'suasor' ('supporter') of measures he favoured?[44] *Auctoritas* is a word loaded with favourable associations and it proclaims the approval of the person who uses it for the form of power that it represents, so it is no wonder that Augustus applied it to his own position. Those who withheld their approval simply chose another word: *potentia* is the mildest, used for the unauthorised power that women and freedmen wielded.[45] In any case, Augustus' *auctoritas* was not fundamental: it was generated by immense powers conferred by law, and he used them, making both aspects of his power less attractive for his peers. Galinsky should not be surprised that Augustus found less political than aesthetic talent among his contemporaries.[46]

A second question concerns what is behind Augustus' ambiguity, the instinctive richness of a statesman of genius or a conscious astuteness that allows a politician who remained a chameleon to evade being pinned down.

Galinsky claims that we cannot penetrate Augustus' motivation to determine what part was played by self-interest, what by disinterested statesmanship. Genuine leadership goes beyond the accumulation of power, and 'ideology' and 'propaganda' are an inadequate foundation for lasting political systems. Certainly we have no privileged access to his, or to any other individual's private thoughts. What we do have is the plain evidence of Octavian's ruthless years, when, if he had been living in modern times and had not been a politician, he could have been termed a sociopath,[47] while we have nothing to contradict the view that Augustus' motivation remained essentially the same, even if his techniques changed. One historian, J. Osgood, who writes graphically of the suffering that the Triumviral Period, 43–30 BC, inflicted, not only on the Roman aristocracy, but on the whole Roman world, argues nonetheless that Octavian did not act merely out of self-interest but had to consider the needs of men and women in Rome, Italy and the provinces: even at this stage, then, 'popular opinion did count'.[48] That is true, but does not put Octavian's purposes into any order of priority or explain the compulsion.

The hypothesis of this book follows lines laid down by Syme and Stevens. They seem to provide better explanations of his behaviour than that of a man who underwent a remarkable change for the better: Octavian/Augustus put his own power and that of his successors first, then worked, other things being equal, for the welfare of his subjects as he saw it – which in any case had a spin-off for his own position. His power, great compared with that of previous dynasts, Sulla, Pompey and Caesar, became entrenched, and his achievements greater. His discretion surpassed theirs, his position became easier and he learned from their and his own mistakes.[49]

I shall also suggest, then, that two other phenomena, the apparent change that took place after the Triumviral Period, and Augustus' apparent imposition on Rome of a vision that has given rise to titles such as 'Augustan Rome', and the 'Augustan Age', stem from his ambitious tuning in to the hopes and fears of his contemporaries, and from their recognition of it and their active response to him. Senators were in the best position to respond effectively, but members of the equestrian order and the people, as well as subjects outside Italy, played their part.[50]

Further, the tide of favourable opinion has carried scholars to an altogether less dramatic view of the Augustan regime itself. It is seen as evolving rather than being jolted along by a series of crises, the result of 'opposition' from one or other individual or group; the Principate was comparatively smoothly installed; its failings and discontents emerged under Augustus' less worthy successors. This view will be challenged (Ch. 4). The regime of Augustus was the central episode in a century that itself represents a convulsion on a grand scale for Roman institutions; the notion that it was itself shaken by smaller crises has an inherent appeal. Divergent opinions and independent ambitions were not forgotten in a commonwealth where the exceptional prominence of one individual lowered his contemporaries to a different level.

The disparity of views among modern scholars is not just the result of changes of intellectual fashion, or of the different circumstances in which authors have written. The disparity, and the events that concern us, will lead to the conclusion that Augustus' special skill lay not simply in opportunistic and improvised duplicity, but in maintaining a purposeful political ambiguity as long as possible – or indefinitely – an ambiguity that would relieve his subjects of anxiety and responsibility, and allow them scope for multifarious expectations. This is an inherent part of his regime and perhaps of his personality, and it is the source of continued modern bafflement. This is the man who wanted to be identified with Apollo, but who did not shrink from allowing other identifications, even with deities associated with his rivals, appropriating Hercules, Antony's ancestor, and even his special patron Dionysus (Ch. 5).

Surviving sources[51]

As to contemporary evidence for the history of Octavian/Augustus and his times, we have the rich literature of the age (Ch. 6). The letters and speeches of the consular statesman M. Tullius Cicero are authentic and vivid, cut short, unfortunately, by his murder in 43 BC. But for continuous and immediate political statement and narrative the full range of Triumviral and Augustan coinage must be put first: it presents the current concerns of those who controlled the mints.[52] It is a question whether a coin can lie; like sculpture, it can certainly mislead, even unintentionally, and misrepresent.[53] Purposeful spin pervades monumental inscriptions such as the *Fasti* – consular and triumphal lists and calendars of festivals and other notable days – compiled under Augustus and set up in Rome and Italy.[54] Those inscribed at Praeneste (Palestrina) were mainly the work of Augustus' friend, the tutor of Gaius and Lucius Caesars, C. Verrius Flaccus. (When Ovid wrote his verse *Fasti* he elaborated on the festivals of the first six months of the year and their significance to the new regime.[55]) Augustus' own *Achievements*, the *Res Gestae Divi Augusti* set up in public immediately after his death, are important and partisan enough to require separate treatment (Ch. 5).[56] Laws and senatorial decrees, to be immortalised in stone or bronze, may be regarded in the same light; like the Princeps' edicts they are statements of policy but also presentations of the issuing authority.[57]

Augustan monumental construction and sculpture were also paid for and controlled very largely by the ruler or his admirers.[58] Besides these public works, though, there are a host of private monuments owed to Roman love of self-commemoration: statue bases and tombstones of the eminent and the respectable that revealingly set out the vicissitudes and careers of lesser men, senators, knights, even freedmen and women. It is one of a woman, the so-called *Laudatio Turiae* (*Eulogy of Turia*), that relates the courage of one whose husband was condemned in the Triumviral proscriptions and all she did to save him; it is a touching monument to private devotion and integrity in the face of public brutality.[59]

A salient feature of the literary sources is the apparent commitment of contemporary writers to the aims of the regime; that faded into varied scepticism and hostility, tempered with nostalgia, after Augustus' death. T. Livius (Livy) of Patavium (Padua), his almost exact contemporary, did not embark on a political career, but was an intimate of the imperial family (he taught the later Emperor Claudius). He wrote a *History of Rome from its Foundation*, which he brought to an end in 9 BC, though he lived on until the beginning of Tiberius' Principate. It was a strange year for closure. In K. Galinsky's view, he ended at a high-point in Roman history, the conquests of Nero Drusus in Germany; better, he ended with the very life of Nero Drusus, whose loss in the field brought on the struggles for the succession to Augustus, which could not be recounted.[60] Livy shared the ideals that Augustus professed, but he may have hoped to see them fulfilled in other ways than through an undeclared monarchy, and he kept his distance. As far as Augustus goes, we have the Preface and most of the summaries of books 117–142. When a topic arose that might be significant for the politics of his own day, Livy was content to repeat Augustus' own interpretation.[61]

Another close contemporary, a friend and servant of Herod the Great, was Nicolaus of Damascus, a diplomat who was in the entourage of Augustus in 20 BC and who wrote a biography of Augustus down to 27 BC, unabashedly laudatory. This work is represented in the surviving writings by sections 1–36; sections 37–139 belong to a general history. The date of the biography is disputed: it was once agreed that it was written in the late 20s and was dependent on, even a Greek paraphrase of, Augustus' own lost *Autobiography* in thirteen books, which concluded with the Cantabrian wars. That view has been challenged: the author mentions Augustus' grant of freedom to Samos, which did not take place until 20–19 BC, and a date even after Augustus' death has been proposed (ancient biographies were usually written after the subject's death).[62]

Men from the Greek East, unless they embarked on political life themselves, were less readily able than Italians and all Latin speakers to appreciate the niceties of Roman political life and traditions. However, Strabo, the historian and geographer, born at Amaseia (Amasya) in Asia Minor in about 64 BC, was an intimate of men close to Augustus, living at least until AD 23. His *Geography* survives and a number of passages display the sympathy with the new arrangements that many provincials felt.[63] Equally enthusiastic was Dionysius of Halicarnassus (Bodrum), who arrived at Rome to teach rhetoric just when Augustus 'put an end to the civil wars' and began publishing his *Antiquities of Rome* twenty-two years later.

A historian of a later generation, C. Velleius Paterculus,[64] born in 20 or 19 BC, was a new man of ancient Campanian descent and from a strong military tradition who reached the praetorship in AD 15. Intensely loyal to the new regime, and especially to his commander Tiberius, in AD 30 he penned a brief *History* that is instructive for the insights it gives into the official point of view at the time of writing. 'Mendacious' was R. Syme's adjective of choice for him; other judgements are more favourable. Velleius' contemporary, the moralist Valerius Maximus, is even more laudatory.[65]

With Cornelius Tacitus, Rome's greatest historian,[66] born in about AD 56, we reach the longer perspectives of the early second century. He was a new man from northern Italy or southern Gaul, but of equestrian ancestry, who reached the consulship in 97 after living through the oppressive end of the Flavian regime. His subject in the *Histories* and then the *Annals* was the Principate after AD 14, and the conduct of senators under it; as we have seen, his references to the founder, Augustus, are cool.

Slightly younger was C. Suetonius Tranquillus,[67] another *eques* by birth, from Hippo Regius (Bône) in north Africa, born AD 70, who in the early second century wrote *Lives* of the emperors, from Julius Caesar to Domitian, organising thematically. His position as secretary to the emperor Hadrian gave him access to documents in the palace archives and he could argue like a scholar, but he had a taste for scandal too. The intimate material he provides is cited throughout this work. Items have to be treated individually. They may be documentary or derived from an annalistic historian and so conveying his viewpoint and judgements.

Poised between Greece and Rome was the aristocratic philosopher L. Mestrius Plutarchus (Plutarch), the sage of Chaeroneia in Boeotia, mainland Greece,[68] who lived from the mid-first century AD to the third decade of the second. He had Roman friends, learnt Latin, though late in life, and studied and wrote on Roman antiquities. He was enlightened enough to give the Romans credit for their achievements, placing Republican worthies alongside Greek in twin political biographies and pointing out the parallels between them. Among the Romans were Julius Caesar and Mark Antony.

Later in the second century came another Greek writer who dealt with the Triumviral period. The origins (and sources) of Appian are uncertain and remain a matter of debate. He came from Asia Minor or Alexandria and may like Plutarch have held an equestrian post. In the mid-second century he wrote a comprehensive history of Rome and her wars, in which the civil wars, down to 35 BC, were conspicuous. There is no doubt of his prime value for the triumviral period.[69] (Lucius) Cassius Dio, of higher status than Appian, wrote a *History of Rome* based on Livy and other sources (much debated); he claims to have spent ten years researching and twelve in writing.[70] Dio, from Nicaea in Bithynia (Iznik), was born in about 164 or 165 into a senatorial family, was suffect consul *c.* 205–206 and consul for the second time in 229 with the Emperor Severus Alexander as colleague, besides being on the imperial council. Books 46–50 deal with the Triumviral period, and the surviving parts of Books 51–56, which are devoted to the aftermath of Octavian's victory and the Principate of Augustus, exist partly in their original form, partly as Byzantine excerpts; the losses are worst in the latter half of the reign. Dio's speeches are not records of what was actually said, and the 'debate' between Octavian's advisers M. Vipsanius Agrippa and C. Maecenas in Book 52 is a composition designed to give the reader Dio's views on government in his own day. All the same, as a Roman senator living though violent dynastic upheavals, he was able to appreciate what the installation of Augustus and his dynasty meant to his order, and he held firmly to the view that Octavian/Augustus was after permanent supremacy from the start.

Pervasive, often anonymous, voices may also be heard in the literary sources for imperial history, entering them at times hard to determine: they are those of rumour and contemporary tittle-tattle, often understandably malicious, on the part of the majority not in the know, or of personal history handed down from one generation to another. Two examples will suffice. In the first category is the story that Augustus' right-hand man Agrippa was sent to the East with *imperium* in 23 BC to keep him out of the way of Augustus' promising nephew Marcellus. Tiberius' Principate provides a famous specimen of the second type. Men of the older generation passed down a tale that Cn. Piso, the governor of Syria accused of poisoning Germanicus Caesar and convicted of treason in AD 20, claimed to possess written instructions from Tiberius that, if produced, would have acquitted him. The first story is implausible and was born or at least kept alive by attested later rivalries in the dynasty between the experienced imperial colleague Tiberius and Augustus' grandsons C. and L. Caesars; the second is believable. Both passed into the works of leading historians, Dio and Tacitus.[71]

Endnotes

1 Caesar's contempt for the Republic: Suet. *Jul.* 77.
2 For Caesar's career, see M. Gelzer, *Caesar, Politician and Statesman* (tr. P. Needham, Oxford, 1968). Brutus: Osgood 2006, 89 and 98–100.
3 Clear survey: Kienast 1982, 1–5.
4 Augustus' birthday: EJ 101; Suet. *Aug.* 5 and 57. 1, with Suerbaum 1980, 334f.; Barton 1995; Feeney 2007, 154f., pointing out that this was also Apollo's birthday.
5 Octavii and patriciate: Suet. *Aug.* 2. 1, with J. M. Carter's n. *ad loc.*; story of early membership concocted when Octavian married the patrician Livia, according to Nisbet 1984, 45. Caesar and patriciate: Dio 43. 47. 3; 45. 2. 7 (Octavius). New men: on Ser. Sulpicius Rufus' attack on Murena: Cic. *Pro Mur.* 15.
6 Macedonia and the Bessi: Suet. *Aug.* 3. 2: *MRR* 2.185 and 191.
7 Equestrian origin: Suet. *Aug.* 2. 3; at 70. 2 he reports a graffito scratched on a bronze statue of Octavian implying that his father was a dealer in bronze.
8 Octavius' early distinctions: Nic. Dam. 4–26.
9 Eulogy on Julia: Nic. Dam. 4 with Bellemore *ad loc.*; Quint. 12. 6. 1; Suet. *Aug.* 8. 1. Caesar's behest: Malcovati 1969, xxx; Caesar the proconsul could not enter the city. Marius' wife: Suet. *Caes.* 6. 1.
10 Prefect of the City: Nic. Dam. 5. 13 (Canfora 2007, 253, regards this item as part of Augustus' claim to have been taken up by Caesar before 45, but he makes excessively sharp distinctions between the stages of Octavius' advancement); honours of 46: Suet. *Aug.* 8. 1.
11 Hereditary position: see Kienast 1982, 4f., noting Dio 43. 44. 3; 52. 41. 4 (*imperator*); 44. 5. 3 (pontificate); these were good stories for Octavian's supporters.
12 Imperator Caesar: Syme 1958; still used as an address by the contemporary Vitruvius 1. 1, etc.; Princeps: Ch. 2.
13 Cf. Syme 1939, 516, on the 'necessary and salutary fraud' of *libertas* and the Republic.
14 Milnor 2005, 12, citing Galinsky 1996, 8.
15 Non-Roman oligarchy: Momigliano 1940, 78.
16 Personality in history: Yavetz 1990, 25–27. Study of systems: Wallace-Hadrill 1996, 285.

17 Insistence on legal aspects: Dettenhofer 2000, 27.

18 Development of Roman historiography: Woodman 1977, 28–56.

19 Allan Massie, author of *Augustus: the Memoirs of the Emperor* (London, 1986), in *Class. Assoc. News* 32 (July 2005), 1. Bibliographical surveys of opinions on Augustus: Schmitthenner 1969, vii–xi; Yavetz 1984, 22–6; Raaflaub and Toher 1990, xi–xxi; Galinsky 1996, 373; Swan 2004, 345; Rehak 2006, xif.

20 The Augustan enigma: Yavetz 1984, 26, citing the laudatory Hammond 1965, 152, and M. Reinhold, 'Augustus' conception of himself', *Thought* 55 (216) (1980) 36; Galinsky 1996, 9.

21 Hostile verdict: Tac. *Ann.* 1.10; Vespasian: *Hist.* 1. 50. 4.

22 Contradictions: Galinsky 1996, 370–5, with the need to distinguish them from conflicting interpretations: Augustus has meant many different things to different people.

23 Kennedy 1992, 26, warns against such 'reifications' as that of 'Augustan ideology'.

24 Division in career: Syme 1939, 2; Augustus' claim: *RG* 34. 2.

25 The Principate in historical writing: Wallace-Hadrill 1982, 32, with nn.

26 Bread and grapes: Suet. *Aug.* 76. Augustus perhaps had in mind Caesar's wish to be seen as a friend of the people.

27 Critics of Augustus: Yavetz 1984, 21; Ridley 2003, 25–50 (survey of treatment of *RG*).

28 Influence on historians of their own time: Dettenhofer 2000, 21f.; 27.

29 Bimillenary celebrated: Alföldy 1993, 103; cf. Arangio-Ruiz 1938.

30 Self deception: F. Adcock in *CAH* 10 (1934) 593.

31 Syme 1939, with Momigliano's review 1940. C. E. Stevens' views: B. Levick, ed., *The Ancient Historian and his Materials* (Farnborough, 1975) 1f.; Cartledge 1975 ('crook' 31); Stockton 1965 and Birley 2000 also offer connections.

32 Syme's 'neglect' of ideology: Alföldy 1993, 110f., drawing attention to the work of Alföldy 1980. The title of Syme's chapter 'The Organization of Opinion', is revealing; cf. Bleicken 2000, 748 on his concept.

33 Propaganda/ideology: the bibliography is immense (in respect of coinage, see Mantovani 2008, 48 n. 120): a useful discussion is given by A. M. Riggsby, *Caesar in Gaul and Rome: War in Words* (Austin, TX, 2006), 207–14; 'propagandistic' at 210. The origin of 'propaganda' in the Church is noted in Levick 1982; for ideology see Santirocco 1995, 225f., and Shumate 2005.

34 Professor J. A. Lobur has kindly allowed me access to his book; he examines recent approaches in the Introduction and offers a comprehensive bibliography; what follows is heavily indebted to him (citation from 13). On 'ideology' he draws attention to Geertz 1964, from whom at 47 critical descriptions are taken ('shady' at 49). At 63 Geertz offers a neutral characterisation.

35 'Representation': Eich 2003.

36 Political agents: Lobur 2007, 15. 'Vacuum': 18. Activity of the educated class: Alföldy 1993, 120.

37 Augustan art seen as propaganda: Zanker 1988, vi.

38 Views of Augustan poetry: Galinsky 1996, 244f.

39 Reassessments of Syme's work and of Augustus: Yavetz 1990; Eder 1990, 71–82; Syme and the Dictators: Linderski 1990, 43.

40 *Auctoritas*: RG 34. 3.

41 Galinsky 1996 on *auctoritas*, two styles of government, and Augustus' commitment to a 'transforming moral program of values and ideals': 4–8; 10–41; 67 (the quotation); 70f.; 80; 140.

42 Nature of Augustus: Feeney 1992, 1.

43 Authoritative government: Galinsky 1996, 39.

44 Repudiation of *auctoritas*: Suet. *Tib.* 27.

45 *Potentia*: Levick 1990, 43; 52.

46 Political and aesthetic gifts: Galinsky 1996, 71.

47 Sociopath: see F. A. Whitlock *s.v.* 'Psychopathic personality' in R. L. Gregory, *Oxford Companion to the Mind* (Oxford, 1987), noting possible amelioration in later life.

48 Public opinion: Osgood 2006, 2.

49 As Prof. J. Rich has pointed out to me, Augustus did not make the Triumvir Crassus' mistake of invading Iraq.

50 Role of subjects: cf. B. Levick, *Julia Domna: Syrian Empress* (London, 2007), 132; 144.

51 Sources: see Wallmann 1989, 19–28 (Triumviral period); Crook 1996, 70–73.

52 Central coin issues: Crawford, *RRC*; *RIC* 1^2; provincial: *RPC* 1. For the handling of numismatic evidence, see Noreña 2001, 146–52.

53 For coinage as an instrument of policy, see especially Sutherland 1951; 1976, 96–101. Unintentionally misleading legend: Kraft 1962.

54 *Fasti*: EJ pp. 32–43; full treatment: *Inscr. Ital.* 13 (1947; 1963), with Feeney 2007, 167–212.

55 Ovid's *Fasti*: Herbert-Brown 1994.

56 *RG*: see Yavetz 1984; Ramage 1987; Ridley 2003; Cooley 2009.

57 Laws, etc.: Rotondi, *LPPR* 434–63; EJ; Crawford, *RS* 60–64; Talbert 1984, 438f.

58 Buildings: Zanker 1988; Torelli 1992; Galinsky 1996.

59 '*Laudatio Turiae*': EJ 357; Wistrand 1976; Horsfall 1983.

60 Livy's terminal point: Galinsky 1996, 285.

61 Augustus as source: Livy 4. 20. 5–11. Crook 1996, 80, n.5, citing 32. 4, says that he plainly did not believe Augustus' case.

62 Nicolaus of Damascus: Yarrow 2006, 67–76; 156–61. After AD 14: Toher 1985. Division of Nicolaus' work: Bellemore 1984, xi.

63 Strabo: Clarke 1997. Provincial feeling: Tac. *Ann.* 1. 2. 2.

64 Velleius Paterculus: Sumner 1970; Woodman 1977 and 1983; Syme 1978.

65 Valerius Maximus: Bloomer 1992; Wardle 2000; he is 'sacralising' the emperors.

66 Tacitus: Syme 1958.

67 Suetonius: Wallace-Hadrill 1983.

68 Plutarch: Jones 1971; Osgood 2006, 8.

69 Appian: Gabba 1956, esp. 207–49; Gowing 1992; Osgood 2006, 9.

70 Dio: Millar 1964; Reinhold and Swan 1990; Rich (*Commentary*) 1990, 1–20; (in Cameron) 1990, on Octavian's ruthlessness; Gowing 1992; Swan 2004; Dio on the imperial council: Crook 1955, 157; his research: 73. 23. 5.

71 Agrippa's departure: 53. 32. 1; Piso's document: Tac. *Ann.* 3. 16. 1.

Chapter 1

Octavian:
Heir of an Autocrat

❧

Entry into politics

Sallust writes in his *Catiline*, a work that belongs to the terrible opening years of the Second Triumvirate, 42–41 BC, that after 70 BC all who harried the Commonwealth used fine pretexts, some that they were defending the rights of the People, others that they were maintaining the authority of the Senate. They made a pretence of the public good, but each was fighting for his own power.[1] Octavian/Augustus made these protestations, but he was an original in that he was the first Roman politician actually to embark on his career with the intention of winning permanent supremacy. If this is accepted, his entire conduct must be seen in that light, as the rational and consistent pursuit of sole power and its perpetuation. That certainly is the aim that Cassius Dio attributes to Octavian: he set out in pursuit of aims of the kind that had led to Caesar's murder. Admittedly, Dio's view of Augustus is very much his own. More decisive would be a pronouncement made on oath by Octavian himself within his first year in politics, in which he overboldly made no secret in a popular assembly of wanting to attain his father's offices, even as he pointed to a statue of Julius Caesar. But Octavian was too clever for that. A better interpretation of this part of Cicero's letter, in

Figure 2 Octavian and Caesar coin (© the Trustees of the British Museum)

which the claim is made, is that he was demanding the implementation of his father's divine status – which he soon achieved. It was only later that Nicolaus of Damascus put forward the claim in its fullest form: it was legally proper and necessary for the son to resume Caesar's responsibilities.[2]

The thirteen years that followed Caesar's murder were full of dispute, espionage, warfare, corruption, treachery and atrocities; Tacitus calls the Dictatorship and Triumvirate, the civil war period that preceded the foundation of the Principate, 'twenty years of unmitigated strife; no morality, no law; all the worst villainy went unpunished, while decency often brought destruction'. For Dio the Triumvirate was a time that made Caesar's Dictatorship seem like a golden age.[3] The youth of many of the key players, notably of Octavian himself, harped on by opponents,[4] and of his closest allies Agrippa and Maecenas, his opponents Sextus Pompeius and Cleopatra, is pointed out by J. Osgood as a factor that contributed to their precipitate behaviour – not mere youth, but the fact that they had not seen the brutal consequences of the civil wars between Sulla and the Marians in the 80s – when advancing years mitigated the brutality not a scrap.[5] Rather the premature deaths of parents brought precocious and ambitious boys to the front, as it had with Pompey the Great. Octavian's ambition and unscrupulousness were to outdo anything that his forerunners displayed.

The diverse sources present impossible choices for the historian at every turn.[6] Whatever the mitigation to be allowed him, or the blame to be attached to his antagonists, Octavian, participant in the Perusine war as well as the campaign of Philippi and the proscriptions, must bear the greatest responsibility – and be credited with systematic and rational efforts to realise his ambitions. Their intensity can be measured by considering the dangers of the course he embarked on. The fourth-century compiler known as the Epitomator of Aurelius Victor, writing imperial biographies, set the failings of his first subject against his merits: Augustus' failings are that he was ambitious beyond belief for supremacy; and that he was a keen dice player.[7] The author was telling us more than he intended.

In the event Octavian was to have a lifetime of seventy-six years, and he came on the stage at a crucial point in a revolution that transformed an aggressive, oligarchical republic with a firm claim on three continents into a monarchic empire. C. Octavius, who from the opening of Caesar's will in 44 and the acceptance of his inheritance down to 27 BC is conventionally known to modern historians as Octavian, had been with Caesar in Spain for some part of his stay there in 46–45, but does not seem to have taken part in the main campaign, of Munda (Montilla).[8] It was during further training at Apollonia (Pojani) in Epirus in preparation for Caesar's Parthian campaign that he heard of his great-uncle's assassination on 15 March, 44 BC; the letter from his mother Atia reached him near the end of the month and urged him to return to Italy. Nicolaus of Damascus gives a graphic account of the views of Octavius' entourage.[9] He crossed to Brundisium (Brindisi) and at Lupiae (Lecce), still in southern Italy, he learned the details of Caesar's will.[10] Despite the pleas of his mother and stepfather L. Marcius Philippus, consul 56 BC and a neutral in the civil wars of 49–45, he decided at once to accept the bequest and the obligation to avenge Caesar that that carried with it, and did so publicly on the day after he arrived in Rome on 6 May,[11] promising the people the games in honour of Venus Genetrix vowed by Caesar at the battle of Pharsalus and the payment of Caesar's bequest to them.

Octavian had had more than a month to think, and advice from relatives and friends, from the cautious Philippus to hold off altogether, from young and ambitious comrades to stage a coup immediately, and from more prudent older followers of Caesar to enter the political arena – which he followed. So it was a considered decision. Caesar had had an agnate relative, Sextus Caesar, but he had been killed two years previously governing Syria as quaestor *pro praetore*. That had removed a possible rival heir, however insignificant he might be.[12] The inheritance left Octavius by Caesar's last dispositions of September 45 was the greater part of Caesar's estate and, more important, the name that he was required to take with it: he was now 'Caesar' and was addressed as such before his arrival in Rome.[13] As to the property, he had to meet charges on it such as the *HS* 300 left to each member of the Roman *plebs* and was forced to raise money by selling properties, as well as showing himself willing to spend all he had from any source in pursuit of political ends.[14]

It was a familiar provision of Roman wills that a main heir should take on the name of a testator whose line and name would otherwise have been extinguished, but it did not have the status of a formal adoption.[15] The original name of a properly adopted son was often attached to his new one, in an adjectival form: the great second-century general P. Cornelius Scipio *Aemilianus* was an Aemilius adopted by a Cornelius Scipio. Caesar's heir dropped his comparatively undistinguished former name completely and enveloped himself in the grandeur of his great-uncle's name. Some refused that and still called him Octavius; so the senior statesman and great orator M. Tullius Cicero, who was devoted to the cause of the Republic, followed the example of Philippus against the practice of the youth's entourage.[16] It was unfriendly too to recall the original name by using 'Octavianus'.[17] Such pinpricks were nothing compared with the fact that the will did not make him Caesar's son, a status worth far more than a name, for it would give him a firm claim to the loyalty of Caesar's clients, his freedmen and other dependants.[18] Octavian was to remedy this as soon as he could, and by unprecedented means.

But if Octavian was to make his way to the eminence that his 'father's' will indicated for him, he first had to play off two sides, both hostile to any such ambitions – but also to each other: Caesar's political ally and consul of 44, Mark Antony,[19] and the assassins ('Liberators') and their natural allies, senators such as Cicero, who were aiming at a restoration of traditional Republican government: a nominal democracy under the guidance of a Senate united in defending its own collective power and interests. These were men known in their own time and to themselves as *optimates*, those who advocated the rule of 'the best'.[20] Cicero's greatest fear and dislike was for Caesar's long-standing ally Mark Antony, the consul of 44 BC, who would remain in power and the possession of legions as a proconsul in 43. That made Cicero vulnerable to the wiles of Caesar's untried heir. Octavian was taken up by Cicero, whatever his misgivings, as the only effective means of saving the state from rule by Caesar's lieutenant. Octavian was aware that he was being used, eventually let Cicero know that he was not going to be disposed of, and made ideas of that kind a pretext for going over to Antony and Caesar's other leading ally M. Aemilius Lepidus, consul in 46 and Caesar's deputy as Master of the Horse.[21] All the same, Octavian had shown Cicero the respect due to an elder statesman and was given strong support, being compared by Cicero with Republican early achievers such as P. Scipio Africanus and Pompey the Great.[22] For long after his early days as a 'butcher boy', Pompey had come to defend the Republic against the usurping Julius Caesar, and could be presented as a model statesman.[23] Octavian's necessarily equivocal and at its worst treacherous role during his rise to power made this part of his life history difficult to put in a favourable light. We do not possess his *Autobiography*, only the material in Nicolaus of Damascus' biography and in other writers deriving from it and the much later formal recital of his *Achievements*, in that the references to his activities in this period are 'lacunose and scattered'.[24]

Since he arrived in Italy Octavian had been raising a private army for his own use, recruiting from Caesar's veterans in Campania (each man received a bonus of 500 *denarii*) and bribing legions away from Antony, the Martia and the Fourth, who had grievances about pay, with his five-fold offers.[25] Emissaries were also working on Antony's legions still on the other side of the Adriatic. When a story went round at the beginning of October that Octavian intended to assassinate Antony, ordinary people put it down as an invention of Antony's; Cicero liked to think that it was true – and approved.[26] On 10 November 44 Octavian appeared in Rome in the absence of the consul Antony and, introduced by the anti-Antonian tribune Ti. Cannutius, held a public meeting demanding recognition (the speech, which alarmed Cicero, was circulated). His troops, however, were more interested in avenging Caesar, and drifted away. It was a weakness of Octavian's that Caesar's veterans were against conflict between Caesar' heirs. Antony was approaching, so Octavian beat a retreat. His rival, after the ineffective march against him, was close to proposing that Octavian be declared an enemy of the state (*hostis*).[27] For the moment Octavian maintained his pose as the champion of senatorial government. In his third *Philippic* oration of 20 December 44, Cicero proposed and carried a vote of thanks to Octavian and the 'liberator' (assassin of Caesar) D. Brutus Albinus, who was consul designate for 42, as saviours of the state, and proposed that measures should be taken to protect the incoming consuls A. Hirtius and C. Pansa.

It was at the instigation of Cicero that the youthful champion Octavian, on 7 January 43 BC, accepted praetorian *imperium*, despite being under-age and having held no previous office; he was to use his legions in a joint attack on Antony.[28] He was allowed consular rank and permission to hold office ten years before the standard age. The precedent of Pompey the Great at the outset of his career comes forcibly to mind, though Cicero found reputable precedents from earlier in the Republic, as well as that of Alexander the Great, and confidently vouched for the future conduct of Octavian.[29] He was over-confident. A gilded equestrian statue was also voted in January, and was later modified to bring Octavian closer to divine models.[30] Antony was besieging D. Brutus, consul designate for 42, who had barred him from his province of Cisalpine Gaul, in Mutina (Modena). As an ex-consul Antony had proconsular *imperium*, and by a plebiscite of 1 June 44 had received the Gauls as his province for five years instead of Macedonia, and the attack on him was illegal.[31] Antony was defeated near Mutina on 21 April, but the consuls both died in the campaign, leaving more troops to be picked up by Octavian. Antony retreated over the Alps, pursued by D. Brutus, while Octavian was predominant in Italy.

There is no reason to suppose that Octavian was responsible in any way for the death of the consuls (that was a hostile fantasy),[32] but it provided a vacancy which Octavian was now intent on filling – twenty-two years before the legal age. His march on Rome outdid in its lack of justification all his main precedents, Sulla, Marius and Caesar. But he began by suggesting to Cicero that they should take a joint consulship.[33] In April and May, after a rebuff from the Senate, which also unwisely refused Cicero's proposal that Octavian should be allowed an ovation for his success at Mutina, cut the rewards promised to his soldiers, and transferred the command to D. Brutus, he was already thinking of an alliance with Antony.

By 9 June it had become known that Antony and Lepidus, who was now governor of Transalpine Gaul and Nearer Spain, had come to terms; the coalition was enlarged by the accession of C. Asinius Pollio from Further Spain (two legions) and L. Munatius Plancus, proconsul in Transalpine Gaul, bringing Antony's legions to a total of twenty-three, against Octavian's seventeen.[34] Theoretically Octavian was the Senate's closest protection, along with D. Brutus. Instead Octavian in July sent a formidable delegation of 400 centurions and soldiers to the Senate demanding a suffect consulship. When the demand was refused (the Senate offered the right to stand for the consulship and five thousand *denarii* to the soldiers but thought better of it when it heard of the arrival of two legions from Africa), Octavian marched on Rome, though he entered the city only with his body-guard.[35] This went beyond earlier usurpations: Marius, Sulla, Pompey and Caesar at least had official power and long service behind them when they forced their way into power; Octavian had one battle and nothing to back him but the loyalty of his troops to Caesar's heir.[36]

On 19 August, providentially swept into office by the sight of six, then twelve vultures, an augury such as had been shown to Romulus, so it was afterwards reported,[37] Octavian entered on his first consulship, with his elderly uncle Q. Pedius (who had handed over part of his legacy from Caesar to Octavian) as colleague, 'no longer just a youth', as he wrote in his *Autobiography,* 'but nineteen years old';[38] Atia lived long enough to see her son's success, but she must have realised that it meant still more danger for him in the long run.[39] For the moment Octavian was in a strong position, with both his potential opponents, Antony and the Republicans, weakened; and the resistance he had met from the Senate gave him the excuse to present himself now as Caesar's avenger. The Lex Pedia passed by Octavian's uncle used a simple formula against the assassins that obviated the need for regular time-consuming trials: all those deemed to have been involved in Caesar's death were declared outlaws and their property confiscated.[40] The decrees against Antony and Lepidus were rescinded and existing appointments in the provinces annulled. It was the State Treasury, the Aerarium, that paid Octavian's veteran troops the balance of Caesar's bequest, ensuring their further loyalty. When he and Antony met Lepidus at the end of October not far from Bononia (Bologna), Octavian was in control of seventeen legions, one more than Antony – the governor of Gaul, Q. Fufius Calenus, had died and his troops had gone over to Octavian; Lepidus had ten.[41]

As we have seen, Caesar's will alone had not done enough for a politician playing for such high stakes. After he became consul, Octavian went through a piece of play-acting that has continued to seduce scholars. The ceremony would have been appropriate if the living Caesar had adopted Octavian formally by the method called *adrogatio*. That entailed the extinction of the family and rites of an adoptee who was his own master (*sui iuris*) and so at least potentially a father of a family (*paterfamilias*), solemnly performed in the curiate assembly of the Roman People (at that time reduced to thirty representative lictors, one for each *curia*) in the presence of priests who were to sanction the sacral consequence of extinguishing the rites. The procedure gave the wishes of the adopter standing in public law. It was controversially undergone by the radical politician P. Clodius Pulcher in 59 BC, to enable him to shed his patrician status and stand for the plebeian office of tribune, and by the future emperor Tiberius in AD 4, to make him the full legal equivalent of a son of Augustus' body. Antony had naturally had the process of 'adoption' vetoed by tribunes in May 44, the month when the two men first met. As to what was done in 43 BC, when Antony was away from Rome, the fact that Octavian went through the ceremony has actually been used as evidence for its authenticity after the death of the 'adopter'. On the contrary, it is evidence of Octavian's desperate wish to legitimate himself as Caesar's heir. At least when Clodius was adopted the adopter was alive and the Pontifex Maximus (Julius Caesar!) was present. In 43 that priest, Caesar's successor in the office, Lepidus, was away with his army.[42]

Octavian and his allies spared no effort to show how far back Caesar's favour to him went. At the time of the battle of Munda (17 March, 45 BC), when Caesar demolished a grove of trees, a palm was spared. It sprang a new shoot, and it would have been natural to connect that with further successes destined for Caesar. Instead, the sign was taken over by Octavian, primarily as a warrant for his 'adoption', then to demonstrate how early Caesar had shown him favour.[43] This justification for the 'adoption' comes from Suetonius, the fully developed version from Cassius Dio, who, like Velleius Paterculus, implies that Octavius took part in the fighting, although he seems to have arrived in Spain only in time for the end of the campaign. So a thread can be traced from official reports about Caesar to Augustus' *Autobiography* and from there to mythologising 'government' history.

Octavian was taunted with owing everything to his name, that is, Caesar's. It is a key item in his relentless advance that he also exploited to the full all the religious connotations of his celebration of the Games voted for Caesar's Victory in July 44: the appearance of a comet, the *Iulium sidus*, as a star to be interpreted as a token of Caesar's divinisation and accordingly displayed on coins and statues, made the connexion clear enough. When he had brought about Caesar's formal deification in 42 that became the justification for his designation as 'Son of the Deified' (*Divi filius*), which appears on coins from 40 at latest; in 38 they present the two men on obverse and reverse, with Julius more youthful than he had appeared for some time and bringing the two men closer together; in 36 Octavian demonstrated his devotion by issuing gold and silver coinage bearing his own full name, Imperator Caesar Divi filius, and titles, all in the nominative case, on the obverse and running over on to the reverse, and showing there a temple with the legend 'To the deified Caesar' in its architrave. Then there was Octavian's proclaimed determination to avenge his death, vengeance for which the troops were also conveniently clamouring, and which survived as a theme in literature and architecture long after the assassins were all dead, and still figures strongly in Augustus' *Achievements*.[44]

The second Triumvirate

By a Lex Titia of 27 November, 43, which was passed without the legally required interval of three market days between promulgation and voting, Lepidus, Antony and Octavian (the *Fasti* followed strict seniority) had themselves appointed a 'Board of Three for the Establishment of the Commonwealth' ('Triumviri rei publicae constituendae causa') for five years. To seal the bargain a marriage was arranged between Octavian and Antony's step-daughter Claudia.[45] These were the terms in which the longed-for goal of a return to political normality came to be formulated. 'Res publica', what belongs to the People, has conventionally been translated 'Republic', but that imposes both limitations and modern preconceptions. It soon acquired the more specialised sense of 'Republic as opposed to monarchy, dictatorship or Principate', and it is best to avoid becoming entangled in that confusion. 'Commonwealth' is to be preferred and has come into use.[46] So the 'Second Triumvirate' became a formal entity; the so-called 'First Triumvirate' of 60 BC was at most an informal pact between Pompey the Great, Julius Caesar and M. Licinius Crassus; only when it was renewed in 56 did the division of provinces between the dynasts foreshadow the division of responsibilities agreed on by Antony, Octavian and Lepidus. When the Triumvirs divided the western Empire between themselves, Octavian's share reflected not only his lack of seniority but also his comparative weakness in legionary troops compared with the joint total of his colleagues. He received Sardinia, Sicily and Africa. Pompey's younger son Sextus Pompeius, who had escaped after Caesar's victory at Munda in 45, was based in southern Spain with seven legions and still controlled the seas under a senatorial commission as Prefect of the Fleet and Seashore. Sextus was condemned under the Lex Pedia, marking out a formidable enemy for the Triumvirs; so the value of Octavian's portion was still further diminished. He also relinquished his consulship to Antony's supporter P. Ventidius.[47]

Whatever the Triumvirs' title said about stabilising the Commonwealth, the Lex Titia defined their *imperium* as greater than that of any other holder, gave them the right to appoint magistrates and to make or annul laws, and immediately initiated a period of absolute rule at Rome, and the repression of free speech.[48] Vengeance was the immediate aim of the Triumvirs against the most prominent of Caesar's murderers, M. Brutus and C. Cassius, who (relevantly) were in possession of lucrative eastern provinces.[49] Antony and Octavian took on this task, while Lepidus remained in charge of their western dominions. To remove Republican sympathisers from the West and to help fund the expedition they instituted proscriptions, Octavian and his colleagues outdoing Sulla. The gains were considerable, seeing that the property qualification of a knight and so of a senator was half a million sesterces. It is not surprising that the protection of private property was a significant part of Augustus' restored Commonwealth.[50] Notoriously, Antony's enemy Cicero was a victim, but the story that Octavian opposed that murder is suspect – it is what Octavian would have said as soon as his relations with Antony began to deteriorate, if not before.[51] Lepidus's brutality was also damned after the event in the *'Laudatio Turiae'*.[52] Octavian had targets of his own, and according to Suetonius was the most relentless of the three; he was severely blamed in one tradition reported by Tacitus.

Second and third century writers would have had sources with divergent views. Julius Saturninus, who is cited by Suetonius, is of uncertain date and social status; it is not even known whether he was a pamphleteer, a biographer or an historian. But he gives us the detail that 'when the proscription was complete, Lepidus in the Senate justified what had happened and held out hope for clemency in the future, since enough punishment had been exacted, but Octavian on the contrary said that the kind of limit he had placed on the proscriptions left everything open to him'.[53] Octavian's childhood guardian C. Toranius, colleague with his father in the aedileship and a former partisan of Pompey the Great, was one of the victims. According to Appian about 2,300 people would eventually be proscribed, many totally innocent, and including women; three hundred perished, senators and knights. That compares with the 2,080 said to have been proscribed by Sulla. (Some who escaped were afterwards restored.) The numbers of the Senate, set at 600 by Sulla in 81, had risen to 900, largely as a result of Caesar's admissions. All the same, the impact of the purge left an ineradicable scar, traceable in all the historians and moralists who dealt with it: Valerius Maximus, Suetonius, Appian and Dio.[54]

The intense hatreds of the period, pre-existing and newly generated, can be seen from the stories that were current about Octavian, as part of the propaganda put about by all sides. True or not, they passed into the historical record.[55] One belongs to 43. It is that of the urban praetor Q. Gallius.[56] Suetonius gives two versions of Gallius' fate. In the first, when he held some folded tablets under his robe as he was paying his respects, Octavian, suspecting that he had a sword concealed there, did not dare to make a search on the spot for fear the object should turn out to be something else; but a little later he had Gallius hustled from the tribunal by centurions and soldiers, tortured him as if he were a slave, and though he made no confession, ordered his execution, first tearing out the man's eyes with his own hands. Then Suetonius gives Augustus' own version, from his *Autobiography*: Gallius actually made a treacherous attack on him after asking for an audience, and was haled off to prison; he was dismissed under sentence of banishment and either lost his life by shipwreck or was waylaid by brigands (so little interest did Octavian have in the fate of his would-be assassin). This version is followed by Appian, who adds details favourable to Octavian: Gallius had applied for a command in Africa; his colleagues stripped him of his praetorship, the people tore his house down, and the Senate condemned him to death, while Octavian simply ordered him to join his brother abroad. The version in the *Autobiography* would hardly have been necessary for so insignificant an event if the first, damaging story had not already been current: Gallius' relatives and friends would be the obvious source. It would have been taken up and elaborated by Antonian partisans. Neither of the versions is wholly acceptable, although Octavian's fear of assassination notably figures in both. The factual basis is that the victim was arrested in public and did not survive. Gallius, linked as he was to Antony and his henchman Ti. Claudius Nero, is likely enough to have been hostile to Octavian. It is an attractive hypothesis that Gallius was the praetor in charge of the court that was dealing with cases under the Lex Pedia and inclined to leniency. The gory trimmings of the first story are not convincing, because there would have been few witnesses to what happened and clearly no body was recovered; that would have made Octavian's version pointless. A like technique was applied, according to Dio. to a senatorial juror in the same court. Silicius Corona voted for the acquittal of M. Brutus and boasted of it and the fact that he was not killed at once gained Octavian a reputation for forbearance. Afterwards he was proscribed and executed.[57] This was not the last time that Octavian was lucky in being freed permanently from a man who was alleged to be implicated in conspiracy against him; the story of Athenaeus, the philosopher from Cilicia who escaped condemnation twenty years later, was similar (Ch. 4). Even a military tribune, Ofillius, who simply championed the demands of Octavian's veterans in 35 for land and money (the crowns and municipal robes of state that he was distributing were only boys' toys) and forced Octavian off his tribunal, disappeared the following day, the story went, never to be seen again.[58] Admittedly such charges are as easy to bring against Octavian as the murderous orders would be to give.

After the defeat and death of the Liberators M. Brutus and Cassius at the two battles of Philippi in October–November 42,[59] Antony was at his most powerful, while Octavian had not distinguished himself. His wing had been defeated by Brutus in the first battle, and there were allegations of cowardice, which he rebutted in his *Autobiography*: he was told by his doctor, who had had a warning dream, to leave his sick bed in camp.[60] But at any rate Octavian had been a participant in the campaign and so gained at the expense of Lepidus, whose very loyalty had somehow become suspect: while Antony took Africa and Gaul in place of the Cisalpina, now a part of Italy, Octavian was allocated all Spain as well as Numidia. He also had to find Italian homes for up to fifty thousand discharged legionaries from the victorious armies, troublesome men who could also, if they were looked after, form a loyal core of support in future political and military struggles.[61] This pattern repeated itself after all his Triumviral victories, and did not disappear under his principate. It was a recurrent and destructive nightmare. On this occasion it meant ruthlessly expelling owners from their lands round the eighteen richest cities of Italy, and there was a revolt led by L. Antonius, brother of the Triumvir and consul 41. It was focused on Etruria, but also involved Umbria, Rome and Campania and it was ended only when in the early spring of 40 BC Octavian captured the hill-top city of Perusia (Perugia) after a lengthy siege.[62] An initial display of clemency was followed by extraordinarily brutal treatment of the inhabitants (even if it has been exaggerated): only a single city councillor survived and one victim was denied burial; other cities suffered too. Octavian's alleged pitilessness after Philippi is mirrored in his acts at Perusia: 'You just have to die!' ('Moriendum est') was his answer to a cry for mercy.[63] But the story that some three hundred men including senators and knights were actually sacrificed on an altar to Julius Caesar set up outside the town is not to be believed: it surely derives from the deaths of the councillors and a metaphorical interpretation of them as a 'sacrifice' to the shade of Caesar; if executions took place anywhere near 15 March, that would give credence to the story. That is not the only tale of human sacrifice in these years and before. Antony is accused of treating the execution after Philippi of Q. Hortensius, whom he blamed for his brother's execution at the hands of D. Brutus, as a sacrifice at the tomb, and another sacrifice (to Neptune) is attributed to Sex. Pompeius. The earliest such story belongs to the civil wars between Sulla and the Marians. Marius Gratidianus was 'sacrificed' by the villainous Catiline at the tomb of Q. Catulus.[64] In later and more conciliatory years the revolt could be treated as understandable, though misdirected by its leaders. All the same, some of the Triumvirs' opponents had a higher regard for Antony; there was mileage to be got out of the story of a man being led to execution after the battle of Philippi who saluted Antony but refused to acknowledge Octavian.[65] The years 41–36 must have seen Octavian's standing in Italy at its lowest. Suetonius reports not only predictable taunts from Sex. Pompeius and Antony and his brother Lucius about his relations with Julius Caesar and A. Hirtius, but also the appreciative reaction of a theatre audience to a line about the world dancing to a pansy's beat.[66] Meanwhile Octavian was honing his own skills as a traducer: lines on Antony's wife Fulvia, who had worked against him in the Perusine War, are preserved by Martial; certainly Octavian's troops got the message: lead bullets have been found with the inscription 'I'm for Fulvia's cunt'. This was precisely the target that Octavian avoided, in spite of Fulvia's pressing invitation: '"Either fuck me or let's fight", she says. Well, my dick's more than life to me. Let battle commence.'[67]

After the Perusine war both Antony and Octavian began to court Sextus Pompeius, the most powerful and prestigious survivor of the Republican cause.[68] Sextus had emulated his father in winning control of the seas between Italy, Gaul, Spain and north Africa, and so of the grain supply to Rome. It was with his co-operation that Antony returned to Italy to recover his position there after his brother Lucius and Fulvia had been defeated. He put Brundisium under siege, but the troops of the two Caesarian leaders refused to fight. Instead they had to conclude the treaty named after the town (October 40 BC) which, while granting Africa to Lepidus, simply divided the rest of the Empire between Antony and Octavian, East and West. The agreement quickly led to the death of Octavian's equestrian commander Q. Salvidienus Rufus, who had actually been designated consul for 39. Antony informed Octavian that Rufus had been in negotiation with him with the idea of changing sides; Rufus was recalled from Gaul, and denounced by Octavian before the compliant Senate. Thanksgivings followed his death (suicide or execution).[69]

In the East, Antony was confronted by a massive Parthian invasion abetted by the Republican Q. Labienus, and needed to make good the losses in material and prestige that it brought. He commanded the loyalties of Rome's dependent monarchs, who included Cleopatra VII of Egypt. She was by far the most important, for the wealth of her kingdom in gold and grain, but Egypt had long been on the point of being taken over by Rome, and Cleopatra also had to deal with her brothers, who claimed their share of the throne. Her only security lay in friendship with the imperial power, and with the individuals who ruled Rome. She had already deployed this strategy when Caesar visited Egypt in 48–47 BC, and the son she had in 47 was claimed as his – an invaluable tie with the central power. Now her links must be with Antony, the new master of the East. Nonetheless, to cement the agreement made at Brundisium, Antony, now widowed, promptly wed his colleague's sister Octavia, who had also just lost her husband C. Claudius Marcellus,[70] while Octavian, with his friend Maecenas acting as broker, married Scribonia, sister of L. Scribonius Libo, Sextus' father-in-law;[71] his only child, the elder Julia, was born the following year. Marriages and betrothals were an essential part of Roman political life, and sentiment had to take second place. Octavian was fully equal to Antony in marital ruthlessness and infidelity. Bad faith (*mala fides*), the worst offence in the Roman book, did not count where wives were concerned, only for kinsmen by marriage.[72]

Ties contracted long since could also be exploited. In the negotiations leading up to the meeting at Brundisium, Octavian complained that Antony's mother, a Julia, daughter of the consul of 90 BC, had left Italy although she was his kinswoman; so he used her to put pressure on Antony.[73]

In 38 Octavian completed another of the procedures that were putting the most outrageous of his predecessors in the shade. 'C. Caesar Divi filius' felt that a modification of his name was desirable, to display his own military merit, which had been little in evidence at Philippi. The banal *praenomen* Gaius was abandoned, and the title 'Imperator' substituted for it. That meant 'general', and successful commanders were saluted as such by their troops; they then added the title to their names, at the end, and kept it until they celebrated the triumph they were hoping for. But Octavian was dissatisfied with such a temporary honour. He was to be supremely and permanently a successful general and took the title as a *praenomen*. Nothing in the way of extraordinary nomenclature had come near this.[74]

Antony was the chief obstacle to Octavian's supremacy, but Sextus Pompeius remained recalcitrant and an immediate threat to his position. Grain shortages in Rome and his own unpopularity (the occasion for stories of his own extravagant feasting) forced Octavian to recognise him in the Treaty of Misenum (Miseno), 39 BC.[75] The treaty conceded him the Peloponnese as well as Sicily, Sardinia, Corsica and the islands that had made up Octavian's original portion. Decades later, in his *Achievements*, Augustus was to claim that they had been 'seized'.[76] In addition, Sextus was given civil advancement for himself (he was to become an augur and hold the consulship in 35), he secured the return of all exiles, some also to political office, except those who were directly implicated in Caesar's murder.[77] This coup won him marked popularity. Later Octavian was to claim, implausibly, that Pompeius, with the support of his 'pirates', was aiming at tyranny; a different strand of thought held that he had been duped.[78] As might be expected, the new agreement added to the familial links that connected Octavian and Pompeius: Sextus' daughter was betrothed to M. Claudius Marcellus, Octavian's little nephew.[79]

But there was one factor in Octavian's activities that was not the result of calculation. This was the passion he developed for Livia Drusilla, his junior by nearly five years, daughter of a man who had killed himself after the battle of Philippi and wife of Ti. Claudius Nero, a patrician exiled after his support for L. Antonius in the Perusine War. Paradoxically the great romance

Figure 3 Livia Drusilla (akg-images Ltd. Photograph by Nimatallah)

of the Triumviral Period was not that between Antony and Cleopatra, but this one of Octavian's. Nero was a complaisant husband – and politician. He gave away his wife to Octavian early in 38. The marriage followed Octavian's divorce of Scribonia, whose intolerable wilfulness was the reason offered in the *Autobiography*,[80] but Octavian was loosening his ties with Pompeius and bringing himself closer to Antony. Livia's attractions went far beyond her beauty and intelligence: she brought connexions with the prominent patrician family of the Claudii Pulchri and with the plebeian Livii Drusi: her father had been adopted by the M. Livius Drusus, tribune 91, the martyred champion of Italian enfranchisement. The marriage with Livia caused scandal at the time, especially as she was pregnant with her second child, giving rise to the rumour that he was Octavian's son, not Nero's. Octavian toughed it out and recorded the birth of Drusus in the public gazette.[81] Each of the two leading Triumvirs had reasons of his own to be grateful to Nero, but he never reached the consulship and soon died, leaving his sons to be brought up in Octavian's house. But the marriage with Livia and the success of Octavian's new stepsons were to cause him and Rome years of trouble later, when the daughter of Scribonia and her children in turn lost ground to them or died (Ch. 4).

It was not long before hostilities broke out again between Octavian and Sex. Pompeius, on what Appian suspects to be a pretext.[82] Octavian's immediate aim was to eliminate Sextus and take over his power base. He was unsuccessful and had to appeal to Antony for help. Antony in turn had to concede it: he needed troops for his campaign against the Parthians, the prestigious execution of Caesar's project of revenging the death of M. Crassus at their hands in 53 BC. Besides, the five-year term of the Triumvirate was expiring at the end of 38, leaving the dynasts without a legal basis for their activities. One hundred and twenty fighting ships and ten skiffs, vital to the campaign against Pompeius, were to be exchanged for a thousand elite troops for Antony's Parthian war, with twenty thousand legionaries to follow.[83] At Tarentum (Taranto) in the summer of 37 they decided to renew the agreement, probably for a further five-year term, to expire at the end of 32 (see the Appendix at the end of this chapter, p. 51). According to Dio, Pompeius was now stripped of his priesthood and his consulship.[84] In token of the intended permanence of the renewed alliance, Antony betrothed his elder son by Fulvia, Antyllus, to Octavian's infant daughter Julia.

In the event, Octavian, taking the ships at once (and returning half later[85]), did not deliver more than two thousand troops to Antony. There is no need to suppose that this was due to thought-out deceit, rather than to the weakening force of an inconvenient promise. The troops accompanied Octavia to the East in 35 when Antony's first Parthian expedition had already proved a failure. Antony accepted them and the other supplies that came with Octavia. But he needed more than them, and his losses could be made up only by Cleopatra. Octavia, reaching Athens, had to go back to Rome without seeing her husband, who was on campaign and returned to Alexandria for the winter. It was a useful item for Octavian's propaganda (expected, as some said), one that outweighed any help she could have given Antony in Rome, and was at its most valuable when Antony finally divorced her in the early summer of 32.[86]

The ships on the other hand had been put to good use and in the summer of 36, after a hard struggle, Octavian's forces, expertly trained by Agrippa, defeated Sex. Pompeius in two naval battles off the coast of Sicily, Mylae and

Naulochus (Milazzo; off Venético, 3 September, 36). After losing ships in a storm Octavian had vowed to win despite Sextus' patron deity Neptune, and at the next circus games Neptune was conspicuous by his absence from the procession on 13 November.[87] Pompeius fled to the East and was captured by Antony's lieutenants; who was responsible for his execution is uncertain, but Octavian put on games in celebration. Nevertheless, when it came in the last four years of the decade to the war of words with Antony, Octavian reproached him for the execution of the son of the great Pompey. There were demonstrations in Rome against Pompeius' killer, M. Titius, who left Antony and carried his bad reputation into Octavian's camp, offending the people when he held games in Pompey's theatre.[88] Pompeius was the only independent and effective actor in the Triumviral period who had a link with the Republic and who had won gratitude when he befriended the proscribed. This was an opponent for Octavian to belittle and forget.[89] His victory over Sextus he misrepresented as the crushing of a nest of runaway slaves and pirates; slaves who had been serving under Sextus were returned to their masters; 6,000 who could not be identified were crucified; Octavian was assimilating Pompeius to the slave rebel Spartacus, whose six thousand followers were crucified after his defeat. The claim that Octavian had freed twenty thousand slaves to serve under himself was suppressed.[90]

The fall of Mark Antony

The third man in the Triumvirate, M. Lepidus, was the next victim. Having contributed to the conquest of Sicily, he demanded that it be added to his territorial share. Octavian, displaying his striking gift for seducing rivals' troops for the last and most spectacular time, courageously presented himself (along with his financial offers) to Lepidus' men and forced him into surrender and resignation from the Triumvirate. He was so little thought of that he was allowed to live on, spending the rest of his life (he survived until 12 BC) at Circeii (Circeo), on the Tyrrhenian sea, except when Augustus humiliatingly required his presence in the Senate. As a useful demonstration of clemency, he was even allowed to keep his position as Pontifex Maximus, taken in hasty succession to Caesar.[91]

After the defeat of Sextus and the deposition of Lepidus, Octavian declared the civil wars over – Appian indeed ends his *Civil Wars* at this point – and in November celebrated an ovation. Octavian had learnt from the Perusine War: problems with the veterans who were demanding discharge were solved by offering them land outside Italy, or else their plots in Italy were duly paid for. At Capua when land was taken for the settlers, the city was compensated with a territory in Crete.[92] (The courageous old jurisconsult A. Cascellius had adamantly refused to collaborate by recognising Triumviral distributions.[93]) Now that civil wars were over, it could be said in November, in well-publicised speeches to Senate and People, normal government would be restored; oppressive taxes levied for the war were already remitted, and magistrates allowed more freedom.[94] Octavian was trying to recover his position at home. A golden statue was set up in the Forum, and its inscription celebrated the return of peace, giving intimations of hope; Italian cities set up statues of him in their temples. Those of Antony and Octavian were erected, significantly, in the Temple of Concord at Rome.[95]

If the civil wars were over, now was the time for the end of the Triumvirate and the restoration of complete normality in government.[96] Instead, in another unprecedented move, the Triumvir was awarded another distinction besides his ovation. He received a grant of the sacrosanctity that tribunes of the *plebs* enjoyed. Their controversial activities made them liable to physical attack, so they were vested in the protection of the gods and made sacrosanct. In the previous hundred years that had not saved Ti. and C. Gracchus and their political heirs; but to attack Octavian physically would be an offence against divine law; even verbal abuse might also be construed in this way. What occasioned the original measure in his favour is unclear, but it may have been connected with a conspiracy, actually hatched against him or alleged. He had good reason to expect attack, whether from the disgruntled remnants of the Pompeians or from the side of Antony. More surprisingly the privilege was soon extended (in 35) to Octavian's wife and sister, putting them on a level, in Roman eyes, far removed from that of any Egyptian Queen.[97] The grant to Octavian's sister was understandable in reparation for her humiliating visit to Athens; to leave out Livia, who needed it more after the scandal of her marriage to the Triumvir, might seem invidious.

After the downfall of Pompeius and Lepidus, Octavian was free now to concentrate on bringing down Antony, whose military misadventures against the Parthians (though he did succeed in annexing Armenia Major in 35) seemed to be compounded by political blunders; and they are sometimes attributed to an uncontrollable passion for Cleopatra. We have already seen that there is no need to assume that she had an uncontrollable passion for Antony; her political needs accounted for the attraction. His position too needs to be reconsidered.

As Roman master of the East – though that did not mean that Octavian was ineffective there[98] – Antony had immense difficulties to overcome: when he took over there it was not quite half a century since Greek-speakers in Asia Minor and mainland Greece had risen at the bidding of Mithridates VI Eupator to shake off Roman rule and taxation and to massacre (it was said) eighty thousand Roman business men and officials in the 'Asiatic Vespers'; and less than half a decade since Brutus and Cassius had financed their campaigns by enforced requisitioning. Cleopatra, last of the Hellenistic monarchs who were heirs to the empire of Alexander the Great, represented authenticity, self-government and self-respect for the Greeks. Antony by 'marrying' her identified himself with the same cause and acquired the key to Egypt's wealth and the resources that Cleopatra's other domains could provide, such as ship timber from Cilicia and the Lebanon. Another advantage was Cleopatra's liaison with Julius Caesar and her son, Ptolemy Caesarion, who was ultimately

Figure 4   Antony and Octavia coin (© the Trustees of the British Museum)

recognised as Caesar's by Antony. A son of Caesar's body could be presented as a rival to the bourgeois Octavian, who was not even a son of Caesar by regular adoption. In Cleopatra's thinking her son, as the embodiment of Horus, son of the murdered Osiris, had his own claim as an avenger of the murdered Dictator.[99]

In order to keep his political authority as an acceptable Roman leader in the Greek-speaking part of the Empire, Antony needed not only the material support that the resources of Egypt could give him but the hearts and minds of his Greek-speaking subjects, in Alexandria and throughout the eastern provinces. That meant presenting himself in the trappings of Hellenistic monarchy, specifically those of the Ptolemies of Egypt, the only monarchy that still survived with some independence from the rapacious and hated Romans. The problem was that Octavian was able to make much of this need. Even the celebration in Alexandria of Antony's takeover of Armenia Octavian could misrepresent as the uprooting into alien soil of a traditional Roman triumph, threatening the displacement of Rome as the centre of the Empire and the loss to Senate and People alike of all the privileges that went with that position.[100] Then there was the affront to Roman dignity and custom: spurning his blameless wife, Octavian's sister, Antony had embarked on an illegitimate liaison, productive too, with an 'Egyptian' who could not be his wife.

Octavian himself spent hard campaigning seasons in Illyricum (35–34), acquiring honourable wounds, winning back standards lost in 48, and training his forces. The successes were duly reported to the Senate and recorded in the *Autobiography*.[101] The year 34 presented him with another opportunity to show Antony up. In the 'Donations of Alexandria', Antony, having entered Alexandria in a parody of a Roman triumph and seated on a golden throne, allegedly allocated regions that had been provinces of the Roman Empire to Cleopatra the 'Queen of Kings' and her children.[102] Antony's recognition of Caesarion, who was to be Cleopatra's joint ruler as 'King of Kings', was met by a sharp riposte from the side of Octavian, written by Caesar's friend C. Oppius.[103] Antony and Cleopatra's sons Alexander Helios and Ptolemy Philadelphus were made kings respectively of lands east and west of the Euphrates, and his daughter Cleopatra Selene of Cyrene. Lesser dependants were also given a share and an interest in the survival of Antony's regime. Useful as all that was in securing the loyalty of Egypt and securing control of areas without the expense of deploying Roman troops (a point made by the geographer Strabo), it gave a supremely effective propaganda weapon to Octavian: whatever was done he would have made the most of it. The hard-won provinces of the Roman People were being given away to foreign kings. Even Antony's legionaries were put at the beck and call of Cleopatra.[104] The reality was different. Cassius Dio gives an account of the changes Octavian made in the East after his victory. Even some of the rulers deposed in 30 were reinstated, and Octavian made some donations of his own when he was in the East again in 20 BC.[105]

At the end of 34 Antony demanded joint abdication from the Triumvirate. It was an answer to the restoration of normality that Octavian offered in 36.[106] He did not intend war with Octavian and meant to tackle the Parthians in 33. But an unremitting exchange of insults and accusations developed, some directly sent by the principals, others inspired by them.[107] Drunkenness and his relations with Cleopatra were the main themes for the variations thought up by Octavian and elaborated by his friends,[108] but the studious litterateur could even reproach his rival with his florid writing style; Sallust would be a better model.[109] Octavian's colleague in the consulship of 31, M. Valerius Messala, was more gross: Antony used golden chamber pots, something to put even Cleopatra to shame. In 33 Octavian had the advantage as consul of chairing meetings of the Senate and being able to use it as his platform; in 32 he went on to sum up the effects of the debauches: Antony was under the influence of drugs and not master of himself.[110] Egyptians were little better than animals and they were the slaves of a woman, as Horace's post-Actian ninth *Epode* has it. Recriminations about sex had continued on Antony's side, notably his hint about Octavian's hasty marriage to Livia and the birth of Drusus soon afterwards and the tale of the banquet from which Octavian removed the wife of a consular, returning her later with her hair dishevelled and her ears burning. A letter from Antony to Octavian himself named four women, one of whom may be Maecenas' wife.[111] But Antony went further: Octavian, besides being a serial adulterer addicted to gambling, owed his 'adoption' by Caesar to their sexual relationship.[112] Octavian's attitude was so threatening that Antony broke off his Parthian campaigns, marched west, and marshalled his troops and ships at Ephesus in the province of Asia.

With the official expiry of the Triumvirate due at latest at the end of 32, Octavian was in a difficult position: Antony in 32 was promising his troops that he would lay down his powers within two or at most six months of victory. Octavian from that year on was relying on the consulship due to him in 31 and on an all-embracing *imperium*, relic of the Triumvirate, that he ought to have laid down on or before the expiry date, but never did, as far as we know, unless it was belatedly and tacitly included in the deposition of power that he made in January 27. In the late 30s he had a plausible excuse: Antony did not come to Rome to join him in the deposition.[113] The consuls of 32, C. Sosius and Cn. Domitius Ahenobarbus, were hostile, and Sosius' initial address to the Senate so virulent that Octavian, for the third time since 44, took to the threat of force against the House. At the following meeting, Octavian came attended by soldiers under arms and civilians with concealed weapons and made himself heard. That was the signal for the consuls to leave, followed by a substantial number of senators. There were now more than a thousand members, thanks to the admission of the Triumvirs' supporters; Augustus' own boasted figures for his seven hundred followers in the campaign of Actium in the *Achievements*, including eighty-three who either before or afterwards (as he guilelessly remarks) attained consulships and priesthoods, let it out that about three hundred senators, men domiciled in the Italy that he controlled, did not rally to him. In any case, the narrative of Dio suggests that some of Octavian's supporters had to be coerced. Some of course were sick or old. Others had fled the Senate, or remained in their country retreats, declaring neutrality or simply keeping quiet; at any rate Antony was able to convene a counter-Senate at Ephesus.[114]

Antony's own support from senators in his camp was being eroded. They were shocked by the oriental state he was keeping with Cleopatra, and by the influence that she had on his strategic and political plans.[115] That was what was said. But they could also see that there were two minds at work, with separate agendas, Antony's to maintain his position as a Triumvir and Roman politician (despite his promises to re-establish Republican government), Cleopatra's to strengthen hers as queen of a powerful and independent allied state. On the other side a single-minded individual was in charge, and one who controlled the traditional seat of government and what were thought of as the limitless manpower resources of Italy. Octavian was the man to back. When it came to the campaign of Actium in 31, even subordinate kings of the East enlisted on Antony's side also deserted: they had no predilection for Octavian's brand of government, but the very changing of the odds forced more and more to reconsider where they should stand. There was a crucial tipping point. Only the obstinate, the despairing, and

the high-principled did not at least think of moving. Cn. Domitius Ahenobarbus the consul of 32 left too, while there was still time.

One of the other senators who deserted Antony in spring 32 was L.
Munatius Plancus, along with his nephew M. Titius. He provided Octavian
with information about Antony's will, of which he had been a witness.
Munatius Plancus may have had to pay a price for his return to Rome, unless
he offered it voluntarily. Useful as he was to prove to Octavian, remaining in
favour for the rest of his life, a descendant, Munatia Plancina, fell from grace
and he more than others incurred an evil reputation as a 'pathological traitor'.[116] Now came another new and unprecedented act of blatant illegality.
Octavian demanded the will, which had been deposited with the Vestal
Virgins in Rome, and forced the Chief Vestal to surrender it. Octavian
claimed to be reading out its contents in the Senate, though he did not
allow anyone else to see it. Scholars have viewed the contents with scepticism, or held that the reading was selective.[117] What was read out was that
Antony asked to be interred beside Cleopatra in Alexandria and (this was
more of a political testament, such as Augustus himself was to leave) 'be-
queathed' tracts of Roman territory to his children by her. These provisions
aroused the righteous indignation of the Italian public, and the clever manoeuvre, besides countering Antony's offer of abdication, confronted him
with a dilemma. If he acknowledged the will he would justify the indignation;
if he repudiated it, he would alienate his supporters in the East. Octavian
could not lose. It did not matter whether he merely suppressed other
clauses or even made up the fatal ones, the effect was the same. It was in 32
that Augustus began the construction of his own Mausoleum: a huge cylin-
drical monument towering over the Campus Martius – in Rome.[118] After
Antony's will was made public rumours circulated that Antony intended to
transfer the seat of power to Alexandria and (even more incredible and more
opportune for Octavian) hand over Rome to Cleopatra.[119]

How seriously are we to take the idea that the Roman Empire might have
split permanently between East and West? The formal administrative divisions that came in with the Tetrarchy at the end of the third century were not
an admission that the Empire had split, and even in the mid-sixth Justinian
was trying to recover the West for Constantinople. Only if Octavian and
Antony had come to a lasting agreement and both had established firm dynasties would such a split have become permanent. Otherwise war won by
either would have restored unity under Rome.

Octavian had the constitutional problem of fighting a war in 32–31 against fellow-Romans, on the basis of an imminently expiring (if not already expired: see the chapter Appendix, p. 51) triumviral power shared by Antony, and from a base in Italy, where he had once practised a brutal confiscation and put down resistance with unforgotten cruelty. His solutions were astute and ruthless. For the final phases of the struggle against Antony the propaganda campaign was stepped up and Octavian, to bolster his power, invoked emergency measures, which of their nature were outside normal legal procedures. With unprecedented ingenuity, he ransacked a whole armoury of weapons, some obsolete.

Octavian's first tactic was to require the whole able-bodied community of Roman citizens, that is, all of Italy – to put on military cloaks in preparation for war (*saga sumere*), an informal act that belonged to times of emergency, especially of threats to Italy. The Senate declared war on Cleopatra – not on their fellow citizen Antony – and Octavian, reviving as he claimed the antique ritual of the appropriate priesthood, the *fetiales*, hurled a spear into a patch of land designated for the occasion as alien, making the declaration of war unchallengeable from the religious point of view.[120] The idea that the ritual was fabricated rather than disinterred is plausible: it depends on what records were available, only something apparently authentic would anchor the movement that was being launched. But it was a long time (to say the least) since Rome was known to have troubled to declare formal war on a dependent monarch who had not attacked Roman territory.

Octavian also exploited an important feature of Greek and Roman political and military life: the oath. The soldiery took their military oath to him, as they had already done to Sulla. But he secured an oath of loyalty from Roman civilians too, who he was later to claim had demanded him as their leader, using it to bind inhabitants of Italy and the western provinces to him and his followers in 32 BC.[121] It was a subsidiary for the Triumviral powers that were now expiring and would be replaced in 31 only by a consulship. If Octavian had had anything else to rely on when he launched the war he would have included notice of it in his *Achievements*. This oath-taking remained important to Augustus, and he recorded it. Its nature and origins are disputed (see Ch. 4), military or civilian; with eastern or western roots. It certainly had military connotations, and may be connected with the solemn taking up of the military cloaks. This was not the first time that a mass movement by the whole of Italy (*tota Italia*) offering an oath to its charismatic leader had played an important part in a crisis in Roman affairs. The most famous occasion was the oath taken by Italians when they banded together against Rome in the 'Social War' of 91–88 BC; then the beneficiary was their champion the tribune M. Livius Drusus. In 57, Cicero found himself carried triumphantly home from exile by the enthusiasm of the townsfolk of Italy. Now Octavian was harnessing the same enthusiasm against the oriental queen. The oath to Octavian was, he claimed, voluntary. That has justly been doubted, for we are told by Suetonius that Bononia was exempted because of its connexions with Antony. Something very much in Octavian's favour and a counterweight to the dispossessed landowners of the Perusine War was that throughout the peninsula men discharged from the armies of Caesar and the Triumvirs were working land that they owed to the efforts of Octavian; in particular discharged centurions had been given seats on local councils. More was expected, however. The demand for a levy of 25 per cent of a man's income for the year was certainly resisted, but the troops exacted it just the same, and from freedmen in Italy whose capital was more than *HS* 200,000 Octavian took an eighth.[122]

The defeat of Antony and Cleopatra at Actium on 2 September, 31 BC was not glorious for Octavian; at best it was due to the poor strategy of his opponents and the skill of Agrippa, but at Augustus' instigation it was made in Syme's words into the 'foundation myth' of the new regime and a turning point in world history. The era that stemmed from it was the model for later sacred eras and the victory is still hailed by Augustus' admirers as obviating the orientalising of Europe.[123] After their death in Alexandria on the capture of the city on 1 August, 30 – Antony was said to have been forced to suicide[124] – Octavian was sole master of the Roman Empire. The execution of Caesarion, who was betrayed as he fled for India by way of Ethiopia, was inevitable. Antyllus, now an adolescent who took the toga of manhood after Actium in token of his political weight, was also killed.[125] The fate of the two sons of Antony and Cleopatra is obscure; Alexander Helios was paraded in the triumph.[126] Octavian claimed to have destroyed the papers (*grammata*) that he found in Antony's boxes, which would have included correspondence that Antony had had with supporters at Rome or even in Octavian's ranks, but that, as in other cases of such leniency, was not strictly true: originals or copies were kept.[127] As to Cleopatra, it was her fate not only to die from the bite of an asp (so it was said), but later to have her lifeblood, even her name sucked out of her by the Augustan poets, who turned her irrevocably into a pallid bogey-woman and whore, an erotic object for male writers and readers and, as a woman ruling in the East, an oriental despot due for taking down. Cleopatra found no place in the other forms of programmatic representation of the victorious Octavian after Actium – a lone woman was thought unfit for a Roman triumph – although measures were taken against Antony's memory before and after his death, and Octavian was still repeating some of his accusations in his *Autobiography*, written in the 20s.[128] Even Cleopatra's ancestors were treated with contempt. When Octavian visited the mausoleum of Alexander the Great after his conquest he showed him due respect (except that part of the body was broken off: there was an accident to the hero's nose); but, invited to inspect the bodies of the Ptolemies, he said he wanted to see a king, not corpses.[129] A fitting male opponent was waiting in the east: the King of Parthia, who was duly humiliated in 20 BC.

A problematical aftermath

Peace was the great and immediate gain from the capture of Alexandria, a relief for Italy and the Empire.[130] But it was now up to Octavian whether he re-established the Commonwealth by laying down his powers completely and retiring to the country as Sulla had done or set up a new form of government. That is a stark and over-simplified dilemma, expounded in speeches that Cassius Dio put into the mouths of Octavian's friends Agrippa and Maecenas under the year 29.[131] Given Octavian's long-held ambitions, there could be no doubt how he would decide, even if his associates had been willing to forgo the prizes that were their due, but the form that the new constitution would take was the problem. Real power for Octavian had to be reconcilable with his professions as a Triumvir for the establishing of the Commonwealth and the aspirations of the mass of his peers who wanted him to be no more than a first among equals.

The political future was extraordinarily difficult, financially and politically, and it was natural to postpone decisions for as long as possible. Octavian allowed a cooling off period in Rome while he toured the eastern provinces – formerly Antony's domain. Egypt's prodigious wealth, which had become available to the Roman state and its ruler, would, if wisely used, help to heal financial wounds and repair physical damage, so restoring morale. For fifty years the kingdom had been hanging like a fruit ripe for the picking, safe because the Senate could not allow it to fall into the hands of any individual member. It was hardly a coincidence that the Roman Republic and Ptolemaic rule in Egypt came to an end simultaneously. Octavian's victories in Illyricum and at Actium and Alexandria were celebrated in a triple triumph held a year later, in August 29. He ordered the temple of Janus to be closed: the world was at peace. In his *Achievements* Augustus could write of himself at that time as 'in control of all things through the common agreement of whole groups of people', a consensus that has been mercilessly described as 'the silence of the exterminated system'.[132]

Giving his own account of his achievements, Augustus had particular difficulties with the events that followed Caesar's death, when for some time he seemed to be the hope of the Republic, with the formation of the Triumvirate and the proscriptions of men involved in the assassination and of sympathisers such as Cicero; and with the alliance with Mark Antony, an enemy of the state – whom he overthrew. The Triumvirate itself, though professedly created to establish constitutional government, allowed its holders such powers that it could be seen as a tripartite dictatorship. An impressive effort has been made by F. G. B. Millar to establish the continuity of government between Triumvirate and Principate. He pointed out that magistrates, Senate and assemblies continued to exercise some of their functions, the assemblies meeting to confirm the Triumvirs' choice of senior magistrates, and actually to choose their juniors, that provinces continued to be governed for the most part by proconsuls.[133] It is hard to accept that the Triumvirs' exploitation of the existing machinery of government allowed the Romans anything that they would have recognised as a *res publica*, and J. Osgood regards the concession of elections and laws as political gesture, and warns that in the case of provincials 'to survive the triumviral period, you needed not just decrees of the Senate but also the help of one of the Triumvirs'.[134] Affairs were in their hands, whatever they had promised. No serious defence can be offered for Octavian's conduct as a Triumvir;[135] the question is how far he changed after he had defeated Antony and Cleopatra. The need for a new persona he acknowledged in 27 when he changed his name once more and became Caesar Augustus.

Appendix: the renewal and end of the Triumvirate

The terminal date of the Second Triumvirate, 33 or 32, is a puzzle that exercised contemporaries, as C. Pelling points out, noting examinations in Livy's history of the ending of other magistracies that required the holders actually to lay them down. It has also given modern scholars scope for ingenuity.[136]

We have the formula used for delimiting the length of the first term of the Triumvirate. The original Lex Titia of 43 used the language that was necessary for indicating dates in the future at Rome: given the Roman practice of marking time in years by referring to consulships rather than years of Rome, there was a difficulty in indicating future dates. It ordained that the Triumvirs should hold office from 27 November, 43 until the sixth time the day before the Kalends (first) of January came round, that is until the last day of 38.[137] This probably followed a format used for previous special five-year commands such as those of Caesar in 59 BC, and of Caesar, Pompey and Crassus in 55 and was probably followed in turn by the ten-year periods of *imperium* granted to Augustus and his associates, without regard for or reference to overlaps between terms. The contention of this Appendix is that the second term of the Triumvirate was couched in the same terms as the first.

A similar formulation drafted in the summer of 37, when the Triumvirate was renewed (or on any day in that year) and ratified by the people (presumably in a second *lex*)[138] would take them to the end of 32. The only reason why the formulation should have been changed was that in November 43 there was such a short period of time left for the first year, but it is hard to imagine the Triumvirs scrupulous about the additional length that a second formulation, made in the summer, would have given them. Octavian in the Senate in 32 seated himself between the hostile consuls,[139] implying that he possessed power at least equal to theirs – though it was not beyond him to assert possession of the *imperium* after he should have laid it down. It is strange too that Antony and Octavian were not to hold the consulship together again until 31, which, with the end of 33 as the terminal date, would have left Octavian in an anomalous position in 32, when the power had theoretically expired again: he would have been without *imperium* in a year in which Antonian consuls were holding office. Appian also implies an end-date of 32, but Pelling and E. W. Gray have demonstrated his fallibility.[140]

Another, very authoritative, formulation of the length of the Triumvirate is that of Augustus himself in the *Achievements*, which claims triumviral power for ten years on end ('per continuos annos decem', borne out by Suetonius' 'ten years'),[141] and this, taken exactly, might seem decisive for the end of 33. However, one should allow for the economical, even misleading, language of the *Achievements* (Ch. 5). The contention is not to be taken as one of Augustus' deceptions: rather it is a reference to the fact that there were two terms of office, each for five years, and the gap before the renewal is ignored. The statement was designed for grandeur and neatness: the Triumvirs received two back-to-back quinquennial grants.

A problem mentioned by Pelling, that the Triumvirs had allocated themselves provinces (ratified by senatorial decrees) which may have survived the expiry of the Triumvirate itself, is less serious; their *imperium* had simply pooled out into the provinces like that of a consul[142] and is unlikely to have been allocated a separate terminal date.

The chronological issue is complicated by the fact that the first five-year grant expired at the end of 38 and the second was not made until the late summer of 37. What of the gap and the legality of any actions taken within it? W. Eck, like Pelling, thinks that this was filled by a backdating to 1 January 37, seeing that the Capitoline *Fasti* mention the Triumvirs at the head of the magistrates of 37 and not 36. This apparently removes the gap that opened up between the first expiry date and the renewal. The insertion would have been made only in the year in which the second term was retrospectively deemed to have begun. This is not a strong argument if the authorities were intent on obliterating the gap.

Perhaps backdating did not come into it: the power was indeed due to expire at the end of each of the two terms but the Triumvirs cannot be shown ever to have laid it down. Indeed, there is a question of how it would be laid down. It was not like proconsular power, which expired when the holder crossed the sacred boundary of Rome, for it functioned within the city as well as outside. Even the proconsul Caesar in early 49 would have kept his *imperium* after the expiry of its official term of five years – until that crossing was made. While the Triumvirate was still in existence an action was necessary, which Octavian required Antony to come to Rome and perform, such as was required of a consul; the same may have been necessary even after its terminal date, namely the laying down of the *fasces* (bundles of ceremonial rods) that were the symbols of office that accompanied magistrates with *imperium*, and the taking of an oath that official actions had been performed according to law. There are parallels for domestic magistrates who failed to lay down their *imperium* after their year was up, notably Ti. Claudius Nero, the praetor of 41.[143] Octavian went on behaving as a triumvir might until the settlement of 28–27, and Antony certainly regarded himself as triumvir in 31 (it was his only power). They never resigned and mere lapse of time was insufficient to bring the term to an end as crossing the sacred boundary into Rome ended the *imperium* of proconsuls, for they enjoyed *imperium* within the city as well as outside the Pomerium.

On the basis of the formulation of the Lex Titia, the renewal would have ordained that the Triumvirs should hold office from the date of its enactment or mere promulgation until the sixth time the day before the Kalends (first) of January came round, that is until the last day of 32. What form of words would have been used if there was backdating is another matter. They could anomalously have specified 1 January 37 as the starting date. It is possible but unlikely that they drew attention to the gap by adding a clause that legitimised anything they had done in it, as was done in the 'Lex de Imperio Vespasiani' of AD 70 to legitimise the acts of Vespasian carried out before he was recognised by the Senate in December 69.[144] It is simpler, though, to hold that they preferred to regard their continued tenure and exercise of power as legitimate, and did not make any such provision.

In 31 Octavian should have been a mere consul – but he was still using the powers that men had accustomed themselves to seeing him use, with the informal resources he had gathered in 32. Augustus himself admitted that after his victory he was holding supreme power 'by the common consent of whole groups' ('per consensum universorum').[145] In thirteen years he had overcome youth, illness, defeat, shortage of funds, mutiny and the hostility of politicians hardly more scrupulous than he was; but a consul behaving like a Triumvir without colleagues could not last for long.

Endnotes

1 Politicians' aims: Sall. *Cat.* 38; cf. *Jug.* 3.
2 Octavian's demand: Cic. *Att.* 16. 15. 3 (mid-December 44) with Gradel 2002, 58, n. 9, who accepts H. Gesche, *Die Vergottung Caesars. Fas* 1 (Kallmünz, 1968), 79–82. Following Caesar: Nic. Dam. 53; cf. Dio 45. 4. 3, with Gowing 1992, 62.
3 Triumviral period damned: Tac. *Ann.* 3. 28. 1; Dio 47. 15. 4.

4 Octavian as 'boy': Cic. *Att.* 14. 12. 2; 16. 8. 1 (early Nov. 44); 11. 6; 15. 3 (April, November, and December 44); *ad Brut.* 1. 15. 6 (mid-July 43); 18. 3 (late May 43); *Phil.* 3. 26; 13. 24. App. *BC* 3. 176 (Antony). Clark 1983, 95f., notes Cicero's emphasis on *spes* (hope) as making up for youthfulness.

5 Youth as a factor: Osgood 2006, 39.

6 For the divergent accounts of Appian and Dio of Octavian's rise, see Gowing 1992, 57–93: Dio is not altogether favourable; his Octavian is markedly ruthless (73 n. 40), and he underestimates the influence of Octavian's friends; he is also hostile to Antony. But 47. 7 exonerates Octavian from guilt over the proscriptions.

7 Augustus' failings: [Epit. Vict.] *Caes.* 1. 21.

8 Octavius in Spain: Nic. Dam. 22–28; Vell. Pat. 2. 59. 3; Dio 43. 41, 3. with Canfora 2007, 245–55.

9 Octavius at Apollonia: Nic. Dam. 37–46. News of the will: 48; accepted against resistance: 53f.; advice of elders followed: 57; cf. Suet. *Aug.* 8. 2; App. *BC* 3. 36–9; Dio 45. 3. 2.

10 Caesar's will: Nic. Dam. 30; Plut. *Cic.* 43. 3; Suet. *Jul.* 83. 2.

11 Brief visit to Rome in April: Osgood 2006, 33, on Nic. Dam. 108; App. *BC* 3. 40.

12 Death of Caesar: App. *BC* 4. 250f.; Dio 47. 26. 3–7, with Canfora 2007, 245, suggesting that Sextus' death prompted Octavius' journey to Spain, and that the dark picture of Sextus comes from the *Autobiography*, answering Antony's allegations about Octavian's own relations with Caesar. Octavian's return and subsequent activities: Lacey 1996, 27f.

13 'Caesar': Cic. *Att.* 14. 12. 2 (mid-April 44); *Fam.* 10. 23. 6 (Plancus, early June, 43); *Fam.* 11. 8 (Jan. 43); *Fam.* 12. 23. 2 ('Caesar Octavianus', early October 44, distinguishing him from the Dictator); 16. 24. 2 (November 44). App. *BC* 3. 38 (assumes name Caesar at Brundisium); Dio 45. 3. 2; 46. 47. 5.

14 Octavian's resources are succinctly examined in Southern 1998, 28f. Selling estates: App. *BC* 3. 77–80. Antony kept *HS* 10m.: Plut. *Cic.* 43. 3.

15 Inheritance conditional on heir taking name of testator (*condicio nominis ferendi*): Weinrib 1968, 251–61. The future emperor Tiberius Claudius Nero accepted such an inheritance, but did not change his name to Gallius (Suet. *Tib.* 6. 3; cf. *Aug.* 27. 4). This was what 'testamentary adoption' amounted to. The legitimacy of adoption of an independent male (*adrogatio*: Gaius, *Inst.* 1. 99; 4. 77) by will is defended by Schumacher 1999, claiming that the will was a substitute for the present wish expressed by the testator; but see Harries 2006, 153–56; so Schmitthenner 1973, 39–90; 104–17; Syme, *RP* 4 (1988) 159; Osgood 2006, 31 n. 71, with bibl., reserves judgement.

16 'Octavius': Cic. *Brut.* 1. 16 and 17 (?M. Brutus, July 44); *Att.* 14. 11. 2; 12. 2; 20. 5; 21. 4 (mid-April); 15. 2. 3 (mid-May). It was still in use by opponents at the siege of Perusia: *CIL* 11, 6721. 11, with Hallett 1977, 152.

17 'Octavianus': Cic. *Att.* 15. 12. 2 (early June 44); 16. 8. 1; 9; 11. 6; 14. 1 (November 44).

18 Clients: App. *BC* 3. 390–92.

19 M. Antonius in 44–43 BC: Kienast 1982, 19–22, criticising Syme's favourable view.

20 'Optimates': Cic. *Pro Sestio* 136–39.

21 Cicero analysed: Osgood 2006, 25–43. Cicero and Antony inadequately treated in Appian and Dio: Gowing 1992, 147–61. Cicero wary of Octavian: *Att.* 16. 11. 6; 14. 1; 15. 3 (November–December 44). Suspicions vindicated: *ad Brut.* 1. 18 (late July 43); he was warned against Octavian by D. and M. Brutus in May 43: *Fam.* 11. 20. 1 (D. Brutus, late May 43, on the saying that Octavian was 'disposable', cf. Suet. *Aug.* 12); *Brut.* 1. 4a (M. Brutus, mid-May 43).

22 Octavian's ostensible respect: Cic. *Att.* 14. 9. 3; 10. 3; 11. 2; 12. 2 (mid–late April 44); 16. 8. 1; 9; 11. 6 (November 44). Cicero's support of Octavian: Cic. *Phil.* 3. 5; 7; 5. 23; 42–52, with comparisons with young Pompey. For this evidence see Eder 1990, 90f., mistakenly thinking that it was bad conscience that caused Augustus to exploit Ciceronian ideology in the aftermath.

23 Pompey the 'butcher boy': Val. Max. 6. 2. 8.

24 Augustus' account: Ridley 2003, 95. The *Autobiography* brazenly admitted that Cicero's oratory had been useful: Plut. *Comp. Demosth. and Cic.* 3. 1.

25 Octavian in Campania: Nic. Dam. 133–39. 500 *denarii*: Cic. *Att.* 16. 8. 1 (early November 44); App. *BC* 3. 164–74 (10,000 men); cf. 179–187 (2 legions, Martia and IV, go over); 178, and Dio 45. 12, and 13. 2 for Antony's partial decimation of mutinous troops. Motivation of troops: Osgood 2006, 43–47.

26 Octavian's alleged attempt on Antony: Cic. *Fam.* 12. 23. 2 (mid-October 44); *Phil.* 3. 19; App. *BC* 3. 157. Nic. Dam. 108–39, with murder plot hatched by Antony: 123–31.

27 Public meeting: Cic. *Att.* 16. 15. 3 (mid-December); veterans against quarrel: App. *BC* 3. 170. Unsuccessful march: Cic. *Att.* 16. 14. 1 (mid-November 44; 15. 3 (mid-December). Possible *hostis* declaration: Cic. *Phil.* 3. 21; 5. 23.

28 Appointment against Antony: App. *BC* 3. 352; Dio 46. 42. 1; 51. 5.

29 Cicero's recommendations: Cic. *Phil.* 5. 46–53, with Kienast 1982, 28, for intimations of Octavian's future titulature.

30 Equestrian statue: Cic. *Ad Brut.* 1. 15. 7 (Brutus, May 43); Vell. Pat. 2. 61. 3; App. *BC* 3. 209; Dio 46. 29. 2, with Osgood 2006, 117 n. 35, comparing *RRC* 490. 1 and 3 and 518. 2.

31 Exchange of provinces: Livy, *Epit.* 117; Vell. Pat. 2. 60. 5; App. *BC* 3. 102–19; Dio 45. 9. 3.

32 Suspicion over deaths of Hirtius and Pansa: Cic. *ad Brut.* 1. 6. 2 (Brutus, mid-May 43); Tac. *Ann.* 1. 10. 2; Suet. *Aug.* 11.

33 Proposed consulship with Cicero: Plut. *Cic.* 45. 3–46. 1 (using the *Autobiography*).

34 Alliance of Antony and Lepidus: Cic. *Fam.* 10. 35. (Lepidus under pressure from troops, late May 43); App. *BC* 3. 340–8; Dio 46. 42. 1. See Osgood 2006, 58. For Plancus in the Triumviral Period, see Watkins 1997, 52–116.

35 Octavian's march: Dio 46. 43, 6; 45. 1f.; his centurions and troops: App. *BC* 3. 88f. See Osgood 2006, 58 n.158 for problems in Appian's account.

36 Failure of precedents: Dettenhofer 2000, 37.

37 Vultures: Suet. *Aug.* 95; App. *BC* 3. 388; Dio 46. 46. 2f.; Obsequens 69; with Gowing 1992, 77, on Octavian's further ambitions in Dio.

38 Pedius' legacy: App. *BC* 3. 388. Octavian's age on taking consulship: Plut. *Brut.* 27. 1.

39 Atia's death: Suet. *Aug.* 61. 2.

40 Lex Pedia: Vell. Pat. 2. 69. 5; App. *BC* 3. 392; Dio 46. 48f.; *RS* 27.

41 Bononia: Suet. *Aug.* 17. 2. Numbers of legions: App. *BC* 3. 364; 381; 399; 4. 9. Lepidus' role: 4. 5–9; Dio 46. 55. 4. Lepidus as Triumvir: Gowing 1992, 123–42, and 1992 ['Lepidus'].

42 Antony's resistance: Florus 2. 15. 2; Dio 45. 5. 4. Octavian's assembly: Dio 46. 47. 4–8. Meeting: Gowing 1992, 65–70.

43 Palm shoot: Canfora 2007, 245–55, on Suet. *Aug.* 94. 11; Dio 43. 41. 2f.

44 Octavian's debt to Caesar's name: Cic. *Phil.* 13. 24 (Antonius). Games and comet: Dr Herbert-Brown notes that 'both astrology and the Julian calendar (two religions) are exploited'. The renaming of the month Quintilis as Iulius and the public sacrifice performed on Caesar's birthday (Weinstock 1971, 157, 206) made obligatory in 42 would also have a powerful impact on the *plebs*. Cicero's disapproval of the games: *Att.* 15. 2. 3 (mid-May 44). See Osgood 2006, 21f.; 40f. Comet: Pliny *NH* 2, 93f.; Serv. on Virg. *Ecl.* 9, 46; Zanker 1988, 34–7. 'Son of the deified': *RRC* 525.1; Caesar's temple: 540. 1f. Cic. *Att.* 16.15. 3 (mid-December 44). Vengeance: App. *BC* 4. 49–60. Galinsky 1996, 211, recalls the end of the *Aeneid* and the Temple of Mars Ultor; Ovid, *Fasti*, 5, 567–78. Troops demanding vengeance: App. *BC* 3. 164 (Brundisium).

45 Second Triumvirate and Lex Titia: EJ p.32 (*Fasti Coi.*); Suet. *Aug.* 27. 1; App. *BC* 4. 4–7; Dio 46. 55. 3f., with *MRR* 2, 337. Titles: *RRC* 492–95. Claudia: Dio 46. 56. 3.

46 Translation of *res publica*: Wardle 2005 ['Dreams'], 30 n. 8 (bibl.); Galinsky 1996, 6; 64. Severus: *ILS* 425, with '*rem publicam restitutam*'.

47 Sex. Pompeius: Powell and Welch 2002. In Appian and Dio: Gowing 1992, 181–205; his motives: 200–2 (legitimate political influence); his legions: Cic. *Att.* 16. 4. 2 (mid-July 44). Commission of 44 BC: App. *BC* 3. 11.

48 Triumvirs' powers: Bleicken 1990, 27–48; Osgood 2006, 60f. Conduct: App. *BC* 4. 10–13; 26–30; Dio 46. 55. 3–56. 2; 47. 2. 1f., with Millar 1973 and Laffi 1993 on the functioning of traditional organs. Absolutism: Pelling 1996, 1. Freedom of speech: Osgood 2006, 86–88, with Val. Max. 6. 2. 12.

49 Even in old age Augustus thought his reply to Brutus' pamphlet on the Republican hero Cato of Utica worth reading out: Suet. *Aug.* 85. 1, with Malcovati 1969, xxxixf.

50 Exactions (42 BC): Eus.-Jer. *Chron.* p. 158 Helm. Protection of private property: Galinsky 1996, 7.

51 Cicero's death: Osgood 2006, 78.

52 Lepidus damned: '*Laudatio Turiae*', EJ 357, II ll. 21–28; see Osgood 2006, 67–76, bibl. n. 18; Birley 2000, 712 n. 5. Lepidus exculpated as a victim of Augustan propaganda: Gowing 1992 ['Lepidus'], and Sumi 2004, 202.

53 Octavian blamed: Tac. *Ann.* 1.10. 2. Julius Saturninus: Suet. *Aug.* 27. 2.

54 App. *BC* 4. 10–146 and Dio 47. 3–17. 6 give accounts of the proscriptions: see Gowing 1992, 247–69. These were authorised by all three Triumvirs (App. *BC* 4. 31), but scholars accept that Antony ensured Cicero's inclusion (e.g. E. Rawson, *CAH* 9², 486). When Bruttedius Niger wrote his account of Cicero's death, he repeatedly inserted the name of Antony; Octavian was concealed in the phrase 'the victors' (Sen. *Suas.* 6. 20f.). Octavian's relentlessness, and Toranius: Suet. *Aug.* 27. 1–5; cf. App. *BC* 4. 47. Other victims: Nep. *Att.* 10. 5; 12. 4; Val. Max. 8. 3. 3; App. and Dio, above, n. 55. See Syme 1939, 187–201; Hinard 1985, 259–300, with tables; Osgood 2006, 63; 67–74 (on the '*Laudatio Turiae*' and the widower as innocent victim); 75 (on problems with the tales told, citing Syme 190 n. 6); 79 (effect on society); 82–4 (women, citing Val. Max. 8. 3. 3; App. *BC* 4. 135–46). Sullan proscription: R. Seager, *CAH*² 9. 198. Propaganda of the period 43–2 is set out by Wallmann 1989, 29–78.

55 Propaganda war: Lacey 1996, 62f.

56 Fate of Gallius: Suet., *Aug.* 27, 4, with Carter *ad loc.* lauding Octavian's conduct; Gallius in Appian: *BC* 3. 95. For the connexion with Ti. Nero see above, n. 15. Gallius presiding over the Pedian court: Bauman 1967, 173–7, followed by Daly 1984, 163f.

57 Silicius: Dio 46. 49. 5.

58 Ofillius' fate: App. *BC* 5. 532f.

59 Divergent accounts of the battles: Gowing 1992, 108–13; 210–18.

60 Octavian's illness and the dream warning: Vell. Pat. 2. 70. 1; Pliny, *NH* 7. 148; Suet. *Aug.* 13. 1; Plut. *Brut.* 41. 3; *Ant.* 22. 1f. (he was ill during the second battle); App. 4. 463 (from the *Autobiography*). Further sources: Malcovati 1969, 90, XIIn.

61 After Philippi: Kienast 1982, 36. Confiscations: App. *BC* 4. 10–13; 5. 48–67; Dio 48. 8f.; Virg. *Ecl.* 1 and 9; Hor. Sat. 2. 2. 112–36. Osgood 2006, 108–51 is cautious on confiscation of Virgil's land and its return. See also Pelling 1996, 14–16 (bibl.); numbers settled: Brunt 1971, 488–98; providing future support: Eck 2007, 20.

62 Perusine War: Prop. 1. 21f.; Livy, *Epit.* 125f.; Vell. Pat. 2. 74. 3 (doing his best for Octavian); Suet. *Aug.* 13f.; 96. 3 (horrors); Plut. *Ant.* 30. 1; App. *BC* 5. 51–203; Gowing 1992, 77–84. Propaganda of this period: Wallmann 1989, 79–135.

63 Pitilessness at Philippi and Perusia: Sen. *De Clem.* 1. 11. 1; Suet. *Aug.* 13 1f. and 15; App. *BC* 5. 203–7; Dio 48. 14. 3–6. Punishment of other cities: Osgood 2006, 172. Loss of life at Philippi: Plut. *Brut.* 45. 1.

64 Octavian's 'sacrifice': Suet. *Aug.* 15; cf. Dio 48. 14. 4. Antony's 'sacrifice' of Hortensius: Plut. *Ant.* 22. 3; Julius Caesar's of soldiers: Dio 43. 24. 3f.; Sex. Pompeius: 48. 48. 5. Gratidianus: Florus 2. 9. 26. A. Keaveney, *The Army in the Roman Revolution* (London and New York, 2007), 15, believes the story about Octavian because it fits the pattern. Human sacrifice at Rome: Plut. *Quaest. Rom.* 83.

65 Contrast with Antony: Suet. *Aug.* 13. 2.

66 Abuse in theatre: Suet. *Aug.* 68. The accusations of cowardice at Mutina belong here: Suet. *Aug.* 8. 2.

67 Octavian's verses: Martial 11. 20. Bullets: Hallett 1977, 152 no. 1.

68 Sex. Pompeius: Osgood 2006, 202–08; versions of negotiations between him, Antony, and Octavian: Gowing 1992, 187f.

69 Salvidienus Rufus: *MRR* 2, 383. Trial: Suet. *Aug.* 66. 1f.

70 Brundisium treaty: Osgood 2006, 187–91. Divergent accounts of the politics surrounding it: Gowing 1992, 85–87. Propaganda: Wallmann 1989, 135–61 on the weakening of the theme of vengeance for Caesar.

71 Marriage connexion of Octavian and Pompeius: App. *BC* 5. 222; Dio 48. 16. 3, adding that Octavian sent Pompeius' mother Mucia (once the mistress of Caesar) to him.

72 *Fides*: Dion. Hal. 2. 75. 2f.; Livy 1. 21. 3; Plut. *Numa* 16. 1.

73 Octavian's exploitation of Antony's mother Julia: App. *BC* 5. 270f.

74 *Praenomen* 'imperator': see Syme 1958 ['Imperator']. 'Pius' and 'Pietas', in use among rivals, were bland. This was so gross that (as Dr Herbert-Brown notes) it is surprising that it was not loudly mocked: Simpson 1998 normalises it by accepting that it was inherited from Julius Caesar (Dio 43. 44. 2–5; 'Divus' was another *praenomen*). Then it is strange that Octavian hesitated to use 'Imp.', waiting until the completion of the Perusine War and his second salutation. Uncertainty about his nomenclature persisted: see M. Beard, *The Roman Triumph* (Cambridge, MA, and London, 2007), 302. It suggests unofficial experimentation.

75 Feasting: Suet. *Aug.* 70. 2 Treaty of Misenum: Vell. Pat. 2. 77; Plut. *Ant.* 32; App. *BC* 5. 304–13; Dio 48. 36. Accounts of the meetings at Misenum and Tarentum: Gowing 192; 190–97; Osgood 2006, 242f.

76 Sicily and Sardinia 'seized': *RG* 27. 3.

77 Return of exiles: Vell. Pat. *loc. cit.*; Dio 48. 36. 3.

78 'Pirates' served by slaves: *RG* 25. 1; App. *BC* 5, 304; 307; Dio 49. 12. 4f. Pompeius threatening Rome with chains: Hor. *Epode* 9. 9f. Duped: Tac. *Ann.* 1. 10. 3. Wallmann 1989, 163–248, analyses the propaganda of 39–36 BC.

79 Betrothal of Marcellus and Pompeia: App. *BC* 5. 312; Dio 48. 38. 3.

80 Marriage to Livia and Scribonia's 'morum perversitatem': Suet. *Aug.* 62. 2; Dio 48. 44. See Osgood 2006, 231f. Dr Herbert-Brown warns against over-stressing Octavian's passion against her political merits (so also Kienast 1982, 44).

81 Drusus' birth recorded: Dio 48. 44. 4. Chronological problem: Suerbaum 1980, 337–53.

82 Peace with Sextus broken: App. *BC* 5. 325–9.

83 Exchange of forces: App. *BC* 5. 396; cf. Plut. *Ant.* 35. 2.

84 Pompeius degraded at Tarentum: Dio 48. 54. 6.

85 Return of Antony's ships: App. *BC* 5. 537; 577; Dio 49. 14. 6.

86 Octavia in Athens: Plut. *Ant.* 53 (ensuing propaganda 54. 3f.); Dio 49. 33. 4. Divorce: Livy, *Epit.* 132; Plut. *Ant.* 57. 2; Dio 50. 3. 2; Eus.-Jer. *Chron.* p. 162 Helm. Final stages of the propaganda war: Wallmann 1989, 249–342.

87 Struggle with Pompeius and Neptune: Suet. *Aug.* 16. 1–3. Allegedly Octavian was asleep when the battle began: perhaps in a state of fugue. Campaign and celebratory aftermath: Osgood 2006, 298f., noting (n. 9) App. *BC* 5. 488–507 as preferable to the Thucydidean Dio 49. 8. 4–11. 1. Pompeius' death and Octavian's reaction: Dio 49. 18. 4–6, with Gowing 1992, 198f.

88 Antony attacked for his treatment of Sex. Pompeius: Dio 50. 1. 4; App. *BC* 5. 525. Titius: Vell. Pat. 2. 79. 5f.; Dio 48. 30. 5f.

89 Sex. Pompeius 'represented a complex of exquisite embarrassments': Powell, '*Aeneid*' 151–57; Seager asks of Hor. *Odes* 1. 9. 7–10 (1993, 25) whether the 'ludicrous exaggeration of the threat . . . was the official line in those years'.

90 Pompeius' forces reviled: *RG* 27. 3; Hor. *Epode* 4. 19; 9. 9f.; Vell. Pat. 2. 73. 3. The charge is analysed by A. Powell in Stahl 1998, 92–94. Comparison with Spartacus: Osgood 2006, 300. Slaves fighting under Octavian: Ridley 2003, 183–5, citing Suet. *Aug.* 16. 1.

91 Lepidus' fall: Dio 49.11. 2–12. 4; 15. 3 (priesthood), with Gowing 1992, 137–41. Fate: 54. 15. 4–8; cf. Suet. *Aug.* 54.

92 Capua in 36: Strabo 10, p. 477; Vell. Pat. 2. 81. 2; Dio 49. 14. 5.

93 Cascellius: Val. Max. 6. 2. 12.

94 Intermittent concessions: Pelling 1996, 19f.; 37, citing App. *BC* 5. 539 (speech publicised); 132; Osgood 2006, 192; 228f., cites *Aphrodisias* 8 for the more significant role of the Senate in 39. Hated taxes: App. *BC* 5. 282f. and 540.

95 Honours to Octavian: App. *BC* 5. 541f.; 548f. ('tribune for life'); Dio 49. 15. Significance: Osgood 2006, 303. Statues in Temple of Concord: Dio 49. 18. 6. Hopes pinned on Octavian: Virg. *Georg.* 1. 498–501, with Osgood 349.

96 Return to normal government: Palmer 1978, on App. *BC* 5. 548; he implausibly believes that Octavian was using tribunician power for that purpose. Promise of these years: Osgood 2006, 298–335.

97 Sacrosanctity of Livia and Octavia: Dio 49. 38. 1.

98 Octavian active in Asia: *Aphrodisias* 10 (Antony is absent) and 12 of 39/38 BC, with Osgood 2006, 229f.

99 Horus the avenger, also exploited by Octavian: Dwyer 1973, followed by Barton 1995, 47.

100 Uprooting of triumph: Plut. *Ant.* 50. 6f.; Vell. Pat. 2. 82. 4.

101 Illyrian campaigns: E. S. Gruen, *CAH* 10² (1996) 172–4. and J. J. Wilkes 549f., with *RG* 29.1; App. *Illyr.* 40–45 (account in *Autobiography, 42*); Dio 49. 35–38.

102 Donations of Alexandria: Plut. *Ant.* 54. 3f.; Dio 49. 41. 1–4, with Fadinger 1969, 150–61 and Pelling 1996, 40–45 for documentation of abuse. Osgood 2006, 182–5 has a realistic account of the relations of Antony and Cleopatra, and at 338f. is sceptical of the mock triumph and the practical effect of any donations: Plutarch and Dio go back to the *Autobiography* and much was 'made up'. Malcovati 1969, 18f. prints Octavian's letters to Antony and cites Antony's to him: Suet. *Aug.* 7. 1; 86. 2 (Octavian); 2. 3; 4. 2; 16. 2; 28. 1; 68; 69. 1; 70. 1 (Antony).

103 C. Oppius' pamphlet: Suet. *Caes.* 52. 2.

104 Cleopatra and Roman troops: Serv. on Virg. *Aen.* 8. 696, with *Autobiography* as source.

105 Changes in 30 BC: Dio 51. 2. 2–3; 'donations' of 20: 54. 9. 2f.

106 Antony's proposal: Dio 49. 41. 6.

107 Propaganda campaign: Osgood 2006, 344–49; 354–56.

108 Cleopatra, drunkenness: Pliny, *NH* 14. 148 (Antony's pamphlet on the subject, *c.* 32 BC); Suet. *Aug.* 69. 2. Chamber pots: Pliny, *NH* 33. 50.

109 Octavian's high tone in literature: Osgood 2006, 346, citing Suet. *Aug.* 86. 2f; and, for Octavian's studies, Nep. *Att.* 20. 1f., and noting the work of Sallust, Horace, Virgil and Nepos during this period: *Histories, Satires, Georgics, Atticus.*

110 Antony drugged: Plut. *Ant.* 60. 1 (32 BC); cf. 37.3. *Epode* 9 'a piece of propaganda': Osgood 2006, 383.

111 Adulteries: Suet. *Aug.* 69–70. 1; Suet. *Aug.* 69. 2; Dio 54. 19. 3; 6; 55. 7. 5.

112 Relations with Caesar: Suet. *Aug.* 68; cf. Plut. *Ant.* 59. 4.

113 Sources and bibliography for 32–29: Osgood 2006, 351 n. 2. Antony's promise: Dio 50. 7. 1. Need to lay down triumviral power: see below n. 136. Antony's absence: Livy, *Epit* 132. For a favourable interpretation of the scene in the Senate, see Lacey 1996, 36–38.

114 Senators with Octavian in 32 BC: *RG* 25. 3, with Brunt and Moore 1970 *ad loc.*; Suet. *Aug.* 17. 2; Dio 50. 2. 6f.; coercion: 5. 10f. Wallmann 1976, 306: 400 fled; he analyses senatorial groups. Senate at Ephesus: Dio 50. 3. 2. See Ridley 2003, 150.

115 The shock of Roman senators at what they found in Antony's camp is accepted by Eck 2007, 37f., though he allows that rational calculation played a part.

116 Plancus' defection: Vell. Pat. 2. 83 ('pathological traitor'); Plut. *Ant.* 58. 2; Dio 50. 3. 2. Plancina: Tac. *Ann.* 3. 17; 6. 26. 3.

117 Antony's will: Suet. *Aug.* 17. 1. Dio 50. 3. 3–5. Scepticism about it: Pelling 1996, 52, with n. 278; Eck 2007, 39, thinks of a probably authentic will, not read out in full; so: Osgood 2006, 353.

118 Mausoleum at Rome: Suet. *Aug.* 100. 4 (dating to 28 BC); an answer to Antony: Yavetz 1984, 6. See Ch. 5.

119 Transfer of *capital*: Dio 50. 4. 1f. Octavian's insistence on Rome as the centre: Nicolet 1990, 193.

120 Declaration of war: Plut. *Ant.* 60. 1; Dio 50. 4. 4f., including assumption of military dress and fetial ceremony, with Pelling 1996, 54; Osgood 2006, 368f. Fetial ritual obsolete: Varro, *Latin Language* 5. 86.

121 Oath: *RG* 25. 2 ('*Ducem me poposcit*'), with Suet. *Aug.* 17. 2 ('*pro partibus suis*'); Dio 50. 6. 3 and 11. 5. Discussion in Osgood 2006, 357–59, explaining how the oath was imposed. Von Premerstein 1937 41–51 and Herrmann 1968 are comprehensive. Linderski 1984 provides Octavian with a legal niche for his military leadership in 44 and 32–31. 'Spontaneity': Ridley 2003, 187–92. There would have been serial oath-taking through the summer: Pelling 1996, 53. Centurions: Kienast 1982, 50f.

122 Exactions: Pliny, *NH* 37. 10; Plut. *Ant.* 58. 1; Dio 50. 10. 4–6; 16. 3.

123 Actian campaign: Osgood 2006, 372–75 ('not decisive'). Mythology: Syme 1939, 297. See Watson 1987 on Hor. *Epode* 9. Augustus creating the vision: Murray and Petsas 1989, 131–51, Eras: E. J. Bickerman, *Chronology of the Ancient World* (2nd edn, 1980), 73. Persistent fears of 'orientalism': B. Levick, *Julia Domna, Syrian Empress* (London, 2007), 124–42, 163.

124 Actium to Alexandria: Osgood 2006, 384–90. Antony forced to suicide: Suet. *Aug.* 17. 4.

125 Killing of Antony's sons: Suet. *Aug.* 19. 5.

126 Fate of Helios and Philadelphus: Flower 2006, 118, n. 7 for differing views. Triumph: Dio 51. 21. 8.

127 Correspondence not destroyed: Dio 52. 42. 8, with Delle Donne 2006.

128 Woman unworthy of a triumph: Prop. 4. 6. 65f. Absence of Cleopatra from post-Actian Rome: Wyke 1992, 112f. Antony's memory: Flower 2006, 116f., with n. 4. His name was later restored: Tac. *Ann.* 3. 18. 1, with Koestermann's commentary (1963) *ad loc.*

129 Octavian and the Ptolemies: Suet. *Aug.* 18. 1; Dio 51. 16. 5.

130 Italy after the victory: Osgood 2006, 390–98.

131 Speeches: Dio 52. 1–40.

132 Control: *RG* 34. 1, with Ridley 2003, 220–22.

133 Continuity of Triumvirate and Principate: Millar 1973.

134 *Res publica*: Wardle 2005, 184f., with n. 9 for bibl. Gestures: Osgood 2006, 59; electoral irregularities: 259f. Senatorial decrees: 228f.

135 Cf. Eck 2007, 4: 'the man who emerged from Tacitus' history was in many respects morally repellent'.

136 Triumviral terminus: see the first four papers in Schmitthenner 1969; Brunt and Moore 1970, 48f.; Ridley 2003, 172–77 (bibl.); Fadinger 1969, 84–136, is for 33, like Gray 1975, 21; Bleicken 1990, 14 (bibl.) and 65–82; Laffi 1993, 80f.; Girardet 1995, taking Augustus' statement seriously and (33) appealing to Syme 1939, 333; Rich and Williams 1999, 188, and Osgood 2006, 352 ('almost certain'); Pelling 1996, 26, n. 115 (full discussion see 67f.); for magistrates laying down power he cites Livy 3. 36. 9; 38. 1; 54. 5f.

137 Form of dating used in the Lex Titia: *Fasti Colotiani*, EJ p. 32.

138 Ratification: App. *Illyr.* 80, which Wilcken 1969 [1925], 44–46, treats as derived from Augustus' *Autobiography*. Gray 1975, 21 accepts the ratification. App. *BC* 5. 398, claims that this time the People played no role, which DuQuesnay 1984, 207 n. 112 regards as propaganda of Sex. Pompeius. (Wilcken *loc. cit.* claimed that the phrase means that the Triumvirs regarded the People as redundant.) Millar 1973, 53 suspends judgement.

139 Octavian between the consuls: Dio 50. 2. 5.

140 32: App. *Illyr.* 80, with Gray 1975, 21, and Pelling 1996, 67.

141 Augustus' formulation: *RG* 7. 1; Suet. *Aug.* 27. 1. Syme 1946, 156 = *RP* 1, 191, dismisses 'overt and pointless mendacity about the duration of the Triumvirate'.

142 Survival of power in provinces is suggested by Osgood 2006, 352, on the basis of Livy, *Epit.* 132 and Dio 50. 4. 3. Consuls' power in provinces: Cic. *Phil.* 3. 9.

143 Lacey 1996, 17; 35f. Nero's retained praetorship: Suet. *Tib.* 4. 2.

144 Retrospective legitimation in the 'Lex de imperio Vespasiani' of AD 70: EJ 364 ll.29–31.

145 'Consent': Instinsky 1940; Fadinger 1969, 304–14: *RG* 34. 1.

Chapter 2

Augustus:
Political Evolution

Transition to normality?

We have seen Octavian's determination to attain to his 'father's' position of
supremacy carrying him through a thirteen-year period of violence and
treachery. Now change was forced on him by the very fact of his blatant supremacy, and it was made possible by his success: Vitruvius in the opening
of his book on architecture expresses it by saying that the council of the
gods transferred the power (*imperium*) of Octavian's father Caesar to his
control (*potestas*). (Only the gods could have done this.) Augustus himself
claims in the *Achievements* that during this period after the victory over
Antony and Cleopatra he was in supreme control, as was universally desired
('potens rerum omnium universorum consensu').[1] We do not know who
proposed the Senate's resolution of 30 BC that a libation should be poured
to Octavian at all banquets public and private, but he was taking his cue
from the honour spontaneously offered C. Marius seventy years before.[2]
Such honours only made it more urgent for Octavian to act, before it
was realised how little had changed since the Dictatorship of Caesar. It was
an easy gesture to allow Cicero's son the suffect consulship as his own
colleague in 30.

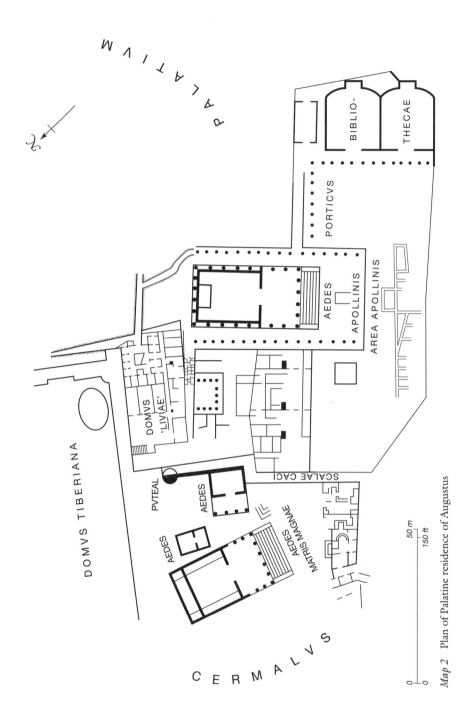

Map 2 Plan of Palatine residence of Augustus

PALATIVM

BIBLIO-
THECAE

PORTICVS

AEDES
APOLLINIS

AREA APOLLINIS

DOMVS
'LIVAE'

SCALAE CACI

DOMVS TIBERIANA

PVTEAL

AEDES

AEDES

AEDES
MATRIS MAGNAE

AEDES

CERMALVS

50 m

150 ft

0

0

Figure 5 Curia Julia (restored) (akg-images Ltd. Photograph by Erich Lessing)

Accordingly a transformation took place in the period 30–27, but one that still left the autocrat with enough power, defined and undefined, to ensure his supremacy. It is not to be believed that a man in his early thirties who had undertaken to follow in Caesar's footsteps at the age of nineteen and had used violence and serial disloyalty to reach a position of supremacy really intended to surrender his power to Senate and People. He was rather adjusting it in ways that looked fine and sweeping, such as the re-establishment of free elections and regulation of the magistracies.[3]

It is in the most celebrated chapter in his *Achievements* that Augustus claims in his sixth and seventh consulships (28–27) to have handed over the *Res Publica* from his power to the *arbitrium* (determination, discretion) of the Senate and People.[4] That is, the power to make decisions and so the direction of government was to be theirs. When that had been achieved, Octavian, like other historical figures, Lenin, Stalin and Tito among them, made a change of name (his second) from Imperator Caesar to Caesar Augustus, the first such change from a human name to one with divine overtones since King Romulus became the god Quirinus. There were many diverse adjustments to come before that final and supreme gesture, involving the redistribution of provinces and armies, was achieved between 13 and 16 January, 27 BC.[5]

It was probably during these years of extra-legal supremacy, based on the consulship, the theoretically expired Triumvirate, and his victories, that stories were circulated of dreams experienced by the resolute defender of senatorial government Q. Lutatius Catulus and by Cicero when Octavian was just a boy (Catulus died in 60 BC; Cicero was also conveniently dead (Ch. 1)). They showed him as the ruler of the Roman world selected by Jupiter, taking the place of the council of the gods invoked in Vitruvius' dedication, but a ruler who would be very different from the Dictator Caesar. The audience destined for the story was probably the apprehensive population of the country towns of Italy; senators would hardly find the idea of a god-sent ruler acceptable, even with Catulus'

Figure 6 Youthful Octavian (akg-images Ltd. Photograph by Erich Lessing)

Figure 7   Leges et Iura Restituit coin (© the Trustees of the British Museum)

sanction. If so, this is a prime specimen of the future Princeps' skill in directing particular messages accurately. Octavian had to appeal to each section of society.[6]

For senators something special was required. In 30 BC a Lex Saenia had given Octavian the right to elevate certain senatorial clans to the patriciate. Once an exclusive set of ruling families, it was by the second century BC merely a social distinction that gave exclusive access to certain priesthoods, while membership kept a man from holding the potent office of tribunate of the *plebs*. Priests had an important position through the sacrifices they offered the gods on behalf of the Roman People, but the posts were not always convenient to hold, at least to the Flamen Dialis, because of their religious prohibitions. Being a patrician might also hinder access to the consulship: it was a rule that there might be only one patrician consul a year. Now Octavian was able to replenish this ancient stratum of Roman society and gratify the social aspirations of some of his followers.[7]

This was a prelude to a shake-up of the Senate. For twenty years senators had been killed in battle, summarily executed or forced into exile or retirement, their families disrupted; all this on top of a low rate or reproduction due in part to fears of splitting family fortunes and especially to the costs of financing a family of ambitious sons and providing dowries for daughters intended to marry well. But new men, ambitious, talented, many unscrupulous and some of descent that before Caesar's coup would never have made them eligible for election to senatorial office, had taken their place and filled

Figure 8   M. Vipsanius Agrippa (akg-images Ltd.)

the House: in 29 BC there were more than a thousand members. This state of affairs had to be remedied if deserving senators were to value their positions and prospects and the public at large were to respect the order. In 29 the consuls Octavian and Agrippa conducted a scrutiny of the list. The 'disreputable' were to go. Only 190 resigned 'voluntarily', and there was angry resistance, notably from a man already designated to a tribunate of the people (see Ch. 4).[8]

The settlement of 28–27[9]

In 28 a restoration of the rule of law was proclaimed. An informative gold coin was minted in the East; two die-linked specimens have come to light, guaranteeing authenticity. The obverse displays a laurelled head of Octavian, with the legend IMP. CAESAR. DIVI. F. COS. VI, while the reverse has

LEGES ET IVRA P.R. RESTITVIT: 'Imperator Caesar, son of the Deified (Caesar), consul for the sixth time; he restored (the) laws and rights to (or, better, of) the Roman People'.[10] Octavian, wearing a toga, seated to the left on a curule stool, holds out a scroll in his right hand, with a scroll box on the ground to the left. With unusual emphasis, Octavian appears on both sides of the coin, and his achievement is commemorated in a fully formed sentence containing a finite verb. The claim is that during 28 Octavian restored laws and their rights that evidently had been lost in previous decades. The stable-mates of these Roman coins are cistophoric tetradrachms struck in Asia and bearing the same obverse legend, with LIBERTATIS P(opuli) R(omani) VINDEX: 'Champion of the Freedom of the Roman People' appended. Peace appears on the reverse: the threat to freedom had come from a foreign power, Egypt under Cleopatra.[11] The capture of Alexandria on 1 August 30 BC had been the signal for the Senate to award Octavian the wreath woven from grasses given to those who had saved a whole army; the calendars show that the day was declared a public holiday (*feriae*), because that was the day on which he 'freed the Republic from the grimmest danger'.[12]

But the 'restoration of liberty' refers to the events of 28 as well as those of 30. With the restoration of the rule of law came a third and closely related feature, a corresponding diminution of Octavian's grip on state affairs. At the end of the year Octavian, on laying down his consulship, took a customary oath that he had done nothing contrary to law during his term of office. Again, Octavian had colleagues in his consulships from 31 onwards, but they were not his equals. From the beginning of 28 he shared with his colleague Agrippa the right to be preceded by lictors carrying *fasces* in alternate months: the two men were made equals in power and so (as far as that could be) in status.[13] The change of posture was retrospective: during the year Octavian issued an edict repudiating his own previous illegal acts down to the end of 29 – the year to which Velleius Paterculus seems to date the reversion to antique normality. The proposal of E. W. Gray, that this repudiation of illegality took the form of opening his acts up for a period to challenge in the courts, remains attractive. Rich and Williams suggest that the coin reverse may present the moment when the edict was issued, and the legend part of the wording of the Senate's response.[14]

Finally, on 13 January, 27 BC, 'every province was restored to our people', as Ovid puts it ('reddita est omnis populo provincia nostro'); that must mean that Octavian relinquished the allocation of provinces to governors to 'senatorial choice' instead of it being left to his discretion, whether as Triumvir or as consul (in Tacitus' words, he abandoned the title of Triumvir and presented himself as a consul): they would be allocated by the use of lots cast between ex-magistrates of equal seniority along the lines of the rule established in 52 BC by a law of Pompey.[15] In the event, the Senate, several of its members well primed, insisted on his being left in charge (while remaining consul), for a period of ten years, not only of his conquest Egypt, but of the three most substantial domains in the Empire, which had been recognised as such by the first 'Triumvirs' in 55 when they obtained five-year commands in them: Spain, once held by Pompey, Gaul north of the Alps (Caesar's sphere of operations), and Syria (Crassus' choice). This disposition was ratified by the People.[16] Such extensive commands by the end of the 50s might be said to have become embedded in the constitution. On the other hand, those commands had naturally been disliked in senatorial circles (Cicero had to work hard for them), and they had played a part in destroying the board game of Roman politics. As to the recently conquered Egypt, Octavian shared the past misgivings of the Senate about allowing individuals command there: he put his equestrian aide, C. Cornelius Gallus, in charge; no other knight or senator was to set foot there without his permission; the very governor proved vulnerable to suspicion.[17] A few other less important but still difficult territories such as Cilicia and Cyprus were also left to Octavian to govern through his chosen legates. He undertook to give up any territory that did not require his military supervision even if that happened before the prescribed ten years was up; the remaining ten provinces were to be governed by proconsuls – all with that title whether they really were ex-consuls, as were the governors of Asia and Africa, or merely ex-praetors. These former office holders applied for posts on a basis of seniority, with the allocation of the separate territories at each level going by the lot. The provinces that were assigned to Octavian contained the bulk of the legions: only Africa, Macedonia and Illyricum of the 'public' provinces were armed.[18] By AD 14 it was only the first that still had a legion commanded by a proconsul: military and economic needs had caused the transfer of the other areas to Augustus' command.

It was ultimately on the basis of his military power, *imperium*, now made legitimate once more, at least in his provinces, that Octavian's extra-legal influence, his *auctoritas*, was to rest. If the *imperium* were withdrawn he could still rely on that power, better called by the sinister word *potentia* in this context: soldiers would follow him whatever the Senate said, as they had already shown. It was already *auctoritas* years before, according to Cicero, that induced Antony's legions to desert to him.[19] Dio contrasts Augustus' 'resignation' of his military powers in 27 – an end to the 'Triumvirate'! – and his reluctance to take more than the specified provinces, as a means of appearing republican, with the reality of the monarchy; but Dio was writing at the beginning of the third century, when the monarchy was an established fact.[20] The outcome depended above all on what use Senate and People were able to make of their *arbitrium* – the discretion to which Octavian had entrusted the Commonwealth at the beginning of 27. The gambler depended on its being minimal or at least harmless.

Is F. Millar right about how slight the change in the running of constitutional machinery was from Triumvirate to Principate?[21] The twists and turns of Triumviral relations made for uncertainty. What returned was regularity and the working of institutions by clear rules – the elections, for example. Moreover, the old metaphor of a lifeless 'façade' of republican government with the despotism concealed behind it is misleading, as N. Mackie showed.[22] Rather, there was machinery working more or less as before, but Augustus manipulated the levers.

What Augustus was to write in the *Achievements,* that after the transfer of the Commonwealth to the discretion of the Senate and People, he enjoyed only the same power as his colleagues in each of the magistracies, was strictly true but thoroughly disingenuous; the 'magistracies' are simply the consulships he subsequently held, those of 26–23, 5 and 2 BC. The boast is grossly misleading: consulships came to be the least of his powers. Nor in 27 did every senator realise (if Augustus himself did) that he would be holding consulships year after year, enabling him to intervene – in virtue of the consulship's ill-defined powers, or of his *auctoritas* – in provinces that had been entrusted to proconsuls. Continuation had long been forbidden, most recently under a senatorial decree of 43; evidently the Senate was induced to waive the ban.[23] It seems that it was the *arbitrium* of Senate and People, with or without prompting from planted speakers, that Octavian should take a leading though unspecified part in affairs of state.

For all Octavian had done for the state, not only was a laurel tree planted on either side of the door of his house on the Palatine Hill, but a wreath of oak symbolising his preservation of the lives of Roman citizens hung above it.[24] And in recognition of his awesome surrender of powers a new name was conferred on him. 'Augustus' rejected the alternative that was bruited about, and which he allegedly desired: Romulus. Its kingly associations were discouraging, and so was the story, which Livy declared 'very obscure', of his being torn in pieces by a group of senators. Whether Octavian really thought of taking that name or not, the story shows that at the time it was realised that he intended to bring in a new constitution under his own supremacy. In any case, with his preferred designation Augustus even got his reference to Romulus, who according to the poet Ennius founded Rome 'augusto augurio', 'with august augury'. 'Augustus' had the advantage of being fresh and above all open to a range of favourable interpretations at the will of audience or user and without unfavourable baggage. The word is associated with success, increase and enhancement (*augere*, to grow) and reverence, and could be rendered 'the august one' (in Greek it was 'Sebastos', 'the revered one'), and it was shared as an epithet by supreme Jove. Its opening syllable also recalled the priests (augurs) who were able to guarantee divine approval, while the ending *-stus* suggested the idea of endowment from outside, so that it has also been rendered simply as 'the divinely favoured one'. This name put the holder above any other Roman – though it is to be contrasted with the blunt 'Divus' on one occasion conferred on Caesar.

The proposal was brought forward by the ever-useful Munatius Plancus. Even senators not in the know would realise that, coming from him, it was the approved brand, and readily acquiesce, not knowing that they were conferring the name that would become the title of the Roman Emperor in the West until the end of the Empire there in 476. This was C. Octavius' final metamorphosis in his lifetime: Julius could be dropped as implied by the *cognomen* Caesar, and it is found only in the names of Augustus' descendants by birth or adoption, among freedmen of the family or provincials enfranchised by them. Besides, the uplifting novelty helped people forget the past and its crimes – at least in their conscious thinking.[25]

'Augustus' was not a title in 27, but a personal *cognomen* not accorded to any of his adopted sons, and it had not quite become a title even in AD 14, when his adopted son and heir Tiberius declined to assume it (perhaps the Senate used it as a form of address and he demurred) and Augustus' wife

Figure 9   Clipeus Virtutis at Arles (akg-images Ltd. Photograph by Erich Lessing)

Livia was 'adopted' as Julia Augusta. Yet it continued to be used of Tiberius and to address him, and he came to use it of himself, giving way to flattering practice; so it was being recognised as the distinctive designation of the supreme ruler, though not yet as '*the* Augustus'. That belongs to later centuries when 'Caesar' designated the heir or secondary ruler.

But there had to be yet another way of referring to and addressing the ruler as ruler, and at Rome the military 'Imperator' would not do, still less the unofficial 'dux', which belongs to war and is the word Augustus uses in the *Achievements* to describe his position as acclaimed 'leader' of the western forces in 32–30.[26] The shift from war to peace was precisely one of the changes that was proclaimed in 27 through the Clipeus Virtutis (Shield of Valour) awarded him by the Senate along with the laurels and oak wreaths. The shield was a type of distinction awarded in the hellenistic age; it was fashioned in gold and hung in the Senate House.

The awards are associated with military success, but the combination on the shield with the non-military merits inscribed on it of *clementia* (forbearance towards guilty enemies), *iustitia* (justice) and *pietas* (devotion to the state and to the memory of his father) transformed it into a reward for a statesman – suitable then for a *princeps*, a leading man in the state (Ch. 5).[27] For this was how Augustus came to refer to himself. Such had Pompey and indeed the younger Cato been: a first among equals. It was an emollient title, nicely ambiguous, because of Latin's want of a definite article: Augustus might be *the* or only *a princeps*, though in the *Achievements* he seems to be using the term as means of dating his supremacy, and so as a unique title. Unlike the novel, faction-based sobriquets for 'leaders' devised by Hitler, Mussolini and Franco, Führer, Duce and Caudillo, it was familiar and cleverly still did not preclude the existence of other, lesser men of the same standing, *principes*, because it was a familiar term in Roman politics. So it is in the calendar known as the *Fasti* of Amiternum, which under the date 13 November AD 16 records a plot to assassinate Tiberius, his offspring, and other *principes civitatis*, 'leading citizens'. On the other hand in AD 20 the Senate referred to Tiberius as 'Princeps noster', '*our* leader': he was unique.[28] Ten years later Velleius was able to say, wildly exaggerating, that Tiberius refused the 'Principate' in 14 for longer than others had fought for it and Tacitus in the early second century could juxtapose the title, anomalously, with that of 'king' or 'dictator' as the basis for a constitution.[29] There is no evidence that it was ever formally conferred, unlike the title 'Princeps Senatus', which was bestowed on the man whose name was given first place in the schedule of senators' names, as Augustus' was.[30] Rather it looks as if Augustus' subjects took the hint of his own usage or a wish informally expressed. Adroitly, Augustus had secured himself a title that was inoffensive and elastic: one that could become what Tacitus says it was. A *princeps* did not exercise official authority to get his way but relied on the influence, *auctoritas*, that his previous achievements had won him. The question might always arise, how far did that influence stretch before beneficent *auctoritas* became authoritarian *potentia*? Augustus hoped that it would not be asked.[31]

Failure of the settlement

Whatever risk Augustus took in reducing his formal powers, he could afford it. The most important feature of the 'constitution' of the Principate as it developed was an elasticity modelled on that of the Republic itself. Reality had never fitted theory exactly, and further theory grew out of varied practice. On one schematic view the Senate began as a mere advisory body to the kings and then to the magistrates who took their place – eventually consuls. The status of the permanent (and jealous) Senate had grown in relation to that of magistrates whose joint term of office, unless prorogued, lasted for only one year, especially through its role in the drawn-out struggle of the Hannibalic War (218–202 BC). The Senate came to see the magistrates as its agents and servants, bound to carry out its decisions. So it became legitimate to see the constitution of the Republic from two quite different ways, as if it were one of the ambiguous drawings popular in nineteenth-century magazines and immortalised by Ludwig Wittgenstein in his 'duck-rabbit'. If such a double conception lived on into the Principate there was ample scope for a whole range of conduct on the part of the Princeps. A comparable change, but in the reverse direction, took place in England as the monarch lost power to Parliament. It is only in law, language, religion and etiquette, that she is truly sovereign; and even there as 'The Queen in Parliament'.[32] Real power rests elsewhere. On this view, assessing the significance of the change that took place in 28–27 lies, not in counting what powers Augustus relinquished or kept during that period, but how he was thought to intend using those that he now had, how little he was expected to intervene elsewhere, and how well his practice conformed to those expectations. It was high expectations and immediate judgements that were the basis of Velleius Paterculus' claim that Augustus brought back the original and ancient structure of the Republic ('prisca illa et antiqua forma reipublicae revocata');[33] again, as in the phrase concerning the elections provided by Suetonius, who states that he brought back the original rule ('pristinum ius') that governed them),[34] the stress on original and ancient practice is marked, invoking an attractive nostalgia. Agrippa's dedication in 26 BC of the Saepta Julia, the people's voting enclosure, made the same point.[35] The public was to think of the state before it had been damaged by party strife at the last decades of the second century BC. P. Zanker notes a sharp change that took place before and after 32–27 in what was expressed in art and architecture, and how it was expressed (Ch. 6).[36]

Velleius' blueprint formulation encouraged the idea that Augustus was actually claiming to 'restore the Republic' ('rem publicam restituere') as Sulla had in 81–80. Scepticism is in the ascendant. J. Rich and J. Williams review the question with clarity, concluding that although substantial concessions were made, we are not entitled to conclude that Augustus either restored the Republic or claimed to have done so.[37] Significantly, a different term was used at the time: in 29 the Senate and People dedicated a monument in the Forum to Octavian for the 'conservation' of the Commonwealth.[38]

For the *res publica* was not defunct: it still existed to be transferred from Augustus to Senate and People. The position taken here is that there is no solid evidence beyond an over-interpreted Velleius that Augustus did claim to have 'restored the Republic', in the sense of bringing back the post-Sullan constitution in its pristine phase. Yet he could make the claim that as Princeps he had restored the workings of that Commonwealth as they had been during the post-Sullan 60s when Pompey the Great was serving it in the East and the Senate was powerful and vociferous. He could hope to convince, because of the elastic nature both of the word 'Princeps' and of the phrase *res publica*, in the sense of 'Commonwealth'. Augustus intended, he said in an undated programmatic edict (K. Girardet convincingly argues for late summer of 29), to lay the foundations of a *res publica*; the formulation presupposed that he would retain power indefinitely. In AD 204 'the restitution of the Commonwealth' was announced once again: the usurping, autocratic and brutal Septimius Severus had been in power for ten years, and had brought the state back to what he claimed to be normality; even in the late Empire the author on military affairs, Vegetius, could salute the revival of the *res publica*.[39] It may not be right then, given the capaciousness of the phrase, to deny a reference to the political events of 28–27 in the private but loyal '*Laudatio Turiae*' (see Ch. 1), 'res[titut]a re publica'). More decisive, if accurate, would be Th. Mommsen's restoration of the *Fasti* of Praeneste, which refer to the Senate's conferment of the oak crown on 13 January, 27, apparently because he 'restored the commonwealth to the Roman People' ('[... quod rem publicam] / p(opulo) R(omano) res[ti]tu[it]').[40] J. Rich and J. Williams, however, acutely appeal to the language of Augustus' own *Achievements*: returning the Commonwealth to the *arbitrium* of the Senate and Roman People left them the option of restoring it to him. How would the Commonwealth work?

This was the context in which Augustus explained, almost excused, what he wrote in the very next clause: 'After that time I had no more official power (*imperium*) than the men who were my colleagues in each magistracy – but I excelled every one in influence' ('omnibus auctoritate praestiti'). It is putting too much weight on the credibility of Dio's account to suppose that

Augustus, overborne by protests, unequivocally accepted any overall responsibility for running the Empire, or the statement of Strabo at the end of his
Geography, which he completed well into Tiberius' principate, that 'the
"fatherland" entrusted Augustus with the leadership of the Empire'. If he
had had such acknowledged control the problems he soon had to face would
not have arisen.[41] When he did have it, it was hard won, gradually, and without any explicit grant. Not everybody allowed himself at the time to recognise what the settlement could mean. Some did, and resented it. One of
Augustus' rewards for his forbearance was to have his bodyguard doubled.[42]

What Augustus claimed to offer in 28–27 is shown with great clarity by
a phrase used by Augustus' successor Tiberius to the Senate when he came
to sole power in AD 14. 'A good and wholesome Princeps, one whom the
senators had equipped with such enormous and unfettered power ("tanta et
tam libera potestate"), should be their slave'. He went on to mention the
claims of the entire state, but this was his opening commitment. It was they
who had conferred power on him, as he acknowledged, and he was promising them a 'minimal' Principate, the best that they could hope for. A similar
promise was made by Nero in AD 54 on his accession, in a speech composed for him by Seneca and likewise acknowledging the initiative of the
Senate. It left little for the young Princeps to do beyond look after the
armies 'that they had entrusted to him'. Whatever Nero's audience made of
his speech, this minimal Principate was what their forbears may have hoped
for in 28–27.[43]

This was no easy option for either party, if it was taken seriously. It demanded self-restraint on the part of the Princeps, and unity, courage and candour on the part of Senate and People. These latter qualities proved to be
found only in a few individuals, while the Princeps interpreted such undertakings less tightly, more as a matter of etiquette, than Tiberius did; in any case
he was fatally used to the exercise of unquestioned power. It is part of F. Millar's
case for continuity between Triumvirate and Principate that, if anything,
Augustus exercised more routine personal jurisdiction as Princeps than he or
his colleagues had as Triumvirs.[44] Perhaps this was development rather than
continuity, and to be expected: the Princeps as the possessor of confirmed
power was a magnet to litigants, and he could not deny them justice.

Still, there were developments in the 20s that limited the authority of
the Senate as a whole. One was an apparently innocuous institution devised
according to Dio in 27. This was the council that was set up to prepare

business for the Senate. It consisted of Augustus and Agrippa (when in Rome), the consuls, one each of the lower magistrates, and fifteen senators serving six months each. These terms of membership prevented any individual or clique from securing permanent influence. Even in this original, apparently innocuous form it enabled the Princeps and his friends to deal quietly beforehand with acrimonious points: the Senate was presented with cut and dried proposals, supported in the House by members of the council.[45]

Then there was the running of the provinces, the management of dependent monarchs and foreign affairs. The year 27 itself saw the edict of Cyme, by which Augustus and his fellow-consul Agrippa regulated affairs in the public province of Asia – for which the proconsul gave Augustus the credit; and an appeal for help from the same province of Asia after an earthquake, to which he dispatched the equestrian P. Vedius Pollio as regulator. This last – emergency – action was carried out not only on Augustus' own initiative, but perhaps without any consultation of the Senate: he was in Spain from 27 to 24, both avoiding the controversies that surrounded his settlement and taking definitive control of provinces that had followed Pompey the Great and his son Sextus (Spain had been a last retreat considered by Antony and Cleopatra). Suetonius also tells of Augustus hearing cases against dependent monarchs such as Archelaus of Cappadocia, who was put on trial before him and defended by the youthful Tiberius – when they were both in Spain. It was to Augustus in Spain that Parthian and other eastern delegations went. It is true that provincial and foreign litigants were supposed to 'approach the tribunal of the consuls', as Nero put it in his accession speech, but these consuls should be at Rome and backed up by the Senate, whose dominant role in foreign affairs had been well-established since the beginning of the second century BC. Augustus, however, was not ready to change his style of management and when it had the opportunity to act the Senate still failed to take advantage of it. A treaty with Mytilene came up for discussion in 24, naturally under the presidency of the consul C. Norbanus Flaccus; the Senate wrote to consult Augustus in Spain, and the city's ambassadors went as well.[46]

The discrepancies between what Augustus had seemed to promise and what he was delivering became clearer as time went on. First, there was no end to his tenure of the consulship, which he had held continuously since 31. As Rich and Williams remark, he probably did not declare himself a candidate and the elections of 27–24 were held while he was away, so that the work of securing his election was done by the presiding officer. This retention, leaving only one post open to competition every year, was probably unforeseen, perhaps even by Augustus, but he tellingly acquiesced in it. Most probably there was a spontaneous demonstration of support for him, in which the officer, the Senate, and Augustus himself (after the election), colluded. The loss to the nobility of one of the only two consulships for the year would be a bitter blow.

The Senate had reason for unease. So did individuals. After 30, Augustus was still afraid of rivals. M. Licinius Crassus, grandson of the Triumvir and consul in 30 BC, had, as governor of Macedonia in 29–28 and in charge of several legions, defeated a people called the Bessi – as had Augustus' own father (see Introduction and Ch. 4). He was saluted *imperator*, and in 27 claimed not just a triumph but an honour awarded only to those generals who had killed an enemy leader with their own hand, that of dedicating to Jupiter Feretrius the *spolia opima* ('most opulent spoils'), Octavian had never achieved anything approaching that and Crassus had also recovered Roman standards from the Getae, rivalling what Octavian had done in the Balkans in getting back what A. Gabinius had lost. The *spolia* were associated with military valour (*virtus*), and displays of that were dangerous; the Princeps, who had been seen lacking it, meant to monopolise that prowess.[47] The claim came to nothing, and perhaps by a coincidence, nothing further is heard of Crassus' career. As a delicious icing to this story, we can read in Livy the story that the *spolia opima* allowed to Cornelius *Cossus* in the later fifth century had been awarded when he was consul (*Cos.*), as 'Caesar' had discovered when he went into the temple and read the report of the award, which was inscribed on a linen corselet. Hence Cossus was acting independently under his own auspices. Despite the acutely argued scepticism of J. Rich, it is hard not to associate this story with the refusal of the *spolia* to Crassus, a mere proconsul, or, as J. Rich convincingly prefers, with his abandoning his claim before it went to the Senate – hardly a lesser ground for resentment.[48]

The second contretemps with an individual was generically similar, though the status of the offenders and the degree of control exercised by Octavian in the two provinces varied. The outcomes were also different: the second ended in suicide. Augustus' Prefect of Egypt, Cornelius Gallus, boasted about his achievements. Augustus withdrew his friendship and there were accusations of misgovernment (Ch. 4). Again the message was plain: the Princeps was asserting that his military supremacy must be unrivalled.

There was also a problem at Rome involving a member of the ruling clique: in 26 or 25 the man appointed Prefect of the City for Augustus' absence in Spain felt unable to continue in office beyond a few days. M. Valerius Messala Corvinus, loyal consular since he left Mark Antony, discovered that his post was unconstitutional and unfit for a citizen (*incivilis*), or perhaps his fellow-senators discovered it and made his tenure difficult (Ch. 4). A man unelected was acting for an absentee consul who had served continuously since 31, when (at least in 26) there was another experienced consul still at Rome – who should have been supreme in the Princeps' absence.[49] Now even the single consulship yearly open to ambitious politicians was threatened by a new office, of powers undefined as far as we know and perhaps not clear to the incumbent when he took it on. Worse, Augustus' repeated tenure of the consulship, which was to go on until 23, would have increased alarm amongst his peers when he was re-elected for 26. Augustus' colleague in that year was another close friend, T. Statilius Taurus, holding office for the second time, in 25 it was M. Junius Silanus, another person of varied allegiance, and given patrician rank by the Princeps.[50] There were serious implications for the consulship here.

The crisis of 24–23

A crucial series of events began when the infringement of the rights of the Senate as a whole and those of individual members with *imperium* were exposed – along with something else: Augustus' plans to perpetuate his power by founding a dynasty. There were signs that he intended to go further than Caesar and provide for continuity of power in his family. He too had a nephew, Octavia's son M. Claudius Marcellus, born in 42. After taking part in the triumph of 29 and serving with Augustus in Spain, Marcellus returned to hold the aedileship in 23, rather than the customary quaestorship, and at the age of 19. At the same time the Senate was invited to allow him to hold the higher offices ten years earlier than was normal. Marcellus was betrothed and married in 24 to Augustus' only child, his daughter by Scribonia.[51] It remains an obvious conclusion that Augustus was making provisional dynastic arrangements. Livia had borne him no child that survived, and she was now in the second half of her thirties.

Augustus had burst through the self-restraint demanded of him by the settlement of 28–27. Effectively, in the words of J. Crook, 'all policy was decided by Augustus'.[52] An outlet for misgivings was naturally sought. If Augustus' encroachments were challenged he might retreat, leaving freer scope for his peers and the Senate as an organ of state. The opportunity came with the trial of a former proconsul of Macedonia, and if that interpretation of the trial is correct, the place for detailed discussion of this and the following trial is in Ch. 4.[53] It is constitutional matters that are relevant here. Briefly, then, the proconsul, whose name is traditionally rendered from Dio's text as 'Marcus Primus', was accused of infringing the majesty of the Roman People (*maiestas Populi Romani*) by making war on a friendly tribe there, the Odrysae, without leave of the People, and his defence was that instructions to do so had come from Augustus, or from Augustus and Marcellus, as he also put it – evidently Augustus' young nephew;[54] perhaps what is meant in the narrative of Dio is that Augustus was claimed to be the ultimate authority and Marcellus his messenger. This defence was an embarrassment to the Princeps: as consul he could claim some authority all over the Empire, but there is no evidence that he had received an official mandate to make war at his own discretion. Had Augustus' inconclusive campaigns in Spain and inglorious rebuffs of his lieutenants in Arabia and Ethiopia (see Ch. 5) justified his usurping of the right? In any case, was this Augustus' idea of leaving the management of the Commonwealth to the *arbitrium* of its supreme council?

Augustus, home from Spain, intervened in court, putting in an appearance without being summoned as a witness, as one might well have expected him to be. Clearly, counsel on both sides knew what Augustus' testimony would be. True or false, he declared that he had not given any such instructions. It was vital that he should not be found to infringe the Lex Cornelia Maiestatis and Caesar's consular law against misconduct in the provinces by making war without the authorisation of Senate and People; it is of course possible that he had not, and that 'Primus' was making up the claim to save himself. The mention of Marcellus was simply inflammatory: nobody would believe that a nineteen-year-old had given the instructions of his own accord. Any order that was given must have come from Augustus, perhaps taken to Rome by Marcellus in 25 as he returned for his marriage. In the event the jury, a panel of senators and knights, voting by secret ballot, was split, and a number voted for the defendant's acquittal. Presumably they accepted his defence and believed that Augustus had given the order. Augustus was now smirched with the suspicion of having infringed the *maiestas* law, and had damaged the authority of the presiding praetor in order to appear in court.[55] Worse was to come.

This trial was followed by another, closely related, for 'conspiracy' against Augustus on the part of a Fannius Caepio, of a well-established senatorial family, and a Murena, who, though also of distinguished antecedents, baffles secure identification (see the chapter Appendix, p. 100), though he is identified by Dio with the man who defended 'Primus'; he is argued by some scholars to be the Murena designated for the consulship of 23 BC who never came into office.[56]

The conspirators allegedly were warned of what Augustus had in store for them and fled. They were not allowed to escape. In Dio's account, 'Since they did not stand trial they were found guilty by default on the supposition that they would become exiles; however, they were killed not long afterwards.' Naturally Caepio's prosecutor Tiberius Nero secured a guilty verdict (had the accused not thrown up their defence?); even so, according to Dio there was another split vote. The conspirators' death in flight, however dangerous they had been as potential assassins in Rome, was contrary to normal practice, which, as the historian Polybius states, allowed accused men to escape a capital penalty by going into exile.[57] If Murena was indeed a consul designated for 23 it was particularly outrageous; elected men were exempt from prosecution, except for electoral offences.

There is scarcely an item in notices of this series of events that is beyond controversy, whether the identity of two leading players or the chronology, which Dio has evidently mangled (see chapter Appendix). However, there can be no doubt of the ever-increasing deviation by Augustus from what he was understood to be offering in 28–27. It is noteworthy that in 23, when a Parthian embassy arrived in Rome, Augustus referred them to the Senate (who proceeded to ask him what should be done). Dio points to this as an example of his treatment of the Romans as a free people, but the gesture came too late to show that he was not depriving senators collectively of their role in foreign policy.[58]

If the date proposed here for the trials (late 24) is correct, they may be brought into connexion with Augustus' resignation of the consulship in midsummer of 23, an untoward action to be taken only in exceptional circumstances, and performed on this occasion on the Alban Mount, probably during the Latin Festival. The Mount offered a Temple of Jupiter, suitable for the abdication formalities, and as it was more than a mile outside the

City it was out of reach of the plebeian tribunes, who might have vetoed his action from the best of pro-Augustan or populist motives.[59] Augustus had carried on in his consulship of 23 with his position becoming more and more uncomfortable, saddled as he was with the Republican-minded colleague Cn. Calpurnius Piso taking the place of Murena.[60]

For the man who took the consulship of 23 apparently had refused office before. Now, we are told, Augustus won him over, a story that suited Augustus and, later, Piso's family (see Ch. 4). When Augustus himself resigned a suffect was elected (under the presiding consul Piso) who was also a friend of the Republican cause: L. Sestius. Augustus was to take his stand on another basis, leaving the consulship to others.

A gradual realisation on his part that he was occupying an excessive number of consulships will not do to explain his retirement in the middle of the year. A simple announcement that he intended not to accept further election would have been adequate. An acute political problem is required, which Augustus came to see he could not brazen out, and that would have been caused by the exposure of his transgressive use of his *imperium* and the brutal illegality of his handling of the 'conspiracy'. Nor was the illness he suffered in 23, serious as it was, a satisfactory reason for resigning. He had been ill before, even as he was campaigning in Spain.[61] In fact, the illness exposes more of the issues that were undermining his position. During it Augustus gave ambiguous indications of his intentions for the state if he did not survive. He dutifully handed over state papers to his colleague Piso, while he entrusted his signet ring to Agrippa: here, then, was his political heir, and no harm in that. After his recovery, however, Augustus offered to disclose the contents of his will in the Senate. Whether this was done in a conciliatory or a defiant spirit is not clear; the offer was refused. What Augustus was evidently going to show was that he had no untoward ambitions for his son-in-law Marcellus, whose premature advancement and figuring in the 'Primus' trial was public knowledge. Admittedly, the Empire was not Augustus' to leave. Even when Gaius Caligula allegedly made a will more than fifty years later 'leaving' the Empire to his sister Drusilla, it is puzzling to conjecture what it could actually have said.[62] But Augustus had the precedent of Caesar, just over a score of years in the past. Caesar's choice of his great-nephew as his main heir, with the change of name, had sent the youth on his way (Ch. 1). Now men must have feared a will written in the same terms for the benefit of Marcellus, with precisely the same dangers inherent in it, an armed struggle between a youthful heir (Marcellus) and an ambitious subordinate (Agrippa). Beyond legacies to his friends, wife, sister and stepsons, provision of some kind must have been made for Marcellus, as well as for Julia. It would have been the omission of the requirement to take the name Julius Caesar that made it possible to offer to open the will.

The makeshift settlement: 23–19

The shift that took place in 23 BC followed political humiliations for Augustus, so it could not be expected to last. Only four years later he reached a position, political as well as constitutional, that thoroughly suited him, but that could not be foreseen. Now, on resigning the consulship, Augustus took a new form of power, that of a tribune of the *plebs* (*tribunicia potestas*). He had enjoyed elements of the tribunician position before 23: in 36 he was granted the religious protection that the holder of the office enjoyed (its *sacrosanctitas*) and perhaps in 31 a right of appeal, but this was the first time he had the full power, notably the power to legislate. It was at this moment, though, that Augustus discovered one of the firmest bases of his future position: the *tribunicia potestas* was conveniently divorced from the actual office of tribune, which, as a patrician, Augustus could not hold. That meant that it was also freed from the constraints of annual tenure and collegiality inherent in the consulship and other offices.[63]

Even more important, the regime was clearly rebranded. Tacitus tells us that Augustus assumed the power 'to defend the people'. The tribunate still carried the flavour of factional Republican politics: reforming (and ambitious) tribunes such as the Gracchi (133 and 123–22 BC), Appuleius Saturninus (103 and 100), P. Sulpicius (88) and Clodius (58) had developed the ideology and could be blamed for the fatal decline of the Republic. At loggerheads with conservative senators and often in conflict with the consuls themselves, they had passed radical legislation (distribution of public land and of grain; electoral reform) and they could bring the entire workings of the state to a halt with their veto. C. Marius as consul in 100 had at least condoned the death of Saturninus and Sulla in 88 had had Sulpicius killed. This was the office that Sulla as Dictator in 81 had tried to cripple (see Introduction). It was one of his strengths that Augustus could shelter the upper class, if he chose, from the fear and rancour of the ordinary people, their want and misery. But the man who had presented himself as the restorer of legitimate and traditional government by Senate and magistrates now flaunted the guise of a protector of popular rights. Of course, Augustus had shown care for the welfare of the *plebs* right from the start. He had to, or they might riot, as they had in 38. The 'son' of the *popularis* Caesar was the restorer of temples and the traditional popular religion which he patronised through the calendar and which involved games, festivities and holidays. Not only spectacles and grain but the very rebuilding of Rome itself was for their benefit (Ch. 5). The people saw that their Princeps had been attacked by the oligarchy, and would rally to the man who would look after their interests. Augustus' famous tribunician predecessors had all been worsted in factional politics before they took up popular causes (just as Augustus had) and all died by violence performing that function and so become martyrs for the *plebs*, as well as bogeymen in conservative senatorial thinking: Augustus did not intend that for his own fate, but his choice of power exposes the depth of the rift that had opened up by the end of 24 between him and the Senate. For all his cultivation of the *plebs* it is an implausible view that Augustus had been planning a 'popular front', and that that contributed to his fall from grace with the Senate. On the contrary, the resignation in mid-year showed haste; Augustus' political change was like that of earlier tribunes, forced and sudden: his reaction was due to his fall from grace.[64] The Princeps was educated and knew his history. The closest parallel to his move of 23 BC was one made precisely a century previously, when the consul of 125 BC, M. Fulvius Flaccus, frustrated in his attempt to enfranchise the Italian allies, was elected to the tribunate of 122 as an ally of C. Gracchus. The anomalous career move was to become a pattern for rising members of imperial dynasties – for Tiberius for example, consul in 7 BC, holder of tribunician power from 6 onwards.[65]

Anger was not all on one side. Augustus could complain that his ambiguous settlement of 28–27 had been generous, compared with Caesar's treatment of the political class. But the ambiguity had misled politicians as to Augustus' true intentions and now he had been found out. His response was not to retreat from power but, on the contrary, take more where he could. If that was difficult in the face of disapproval at what he was already using, this was the man who, only nine years before, on being attacked in the Senate, had entered it with the support of men-at-arms. He could still call on them, a potent threat, and on senators who accepted and hoped to benefit from his lack of scruple.[66]

If enhanced by improved rights to summon the Senate and a higher place in the speaking order, as it was now for Augustus, the tribunician power was a viable substitute for the consulship. Its scope though was limited to one mile outside Rome and it did not confer *imperium*. In the provinces that the Senate had allocated to him when he was consul, Egypt, Spain, Gaul and Syria, Augustus accordingly now became proconsul, but he had lost that indeterminate right to oversee the entire system that belonged to the consuls. It seems strange that it was restored to him at once in the stronger, unchallengeable form of a proconsular *imperium* that was Empire-wide and superior to that of all other governors.[67] It meant that when Augustus entered a province, or even wrote to its proconsul, there would be no doubt of his right to issue instructions to him; troops in public provinces were regarded as Augustus' no less than those in his own. But there was a good reason for his impudent champions in the Senate to offer: a proconsul had recently been convicted for treason (*maiestas*) for making war without the People's authority. If Augustus had had overriding authority, he could have prevented the man's illicit action. By such effrontery could Augustus' reverse be turned to his advantage.

There was a conflict, though, between the tribunician power and the enhanced *imperium*: tribunes could not exercise their power beyond the first milestone outside Rome: it was a position that concerned the urban *plebs*; but a proconsul's *imperium* lapsed when he crossed the sacred boundary of the City, the Pomerium; only in a narrow mile-wide ring round the City could Augustus exercise both powers at the same time. The problem was resolved by making it possible for Augustus to deploy his *imperium* in the Empire *from within* the City. The one part of the Roman world that was not subject to Augustus' power in this period was Italy itself.[68] That was a serious lack for a man who had largely based his political position on the support he received there in 32–31, and it would have to be remedied.

In 23, Augustus' associate Agrippa was accorded a command, perhaps proconsular *imperium* rather than a mere legateship, over Syria and other eastern provinces. The idea that this work was devised to take him away from Rome and rivalry with Marcellus is absurd; it is anachronistically based on the story of Tiberius' retirement to Rhodes in 6 BC. Agrippa proceeded to the 'free' island of Lesbos, which, though within sight of Asia Minor, also gave access to the armed province of Macedonia, and he governed Syria through legates. The appointment diminished the authority of other senators serving in the East, but Agrippa's presence there was necessary: above all it was an insurance policy on Augustus' life at Rome, as well as a variant, however subdued, on the theme of division of the Empire between East and West and a sign of Agrippa's potential advance to partnership in the Augustan 'firm'.[69]

The events of 24–23 show how far Augustus had deviated from his constitutional undertakings of 28–27, and how determined he was to hold on to his supremacy. His enhanced *imperium* as a proconsul remained the core of imperial power as long as enquiries might still be made as to what that was.[70] Probably well before the end of the Julio-Claudian dynasty in 68, the significant imperial powers came to be seen as an indissoluble unity: on Gaius Caligula and Claudius they had already been conferred all at once. Most importantly, Augustus in 23 took a step that was decisive in the evolution of the Principate and gave the lie to his professions. The Republic had been built on power limited in time and scope: the consulship, with which Tacitus vehemently identifies *libertas* in the first sentence of his *Annals*, lasted for a year and was shared with a colleague. Now Augustus took the power that belonged to another office that was similarly limited, this time with nine colleagues; but instant renewal of the office had never effectively been denied, as it had been for the consulship. But Augustus' tribunician power was for life. He was sidestepping the constitution and beginning to build up a separate structure.[71]

Much of the period 23–19 was spent abroad: in 22 Augustus was in Sicily, concerned no doubt with the security of grain supplies from there, and 21–20 saw him in the East, dealing effectively with the Parthians. Magistrates and Senate would have to manage as best they could, and when they realised in 21 that they had failed and asked him to return he refused.[72] The gods were kind to Augustus and sent flood, famine and fire during these years.[73] The Tiber overflowed, bringing destruction and disease; the grain supply had already failed in 23, threatening hunger. Any suggestion that Augustus contrived shortages must be firmly resisted. There is no evidence for that, and he would have been found out. Grain shortages persisted even under emperors who had every reason to prevent them.[74] However, the fact that reports of natural disasters peak in years of difficulty for Augustus, 23–22 BC and AD 5, suggests that writers were on the alert for them and saw them as chiming in with the political situation.[75]

Two factors contributed to political disorder of these years: first, these material privations of the people and their correct conviction that only their defeated favourite could remedy them. The People proved ungovernable even when Agrippa was sent to calm them in 21.[76] The power vacuum at Rome that Augustus' abdication of the consulship left sucked in ambitious senators who now saw a chance of reaching the supreme magistracy. There were wrangles over the consulship, even over the honorific post of Prefect of the City for the Latin Festival. In 22 quarrels between candidates for the consulship brought an end to the electoral process: the year 21 opened with only one in office. A delegation to Augustus in Sicily brought about a superficial reconciliation and the election of one of the candidates. The very year after his abdication of the consulship, Augustus was forced to refuse offers of the Dictatorship, the office that had been abolished in the aftermath of Caesar's murder. He fell to his knees, tore his clothes and bared his breast. This was theatrical, but no doubt sincere in its aim: the Dictatorship and ensuing martyrdom were no part of his plans. To have accepted it would have been to take a fatal road, but the people were not to know it – or they did not care. An alternative offer of 22 was of an annual and perpetual consulship. Perhaps it was in token of one of his refusals that Augustus began numbering the years of his tribunician power, enhancing its status.[77] However, Augustus did take on a charge of the grain supply, and relieved that shortage remarkably fast; for, providentially, he was not far away.[78] At some point, in 23 or 19, there was a proposal from Augustus himself that in years when he was consul there should be three colleagues, obviating the problem that his tenure kept other men out. That was refused by the whole Senate, which clamoured that his greatness (*maiestas*) was already too much diminished by having to share the office at all. It would be interesting to know when this scene took place, and whether we are dealing with servility, irony or a simple fear of diminishing the value of the supreme magistracy for men who would become secondary members of a board.

The *Achievements* also record refusals of offers made in 19, 18 and 11 BC of a 'charge of the laws and customs' ('cura legum morumque') with supreme power and without a colleague, and of the censorship (Dio reports, mistakenly, that Augustus accepted a five-year term in 19). That would have given him blatant control over the membership of the Senate. Instead, two eminent senators were entrusted in 22 with that job, which was to assess the numbers and property of Roman citizens and, more controversially, to scrutinise the Senate. These censors proved incapable of carrying out their duties; in fact, by an extraordinary coincidence, when they ascended the tribunal on the first day of office it proved to have been ill constructed and collapsed.[79] Not all the abortive offers would have restored Augustus his *imperium* within the Pomerium, but they are to be taken as intended substitutes for the consulship that he had renounced, offered by the people (formally assembled or in crowds) as a desperate alternative, or by the Senate to placate the man and his supporters.[80]

As the year 22 showed, this was a time for opportunistic politicians to make careers out of the People's discontents. One ambitious individual, M. Egnatius Rufus, planned a consulship for 19, without leaving the required two years empty after his praetorship. Augustus was still away. A determined consul, C. Sentius Saturninus, resisted his candidature and he was arrested and executed (Ch. 4). This year it had proved impossible to find a substitute consul for Augustus: the people wanted him back and the elections were abortive. The Senate House itself was threatened by arson, for the first time since the funeral of Clodius in 52. Indeed, these events recalled Clodius' turbulent feuding with T. Annius Milo and the appeal made to Pompey in 53 to assume the sole consulship. The Senate could not govern. An embassy of Saturninus, other magistrates and leading senators went to greet the Princeps in Campania. Augustus came back to Rome quietly, without even an ovation, still refused the consulship and instead saw to the election of an acceptable colleague for Saturninus, an elderly senator with an unimpeachably republican history and the grotesque name of Q. Lucretius Vespillo, 'Undertaker'. An altar to Fortuna Redux celebrating vows taken for his return, and commemorating his modesty in refusing a triumph, was decreed on 12 October at the humiliated Senate's orders; she was further celebrated by being represented on contemporary coins of the Triumviri Monetales. The day of Augustus' return was proclaimed a holiday, and a festival instituted which became the Augustalia, the first to be named after an historical human being. The brief unhappy interlude was over.[81]

The settlement of 19

It was in everyone's interests that there should be a settlement of present discontents, but Augustus made a positive gain, while Senate and People found only relief. In place of the proffered consulship he allowed his

Empire-wide *imperium* to be made equal to that of the consuls: that is to say, made applicable within Rome and Italy. He was now to sit between the incumbent consuls on the curule chair – as he had in 32 – and again to have the twelve bundles of rods and axes that consuls were entitled to carried before him by lictors. These were not empty displays (why should the Romans have devalued their ancient and graded symbols of *imperium*?), but the outward representation of substantive powers. Augustus now had all that he had enjoyed before 23, but again, as with the tribunician power, without the annual time limit and free from the nuisance of collegiality, not magistracies but the powers of magistrates. H. Cotton and A. Yakobson rightly insist on the delicacy of formulating this enabling measure. However, there should be no doubt of his possessing the full power of the consuls: the sensitivity that emperors occasionally demonstrated about its use is sufficient to illustrate that: Tiberius invoked his tribunician power to summon the Senate on Augustus' death (the consuls were in Rome); and Nero on his accession renounced intervention in Italy.[82]

This was the turning point in the Augustan Principate, a victory for the Princeps that changed his relationship with the Commonwealth and its leading members. It was symptomatic that, according to Dio, the Senate, after voting him his powers, invited him to pass whatever legislation he chose.[83] For our purpose it means that he was no longer on the attack, using every means to entrench himself; his future efforts went towards consolidation, the recognition of his position, even its celebration: 17 BC saw games initiating a new age (Ch. 3).

Augustus was now free to take measures that might previously have met resistance. Political changes in the relationship between Augustus and the Commonwealth took four forms, not mutually exclusive. There were further honours for Augustus, which were harmless in themselves but cemented his position; more important, further encroachments on the prerogatives of the Senate and its members, some of which gave a hint of the iron fist. These were mitigated by apparent concessions to senatorial feeling. Finally came a major development which was made possible by Augustus' own entrenchment: a shift of attention away from Augustus himself to his partner Agrippa and to a series of potential successors who could share his new powers: the development of the imperial house (*domus Augusta*), something different from and, with the place it had for

Figure 10 The foundation of a dynasty (Bibliothèque Nationale de France, Paris)

women, larger than the agnatic family of the Julii Caesares. That had already manifested itself when Marcellus was buried in the mausoleum on his death in 23 BC, and it was embodied in the procession represented on the Ara Pacis. Now began the celebration of the family in monuments Empire-wide.[84]

First, then, new honours, some with religious connotations. The first formal advance came in 12 BC, after the former Triumvir M. Lepidus, still Pontifex Maximus, died at last and Augustus took the place that had been his father's and was thought by men of good will to be rightfully his. This was a high point of Augustus' Principate, with Vesta taking her place on the Palatine; and it initiated a new phase in Augustus' penetration of religious institutions (Ch. 3).[85] Only the year before, in 13, when Augustus returned from Gaul after an absence of three years, the Senate determined on 4 July that a massive altar to the Augustan Peace should be set up in the Field of Mars. The imperial family played a prime role on the sculptures (Ch. 5).[86]

Entitling Augustus 'Father of his Country', as the Senate and Roman People formally did on 5 February 2 BC, might have been thought purely honorific, but the title – or *cognomen*, as Suetonius called it – was important enough to be taken by all Augustus' successors after they had been in power for varying lengths of time, all but Tiberius, who thought that only exceptional acts justified it. It conferred the moral authority of a father and came close to implying a supreme *auctoritas*, virtually emancipating Augustus from the restrictions of the defined powers that had been conferred on him.[87] It had been used of Cicero the consul after he had dealt with the Catilinarian conspiracy, but not for long: his *auctoritas* collapsed. This time elaborate ceremony, even fuss, surrounded an official conferment, setting it in stone. First of all a delegation from the *plebs* came to Augustus, and he refused the offer; it was then renewed in theatre or circus, and in the Senate, with the prominent quondam Republican Messala Corvinus being mandated to make it (his son Messala Messalinus was to play a servile role in the 'accession debate' of 14). Perhaps a formal decree embodied the Senate's wish, but the spontaneous acclamation may have seemed enough in itself. In any case Augustus in the *Achievements* could write that 'the Senate and equestrian order and the whole Roman People designated me Father of my Country'. The name that represented the summit of Augustus' ambition (so he said) was then propagated on other monuments. It was indeed the seal of approval from the state, every rank implicated in a carefully engineered piece of theatre.

If Augustus invoked Concord on 5 February, when the same unanimity manifested itself as it had in the period after the defeat of Antony and Cleopatra, the deity and what she stood for were to play a more prominent part than before as the regime was shaken in its last ten years. Her temple, initiated by Tiberius, was under construction, and after his return to power in AD 5 the Ciceronian slogan of 'Concord between the orders' ('Concordia ordinum') was to be in the air when a Lex Valeria Cornelia modified the voting system in favour of senators and knights (Ch. 3).[88]

There were lesser areas of state religion on which Augustus and his family bore down. The ancient twelve-man body of the Arval Brethren, who were concerned with the fertility of the fields, came not only to be headed by the Princeps (as were the three great priesthoods beside the Pontificate – the Augurs, the Board of Fifteen in charge of Sacrifices and the Board of Seven in charge of Feasts) but to have sacrifices of the most expensive type of animal, bovines, offered for his safety and that of the members of his family every year, and on special occasions (such as the uncovering of conspiracies).[89] The entire dynasty became numinous, a development that needs no lengthy explanation: Romans worshipped power and did it homage – enhancing it further thereby.

Now for Augustus' use of his restored powers and his encroachments on the rights of his peers. Normally he does not seem to have usurped any of the functions of the actual consuls, such as presiding over elections (as has sometimes been suggested), but his presence nonetheless must have limited their scope for unfettered action. It is elsewhere that his tightened grasp on affairs may be seen. In 18 he initiated another scrutiny of the Senate, though this time it was conducted by the members themselves: a caucus of worthy men was trusted to put forward their own candidates, who did the same in their turn. Even this did not go well: there was faction, favouritism and disorder. Augustus was nonplussed to find Lepidus nominated. He ended by conducting the selection himself, and this time succeeded in bringing the Senate down to 600 men – though he said, hardly seriously, given the number of administrative duties there were to be performed, that he would have preferred 300. Probably it was at this point that the senatorial census was imposed: HS 1 million, (or possibly HS 800,000, rising in 13 BC); previously senators had to possess only the same amount as members of the equestrian order, HS 400,000.[90]

The realisation that proconsuls were no longer going to be allowed to triumph came more gradually. Suetonius, whose perspective was that of a second-century servant of the emperors, presents Augustus' conduct as evidence of his merits: Augustus allowed more than thirty triumphs to be decreed (even if they were not all celebrated), and still more 'triumphal decorations' (*ornamenta triumphalia*), for what they were worth.[91] The last time a man who was not a member of the imperial family held a regular triumph was precisely in 19 BC. He was Cornelius Balbus of Gades (Cádiz), who triumphed from Africa. Son of a faithful follower of Pompey and Caesar, a provincial, he was harmless to the regime. The shut-down was cleverly managed. Agrippa in Spain, also in 19, brought an end to the obstinate war there. However, he failed to report his successes to the Senate, so he could not be offered a triumph. Instead, Augustus was given the salutation of '*imperator*' that Agrippa had earned. Another triumph was refused in 14.[92] The successes of Tiberius and Nero Drusus in the Alps, Germany and the Balkans, 16–9 BC, apparently were reported, and the Senate hopefully offered them triumphs, refused on their behalf by Augustus. Only after the death of Nero Drusus in 9, when Tiberius' *imperium* was enhanced, was he allowed the celebration, held in his second consulship of 7 BC. Other generals could not expect to do so well. L. Calpurnius Piso, *cos.* 15, for his successes in his three-year tenure of Macedonia, 13–11 BC, was offered and accepted a newly devised lesser honour: the 'triumphal decorations' (*ornamenta triumphalia*), which allowed him a statue in Rome and distinction of dress, but no chariot procession. The example of Piso, a co-operative member of the nobility, was followed in future by all successful generals outside the imperial family. Admittedly, most but not all were not proconsuls but legates of Augustus in imperial provinces and so without independent *imperium*. At the beginning of Augustus' Principate there were on W. Eck's estimate five such imperial provinces, at the end about thirteen.[93]

This was a blow to high-flying senators in their public life. Then there was a crop of drastic legal measures introduced in 18–17, almost immediately after Augustus' accession to undisputed supremacy, though he used his tribunician power to put it through the popular assembly. There was the law against electoral corruption (*Lex Julia de ambitu*) and measures even more serious, because they invaded private life and conduct in an unprecedented way, which will be treated at greater length in the next chapter: the social legislation. Political advancement was to depend on marital status and even inheritance was affected (*Lex Julia de maritandis ordinibus*); adultery was criminalised if a married woman was involved (*Lex Julia de adulteriis*); and there was a sumptuary law (*Lex Julia sumptuaria*). The iron hand was clearly felt. Whatever other statesmanlike motives may be ascribed to Augustus in bringing forward this legislation, one is obvious: he was disciplining, if not punishing, the Senate.[94]

Concessions to the Senate took the form of enhancing its dignity, and that was one of the intended consequences of Augustus' social legislation. Under Augustus the Senate developed the *maiestas* ('greatness', 'majesty'), which had been the sole prerogative of the Roman People and its magistrates. Its power, too, seemed to be enhanced. Gradually decrees of the Senate, because they were never challenged in popular assemblies, obtained the force of law; their confirmation was no longer felt necessary except for such essential items as the conferring of imperial powers, which had to be legally watertight.[95] It seems to have been after 19 BC that the right to try cases of state importance – treason, misconduct as governor of a province, especially extortion (*res repetundae*) – was handed over to the Senate.[96] This looked like a marked extension of the Senate's authority: the courts had been one of the major issues that divided senatorial and equestrian orders since the tribunates of C. Gracchus. There was more to it than that, however, as we shall see (Ch. 3). Less sensational, because they were noticed only in passing and not systematically charted, were the changes that Augustus eventually introduced into electoral procedure (including even the reduction of days available for elections by the introduction of new Augustan festal days), and which led in AD 14 to the transfer under Tiberius of all elections to the Senate (Ch. 3). In any electoral wrangles or deadlock after 19 BC it would have been in collaboration with or at least with the agreement of the Senate that Augustus 'appointed' candidates. Then, in AD 5 as part of the funerary honours for Augustus' dead grandsons, came the creation of the ten new voting units (centuries) in which senators and knights were to vote first.[97]

Augustus seems to have made a minor concession at this time if it was in about 19 BC that the junior magistrates called Triumviri Monetales, who held this post at an early age, perhaps eighteen, began to strike their own coins again, and with designs that might refer to the achievements of their own ancestors; or to those of Augustus. One member of the college of 15 BC was Cn. Calpurnius Piso, son of the consul of 23. Piso's issues showed his legendary ancestor Numa, the king who succeeded Romulus.[98] The letters S(enatus) C(onsulto) ('by decree of the Senate') which figure on base-metal coinage from now on are variously interpreted: they show some authority of the Senate over that coinage or indicate its decision to coin aes in brass and copper or they refer to a decree that conferred the corona civica on Augustus, the oak-leaf crown awarded for saving the life of a fellow-soldier. Most satisfactory is the explanation of C. H. V. Sutherland, that the letters marked the withdrawal of stocks of metal from the Aerarium, of which the Senate was so long the literal key-holder; it was 'a polite and harmless fiction which could continue . . . for some three centuries'.[99]

Finally the question of the succession to Augustus' power, a cause of dissension and speculation in 24–23: he could now proceed at will. A decisive step was soon taken. Collegiality after all was to form a vital part of the plan. In 18 Augustus renewed his own imperium for five years, and whatever reluctance he showed at subsequent renewals, it was to be his for life.[100] It is noteworthy that the renewals of 18 and 13 BC are the only five-year conferments: the rest were for ten years; perhaps Augustus still felt the need for caution. He took Agrippa as his colleague in the tribunician power and had the imperium that Agrippa had enjoyed in the East prorogued and perhaps extended to cover western provinces such as Spain (both for a five-year term); in 13 it was to be defined as greater than that of all other proconsuls, like Augustus'.[101] From then on, when Augustus died there need be no hiatus. Agrippa would already be in an unchallengeable position, and tribunician power was on its way to becoming an innocuous token of supremacy.

A different step was taken in 17 to prolong the dynasty's supremacy into the next generation. Marcellus' widow Julia was married to Agrippa in 21 and in 20 and 17 she gave birth to sons, Gaius and Lucius. Now (and only now) Augustus adopted both boys as his sons, conferring on them, as he had not been able to do on Marcellus, the illustrious name of Julius Caesar, and showing that his scheme of unbroken partnerships was to continue. Agrippa in Spain and the Balkans was as good an insurance for Augustus' safety as he had been in the East. If M. Torelli is to be believed, the two sides of the procession on the walls of the Ara Pacis, the altar of Augustan Peace in the Campus Martius, represent primary and secondary lines of succession, so embodying Augustus' plans as they were after Agrippa's death in 12 BC.[102] However that may be (see Ch. 5), when the altar was dedicated on 30 January 9 BC – Livia's birthday – plans for the succession had changed. Agrippa, who appears in the altar's sculptured procession, had been dead nearly three years. Augustus had brought the two sons of Livia, Tiberius and Nero Drusus, into the scheme, and Tiberius was married to Agrippa's widow Julia. The stage was set for conflict within the dynasty (Ch. 4). He would have been rash to set his plans in stone.

The last decade: autocracy

According to Dio, assigning the remark to AD 3, which he attaches only to the renewal of powers made in that year, and perhaps connects with Augustus' pretended reluctance, the Princeps became more conservative with age and reluctant to risk causing offence to senators.[103] Rather, Augustus' gradual entrenchment and his customisation of power ended in a decade of autocratic behaviour. We have noticed the language of Tiberius in his accession speeches: only the divine mind of Augustus was capable of governing the Empire by himself; he himself needed help.[104] The speeches of Prime Minister Gordon Brown, made to the Commons on 3 July 2007, and on other occasions, undertaking to offer Parliament a greater role, were a similar tacit repudiation of the government of his predecessor.

By AD 14 causes for discomfort among senators, Roman People and even provincials had been accumulating. In part they were external, even natural: earthquake, flood, fire, persistent grain shortages (and it is highly significant for the way the decade was perceived that they are so prominent in Dio's account). Then there was difficult, even threatening, warfare in the Balkans and Germany, revolts and protest from other parts of the Empire, and at the core of his regime unrest amongst the troops and unrest at the shortage of grain.

To start with changes in Augustus himself, there was inevitable physical decline. He did not leave Italy again after 8 BC, even though he lost one of his two front-rank generals, Nero Drusus, on campaign in 9 BC and the other, Ti. Nero, to political dispute in 6. But there were other men, and he no longer needed to demonstrate his own military capability. There is no indication of real physical weakness until AD 8, when he stopped canvassing in person at elections (see Ch. 3). In the same year Dio notices an apparent liberalising of the regime: Augustus told the Senate that they might take decisions without him. M. Dettenhofer draws the conclusion that the Senate's proceedings, like those of the public assemblies, which he also gave up, had been closely supervised by Augustus and his deputies. But we do not know the circumstances of this pronouncement. Eight years later senators tried to bring proceedings to an end when Tiberius went to Campania for a short visit.[105] Perhaps we have now Augustus proposing his own retirement, senators protesting that the House could not function without him, and Augustus denying it. In that case not too much should be made of the exchange, and the only implication is that senators were always careful to speak with an eye on the Princeps, which is obvious. More probably he too was intending a short break from Rome, and the Tiberian scene was a recapitulation of one with Augustus. But the saying may have been a mere casual remark that some admirer (or ironist) has captured and preserved for Dio.

Whatever Augustus said, authority, even prestige, was passing away from the Senate. There were symptoms before the last decade, for example, in about 4 BC the disappearance from the coinage of the names of the young aristocrats who were charged with the striking of coins at the mint of Rome. Nothing, perhaps, must detract from the brilliant entry into public life of C. and L. Caesar in 5 and 2 BC.[106] This faint sign is hardly worth mentioning in comparison with the blatant development of AD 13. The 'probouleutic' council, a sub-committee of the senate, as J. Crook describes it, underwent a radical change. First, it was permanently afforced by leading members of the imperial family, notably Tiberius and his sons, when they were in Rome. Far more startling is the fact that its recommendations were no longer merely to be added to the Senate's agenda but were to be taken as having the force of senatorial decrees. Augustus' increasing weakness was given as the reason. So the usurpation of the Senate's ancient rights was the price of sparing the enfeebled Emperor attendance in the complex of Apollo on the Palatine, where senatorial meetings were already being held. Crook sees the change also as promoting a quiet transfer of power to Tiberius. Not least perhaps, it made dissent on important matters in the full House little more than mere noise.[107] It is no surprise that on Augustus' death, Tiberius, with his stress on the importance of the Senate's role in decision-making and the programme of 27 BC, seems to have given up the council and instead constituted an informal body of twenty senators whose job was to advise him in carrying out his duties.[108]

Misfortune in his family was another and crucial cause of deterioration in the Senate's position and so in government as it had once been understood (Ch. 4). The start came with the death of Nero Drusus in 9 BC. The ageing Augustus needed a real partner again, not a youthful heir. In the next three years Tiberius Nero was raised by grants of power, his triumph, a second consulship (7 BC) and immediate accession to the tribunician power in 6 (Augustus was mimicking his own progress in 23 BC), with *imperium* in the eastern provinces to follow. Tiberius was the new Agrippa and the man who would take over when Augustus died. The struggle for power within the imperial family that broke out as a result affected the Senate too, not only individuals who supported one member of the family or another, but the entire body, where enmities found expression and could now be resolved by prosecution. It continued after Tiberius' adoption in AD 4 and into his own Principate (Ch. 4).

It was an aggravating factor that austerity was now looming large, for the boom brought by the peace of 30 BC and the injection of Egyptian gold into the Treasury, with its expenditure on building projects at Rome and elsewhere, was coming to an end.[109] An early sign of this was the resurgence of the debt problem in 7 BC: debtors were suspected of causing a fire in the Forum.[110] Wars of conquest were being carried on, but Germany was not Egypt, and Augustus had to meet the cost of sustaining the army and above all of providing for the retirement bounties of legionaries. The massive recruitments that preceded the campaign of Actium will have produced a huge crop of land-hungry veterans in 13 BC, and there were further surges in 2 BC. Thoughts of Perusia and the disturbances that followed the end of the civil wars came to landowners' minds. In 13, Augustus introduced a system of cash payments for discharged soldiers which relieved their anxieties. Sometimes Augustus paid bounties from his own property, as in 7, 6, and 4–2 BC, but in AD 6 he had to find fresh public resources: new taxes fed into a special military treasury (see Ch. 4). Perhaps to relieve problems of the State treasury itself, a three-man economy commission was established and in the following year state expenditure on shows was cancelled to save money.[111]

Natural disasters were bad enough, especially as they were ominous. Persistent grain shortages at Rome were an embarrassment for which Augustus could be held responsible. The drastic measures that Augustus took in 6 to counter the shortage – exclusion of gladiators and slaves for sale to a hundred miles' distance from Rome, and the like – were not effective. Romans may have been pleased to see the German bodyguard go. In 7 he also had to cancel the customary parade of *equites*.[112] But it is noteworthy that Augustus' eventual reaction in AD 8 was to break out into a takeover of the grain supply, which he entrusted to a procurator, and he responded to a fire in the same way (Ch. 3).[113]

The provinces likewise found themselves in difficulties. In the new conditions, pressure from tax collectors must have increased, and the first two decades of the new millennium were marked by protests and rebellions, several attested as due to debt or rapacity. By far the most serious and costly were in the Balkans and Germany. The Pannonian revolt broke out in AD 6, alongside revolts in southern Asia Minor and Judaea. It lasted for three years, to be suppressed only by the most strenuous efforts of Tiberius, using troops that were sometimes near mutiny. Immediately upon it came the traumatic loss in the Teutoburg in Germany of three legions under P. Quinctilius Varus.[114] These events should radically have intensified the feel-bad factor that developed towards the end of Augustus' reign and under Tiberius as he too tried to save money by economising on expenditure. It is hard to believe P. Zanker's claim that none of the disagreeable facts of the last decade impinged on the consciousness of the Romans themselves: 'An image was more powerful than the reality, and nothing could shake their faith in the new era.'[115] On the contrary, seeing that the Varian disaster was not a catastrophe that could be hidden, Augustus showed himself a participant in the people's anguish (the men lost were largely Italians), and during the grain shortage let it be known that he was contemplating suicide: he went without food for four days.[116] Augustus found nothing to add to his personal record, the *Achievements*, after AD 6–7 except the formality of a census, and possibly mention of Armenian affairs.[117]

The 'evolution' of this chapter's title should not be taken to imply a smooth trajectory; natural evolution too has been credited with irregular leaps and bounds. Two types of change marked the principate of Augustus. His own formal powers were modified or advanced in extemporised jerks, two, those of 28–27 and 23 BC, carrying extremely diverse, even conflicting ideological content. Some new institutions and equestrian posts (Ch. 3) might be described as revolutionary: they added to one man's power and were alien to Republican ways of thinking. Augustus' supremacy, accepted at once or in the course of time by Senate and People, and by the population of the Empire at large, remained for some a thing to resent (see Ch. 4).

An undated anecdote attests Augustus' professed reverence for the arch-conservative Cato of Utica. To a man who spoke ill of Cato he delivered a snub: 'Whoever is unwilling for the existing state of the community to be changed is both a good citizen and a good man.'[118] One might suspect that that anecdote belongs to the period 28–27, but if the man snubbed and named as 'Strabo' is the Prefect of the Guard in office in AD 14 the anecdote belongs late in Augustus' Principate and is highly significant. Pompey the Great too was commended by Augustus to his elder grandson for his 'good will' – whether his own or of others towards him.[119] By then success, for Augustus, had obscured the issue that had dominated the late Republic: whether the Senate or some individual should control the state. That question had been settled: in Ovid's words from exile, 'The Commonwealth is Caesar.'[120] Stability was now paramount – the stability that Augustus claimed to have provided.

Appendix: chronology and personnel of the 'conspiracy' of Caepio and Murena[121]

This conspiracy is apparently dated by Dio to 22 BC, though all he does is embed his account in events of that year, by making it follow the trial of 'Primus', which itself is brought on as an example of Augustus' conduct towards his friends. Velleius' language does not forbid the same date.[122] E. Badian[123] has trenchantly argued against rejecting it and assigning the trials of 'Primus' and Murena to 23. Equally he rejects the identification of the conspirator with the Murena, consul (designate) of 23, who vanishes from the record after being mentioned solely on the Capitoline *Fasti*, putatively as a result of his conspiracy. Accordingly, Badian rejects the view that Augustus' retirement from the consulship in mid-23 has anything to do with this conspiracy. The retirement was planned well beforehand because continuous tenure of the consulship was unsatisfactory; the solution reached in 28–27 was always an interim one.

The main evidence for the date of the conspiracy and the identity of the alleged conspirator is as follows. Dio, relating events of 22, says that, although Augustus played the ruler and lawgiver, *in other respects* he was moderate, even standing by friends when they were undergoing scrutiny; and when 'Primus' was on trial he came voluntarily into the court to deny giving orders to him. The account of the conspiracy follows on from this trial. This is an extraordinary sequence: Dio is (a) speaking generally of Augustus' moderation and strangely (b) giving an instance (originally one of several?) in which Augustus in this case precisely did *not* stand by someone. The notice of the conspiracy is severed in thought from the narrative of 22. That is resumed after the conspiracy with the notice of the handing back to proconsuls of the provinces of Narbonese Gaul and Cyprus and the dedication of the temple of Jupiter Tonans at Rome, events not datable by other means, although the handing back to proconsuls of minor provinces goes well with the constitutional changes of 23 and the taking of *imperium* over the entire Empire.

Augustus' colleague (designate or actual) for 23 BC was A. T[erentius Var]ro Murena (*Fasti Cap.*, EJ p. 36). His place as regular consul in all the other lists is taken by Cn. Piso, but it is not clear from the damaged Capitoline *Fasti* what happened to him, whether he died in office, was condemned in office, was removed from office or died when designate. The conspirator's name is variously given as Murena (Strabo 14, p. 670), L. Murena (Vell. Pat. 2. 91. 2), Varro Murena (Suet. *Aug.* 19. 1; *Tib.* 8), Varro (Tac. *Ann.* 1. 10. 4), Licinius Murena (Dio 54. 3. 3–5, with Maecenas as brother-in-law and Proculeius as brother). Attempts have been made to reconcile these versions with each other (e.g. Syme 1939, 325 n. 5) and to show that the two men were identical, but no ancient writer connects the conspirator with the consulship, which is surprising: it would have given additional dramatic point to the story, as well as recalling the fate of Salvidienus Rufus, consul designate in 40 BC (Ch. 1). They may rather have been kin, even brothers, the conspirator, a Terentius Varro adopted as a child by L.

Murena, consul 62 BC (so A. J. Woodman on Vell. Pat. 2. 91. 2, citing Atkinson 1960 and Sumner 1978; rejected by Arkenberg 1993, 484). That involves a coincidence, not far-fetched: two kinsmen receiving a check in their careers, one fatal, within two years.[124]

It seems unlikely that an incumbent consul was removed from office in 23 during Augustus' own consulship: a fourth- or fifth-century source, Obsequens *On Portents* (who may have extracted his material from Livy or directly from lists of prodigies on which Livy drew),[125] claims with examples that any magistrate who had removed his colleague did not survive his own term. Dio (46. 49. 1f.) makes the same observation in connexion with the tribune P. Servilius Casca, deprived of office by his colleague P. Titius and proscribed in 43; Titius died soon afterwards. If the consul designate was the conspirator he was removed ('condemned' or 'died') before he came into office, for the consul Augustus survived 23. As Swan 1968 showed from other examples on the *Fasti*, Varro Murena never acceded to his consulship.

If conspirator and consul designate are distinct, both 23 and 22 are available for the conspiracy; if they are still to be identified, say as a polyonymous A. Terentius Varro (L.) Licinius Murena, it would mean that the conspiracy came late in 24, an idea said to be too unacceptable to have been suggested: allegedly it is at variance with all the other evidence.[126] Yet the prosecution of 'Primus' might have come in 24. We do not know the year of his governorship of Macedonia. If it was 25–24, he could have received instructions from Marcellus when the latter returned from his time with Augustus in Spain to marry in 25 (Dio 53. 27. 5). The year of office would have ended in mid-24, and 'Primus' could have been prosecuted in the late summer of that year, with the conspiracy following directly afterwards (Augustus on this occasion neglecting his motto 'Make haste slowly').

It is an argument in favour of 22 for the first trial that Marcellus is not said to have been called as a witness: in 22 he was dead and could not be called. But Augustus himself was not called: neither side wanted him in the court: he was going to deny responsibility (Levick 1975). There was no point, then, in calling Marcellus, who had no independent authority to give orders. Another point makes Dio's apparent dating of the conspiracy highly uncertain. Dio says (54. 3. 3) that after the conviction of 'Primus' Augustus received a special privilege as a reward: that of summoning the Senate as often as he wished. As Badian points out (1982, 20, n. 7), the privilege of summoning the Senate was inherent in the tribunician power, which he was granted in mid-23: Dio reports that grant separately, at 53. 32. 5f. So the new grant is most easily explained as some dispensation from procedural formality (cf. EJ 364, ll. 7–9). Why was it necessary? The right of tribunes to summon the Senate was limited; there was a pecking order, in which consuls and praetors took precedence (Gell. 14. 7). Without a special clause Augustus' tribunician power was in that respect ineffective. Moreover, Dio reports another privilege, that of putting the first item on the senatorial agenda even when he was not consul (53. 32. 5). This comes in a packet with his report of the tribunician grant, but logically presupposes the enhanced right actually to summon the Senate. There is something wrong with Dio's account, explicable if he were unsuccessfully combining sources. The fact that Dio puts the grant of the right to convene the Senate as a consequence of the trial of 'Primus' and before the conspiracy (54. 3. 3) may be taken as part of Dio's mangling of the chronology, not as a reason for placing the conspiracy in 22.

One source, exceptionally favourable to Augustus, can be traced in Dio. It claims that he stood by friends and denied having ordered 'Primus'' actions (that is, the defendant was not a friend); 'Primus'' advocate was impudent to him; Augustus came into court and was praised by men of good will (evidently the *boni*). After the trial of Caepio and Murena Augustus made his new regulation on voting in *maiestas* trials, which was for the public good; the same public spirit was shown by his forbearance towards Caepio's indignant father. There is one judicious note of criticism: the 'victory celebrations' on the unmasking of the conspiracy.

It is feasible and economical, then, to identify conspirator and consul designate and to assign the trial of 'Primus' and the 'conspiracy' to the end of 24. If the men are not taken to be identical 24, 23 and 22 are all available for trial and 'conspiracy'; but 24 or the early months of 23 still make it plausible to interpret the trials as causes of Augustus' surrender of the consulship in mid-23.

Endnotes

1 Octavian's supremacy: *RG* 34. 1, reading '[po]tens',' controlling', as preferred by Krömer 1978, 133–44 ('potitus', 'having gained control' was an accepted conjecture): Drew-Bear and Scheid 2005, 225. The participle can be causal, concessive, or chronological and refers to the period after Actium. Echo in Vitr. 1. Pref. 1f. of 29–28 (Girardet 2000 ['Edikt'], 242 n. 85); *potitus/potens.* which can be causal, concessive, or chronological, refers to the period after Actium; Adcock 1951 implausibly thinks of a temporary grant of power in 28 intended

to prevent an irruption by Licinius Crassus. On 29–27, see Bleicken 1990, 82–93. Powerful interpretations of the settlement: Rich and Williams 1999, 204–13 (the changes of 28 were important in making the whole package acceptable); Mantovani 2008 (convincing modifications).

2 Libations: Dio 51. 19. 7, with Gradel 2002, 207, citing Val. Max. 8. 15. 7. and Plut. *Mar.* 27. 9 for precedents; shown in practice in Hor. *Odes* 4. 5. 31–36 (12 BC).

3 Rich and Williams 1999, 200f., postulate a *lex annalis* of 28 and the ending of suffect magistracies (Dio 53. 21. 6f., suggests 27), comparing the language of Suet. *Aug.* 40. 2: '*comitiorum quoque pristinum ius reduxit*' ('he brought back the ancient right of election also'; canvassing: 56. 1). How Octavian and Agrippa were elected to the consulships of 27 after the passing of new regulations on the magistracy is not immediately clear, but, as Rich and Williams suggest, it was presumably by an expression of the Senate's wishes (which made it futile for other candidates to stand).

4 Handover: *RG* 34. 1, with Ridley 2003, 139–41.

5 If Dio tampered with chronology to expose Octavian's hypocrisy, as Rich and Williams suggest, rather than through being misled by the variety of his sources, he was misguidedly undermining a good case. See Simpson 1994. Day of conferment of 'Augustus': 16 January *Fasti Praen.* (EJ p. 45 and sources cited by T. Mommsen, *Res Gestae Divi Augusti* (2nd edn, Berlin 1883), 149; *Fer. Cum.* (*ILS* 108) has 15th, like Ovid, *Fasti* 1. 587–90).

6 Dreams: Suet. *Aug.* 94. 8f.; Dio 45. 2. 2–4 (ironical: Gowing 1992, 160 n. 48); Tertullian, *De Anima* 46; cf. Plut. *Cic.* 44. 2–6, with the interpretation of Wardle 2005 ['Sponsors'] (bibl. of presages 29 n. 1). Lorsch Wildfang 2000 assigns the propagandistic dreams of Cicero and Catulus to the West, just before the Actian campaign and when funds were being collected.

7 *Lex Saenia*: *LPPR* 440. Intermediaries: Eck 2007, 49.

8 Enrolment of Senate in 29: Suet. *Aug.* 35. 1f.; Dio 52. 42. 1–5 (tribune at 3); cf. EJ[2] p. 35 (*Fasti Ven.*, completion of *lustrum*, 28); with Jones 1960, 19–26.

9 Bibliography of settlement: Rich 1990 *ad* Dio 53. 2. 6–22. 5.

10 Coin: Abdy and Harling 2005; Rich and Williams 1999, 170, for the authenticity and the constitutional implications (*leges et iura* at 181f.); Mantovani 2008 offers a very exact interpretation of the traditional phrase, assigning the legend a more negative and restricted, technical sense, and discussing *restituit* ('set on its feet'), and the case of 'P.R.' at 24–30.

11 Rich and Williams 1999, 173–76, on joint striking of Roman and local coins in the East.

12 Dio 51.19. 5 (Antony not mentioned); EJ p. 49, cited by Rich and Williams 184 n. 54. Cf. Pliny *NH* 22. 13: Senate honoured Octavian with the 'siege' crown on 13 September 30). Danger: *Inscr. Ital.* 13. 2, p. 559.

13 *Fasces*: Dio 53. 1. 1, with Noè 1994, 60f. ('ritorna alla normalità'); cf. *RG* 34. 3 on collegiality: 'post id tempus . . . potestatis . . . nihilo amplius habui quam ceteri qui mihi quoque in magistratu conlegae fuerunt'. (Note Brunt and

Moore 1970, 78f. on the ambiguity of 'quoque'.) But Vell. Pat. 2. 89. 3, on the reduction of magistrates' *imperium,* is better seen as a precaution against the rise of new Caesars and Pompeys than as a restraint on Augustus himself.

14 Return to law: Rich and Williams 196–99, using the *aureus* against Dio's over-simplified chronology. Oath: Mommsen, *St.* 1. 625. Tac. *Ann.* 3. 28. 2; Dio 53. 2. 5, with E. W. Gray, *Gnomon* 33 (1961), 193, and Rich 1990 *ad loc.* However unreal the offer, it is preferable to believe that some redress was available rather than that the edict was a manifestly empty declaration. Return to normality on Octavian's return, 29 BC: Vell. Pat. 2. 89.

15 Provinces: Ovid, *Fasti* 1, 589, with Simpson 1994 for the role of the People. Livy *Epit.* 134 calls this 'giving the provinces a fixed structure' ('*omnibus provinciis in certam formam redactis*'). Lacey 1996, 16, against Crook 1996, 78, denies that there was a formal decree of the Senate on this subject; but Augustus' own provinces must have been the subject of one. At 85, 89, and 97, he argues that the arrangements for the provinces were not finalised until 15 or 16 January. From Triumvir to consul: Tac. *Ann.* 1. 2. 1. *Lex Pompeia: LPPR* 411, with Ferrary 2001, 110.

16 Ratification: Dio 53.12. 1. It is an implausible view (Lacey 1996, 90 and 102) that Augustus' choice was intended to avoid monopolising military power while assuring the Senate there would be no further triumviral quarrels. He also writes (212) that control of the armies was an area from which there was never any retreat from sole charge; but the proconsuls of Africa, Macedonia, and originally Illyricum had independent *imperium.*

17 Egypt: E. S. Gruen in *CAH*[2] 10, 148, with bibl. n. 4.

18 Public and imperial provinces: Suet. *Aug.* 47. For 'public', see Millar 1989. 'Senatorial' is misleading: in law Octavian was a proconsul on the same basis as the rest, though in control of huge territories, and should like them report to the Senate.

19 *Auctoritas:* Magdelain 1947. In youth: Cic. *Phil.* 3. 7.

20 Contrast of appearance and reality: resignation: Dio 53. 2. 6; 11, and 21. 1; provinces: 53. 12. 1; 13. 1; 16. 1; 17. 1; Rich and Williams 1999, 194f., note exaggerations and inaccuracy. For the chronology of the compromise and the honours of 27 BC, see their 202–04.

21 Slightness of change: Millar 1973.

22 Façade: Judge 1974; Mackie 1986.

23 Power of consul: Cic. *Phil.* 4. 9 (*auctoritas:* Ferrary 2002, 133); Birley 2000, 721f.; Kienast 1982, 74, still considers the consulship purely domestic since Sulla. Dettenhofer 2000, 79, thinks that Agrippa, presiding over the elections of 27, brought Augustus in. Continuation forbidden: Dio 46. 39. 3.

24 Oak crown: *RG* 34. 2; Ovid, *Fasti* 1, 614; *Trist.* 3.1. 36–48; Dio 53. 16. 4, with Rich 1990 *ad loc.* See also Kienast 1982, 81.

25 'Augustus' chosen (and 'Romulus' rejected): EJ p. 45 (date); *RG* 34. 2; Vell. Pat. 2. 91. 1; Suet. *Aug.* 7. 2; Dio 53. 16. 6–8, with Rich 1990 *ad loc.* for

further refs.; Florus 2. 35. 66, with Scott 1925, who stresses (82–84) the connexion between Romulus and Caesar. Plancus under Augustus: Watkins 1997, 143. Bibliography: Wardle 2005 [Edict'], 191 n. 38. Professor Wardle reminds me that views differed as to the correct syllabising and thence the origin of *augustus*: some connected *au-* with *avis* in some form. 'Most modern philologists may prefer *aug-* with *augeo* (*e.g.* A. Koops, *Mnem.* 5 (1937), 34–9, G. Dumézil, *REL* 35 (1957), 126–51; *contra* G. Neumann, *WJA* 2 (1976), 212–29: *au* from *avis* and *-gur* comes from an Indo-European root **geus* which corresponds with *gustare* ('test' or 'evaluate') and the *-tus* suffix indicates a passive meaning, *e.g. divinitate auctus* (Zecchini 1996, 130; cf. D. Moreno Morani, *Glotta* 62 (1984), 65–71).' He concludes that the uncertainty of the ancients should encourage us not to imagine a narrow or exclusive interpretation. Romulus in tradition: Herbert-Brown 1994, 49–55; reasons for rejecting him: 58–62. The story that Romulus killed his brother Remus for jumping over the unfinished wall of Rome is notably not accepted in Ovid's *Fasti* 4. 813–58; where there is another culprit. Romulus' fate: Livy 1. 16. 1 with Syme 1959, 56 = *RP* 1 (1979), 431. Connotations of name: *Augusto augurio*: Ennius in Varro, *De Re Rust.* 3. 1. 2, Ovid, *Fasti* 1, 587–616, with Livy *Epit.* 134 (*cognominatus*); Florus 2, 34. 66 (*sanctius, reverentius*, compared with Romulus). Brunt and Moore 1970, 77f.; Zanker 1988, 98–100; Galinsky 1996, 315–18, and Gradel 2002, 113f., noting Ovid's association of the word with the holy and the divine. Conscious thinking: Dr G. Herbert-Brown reminds me that Augustus may have depended on their memory of the past to keep men subdued.

26 *Dux/princeps*: Cic. *Off.* 2. 16; Vell. Pat. 2. 113. 1 (Tiberius). Demand for Octavian as *dux*: Ch. 1.

27 Clipeus virtutis: *RG* 34. 2, cf. Vitruv. *De Arch.* 1. 1, from the same years; transformation of *virtus*: M. McDonnell, *Roman Manliness: Virtus and the Roman Republic* (Cambridge, 2006), 386; V. A. Maxfield, *Military Decorations of the Roman Army* (London, 1987), 97.

28 'Me principe': *RG* 13; 30. 1; 32. 3; 'te principe' in Hor. *Epist.* 2. 1. 256 (mid-teens BC); *princeps* already in use by Hor. *Odes* 1. 2. 50; in 4. 14. 6 he is 'the greatest of the *principes*' ('maxime principum'). Others: Pompey: Cic. *Att.* 8. 9. 4; EJ² p. 52 (*Fasti Amit.*): *Principes viri* in *RG* 12. 1; future *principes* (ambiguously) in an edict: Suet. *Aug.* 31. 5. Cf. Eck 2007, 57f. ('Now there was only one') and noting (88) *Principi suo* (the Senate's) in *SC de Pisone patre* l.15. Other Tiberian uses: Suet. *Tib.* 29; Dio 57. 8. 2.

29 Tiberius' refusal: Vell. Pat. 2. 124. 2. Status of 'princeps': Tac, *Ann.* 1. 9. 5.

30 'Princeps Senatus: *RG* 7. 2 (for forty years); Dio 53. 1. 3 (28 BC) with Rich 1990 *ad loc.*, comparing 52. 42.

31 *Auctoritas* is prime for Galinsky 1996, *e.g.* 376–89: naturally, for Augustus is a leader who 'transforms society' (see Introduction).

32 King succeeded by consuls: Tac. *Ann.* 1. 1. 1. Senate advisory: Cic. *Pro Rabirio perd. reo* 3. Supremacy of the Senate: Cic. *Pro Sest.* 137f. It was C. E. Stevens

(see Introduction) who drew my attention to these passages and their signifi-cance. Duck-rabbit: L. Wittgenstein, *Philosophical Investigations* (Oxford, 1953), 194.

33 Vell. Pat.'s summing up of 28–7: 2. 89. 3. (Dr Herbert-Brown suggests that he may be retrojecting Tiberius' plans.)

34 Elections: above, n. 3.

35 Saepta Julia: Zanker 1988, 142f.; E. Gatti, *LTUR* 4 (1999), 228f.

36 Change in representations before and after 32–27: Zanker 1988, 33f. His account of the change (100) is puzzling: 'The "restoration of the Republic" was not simply a sham intended to fool the Roman public . . . Even before 27 it was clear that Augustus' new political style did not represent a departure from the sense of mission that had always motivated him. It was simply that as sole ruler he conceived of his role somewhat differently from before.'

37 For *restitutio* see Strothmann 2000, 23. 'Restoration of the Republic': Eck 2007, 50, uses this phrase, although he notes that Octavian had no intention of really surrendering power; cf. 55: 'An appearance of a return to the old ways was achieved, accompanied by a glimmer of liberty.' See Rich and Williams 1999, 208–13, citing (n. 113f.) Millar 1968 (justifiably denying any evidence of division of power or responsibility between Emperor and Senate in 28–27; that was not the way the change was formulated) and 1973; Judge 1974, who analyses the phrase *res publica* and proposes a different restoration of *Fasti Praen.* and a different interpretation of the phrase 're publica res[titut]a' in the '*Laudatio Turiae*' (EJ 357; see Ch. 1), l. 35; his negative arguments are more persuasive than his positive proposals; see also Brunt 1984; Mackie 1986. Hut-tner 2004, 81–105, has a good survey, finding 'Kompromiss' (98).

38 'Re publica conservata': EJ 17.

39 Laying foundations: Suet. *Aug.* 28. 2, with Girardet 2000 ['Edikt']; *res publica* under Severus: ILS 425; Vegetius, 1. *Prol.* Meaning of *res publica*: Judge 1974, 279–88. Date of edict: 23 according to Birley 2000, 737; but Augustus' use of the words 'promoter of the best state of affairs' ('auctor optimi status'), recall-ing Cic. ad *Q. fr.* 3. 5. 1, suggests the 'optimate' period of his reign (queried by Lacey 1996, 86); Ceauşescu 1981, and Wardle 2005 ['Edict'] argue for 27, Girardet for 29.

40 Oak crown: EJ p. 45 (*Fasti Praen.*), with Mommsen, *CIL* 1^2 231; 307 (13 Jan. Verrius Flaccus), but see Judge 1974, 288–98. The connexion of the oak crown with the preservation of citizens' lives (Gell. 5. 6. 11, with Gradel 2002, 49–51) should not be forgotten: cf. coins commemorating it ('OB CIVES SERVATOS', *RIC* 1^2, 62 no. 278f.; 63 no. 312; the deaths had ended after Ac-tium, as Lacey 1996, 82, notes, citing Dio 51. 2. 4.

41 Formal leadership: Strabo 17, p. 840; Dio 53. 12. 1, with Rich 1990 *ad loc.* cau-tiously inclined to accept what they say; Ferrary 2001, 144–54 rebuts the notion. The notion of such a charge (*tutela rei publicae*) in 27 could have arisen from senatorial verbiage when Octavian resigned his Triumvir's powers and became a

consul with provincial responsibilities (bibl. Wardle 2005 ['Dreams'] 39 n. 45). Generals in the field making war: J. W. Rich, *Declaring War in the Roman Republic in the Period of Transmarine Empire*. Coll. Lat. 159 (Brussels, 1976) 15, n. 10.

42 Doubled bodyguard: Dio 53. 11. 5.

43 Tiberius' interpretation: Suet. *Tib.* 29f.; Nero: Tac. *Ann.* 13. 4. 2 (the Senate had 'entrusted' the armies to Nero).

44 Jurisdiction: Millar 1973, 59–61.

45 Council: Suet. *Aug.* 35. 3 (linked with the *Lex Julia de senatu habendo*); Dio 53. 21. 4f. (27 BC).

46 Intervention at Cyme: *IK Kyme* (1976) 46 n. 17; Augustus given credit (l. 19): Giovannini 1999, arguing that Augustus and Agrippa made this general ordinance in consequence of a senatorial decree; Ferrary 2001, 134–36. Vedius Pollio: *RPC* 1. 2634f.: Augustus' agent on coinage of Tralles (cf. K. M. T. Atkinson, *RIDA* Ser. 3, Vol. 7 (1960) 227–64; 9 (1962) 61–89 for innocent interpretations). Augustus' reasons for his Spanish expedition and events during his absence: Schmitthenner 1962. Campaigns: Dio 53. 25. 5–8, with Rich 1990 *ad loc.* (bibl.). Lacey 1996, 212f., notes that (presumably as consul) Augustus referred Parthian delegations to the Senate – who referred them back to him: Dio 53. 33. 1f., dating to 23 BC, but it is a specimen of his good behaviour. Trial of Archelaus of Cappadocia and appeal of Asia: Suet. *Tib.* 8; Agathias 2. 17. Parthians: Justin 42. 5; cf. Oros. 6. 21. 19f. No longer consul, Augustus received envoys in Samos and Athens: Dio 54. 9. 7–9; cf. *RG* 31–3. Nero's promise: Tac. *Ann.* 13. 4. 2. Treaty with Mytilene: EJ 307, with Badian 1982, 28.

47 Crassus' campaigns: Dio 51. 23. 2–27. 1; recovery of standards: 26. 5, with J. J. Wilkes, *JRS* 95 (2005) 137, for their importance, and Flower 2006, 124. *Virtus* monopolised: McDonnell 2006, 235f.

48 Cossus corselet: Livy 4. 20. 5, cf. 32. 4. Chronology of campaigns (29–28), discovery of the corselet in 32 and revelation of what its text meant in 27: Badian 1982, 25 and 27; at 38–41 he refutes Dio's claim (51. 25. 2) that Crassus was not allowed to keep his title of *imperator*, attested on *ILS* 8810. His triumph: *Inscr. Ital.* 13, 1, p. 345. 'Voluntary' abandonment: Rich 1996, 106–09: Augustus' interest in the corselet was antiquarian; but see Tac. *Agr.* 42. 1f. Eck 2007, 60f., accepts the sinister interpretation, and assumes Crassus' retirement. Auspices: EJ 43 (when Augustus had Empire-wide *imperium*).

49 Messala's prefecture: Sen. *Apocol.* 10. 2; Tac. *Ann.* 6. 11. 3; Eus.-Jer. 164 Helm (26 BC); Schmitthenner 1969, 471–4; 479–85, arguing for 25. There were precedents, when both consuls were absent – or from the dictatorship of Julius Caesar. See Sattler 1969 ['Senat'], 58–61; Syme 1986, 211f.; Crook 1996, 82, implausibly suggests that Messala heard of the anomaly from Livy (31. 50. 7).

50 Silanus: *PIR*² I 830; Schmitthenner 1969, 474 and 485, thinks he was elected without Augustus' approval.

51 Career of Marcellus: *PIR*[2] C 925.

52 Augustus deciding: Crook 1996, 113, citing Millar 1977, 616.

53 Trial of 'Primus': *PIR*[2] P 946; Dio 54. 3. 2–4. Dettenhofer 2000, 96–100, dating to early 23 (97 n. 49); Eck 2007, 62f., succinct and judicious. Crook 1996, 87f., like most scholars, dates to 22.

54 Atkinson 1960 implausibly claimed that M. Marcellus Aeserninus, consul 22 BC, was meant.

55 Princeps in a praetorian court: Tacitus (*Ann.* 1.75. 1) regards Tiberius, even seated in silence, as infringing the praetor's authority; and see Augustus doing the same at the trial of L. Nonius Asprenas on the advice of the Senate: Suet. *Aug.* 56. 3, with Ch. 4.

56 Murena: Dettenhofer 2000, 97 n. 52 (bibl.) and see Appendix. Lacey 1996, 104 denies any plot in 23: the consul designate simply died in the autumn of 24.

57 Escape into exile: Pol. 6. 14. 6f. Daly 1983, 260, thinks that the men were found guilty *in order that* they might go into exile.

58 Parthian embassy: Dio 53. 33. 1f.

59 Resignation on Alban Mount: *Fasti Lat.* EJ p. 36. The significance of this site as the place for disgruntled commanders to celebrate unofficial triumphs was first pointed out to me by C. E. Stevens; see now Brennan 1996, 315–37.

60 Cn. Piso consul 23 BC: EJ p. 36 (*Fasti*; on *Cap.* replacing Murena).

61 Augustus' illness: Dio 53. 30. 1: in Spain, 24 BC: EJ p. 36 (*Fasti Lat.*); previous illnesses: Ch. 1. Crook 1996, 77f., cf. 81 and 84f., is inclined to accept them as genuine (but cf. 100). Birley 2000, 730, thinks of hepatitis contracted in Spain.

62 Offer to open will: Dio 53. 31. 1. Caligula's will: Suet. *Cal.* 24. 1. (Opening the will would invalidate it, but the dispositions could be made afresh.)

63 Tribunician power: EJ p. 36 (*Fasti Cap.*); *RG* 10. 1; Dio 53. 32. 5 with Rich 1990 *ad loc.* (bibl.); Last 1951 (classic account); privileges before 23 BC: Kienast 1982, 88–91; Pelling 1996, 68f. (sacrosanctity); Dettenhofer 2000, 103–09. Resignation 1 July: Crook 1996, 85.

64 Augustus as *popularis*: Cuff 1973, 466–9; Bosworth 1999, 17, draws attention to Livy 38. 56. 10 on the rights of tribunes; Dettenhofer 2000, 205–16. Defending the *plebs*: Tac. *Ann.* 1. 2. 1. Importance of *plebs*: Galsterer 1990, 14. Griffin 1991, 24–32, denies that the power was aimed to win favour from the *plebs*; the whole people were involved; that would be the situation by the end of Augustus' principate. Festivities: I owe this point to Dr Herbert-Brown. Popular front: Lacey 1996, 105–08; 116. He implausibly denies (1985 and 1996, 16) that existing power was formally conferred in 23 and thinks that it advanced in importance; rather it changed from a significant power that was used to one that indicated supremacy (Tac. *Ann.* 3. 56. 2). Saving the state from the People: Dio 56. 43. 4; cf. the imposing Hor. *Odes* 3. 14. The Gracchi blamed for decline: Birley 2000, 726–28.

65 Flaccus: *MRR* 1, 517.

66 Octavian in the Senate in 32: Dio 50. 1. 6.

67 Grant of *imperium maius*: Dio 53. 32. 5 (Augustus is 'proconsul' in a (suspect) document from Spain dated to 16–15 BC: *AE* 2000, 760). Earlier bibl.: Kienast 1982, 89 n. 84. For the view that the *imperium* in this period was not *maius*, see Dettenhofer 2000, 111 (bibl.); full discussion: Girardet 2000 ['*Imperium maius*']; Ferrary 2001, 131–33, rejecting *imperium maius* as such and allowing only *superiority* to other holders, plausibly thinks of a gradual spread of the power from an original specific grant for Augustus' travels of 23 onwards (136).

68 *Imperium* exercised from within the Pomerium: Dio 53. 32. 5: see Dettenhofer 2000, 105f., on the grant made 'once for all'.

69 Agrippa in 23: Vell. Pat. 2. 93 (Marcellus motive); Jos. *AJ* 15. 350 ('Caesar's *diadochos*', 'deputy/heir'); Suet. *Aug.* 66. 3; Dio 53. 32. 1, with Rich 1990, *ad loc.*; Roddaz 1984, 339–51; Wardle 1994, 58; Crook 1996, 84f.; Dettenhofer 2000, 109f., dating to the months of Augustus' consulship; so Ferrary 2001, 138f. (he too had 'superior' *imperium*; bibl. n. 154). Survey of theories: Southern 1998, 238f.; earlier bibl. Kienast 1982, 91 n. 98. Agrippa owed his advance to Augustus' favour as well as to his own merits, as Augustus himself said: Gronewald 1983.

70 All usual powers conferred at once on Vespasian, says Tac. *Hist.* 4. 3. 3:

71 Augustus building a separate structure: Dettenhofer 2000, 109.

72 Refusal to return: Dio 54. 6. 3.

73 Disasters and rioting 23–19 BC: Dio 53. 33. 5–10. 5; censorship: Dio 54. 10. 5; Egnatius: Vell. Pat. 2 92. 4; 93. 1; Dio 53. 24. 4–6. Interpretation of events of 19: Dettenhofer 2000, 125f.

74 Grain shortage deliberate? So Sattler 1969 ['Senat'], 77f., with Dettenhofer 2000, 114. Augustus able to foresee such problems: Ridley 2003, 101.

75 Peak years in famine, flood, fire, earthquake: Favro 1996, 113.

76 People ungovernable: Dio 54. 6. 1f.; Agrippa appointed: 6. 4–6. Recollections of Pompey's sole consulship: Dettenhofer 2000, 127.

77 Refusals of powers in 22: *RG* 5. 1 (Dictatorship); Suet. *Aug.* 52; Dio 54. 1. 2–5; 6. 2. Perpetual consulship: *RG* 5. 3; consular power: Dio 54.10. 5; Crook 1996, 85f. prefers 23.

78 Charge of corn supply: *RG* 5. 2; Dio 54. 1. 3, with Rich 1990 *ad loc.*

79 Censors of 22 BC: Vell. Pat. 2. 95. 3; Dio 54. 2. 1, with Rich 1990 *ad loc.*

80 *Cura legum*: Ridley 2003, 101–08, gives a summary of offers: 22 BC, perpetual consulship refused (*RG* 5. 3); censorship refused (Dio 54. 2. 1); 19 BC, *cura* refused (*RG* 6. 1); 5-year *cura* accepted (Dio 54. 10. 5, with Rich 1990 *ad loc.*); Dio is mistaken, cf. 18 BC, *cura* refused (*RG* 6. 1, see Brunt and Moore 1970, 45f.); 12 BC, *five*-year *cura* accepted (Dio 54. 30. 1); Dio is mistaken, cf. 11 BC: *cura* refused (RG 6. 1). Professor Wardle has kindly allowed me to read the draft of his forthcoming commentary on Suet. *Aug.* He notes that it is consistent with Augustus' wider practice in *Res Gestae* that he should emphasise his rejection of the non-traditional, but conceal the real powers he

did receive, so to believe that Augustus did accept some power is plausible. 'The most likely scenario is that in both 18 and 13 BC Aug. accepted *censoria potestas* for five year periods.'

81 Altar set up '*pro reditu*': *RG* 11; modesty: Torelli 1992, 29; Dio 54. 8. 3 (with ovation); cf. 10. 3f.; coins: *RIC* 1², 45 no. 55–56b. 12 October saw a festival annual since 14 BC: EJ p. 53 (*Fasti*); Hor. *Odes* 4. 2. 41–44; *RG* 11; Tac. *Ann.* 1. 15. 2f. The transactions elucidated: Rich 1998. Vespillo: see Birley 2000, not suggesting that grim humour may have been behind Augustus' choice.

82 Consular power: Dio 54. 1. 5, with Rich 1990 *ad loc.* (bibl.); cf. the silence of *RG* 6. Dettenhofer 2000, 125f. and 189, is sceptical, Eck 2007, 68f., judicious and brief; Ridley 2003, 143–45. Arguments reviewed: Southern 1998, 240f. In an interesting discussion Cotton and Yakobson 2002, 199f., argue that when Dio claims that the power was for life (*dia biou*) he is referring to the fact that domestic *imperium* (held since 23) did not lapse when Augustus entered Rome. Augustus had this authority in 18–11 BC when he issued an edict concerning the aqueduct at Venafrum (Venafro): EJ 282; *AE* 1999, 460. Ferrary 2001, refining on what it meant, asks (123) why the tribunician power became so prominent. But there was sensitivity over use of consular power, which impinged on the consuls (a point stressed by C. E. Stevens): Tiberius: Tac. *Ann.* 1. 7. 3; Nero: 13. 4. 2.

83 Augustus to legislate: Dio 54. 10. 6f. Turning point: cf. Dettenhofer 2000, 211, on the social legislation of 18 BC.

84 Succession: Dettenhofer 2000, 146–50. Women's place: Corbier 1995. *Domus Augusta*: Wardle 2000, 479f., noting Marcellus; Severy 2003, 214–18. Epigraphic celebration of the family: R. Gordon, J. Reynolds, M. Beard and C. Roueché, *JRS* 87 (1997) 210f.

85 Lepidus as Pontifex Maximus: Gowing 1992, 125 n. 4. Augustus' election: EJ p. 47 (*Fasti Maff., Cum., Praen.*); *RG* 10. 2; Ovid, *Fasti* 3. 415–28; Dio 54. 27. 2 (dating to 13 BC).

86 Torelli 1992, 27–61 (bibl.): 'A new start'. It was too soon after the Secular Games for that; continuity was the theme.

87 'Pater Patriae': *RG* 35. 1, with Brunt and Moore 1970, 80; *Fasti Praen.* in EJ p. 47 (Senate and People); cf. *ILS* 101 and 96; Ovid, *Fasti* 2, 127f. ('plebs . . . curia . . . eques'); Suet. *Aug.* 58. 1 (omitting knights), with Dettenhofer 2000, 173–76, citing (n. 58) Dio 53. 18. 3 for contrast with 'Augustus'; Lacey 1996, 193–97 (order of events); Stevenson 2007, 120f. (coins and refusals). Cicero's appellation: *Pro Sest.* 121; *In Pis.* 6; cf. Suet. *Caes.* 85; Dio 44. 4. 4; Livy 5. 49. 7 (Camillus); Hor. *Odes* 1. 2. 50; [Sen.] *Octavia* 477f., discounting earlier claimants. Moral authority: Herbert-Brown 1994, 57. Proposal of Corvinus: Eck 2007, 75; Messala Messalinus in AD 14: Tac. *Ann.* 1. 8. 4, where C. E. Stevens pointed out the parallel in tutorials, the same verb 'mandate' being used in both passages (and Tiberius implying that Augustus assigned Corvinus his role in 2 BC). Strothmann 2000, 73–108, provides exhaustive discussion.

88 Concord: Levick 1978; Lex Valeria Cornelia: Brunt 1961.

89 Arval Brethren: Gradel 2002, 18–22, bibl. n. 21.

90 Revision of the senatorial roll: *RG* 8. 2; Suet. *Aug.* 35. 1f.; Dio 54. 13f., with Rich 1990 *ad loc.* Also in 13: Dio 54. 26. 3–9 and 35.1. Census: Dio 54. 17. 3, and 26. 3 (cf. Suet. *Aug.* 41. 1), with Rich 1990 *ad loc.* for interpretation; cf. Nicolet 1976.

91 Augustus and triumphs: Suet. *Aug.* 38. 1.

92 Agrippa refuses triumph: Dio 54. 11. 6, with Simpson 1991 (due to dislike of the Spaniard Balbus' triumph); Wardle 1994 (Agrippa was only a legate, and Augustus was bent on diminishing opportunities); Rich 1990 *ad loc.* noting his refusal of 37 (Dio 48. 49. 4). Refusal of 14: 54. 24. 7.

93 Piso's *ornamenta triumphalia*: Dio 54. 34. 7. Number of imperial/public provinces: Eck 2007, 96. Proconsuls who might have claimed triumphs: Rich 1990 *ad* Dio 54. 24. 7f.

94 Legislation of 18: *RG* 8. 5; Suet. *Aug.* 34. 1; Dio 54. 16 (*ambitus; de maritandis ordinibus*), with Rich 1990 *ad loc.*

95 Senate's *maiestas*: Levick, *JRS* 73 (1983) 101. Decrees with the force of law: cf. Cic. *De Leg.* 3. 3. 10.

96 Late republican jury courts: A. H. M. Jones, *The Criminal Courts of the Late Republic and Principate* (Oxford, 1972) 445–84. Senatorial court: Levick [1976] 1999, 184f.; Eck 2007, 86, favours the trials of Julia's lovers in 2 BC as the starting point but the *SC Calvisianum* of 4 BC (EJ 311, V) seems to presuppose the process.

97 Appointment: Dio 55. 34. 2. Reduction of days available for elections: this point has been made to me by Dr Herbert-Brown.

98 Date of *monetales'* coinage: *RIC* 1², p. 32. Piso's coinage: p. 70. For the view that the development enhanced Augustus' *auctoritas*, see Galinsky 1996, 31–35.

99 '*SC*': Kraft 1962, with appendix 1969; Bay 1972; Sutherland 1976, 11, and RIC 1² 32).

100 Renewals of power: Dio 53. 16. 2; 12. 4f. (18 BC); 55. 6. 1 (8 BC, 'with reluctance'); cf. 55. 12. 3 (AD 3, 'under compulsion'). 56. 28. 1 (13, 'with seeming reluctance'). Timing: Ferrary 2001, 141.

101 Agrippa's tribunician power and *maius imperium*: EJ 366 with *PKöln* 6. 249; *RG* 6. 2; Dio 54. 12. 4 (18 BC); 28. 1 (13 BC), with Roddaz 1984, 477f.; Rich 1990, *ad* 53. 32. 1; *contra* Ameling 1994, 5; 12 (for *imperium aequum*).

102 Pictorial commemoration of succession plans: Zanker 1988, 215–30; Ara Pacis Augustae: dedication: *Cum., Fasti Cae., Prae.*, EJ p. 46; constitution: *Amit., Ant.*, p. 49; *RG* 12. 2, with M. Torelli, *LTUR* 4 (1999) 70–74. Processions: Simon 1967, 15–21; Bonanno 1976, 23–34; Syme 1984 ('Children'); Torelli 1992, 27–61 (bibl.): new Romulean age, rebutting the idea that the processions depicted reflect any real event, 43; 'secondary line of succession', 51. Rehak 2006, 132f.: the friezes represent Augustus' extended

family, and 'power in the aggregate'; he accepts the view that a *supplicatio* is represented; a *supplicatio* on the accession of Augustus to the supreme pontificate was already proposed by Van Haeperen 2002, 416–19. Agrippa's death: Dio 54. 28f.

103 Augustus conciliatory: Dio 55.12. 3.

104 Augustus unique as sole ruler: Tac. *Ann.* 1. 11. 1 (citing a speech).

105 Decisions without Augustus: Dio 55. 34. 1f., with Dettenhofer 2000, 198. Tiberius' absence: Tac. *Ann.* 2. 35.

106 Moneyers' names: *RIC* 1², p. 78. Two former (named) moneyers were disgraced with the elder Julia in 2 BC: T. Quinctius Crispinus: *RIC* 1², 65f. no. 327–36; Ti. Sempronius Gracchus: 67, no. 348f.

107 Reorganised *consilium*: Dio 56. 28. 2f. Crook 1955, 14–18; 1996, 111, citing EJ 379.

108 Suet. *Tib.* 55; see Crook 1955, 18f.; Dettenhofer 2000, 157, citing various datings n. 63; Eck 2007, 84.

109 Alexandrian gold bringing down interest rates: Suet. *Aug.* 41. 1; Dio 51. 21. 4f., with Osgood 2006, 396–8.

110 Debt problem: Dio 55. 8. 6.

111 Military unrest: Dio 55. 23. 1. 13 BC: 54. 25. 5, with Galinsky 1996, 119, cautious on Augustan rural prosperity. Cf. Vell. Pat. 2. 89. 4, on Augustus' concern for property rights. Economies of AD 6–7: Dio 55. 21. 6 (consular commission); 31. 4 (gladiatorial shows).

112 Cancellation of *travectio*: Dio 55. 31. 2.

113 Natural disasters: Dio 55. 22. 3 (with famine). Grain shortages: Pliny, *NH* 7. 149; Suet. *Aug.* 42. 3; Dio 55. 26. 4 (fire); 27. 1; 31. 3; 56. 12. 1; Eus.-Jer. p. 170 Helm. See G. Rickman, *The Corn Supply of Ancient Rome* (Oxford, 1980), 63–66; 218; P. Garnsey, *Famine and Food Supply in the Graeco-Roman World* (Cambridge, 1988) 218–43 (survey); Dettenhofer 2000, 201. Augustus' reply to grain shortages: Suet. *Aug.* 42. 3; Dio 55. 26. 1f.; 33. 4 (games). Removal of the German bodyguard: 56. 23. 4. Fire of AD 6: Dio 55. 26. 4f.

114 Revolts: Dio 55. 8. 1–4; 6 (Sardinia, Asia Minor, Africa, AD 6); Jos. *BJ* 2. 117f. (Judaea, 6); Vell. Pat. 2. 110–116, with Augustus' response 111. 1; Suet. *Tib.* 16–17. 1; 21. 5, where Augustus writes of 'difficultates'; (Pannonia and Dalmatia 6–9); Vell. Pat. 2. 120–122; Dio 56. 18–24 (Germany, 9, with Murdoch 2006); Eus.-Jer. p. 170 Helm (Athens, 9). Protests: Tac. *Ann.* 1. 76. 2; 80. 1 (Greece, AD 15); 2. 42. 5 (Syria and Judaea, AD 17).

115 Feel-bad factor: Newbold 1974; cf. Zanker 1988, 238. Tiberius' parsimony: Suet. *Tib.* 46f.; but cf. (*e.g.*) Tac. *Ann.* 4. 6. 4.

116 Intended suicide: Pliny *NH* 7. 149; *Epit. Caes.* 1. 29.

117 Census of 13: 8. 4; Armenia: 27. 2.

118 Augustus on Cato: Macr. *Sat.* 2. 4. 18; he composed a *Reply to Brutus on Cato*: Suet. *Aug.* 85. 1.

119 Pompey's *eunoia* commended: Plut. *Mor.* 207B; 319E.

120 Caesar as *res publica*: Ovid *Trist.* 4. 4. 15.

121 Dio's narrative: Rich 1990 *ad loc.*, noting the mangled chronology. Survey of views: Arkenberg 1993, 471; Southern 1998, 236f.; bibl.: Birley 2000, 731 n. 69.

122 Date of 'Primus" trial and subsequent conspiracy: Dio 54. 3, with Rich 1990 *ad loc.* (bibl.); Vell. Pat. 2. 93. 1, setting M. Marcellus' death (23) '*around* the time of' the conspiracy; see Badian 1982, 22 claiming that 22 is meant, with parts of 23 and 21 included; A. J. Woodman *ad loc.* goes for 23, emending the MS.

123 Date and composition of the conspiracy: Badian 1982, 28–36; his main target is Jameson 1969. Syme 1986, 388–92, is magisterial and cautious; Bleicken 2000, 346 (bibl. 728) adheres to 23.

124 According to Dio 53. 25. 3–5, a Terentius Varro, perhaps the future consul designate (Sumner 1978, 194) on Augustus' order conquered the Salassi in 25.

125 Date and sources of Obsequens: S. Butler, 'Notes on a *membrum disiectum*', in S. Joshel and S. Murnaghan, *Women and Slaves in Greco-Roman Culture: Differential Equations* (London and New York, 1995) at 236–39.

126 24 BC was suggested for the 'conspiracy' by E.W. Gray in a paper read at Christ Church, Oxford; rejected: Badian 1982, 29 n. 28; Woodman *loc. cit.*

Chapter 3

Techniques of Management
and the Feel-Good Factor[1]

Augustus relied for his position on the perception of him in the minds of men. It is conventional to think of dependence on the army, and to recall the sophist Favorinus of Arelate (Arles) who was reproached by a friend for letting the Emperor Hadrian win a literary argument: sense, he replied, when his opponent controlled thirty legions.[2] Their loyalty was due to their belief in Augustus, his commitment to themselves, and his ability to supply their needs in the form of pay and bounty; and this ability, they knew, depended directly and indirectly (for they could enforce exactions of money) on themselves. It was a mutually supportive and dependent relationship, familiar to other sections of Roman society. But if fear of force was the foundation of Augustus' power, it was normally concealed. Seneca assured Claudius that it was through acts of generosity that imperial power was most effectively exercised rather than through arms.[3] Without being a patron in the Roman sense of a superior bound by the formal ties of *patrocinium* to help his clients, Augustus was one in the modern sense familiar in societies with inadequately developed formal structured methods of advancement and security.[4] He had more to offer, over a longer period, than any Roman before him.[5]

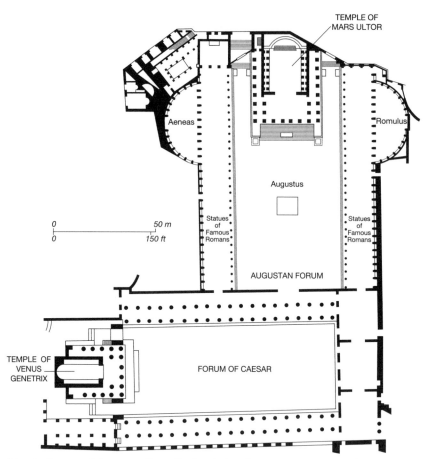

Map 3 Forum of Augustus (from Heslin, P. J., 'Augustus, Domitian and the so-called Horologium Augusti', *Journal of Roman Studies*, 97, p. 7. Courtesy of The Roman Society)

There was tension between Octavian/Augustus' supremacy and his need to win loyalty. He was aware of it and dealt with it pragmatically. We shall begin (as Augustus did in 28–27) with conciliatory moves, repudiating any Caesarian or Triumviral style, followed by a gradual hardening of control in one area or another. Then there were transformations, unconnected with Caesar, that were pleasing to the apparent beneficiaries – but poisonous to freedom: changes to judicial procedure. Next came the social legislation of 18–17, where the leader's control was dominant and the 'feel-good factor' recessive. Different in kind was the pervasive and beneficent Augustan voice, notably in legislation, and in the saturating presence of his new name, in legionary titulature, religion and the calendar. Finally, Augustus had to deal with the complication that the conflicting interests of the different ranks of society brought their own tensions. It was Augustus' achievement, by addressing needs at each level, to weld them all into his new order and find them all a place, from patrician senators to slaves.

The relegation of Caesar

While the Triumviral soldiers served under 'Imperator Caesar, son of the deified Julius', civilians later encountered the new and malleable 'Augustus'. Another preliminary answer may be given to an enquirer who asks how this Augustus managed the people he ruled: 'Differently from Julius Caesar'. Items reported by Suetonius or publicised in Augustus' own *Achievements* seem to be repudiations of the Dictator's measures, notably those listed by Suetonius in a late chapter of his biography that leads up to Caesar's assassination. Augustus learned from Caesar what not to do.[6] During his principate, whatever respect was accorded Julius Caesar, he is not cited as a precedent except over the funding of the proposed new Military Treasury in AD 6–7 (Ch. 4). That was a notable incident, explained by G. Herbert-Brown with the suggestion that Augustus was currently suffering by comparison with Caesar: he was failing to deal with dissatisfaction over discharge and bounties amongst the military. In these difficult years a comparison between the two rulers may well have been made. It was a cruel play on such comparisons for Augustus in response to present the Senate with Caesarian plans. The Dictator's appearance in the Princeps' *Achievements* is only as initiator of building schemes left incomplete (Ch. 5) or as victim, slaughtered by men that young Octavian had brought to justice.[7]

It was Octavian who had carried through the definitive consecration of Julius Caesar in 42, two years after a comet had appeared at the games that were being held in his honour at Rome.[8] Caesar was thus removed from his embarrassing historical role to that of a protecting deity. Ovid can even claim that it was a shade that fell victim to the impious assassins: Caesar himself was placed in the heavens and occupied the temple in the Forum festively dedicated to him in 29 (Octavian was prevented by illness from being present).[9] So there was no reason why the safely dead and deified Dictator should disappear from Augustan ideology. In 29 a new Flamen Divi Iuli was duly inaugurated – the original, Mark Antony, being deceased. Even after the constitutional changes of 28–27 BC Caesar features, with the star that signalled his consecration, on the reverses of *denarii* from Spain (19 or 18 BC); on obverses of 17 BC connected with the celebration of the Secular Games (the features are thought to resemble those of Augustus); and on those of 12 BC.[10]

Even so, there remained something anomalous or awkward in the cult, which had gone further before his death than Augustus was prepared to allow his own. Caesar was not taken to be first in the line of Divi as construed in state cult under the Empire. His cult was 'self-contained'. The Arval Brothers never sacrificed to him and their list of Divi began with Augustus. Only Caesar's *flamen* (there were no *sodales*) and personnel were involved in the cult at his temple.[11] On the other hand Divus Julius (Caesar) was included in the ritual of the third century *Feriale Duranum*, a calendar of festivals from an eastern military base that originated under Augustus: Caesar was celebrated in the army without interruption. In the minds of emperors (and their subjects) he was relegated to the gallery of military heroes, where he is to be found already in Ovid's *Fasti*.[12]

There was little that Caesar achieved in controlling the state in which he was not equalled by Augustus: it was essentially a matter of style, less about what ends were to be achieved than how it was to be done. Simple matters of etiquette may be disposed of first. In 9 BC lightning damaged the Temple of Jupiter on the Capitol. Restoring it, Augustus made a point of keeping his own name off the building, as Caesar had failed to do when after his own repairs he allowed his name to replace that of his old enemy, the stout defender of senatorial rights, Q. Lutatius Catulus.[13] In the eyes of the people, Augustus was lavish in his celebration of games and avoided a gaffe of Caesar's by paying attention when he was in the audience; if he had to be absent he apologised and appointed a deputy to preside.[14] Of real importance were matters of finance, elections and a related issue, control of senatorial membership and the introduction of new men, especially provincials, into the Senate. Finally there was the question of Caesar's friends, their status, and the advice he might take from them, which remained a potential grievance beyond the Julio-Claudian age. These issues expose the real and merely apparent differences between the techniques of the two rulers.

Promises and practice: finance, political advancement and political friends

Financial arrangements must come first: perceived control of state funds and vast private wealth to be used for their benefit won the confidence of the troops and of humble subjects. Caesar made the Senate powerless when in 49 BC he broke into the Aerarium, the state treasury, and commandeered its contents for his civil war needs. For the first time, as the poet Lucan put it, Caesar (or, 'a Caesar') was richer than Rome. According to Suetonius, the Dictator also put his own slaves in charge of the mint and the tax system. Under Caesar's regime the traditional Triumviri Monetales were still in office, and were even given an additional member; quaestors still supervised the Aerarium itself. His slaves may have been charged with the routine work and proved more expert than the men nominally in charge wanted them to be.[15]

Augustus on the contrary stresses in his *Achievements* that he had four times helped the Aerarium; and Dio has Augustus claiming (speciously, we shall see) under the dispensation of 27 BC to be handing over not only provinces and armies but revenues too.[16] Shortage of funds was weakening, even crippling, the Aerarium, and so the Senate's ability to act and empower its agents. As Lucan's phrase makes clear, the Princeps' modest direct contributions, and even the vast subventions listed in the Appendix to the *Achievements*, which amounted to *HS* 2,400 million, did not end the state's financial difficulties, which were worsened because a large part of state revenue accrued to the armed provinces controlled by Augustus himself, and was spent there. These contained most of the legions and auxiliary troops, the costliest item on the debit side; revenues never reached the Aerarium but merely moved round provinces in the form of tax and soldiers' pay; the imperial organisation that controlled these funds came to be known as the Fiscus, and Augustus' clerks were able to produce accounts for the whole Empire.[17] Even if Augustus' huge private fortune, which prompted Dio to claim, perhaps anachronistically, that he had removed the difference between public and private funds, is left out of account, the provincial tail was wagging the metropolitan dog in financial matters. It was an early sign of Augustus' encroachment that when his friend Cornelius Gallus was damned by the Senate it decreed that his property should go 'to Augustus'; whether this meant to Augustus personally (because he had made gifts to Gallus) or to the Fiscus (because Gallus had embezzled public funds) is unclear, as often in later cases.[18]

Augustus' property included booty legitimately taken from his victories in the Triumviral period, from the Balkans, but especially from Egypt. But we also need to take into account what happened to the public funds that Caesar had commandeered. Caesar's prime heir was Octavian. Part of what Augustus contributed to the Aerarium may be seen as having been filched from it in the first place. But that was beyond calculation. The conquest of Egypt also enriched the Aerarium, as the conquest of Gaul had, but much of Egypt's later tax contributions were in the form of grain, absorbed by the people of Rome. The Princeps' subsidies looked good and were kept up, either directly or indirectly in the form of disbursements on state enterprises, by emperors keen on their image, including Nero.[19] Naturally his gifts earned the Princeps a decisive voice on matters that involved state expenditure, including coinage.[20]

As to the Triumviri Monetales, even after the end of their remarkable efflorescence on the coinage (Ch. 2) the office survived, functions unclear, as a prestigious opening post for young men of good family. Such junior annual post-holders could hardly take on the task of guiding the mint and choosing the designs for Roman coins. Even the more senior senatorial officials who were in control of the Aerarium itself, whether praetors, prefects of praetorian rank, or selected quaestors (the officials were changed from time to time in efforts to enhance their authority and ability to resist demands for expenses from senior magistrates), were not capable of supervising the revenues and expenditures of the entire Empire; they were presumably provided with state-owned slaves or freedmen for what concerned the Aerarium.[21]

Hard-pressed taxpayers such as the fishermen of Gyaros knew already in 30 BC to whom they should apply for relief.[22] Augustus' own organisation of his vast public funds, which served most of the army, was part of his official functions, as a governor of four major areas and any that accrued, and he made use, as governors customarily had, of his own slaves and freedmen, as he naturally did also for his private funds. At the head of these men was the freedman whose title emerges as 'Chief of Accounts' (*a rationibus*). M. Antonius Pallas was the most important and powerful man in the court during the reign of Claudius and the first years of Nero, and certainly one of the richest. By the time of Domitian this post-holder could be said to be charged with the management of the entire financial system of the Empire.[23]

Naturally the interest of Augustus' officials extended to the doings and needs of the declining Aerarium and its revenues. When Augustus died, advising that all the figures for the contents of official chests Empire-wide, and what was owed them, could be obtained from his staff of slaves and freedmen, we arrive back at the Caesarian state of affairs, but perhaps with better book-keeping and now no open signs of resentment. What was bitterly hated was the political clout that their charge of vast sums of public money and their closeness to the Princeps gave his servants, especially under Claudius and Nero. Augustus never flaunted them.[24]

Next, elections and membership of the Senate.[25] If we think of Roman political life in terms of a competitive board game such as Monopoly, Caesar not only controlled the Bank and could disburse or withhold funds as he chose, but he could advance men round the board, helping them at will to lucrative and prestigious positions or blocking their way, in some cases removing them from the game altogether by keeping them in exile. His 'prefecture of morals' enabled him to determine whether men should take part in the game or not. The Senate lost recalcitrant aristocrats, but Caesar was also accused of bringing in new citizens, even Gauls who were still 'half barbarians' – unjustly, for known provincial senators were descended from Italian emigrants.[26] There were military men to be rewarded, and his Dictatorship saw numbers rise to nine hundred. At the highest level his appointment of a suffect consul for the last hours of 45 caused particular offence. In 44, given his intended campaigns in Parthia, which were expected to last for three years, he was given the right to nominate half the magistrates every year, except for the consulship, and to appoint the magistrates for several years ahead, a practice blatantly imitated by the Triumvirs. For serious participants in politics such interference made the game not worth playing.[27]

Augustus' way of coping with the Senate's membership was more delicate. The *Lex Saenia* of 30 BC that gave him the right to create new patricians and appoint to priesthoods was presumably intended by its proposer to deal with immediate needs. It was a tacit criticism of Caesar, as well as of the Triumvirs, especially Antony, that he had to make efforts in 29 and 19 to reduce the Senate's size from the thousand or more that it had now reached, and that he refused the 'curatorship of morals' that would have given him the same powers as Caesar's prefecture. It is a boast of the *Achievements* that that would have been an office 'contrary to ancestral practice'. As part of his restoration of civic rights, Augustus pointedly renounced the direct methods that Julius Caesar and the Triumvirs had used to ensure that his favoured candidates reached the highest office: according to two passages in Suetonius' biography, he brought back 'old style', that is, free-for-all, elections and behaved like an old-fashioned canvasser. This restoration of the old game was important to senatorial players (Ch. 2).

It is worth noting Augustus' subtlety and resourcefulness in getting round the inconvenience that free elections presented, so that men came to talk routinely about him 'giving' the consulship to a certain candidate. By AD 14 it was appropriate to thank the Princeps for the post.[28] The effectiveness of canvassing like any Republican grandee was revealed when in AD 8 physical weakness forced him to give up pressing rough plebeian flesh at elections; instead he posted up a list of the candidates, trusting that his *auctoritas* would stand the favoured ones (*commendati*) in good stead. Candidates whose names appeared on that list might call themselves 'commended', since Augustus was 'entrusting' the electorate with their advancement, a subtle form of pressure. Writing of the elections that took place immediately after Augustus' death, Tacitus casually remarks that 'commended' candidates (*candidati Augusti*) were certain of election; they had no need to canvass. Augustus had a negative power as well: he could make promises and threats to deter an unwanted candidate. There is no evidence that he had any right to reject a man's candidature for office, as was once supposed, just as he did not take over the running of elections from the magistrates whose function it was. Rather a mere hint of future disfavour or a promise of a good post in an imperial province meanwhile might make a man defer his candidature.[29]

Augustus' use of his *auctoritas* during elections does not seem outrageous: he probably wanted to help unattractive protégés who, for lack of ancestry, would not find favour with a conservative electorate, still less with rival senators. A few of these men were from the provinces, one even an aristocrat from the Greek-speaking East, Pompeius Macer of Mytilene, descended from a friend of Pompey the Great. After the promotions of the Triumviral period Augustus could get away with more than Caesar. Even so he was cautious and when Claudius addressed the Senate on this matter in AD 48 he passed over Caesar altogether and claimed only that Augustus and Tiberius were aiming to bring into the Senate 'the flower of the country towns, wherever they were to be found'; the phrase he used normally referred to the country towns of Italy. For as late as 48, the Princeps' proposal to admit chieftains from northern Gaul to the Senate met resistance, and it was only the traditionally loyal Aedui who in the first instance were granted the privilege.[30]

All this did not prevent occasional electoral disorder, even after the brouhaha that Egnatius Rufus caused in 19 BC had been put down so ruthlessly (Ch. 2). Nobles thought that office was their prerogative and new men fought with all they had (money) for advancement. It was presumably to ease competition for the post that in 5 BC 'suffect' consulships were introduced: from then on, most consuls came to hold office for six months only. More men could be satisfied with the outcome of their careers, and more ex-consuls were available for crucial provincial posts, but the importance and prestige of the consulship was reduced. After the Triumviral period Augustus never practised the designation of magistrates more than one year ahead; and when in AD 16 Tiberius was invited to do so he indignantly refused what he took to be an enhancement of his power, as well as a source of long-term frustration and jealousy.[31]

Electoral bribery, a constant of Roman politics, recurs in Dio's account of the Augustan Principate. The *plebs* as ever was up for hire, not necessarily for demonstrations, but simply as voters. In 8 BC Augustus, perhaps supplementing the law on bribery he passed in 18–17, refused to investigate an electoral scandal, merely exacting a deposit from future candidates, to be forfeited if they misbehaved. Besides enacting that law, Augustus less reputably offered *HS* 1,000 to members of the two voting tribes of which he was a member, by birth or 'adoption' – to prevent them being influenced by bribery; we do not know when or how often. In AD 7, after electoral struggles reached an impasse, the consuls had to be appointed by Augustus; his choices presumably were ratified by the electoral assembly. Significantly, this happened after Tiberius became the accepted heir in AD 4 and only two years after a law had been passed which set up new arrangements for praetorian and consular elections. The *Lex Valeria Cornelia*, commemorating the deceased princes Gaius and Lucius, provided amongst other honours for the creation of ten additional voting groups ('centuries') in the 189 century-strong voting assembly, the Comitia Centuriata, consisting of senators and knights who had sat on jury panels, a few thousand men in all; their votes would be counted and announced first, giving a strong lead to the remaining centuries.[32]

What happened in 7 showed that this measure was inadequate. When Augustus died his political testament, left for Tiberius to read to the Senate, proposed that they should hold preliminary elections, and that only the candidates who were successful there should be considered by the people's assembly. The Senate was delighted, and the people could greet the changes only with helpless grumbling. In short, Augustus ended by effectively abolishing free elections of the Roman People. This measure, the more effective as Augustus' dying wish, exposes how far he had been able to go in eroding free elections after he had ostensibly restored them, not so much by extempore answers to crises as through the continuous exercise of his vast political influence.[33]

In the praetorian elections of 14 Tacitus reports Tiberius' announcement that he was limiting himself to recommending no more than four candidates for the twelve places available; that would relieve them from the danger of being rejected, and so from the trouble of canvassing. Evidently Augustus had not so restricted himself, but Tiberius considered that that was a fair proportion. The numbers of praetorships available had expanded during Augustus' reign (they had been set at eight at the beginning), partly to satisfy senatorial ambitions, but Tiberius refused, this year at least, to allow more than twelve, the standard Augustan number.[34] In effect, then, by the end of his Principate Augustus was choosing a third of the praetors. The consulship was much more difficult. Subtle methods were needed when twelve ex-praetors, if they all survived and wanted to stand, were competing for four places a year. Ancestry and service both had claims. The Princeps would have to meet and negotiate with candidates, with encouragement or the reverse, in some cases mortgaging future places to mitigate disappointment. When it came to the public presentation of the results of these negotiations, we have another vivid picture from Tacitus, this time from AD 15, the first time the consular elections were held under Tiberius and in the Senate instead of the Comitia. Tiberius concealed his embarrassment behind elephantine delicacy. On this occasion and later he might mention candidates' comparative qualifications (and disadvantages) without naming them. Sometimes he would say nothing about them and simply warn against misbehaviour. Most often he would produce the list of candidates and invite others who thought that they were deserving to put themselves forward. This sounds surprisingly as if there was a shortage of candidates, giving rise to Tacitean suspicions that Tiberius was restricting candidatures for his own purposes. In fact, it means that leading candidates did their own bargaining beforehand and deprived Princeps and electorate of any choice; such compacts were not invented in 15. Competition of whatever sort for the higher magistracies was not stifled by Augustus and his successors. It was a vital element in the politics of the Commonwealth; consuls were not dangerous, and the Princeps needed only to get his men their reward and qualification for further service.[35]

So to the issue of the Princeps' friends. It was a bitter complaint against Caesar that he excluded from his counsels first-rank senators such as Cicero – who was compelled to queue for an audience and found his name cavalierly inscribed on the list of men who had voted for a decree passed during his absence – and instead took in new men of undistinguished origins, such as C. Matius and the Spanish knight L. Cornelius Balbus from Gades in Spain who owed his citizenship to Caesar and Pompey. It was to the malign influence of Balbus that biographers attributed Caesar's failure to rise when he was approached with offers of honours by consuls and other distinguished senators – hardly a coincidence; Balbus was one of those who warned Cicero against sending Caesar a letter of advice.[36]

But young Octavian needed help, even from men of comparatively low status and repute: suspicions were soon voiced by Cicero of his earliest allies, who included Caesar's Matius.[37] Of Octavian's long-term supports Agrippa (63–12 BC) and Maecenas (d. 8 BC), the former was a first class general of obscure origin, outspoken views and little respect for senatorial traditions, while Maecenas, a knight of Etruscan descent who became patron of the greatest poets of the age (Ch. 6) was blatantly luxurious, even dissolute. The failings of both, as reported, show dislike for their influence and success, Maecenas was pilloried even for his louche manner of dress. Men believed, rightly or wrongly, that Maecenas' influence waned, and gloated. So did Tacitus over the supposed eclipse of Maecenas' successor Sallustius Crispus, nephew of the historian Sallust. But Augustus felt their loss: his daughter would not have brought him so low in 2 BC if they had still been alive, he complained; or was this story invented to explain the decline of Augustus' later years? The philosopher Seneca wrote that monarchs attribute the virtue of speaking the truth to those from whom they no longer are in danger of hearing it.[38] This issue of confidants did not go away. Tiberius constituted a formal advisory council, but the Senate and all but a few of its members lost pre-eminence as advisers to Crispus, the equestrian Guard Prefect L. Aelius Sejanus, and the freedmen whom Tiberius rightly suspected of being liable to corruption, and who became notorious under Claudius. The struggle to command the ear of the Emperor, even by factions in the Senate, continued at the beginning of Vespasian's reign and into Trajan's: this 'best of Emperors' was told – by a candid friend – that, bad as Domitian had been, he at least had good friends. In the long perspective, Augustus emerges well, and better than Caesar, probably because he paid attention to public opinion rather than because he lacked humble confidants.

Augustus needed friends, especially members of the Senate to hold vital offices, in particular when he was away from Rome, and humbler aides to advise on day-to-day decisions. His absences were frequent, starting in the spring of 27 BC after the first settlement was reached.[39] Augustus went to Gaul and Spain and did not return for three years. There was work to be done in Gaul and warfare to be undertaken in north-west Spain,[40] and that if successful might be extended to a glorious invasion of Britain. Absence itself was an advantage, as General de Gaulle proved in retirement at Colombey-les-deux-Eglises during the period leading up to his presidency. When Caesar was assassinated in 44 he was close to departing for campaigns against the Parthians, perhaps in the hope that after three years his rule might have proved acceptable and that the city would have settled down. With senatorial scapegoats to blame for the chaos of 23–19 (Ch. 2), Augustus was playing a safe game, hardly available to British prime ministers, who have made themselves responsible for everything and are liable to be removed by party or electorate: they have to be seen perpetually present and busy with the country's welfare. There was another period abroad, in Gaul after the reverse that M. Lollius met there in 17, and according to Dio also due to Augustus' current unpopularity. The Princeps returned in 13, again to formal acclaim.[41] There were legitimate reasons for Augustus' expeditions abroad, but these too became less pressing as time went on – his young kinsmen had to win their glory – and Augustus never left Italy after 8 BC.

So much for the non-Caesarian tone of the early Augustan Principate. Reasons for repudiating him became less strong as the Princeps entrenched himself, but the *Achievements* offers plentiful examples of Augustus' restraint (*moderatio*) in accepting unusual offices (Ch. 5). This fair-seeming posture had been well practised by Caesar's rival Pompey the Great.[42] The refusals do not necessarily signify that Augustus really did not want the positions (or, better, the power they conferred), only that he realised that they were unacceptable to senatorial opinion, much as the people cried out for them. His extra-magisterial powers brought increasing overall dominance.

Tacitus' summary of Augustus' rise as a 'gradual encroachment' goes on to explain it as the taking over of the functions of other men, institutions, laws and magistrates alike.[43] Overall ascendancy was gradually acquired almost imperceptibly as it became accepted, like that of British prime ministers during the last quarter of a century over Cabinet colleagues, notably foreign secretaries. As Augustus came to occupy public space and literary attention, lesser senators lost traditional chances of self-presentation and the preservation of their name through legislation, triumphs, buildings and sculpture, and that led in turn to the increasing identification of Augustus with the Commonwealth. It is only the most favourable view of his regime that can interpret this development merely as his response to senators' failure to transcend their narrow traditional compass.[44] Not all the pleasing changes that Augustus brought about had anything to do with avoiding the example of Caesar. The difficult, multi-tracked, occupation of the religious sphere will be considered later; the judiciary offers an adequate and instantly clear example.

The judiciary

The last century of the Republic saw the establishment of jury courts, presided over by a praetor, for the trial of defined offences, such as the misconduct, especially extortion, of senatorial officials in the provinces (*res repetundae*). The law prescribed the penalty; juries only balloted on guilt or innocence.[45] These courts were politically controversial because of the composition of the juries, which changed with every major swing of power: the knights put in charge by Gaius Gracchus and his allies in 123–22 BC were unfriendly to senatorial defendants; Sulla installed senators. Mixed courts were re-established in 70 BC and by the time of Caesar's death a compromise on proportions had been reached: perhaps half from each of the two highest orders of the state, senators and *equites*.[46] Over private actions a praetor also presided, assigning judges (*iudices*) to hear the cases when he had decided the issues involved. But magistrates and pro-magistrates with *imperium* also had wide powers of their own to hear cases and take decisions, even to impose death sentences on those who were not Roman citizens: they could take account of (*cognoscere*) actions, even those not already criminalised; the line between judicial and administrative action was thin. The Senate too on occasion might take action, especially in what the consuls deemed emergencies, such as the 'conspiracy of Catiline' exposed by Cicero in 63 BC, which, after a brief hearing, ended in the death of five senators, one a praetor in office. Cicero was made to bear responsibility for that illegal action (the Senate's vote had been only advisory): he went into exile five years later. Nonetheless, the Senate occasionally took similar action in later 'emergencies' such as those of Salvidienus, the younger Lepidus and Egnatius Rufus, with presiding magistrates escaping punishment.

Octavian was keen on dispensing justice,[47] and, according to Dio, in an unclear and controversial passage, was given a special power of appeal (*ius auxilii*, a prerogative of the tribunes in Rome) in 30 BC, presumably to function all over the Empire, as well as a casting vote in case of a tie.[48] At any rate, Augustus continued free exercise of his *imperium* in deciding the fates of dependent monarchs (Ch. 2). Yet in 28–27, says Velleius Paterculus, the rights of magistrates and judges were restored. It is to this 'conservative' period that J. T. Ramsey plausibly assigns the repeal of Antony's jury bill of 44 BC, so detested by Cicero, which had created a third panel of jurymen who could include centurions and the like.[49] The next we hear of the jury system was of an outrageous modification made in 23, no doubt by the Senate on Augustus' recommendation, when juries proved unsatisfactory to him: votes for acquittal had been cast for 'Primus' and for Caepio and Murena: henceforward in cases where the majesty of the Roman People was held to have been damaged (*maiestas minuta*) they had to be cast openly and had to produce a unanimous result.[50] It may have been in 17 BC that Augustus introduced a fourth jury panel to try lesser cases. That may have been for practical purposes, to ease a log-jam in the courts, but it may also have been a gesture towards lower strata in society that he could now afford: men with only half the equestrian census were eligible to serve in this court.[51]

The ruling that followed the trial of Caepio and Murena was gross. Something even more radical followed after the settlement of 19: the Senate, either by a single measure or by gradual development, took over cases involving its own members, or high matters of state, with consuls or Princeps presiding.[52] It was a regularisation of the procedure that Cicero had adopted in 63, and on the face of it showed high optimate spirit: the Senate was to be supreme arbiter in the Commonwealth and master in its own house, as it had been in the second century, before the Gracchans intervened. The jury courts were not abolished, simply bypassed in some cases. It must have been pointed out when the question was debated that the system had not worked well in the recent past: in two cases blatant offenders had

had votes cast for acquittal. In the Senate, where members gave their opinions openly, there would be no room for such irresponsibility.

There can be no doubt that this move was as welcome to the Senate as the nullification of free election in the Comitia was to be in AD 14. The results were pernicious. Routine cases of extortion tended to lead to acquittal, or at least to mitigated penalties ('There but for the grace of God go I'), for the House did not just decide guilt or innocence by delivering a verdict; it also came to determine penalties, though with an eye on the legal tariff. When it came to treason, however, that is, to capital offences against the regime and its supporters, all but the strongest-minded were anxious to speak and vote in such as way as to demonstrate orthodoxy and patriotism: careers depended on it. By pitting one member against another and subjecting judicial procedure to factional politics, with property and lives at stake, this change did more than anything else to undermine the House; it was the imperial voice that echoed round the chamber.[53]

It did not take only cases on the statute book and defined by law, either. The right of magistrates and Senate to inquire (*cognoscere*) into what they chose, as in 63 BC, freed them from other legal constraints and opened the way to the ingenious terrors of later reigns, whether presided over by the Princeps or by the consuls. Besides this, the Princeps himself, as a holder of *imperium*, conducted hearings on his own. Augustus is praised by Suetonius for his assiduity, for hearing cases even in his private apartments, and gives examples that demonstrate benefits of the system, but it became a profound grievance in the reigns of Claudius and Nero, when capital political charges were heard in private, and in the presence of women and freedmen, instead of before the Senate, as had by then become traditional.[54] How Augustus acquired his judicial powers is a question. It was a complex process in which the *auctoritas* of the Princeps played as great a part as his possession of *imperium* and, as J.-L. Ferrary insists, the fact that tracts of the Empire were governed by his legates, from whom there was appeal to him.[55] Given that that was the case, it was a sound basis for further encroachment.

Social legislation and the feel-good factor

It had been more than harmless and emollient to restore the state religion and its houses: only that would allow healing of the body politic. It had the additional benefit of providing aristocrats with prestigious offices. There was no reason in 28 for delaying the implementation of a reassuring project.[56] But, following a plan adumbrated by Caesar, in 18–17 Augustus brought out a whole 'raft' of reforms: laws imposing exile for adultery between men and married women, penalising celibacy and regulating marriage between the orders and forbidding the intermarriage of those of senatorial rank with persons of servile origin or ill repute.[57]

Augustus' social legislation was paradigmatic for K. Galinsky's 'transforming' leader (see Introduction). When in 5 BC Augustan records noted a commoner of Faesulae (Fiesoli) who had an exceptionally large family they were drawing pointed attention to neglected obligations of privilege. *Noblesse oblige*, and ordinary people, seeing such rules imposed, would acquiesce in the superiority of their rulers, so it could be claimed in the House and at upper-class dinners. Besides, the legislation on marriage and inheritance helped to keep wealth within the family by encouraging the propertied classes to raise true heirs, putting off disreputable legacy hunters. The more children a man had the less property, under Roman rules, each would inherit. That was unfortunate, and a contributing cause to the decline of senatorial birthrate. Hence a notion that Augustus reckoned that the less property a man had the less likely he would be to become a potential rival. That is implausible. Children were hostages to Fortune and to the ruler; with an eye on his sons' future, a man might guard his tongue. The legislation was hardly part of a Machiavellian scheme to weaken the aristocracy. Its demonstrable replenishment and self-respect was the aim, with inheritances passing within the family. This would reassure every section of society that Rome had finally turned back from the fast track to destruction that had been before its eyes for more than a century and had been lit up for it by the monographs of Sallust. It was a part of spreading the sense of well-being throughout society that each of its ranks should be given well-defined privileges and duties, indicating its special value.[58]

G. Williams takes a different view: Augustus was 'obsessed' with sexual reforms over three decades; in 19 he took over control of the age as far as literature was concerned; in preparation for the social laws of 18 he even forced a favoured freedman to suicide for seducing Roman ladies of rank (*matronae*).[59] This view will not do. Augustus' intervention was intermittent and both the legislation and the assumption of patronage were part of a tightening of control after the political crisis of 19. The women were of high status, and married; Augustus was obsessed not with sexual reform but with class stability and decorum. Something of the same kind of thinking (besides concern for health and safety) is shown by the rule introduced on the height of buildings at Rome – 70 Roman feet or 20.67m. Here again Augustus cited precedent. He read volumes to the Senate and issued edicts to the People. The precedent cited on this occasion was the speech of Rutilius 'On the limits of building heights'.[60] Competitive jerry-building by money-grabbing landlords was the target here. Even more obvious were the regulations against ostentatious luxury and so unfair competition. Those had a long history and Augustus' were no more successful than their predecessors.[61]

The rules on marriage and the criminalisation of adultery restricted freedom, though in the case of the second it was only the freedom of *matronae* that was restricted, and the fancies of men about married women: a Venus yoked to a repulsive Vulcan would now find herself in chains if she gave way to Mars, as in Ovid's *Art of Love*. Ovid himself programmatically cast aside the dreary garment recommended for married women, the *stola*, in the opening of his *Ars Amatoria*. Resistance is a topic for Ch. 4, and the laws are agreed to have been a failure, like the sumptuary rules. All the same, they remained on the statute book until the sixth century. They had programmatic value, and no right-thinking ruler could repudiate them, although the old-fashioned Tiberius leaned towards the previous method of dealing with female adultery: trial in a family council. Certainly, they had taught a lesson: the state could interfere in private lives (even the interrogation of slaves under torture was allowed).[62]

Augustus promoted orderliness, as far as he could: new ranks, new posts, new voting centuries, new privileges. He certainly promoted it in public meetings. Agrippa's *Saepta Julia*, the covered voting enclosure in the Campus Martius, was completed in 26, making for an orderly procedure (Ch. 2). In the same spirit Augustus banned men from the Forum and its surroundings unless they put on their togas – the defining garb of the Roman; he himself never wore anything else, his admiring biographer tells us.[63] In the theatre ranks – and sexes – were visibly separated, facilitating control. Members of the Senate, who had long enjoyed seating privileges, sat in the orchestra, and since the *Lex Roscia* of 67 BC members of the equestrian order had the first fourteen rows reserved for them. Now came further segregation. Boys with their *paedagogi* (attendants) were assigned to a special block; soldiers too, a potential source of disorder, were assigned their own place. Women were sent up to the top of the viewing space, to the 'gods'. Augustus did nothing to purge the content of the performances and the gender segregation merely reflects women's place in society. The Vestal Virgins, Suetonius says, had seats in the front, but their gender status was ambiguous; the imperial women would sit in the imperial box.[64]

This legislation does not obviously have much to do with the feel-good factor. Indeed, the tension between that and Augustan control is most obvious here. It lay in the reassurance it gave the upper classes about the stability of their position. But under the programmatic aspect of this legislation and the social cohesion that it was to promote lies something closer to the legislator: the securing of his own position, firmly anchored in that cohesive society. The philosopher Seneca made a public point in his essays of including slaves among his own. Dining with them, except at the Saturnalia, would have been another matter.[65] Augustus showed himself sensitive to social distinctions: he never admitted freedmen to his table, though he wrote that he had once invited to dinner a man in whose country house he was staying who had previously been his secret agent (*speculator*). He refused to allow Menodorus, the admiral who had defected from Sex. Pompeius and was instrumental in his downfall in 36 BC, to dine at his table until he had acquired, by a legal dodge, the status of a free-born person. The story, as R. Nisbet notes, was recounted by the patrician Valerius Messala Corvinus.[66]

There need be no doubt of Augustus' sincerity on these matters. He was as vulnerable to social prejudice as the next man, however revolutionary his political aims and methods. Here there are parallels with the European dictators, who ardently espoused retrogressive views on family and morality that comforted their subjects and strengthened their own positions, without constraining their own activities. Subjects felt their fellow-citizens under a control that they approved, and saw themselves exercising it.

The Augustan voice

The hidden transactions of the Augustan state were already an issue. It was a secret of the imperial power that so much was decided behind closed doors, Dio complained. There had always been cabals, but their plans had to be brought into the open and approved in the Senate. Now decision making was restricted to those who needed to know. Augustus even ended publication of the senatorial minutes, begun as a political gesture by Julius

Caesar. Evidently they were put in the charge of a trusty senator, giving the Princeps the chance to tweak them if necessary. Augustus punished breaches of confidence ruthlessly: a secretary who sold the contents of a letter had his legs broken. The populace, Italy and provinces were treated to a gazette, the *acta diurna,* which recorded festive doings and events at the court; there was no need to suppress that; the contents, presumably drawn up by public slaves, were easily manipulated by the Princeps.[67]

Suppression of information is the negative side of 'propaganda'. Every arena was pervaded by the Augustan voice, varying from one time to another but consistent overall in its self-righteousness, and intended to conciliate public opinion. 'Augustus rewrites everything', says A. Barchiesi.[68] The political language of modern Britain directs the public's attention to the future, for it expresses hope for improvement in the condition of 'our'/ 'ordinary'/'hardworking' people/families, and for achievement where there has been none before, through 'rafts' of reforms or 'initiatives' 'rolled out'; there is 'investment', which gives hope of returns for the future, rather than mere spending; so politicians 'move (things) forward' or, most neatly, 'progress them'. Augustus on the contrary intended his Romans admittedly to look forward, but only in the sense that an imaginary age of the dim past might somehow be recreated, or was indeed in the process of recreation. The posture, not being Marxist or revolutionary, approached that of Mussolini and Hitler rather than that of Lenin and Stalin. It could be as generalised, emollient, or hortatory as that of present British politicians. It was office that was contrary to ancestral practice (*contra morem maiorum*) that Augustus had refused. He hoped that when he died he would prove to have laid the firm foundation of the optimum condition of the Commonwealth (*optimi status*), and explicitly shared the view of Cato that a good politician was one who left the *status quo* undisturbed. His concern for the current Roman birth-rate was nothing new; he expressed it by reading out to the Senate the speech uttered in 131 BC by a conservative censor, Q. Caecilius Macedonicus (the same theme was dealt with by the equally conservative Metellus Numidicus, censor 102–01). Where Macedonicus spoke in favour of marriage, as a way of countering the shortage of manpower, the radical tribune Ti. Gracchus had legislated for the distribution of public land; and even Gracchus claimed to be renewing a law of the mid-fourth century.[69]

It has been pointed out that laws promulgated by their rulers would have been the principal means that subjects had of visualising the imperial political image. That meant that legal language aimed to communicate both the content of the law and the character and policy of the lawgiver: 'It was both rhetoric and legislation.'[70] There are fine examples from Augustus' time, and we need not be strict about what constituted 'legislation':[71] after 30 BC what he said went, and even before, when he wrote in 39/38 in support of the privileges and property of the people of Aphrodisias (Geyre), he was effective. Octavian wrote letters to Rhosus (Arsûs) in Syria concerning the privileges of Seleucus, a naval officer who had fought for the Triumvirs and on the basis of rights granted to them he was given Roman citizenship for his work. In the last letter (30 BC) Octavian encourages the people of Rhosus to put any requests to him; men like Seleucus generate good will towards their native communities. Everyone benefited, then, from the transaction. We may also notice Octavian's letter of 31 to the people of Mylasa (Milas) in Caria, who had suffered dreadfully in 40 BC when Q. Labienus, the republican who had enlisted the Parthians, invaded Asia Minor. Octavian, granting whatever request was put to him, catalogued those sufferings. Then, the fifth Cyrene Edict of 4 BC, which embodies a *Senatus Consultum* aimed at shortening the length of time necessary for the prosecution of offending provincial governors. The Princeps boasts of the care (*kedemonia, cura* in Latin) that he and the Senate have for their subjects and expresses sympathy for the age and frailty of some witnesses. That may have been genuine; the point is that it was expressed. The earlier edicts present comparable attention to relations between Greek and Roman citizen communities in the province of Cyrenaica. As A. Momigliano writes, the monarch was, inevitably, monarch of everybody.[72]

So determined was Octavian/Augustus to make sure that his self-justifying voice was heard that he was ready to disclose material that diminished his wife in the eyes of her protégés and others. He wrote to the people of Samos refusing them the privilege of 'freedom', which would have exempted them from interference by the governor of Asia; and he did it in spite of the efforts made on their behalf by Livia. Aphrodisias, which had been granted the favour, was a special case. The people of Aphrodisias duly copied this reply to Samos and made it permanently visible by setting it up in their archive wall.[73] There were also individuals whose cases were unsuccessfully put to the Princeps by members of his family, for example a Greek for whom Tiberius wrote asking for citizenship and who was turned down; he must appear in person and justify his claim. Livia is refused again in another case, also mentioned by Suetonius in a passage specifically designed to show how admirably careful Augustus was not to degrade Roman citizenship: she made a plea for a provincial Gaul – who was liable to tax. Augustus said that he was ready to remit the payment rather than cheapen the citizenship.[74] It might be tempting to believe that Augustus himself made this material public. But there is another case under Tiberius of Livia foiled in an attempt to extract favours from her son.[75] Such items were available to Suetonius from the imperial archives; the unsuccessful Samians had the misfortune of having their letter of rejection publicised by the people of Aphrodisias. The applicant's advocate had to be mentioned, or it might look as if she had done nothing for her protégés.

Something must be said about lying and related techniques. R.T. Ridley has been forthright on the subject, listing cases he found in the *Achievements*. They belong to Ch. 5, for they concern Augustus' presentation of his past for the sake of his reputation. What belongs here is misrepresentation of present action for future gain, seen in its grossest form in the terms of the law that established the Second Triumvirate as a means of establishing the Commonwealth and in the proffered resignation of 27 BC. But there are grey areas in both: truth almost unvarnished (though liable to provoke the response 'well, that's one way of putting it') can jostle half-truths, omissions, ambiguity, *suggestio falsi*, misleading language, tendentiousness and out-and-out lies (used only when they seem safe from exposure).

Augustus remarks in the *Achievements* that he five times asked the Senate for a colleague – he means in the tribunician power: Agrippa in 18 and 13 BC, Tiberius in 7 BC, AD 4 and AD 9. He is looking back here, but something must have been said at the time to justify the grants. The context is the moderateness of his claims to power, and it is plausible as a justification, since collegiality was a prime characteristic of the Republican magistracy. Suetonius tells us that already Augustus had asked the Senate whenever he was elected consul for two others to hold the office as well.[76] This was clearly intended to show moderation and concern for the careers of lesser men. There was an outcry from the Senate: they all protested that it was enough of an infringement of his majesty (*maiestas*) that he should have one colleague, that is, one momentarily equal to himself. However much Augustus made in putting forward the proposal of his willingness to share the burdens and responsibilities of office, the truth was that in securing himself a colleague in the tribunician power Augustus was securing his own position (Ch. 2).[77]

Pervasive as the Augustan voice was, persuasion need not be verbal. Wordless saturation by portraiture of the leader, in statuary and coins, in all autocracies ancient and modern has gone far beyond the conventional representations of the monarch routinely presented in British government offices and on coinage and stamps: there was something to prove, people to be convinced. Symbols can be equally potent, as the swastika showed, plastered in the Nazi era over the most homely objects in Germany (Mussolini had his emblem, the Fasces, ready-made).[78] There is no moral equivalence, but in technique there is something comparable in a small way in the deployment of Augustus' star sign, Capricorn, under which he had been conceived. Some legions (II Augusta, XIV Gemina, XXI Rapax, IV Macedonica and perhaps IV Scythica), had that emblem on their standards.[79] The leader's name functioned as an explicit tie: the adjective 'Augustan' came to be conferred on legions reconstituted by Augustus or serving him (so it is implied) with special distinction, such as the Second, first in Spain, then on the Rhine, the Third in Africa, the Eighth on the Danube, and perhaps a First in Spain that lost the title after disgracing itself.[80] Cities incorporated his name, such as the present-day Saragossa, Autun, Aosta and Augst, in Spain, Gaul, northern Italy and Germany (respectively Caesaraugusta, Augustodunum, Augusta Praetoria and Augusta), with the corresponding use of the Greek 'Sebastos' in the east, as at Sivas and Sabastiyah in Asia Minor and Palestine (both Sebaste); some three dozen names are prefixed or compounded with 'Augusta' in the *Barrington Atlas* index, and eleven with 'Sebaste'.[81] Months and games were named after the Princeps throughout the Empire, as with August in the Roman calendar (8 BC), and so eventually were deities in the western provinces, the name now an honorific and empowering title.[82]

Manipulating the orders: the Senate

A complicating factor in Augustus' winning both control and acceptance was the varied and competing interests of the orders in a hierarchical state. The last century of the Republic had seen Senate and *equites* at loggerheads over exploitation of the provinces and the courts; the *plebs* had to look hard for employment, their daily bread and a role in politics; slaves were of no account, and the privileges and status of freedmen were limited.[83] Complex problems remained: when the Senate took over cases at law equestrian jurymen lost status and power.

Figure 11 Compital Altar (Bridgeman Art Library Ltd. Photograph from Galleria degli Uffizi, Florence, Italy/Alinari)

Even at the last, from beyond his own death – a strong position when he had a loyal heir – Augustus was capable of manipulating the Senate. He desired deification and a state cult and may have gone so far, in one of the documents he left behind to be read in the House, perhaps in his funerary instructions, as to specify the form the honours should take. The Senate in its appreciation decreed him cult, priests and temple, just as in 43 BC it had granted him his first *imperium*.[84] This event, like others from the reign of Tiberius, allows us to understand earlier precedents and initiatives from Augustus' time. In 7 BC, it had been the Senate's decree that had regulated the cult of the *Lares Compitales*, which had already received offerings of incense, candles, and wine for the popular politician M. Marius Gratidianus in 80s BC. It had christened them 'august', and linked them with the Princeps; the novel sacrifice of a bull in this cult is interpreted as a preparatory step towards introducing Augustus' Genius into state cult, a step never taken in his lifetime (Ch. 7).[85]

Throughout his career, all the measures that conferred Augustus' powers on him must have passed through the Senate, emerging as senatorial decrees (*Senatus consulta*), to be ratified by the People. There was complicity between senators and between the Senate and Augustus, and their political relationship was symbiotic. Senators knew that their voting record was open to scrutiny. Most men would vote as required by the Princeps. Augustus gave them prestige and entrenched superiority (*dignitas, maiestas*).[86] Their votes advanced his power and position, often by stages that seemed harmless, until he was supreme and his supremacy acknowledged. So they had the illusion of control, provided they disregarded his ability to use other devices such as his own edicts, or the popular assemblies: he was in their debt. Sometimes it was a known friend of Augustus who drew up honorific proposals and useful measures, a Plancus or a Messalla (Ch. 2). We are not told who proposed the decree that made Mark Antony's birthday a black day (*vitiosus*); the vindictive victor did not forbid it. As Dr Herbert-Brown has reminded me, advice on the calendar must come from the pontifical college, and the Pontifex Maximus was in virtual exile from 36 BC.[87] On other occasions the initiative may have been unprompted, a venture that the proposer thought would help his own career. Under Tiberius, helpful friends of the Princeps stood up with proposals to his advantage; some men less well disposed inserted others that carried irony in their exaggeration. There could also be blunders and the proposer could be snubbed, later even punished. The beginning of a reign and moments of crisis invited particular ingenuity, as the first debates after the death of Augustus showed: Tacitus took pleasure in recording particularly helpful contributions.[88] It would take a strong-minded senator to resist. Unavailingly Augustus questioned the jurist M. Antistius Labeo about his selection of the former Triumvir Lepidus when membership of the Senate was being scrutinised in 18. Labeo, notoriously strong-minded, never reached the consulship.[89] Under the Principate, senators might admit, nothing was done by the House of which the Emperor did not approve. One who acted on an initiative of his own would be careful to find out whether it was likely to be acceptable. At worst Augustus and his successors always had their tribunician veto. Tiberius certainly used it, but a mere expression of intention or even of opinion would be enough.[90]

There were lesser men than Labeo not destined for the consulship (there were twenty entrants to the Senate each year and four consulships available from 5 BC onwards). They had the lesser opportunities of new offices created under Augustus, such as the curatorship of a minor road. These would appeal to men who were new to the Senate, whose expectations of a speedy rise might not be as strong as those of well-established aristocrats. These posts took care of work that had never been properly done under the Republic, and provided titles for men whose posts in the regular career ladder would have looked thin: tribunate, aedileship, praetorship at best.[91] They filled the interstices of the regular senatorial career to serve really useful, if not always glamorous, functions and, if performed well, could lead to higher office.[92]

Advancement through kin and friends

Augustus need have felt no hesitation in bringing on allies and young relatives. In AD 22 Tiberius himself asked for the tribunician power to be conferred on his son Drusus, and accompanied the request with an elaborate letter.[93] That was permissible, and based on Augustus' method of working for the promotion of his intended successors. The first example is M. Claudius Marcellus, a blood connexion (not a stepson like Tiberius) with his early aedileship and ten years' seniority. It is possible that this proposal was made by Augustus' colleague in the consulship of 24, C. Norbanus. But he would have to be carefully primed about the details, including the lesser privileges granted to Tiberius at the same time as a tribute to his talents and an act of grace towards Livia.[94] The request, displaying intimate knowledge of what was required and insight into the Princeps' mind, would have been an embarrassment for the consul. It is more likely that Augustus wrote to the Senate as Tiberius did for his son.

When we reach the promotion of Gaius and Lucius Caesars, fifteen years later, there were many in every rank of society who looked forward to their rise and accession to power. Some senators would have had no hesitation in bringing forward measures in the boys' honour, even hustling the Princeps along if the proposals did not always quite fit the timetable that Augustus had envisaged: hence the report of his fine-sounding response to untimely demands for their advancement: 'When they have earned it.' (We are entitled to ask what Gaius had done in 1 BC, when he received his command against the Parthians.)[95]

There were also kinsmen by marriage to benefit. For a man with only one surviving child of his body, and that a daughter, Augustus spread his marital net widely. He had female relatives beside Julia to dispose of who gave ambitious young nobles access to the imperial family itself, and so to a share of its power and prestige. Before she wed Mark Antony, Octavia had been the wife of M. Claudius Marcellus, consul in 50 BC, who had not long survived; but she had not only her son Claudius Marcellus, who in 25 became Augustus' son-in-law,[96] but two daughters, the elder and younger Marcellae.[97] The elder was given to Agrippa as his second wife, the younger in succession to Paullus Aemilius Lepidus, consul in 34 BC, and to M. Valerius Appianus, who died in his consulship of 12 BC, then to Iullus Antonius, son of Mark Antony and Fulvia, who lost position and life when he came too close to Julia, sexually, politically or both (Ch. 4).[98] The daughter of Marcella and Appianus, Claudia Pulchra, married P. Quinctilius Varus, consul 13 BC, who went on to govern provinces of the first importance and died in the disaster of the Teutoburg Forest in AD 9. There were also Octavia's two daughters by Mark Antony, Antonia Major and Minor. The second wed Augustus's stepson Nero Drusus, but the first was allocated to L. Domitius Ahenobarbus, consul 16 BC, the man also entrusted with the dangerous campaigning in the Balkans and Germany after Tiberius' retirement (6 BC–AD 1). Their half-brother, Iullus Antonius, was also a consul (10 BC). The other consul of 16 BC was P. Cornelius Scipio, Julia's uterine brother, the son of Augustus' divorced wife Scribonia.[99] In the next generation the younger Julia, granddaughter of Augustus, was married to L. Aemilius Paullus, consul in AD 1; their daughter Aemilia Lepida, married to M. Junius Silanus, the consul of 19, produced a brood of five, who survived into the reign of Claudius and outdid him in their share of Augustus' genes (two of the progeny were to be carried off in 49 on a charge of incest); none survived Nero.[100]

In 21 BC Agrippa, the Princeps' friend, was important enough to marry Julia, benefiting for the second time from the Augustan marriage network. And he in turn had prizes to dispense, in spite of his humble origins, that is, two daughters worth marrying. One Vipsania came from his first marriage, to Caecilia Attica, daughter of Cicero's equestrian friend Atticus, and she was given to Tiberius, and then, when in 11 BC Tiberius was reallocated to Julia, to C. Asinius Gallus, consul in 8 BC; their sons were numerous and successful. There was another, born of Agrippa's union with Augustus' daughter Julia, who is known as Agrippina the Elder, and who eventually became the wife of Germanicus. So Agrippa was the grandfather of their huge and hopeful brood, including not only Gaius Caligula and his sisters Drusilla, Julia and Agrippina the Younger, but also of Tiberius' son Drusus Caesar, a fact that told against Drusus.[101]

Senatorial pensioners

At the other end of the scale were men who, in the aftermath of decades of civil war and proscription, needed help to stay in the senatorial order. Augustus was forced to give direct help. They were short of cash, as senators had already been in the landowning aristocracy of the Republic. It was a bitter contrast to the wealth of their leading peer and his intimates. Some found that they could not even meet the census qualification that Augustus imposed in the teens BC, *HS* 400,000, rising soon to one million. Men of ill-repute, or those not favoured, were allowed to resign; the deserving became pensioners of the Princeps and a prey to lack of candour in offering their opinions. Subsidies to deserving but impoverished senators looked well and nobody would complain, however much the wealthy privately disdained the recipients. These should have become usefully loyal, but, a prey to resentment at their plight, they might go on to make further public demands. Augustus encouraged Marcius Hortalus, descendant of the celebrated orator Q. Hortensius, Cicero's rival, to perpetuate his family. So he did and early in Tiberius' reign presented himself and his boys at the doors of the House with his petition for more. Tiberius acceded, but ruled that other requests should be taken formally to the Senate. Hortalus evidently thought the humiliation was worth it, if the money was forthcoming. He and others may also have enjoyed exposing the plight of members of their order in the face of immeasurable imperial wealth.[102]

Gratification of the knights[103]

At first sight, the *equites* lost under the new order. Not only did important state trials pass into senatorial control, but wealthy members of the order were as exposed to the social legislation as their betters. They became subject to scrutiny from the Princeps as to birth, property and conduct. On the other hand, this sifting of the membership and the annual parade (*transvectio*) of those who, as members of the eighteen 'centuries' of knights who had their horse supplied at public expense (*equites equo publico*) enhanced the dignity of the rank. So did the common membership of the voting centuries that equestrian members of the jury panels shared with the Senate under the new voting regulations of AD 5.[104]

But Augustus also found the *equites* military positions of real importance and power in areas in which there had been no will under the Republic for management by the state, since senators were jealous of any individual who undertook them. Attempts to exploit Egypt had been frustrated under the Republic. Cornelius Gallus was only the first of the equestrian prefects to whom Augustus and his successors entrusted it. Small military prefectures, under the command of Augustus as holder of *imperium*, were to follow, in other areas with tough districts (as in the Balkans); most famous is the prefecture of Judaea, created in AD 6 when the kingdom of Herod the Great was annexed. Pontius Pilate (*c.* 26–37) used the title on a commemorative inscription.[105] Such provinces could be seen as too small for the attention of a senatorial governor. Nor would senators grudge lesser prefects their posts: the man who was put in charge of the Italian courier service and system of relays that provided the speedy transmission of news and officials to and from the provinces, the *Praefectus Vehiculorum*, was vital, but he could not sustain the dignity of a senator.[106]

The right to extract profit from the provinces had contributed to the issues fought over in the late Republic (see Introduction). The knights' formidable functions as contractors of tax revenues (*publicani*) continued, and they were enhanced by a novelty: the appointment of *procuratores Augusti* to supervise taxation in imperial provinces; in public provinces the Princeps also had procurators, his private but authoritative agents, to manage his estates.[107] Procurators had been the private agents of landowners and businessmen; as agents of Augustus they acquired status, and the presence of an imperial procurator indicated the presence of imperial power. It was still prudent for a governor to keep on good terms with such men. Even in Judaea, whose governor's official title was 'Prefect', the preferred title came to be 'Procurator'.[108] Under Augustus and his successors access to the Senate became easier for knights, but some preferred the profits and security of equestrian service.[109]

At the centre we find equestrian posts devised by Augustus late in his principate to deal with fire-fighting, security and the grain supply. As to fires, no measure proved adequate (Ch. 2). Aediles and tribunes had been responsible for protecting the ramshackle and flammable fabric of Rome, but they lacked staff. Republican profiteers such as M. Licinius Crassus had made it their business to save buildings – and acquire them cheaply from distraught owners. The example of the ambitious Egnatius Rufus, who had won his popularity by using his own fortune and his own slaves as aedile to supply fire-fighters (Ch. 4) was not going to be followed by any other politicians of Augustan Rome. Augustus developed the idea, and the aediles, later the officials in charge of each district of the city (the *magistri vici*) are found in charge of a force of 600 slaves. But the reorganisation of the city in 7 BC into 14 districts, each under a senatorial magistrate, proved inadequate. After another fire, in AD 7 Augustus set up a brigade of freedmen divided into seven cohorts, 3,500 men under an equestrian commander, the *Praefectus Vigilum* (Prefect of the Watch); it was funded by a new tax, 2 per cent on the sale of slaves.[110] The way Augustus developed these solutions, through a series of improvisations prompted by blatant failings, invites reflections on the development of the Principate itself: not as smooth as it has been painted (Ch. 2).

The origin of the greatest prefecture (except the governorship of Egypt), that of the Praetorian Guard, is obscure: Republican generals had had troops at their headquarters (*praetorium*). Augustus kept nine cohorts stationed throughout Italy as a security measure. The command structure remains unclear until Dio tells us that in 2 BC Augustus appointed a pair of prefects (see Ch. 4);[111] one prefecture in this office was an exception, and possibly a concession. The Prefect of the City was a consular appointed by the Senate to ensure public safety in the city. He too commanded a quasi-military force of three cohorts of 500 men each. At the same time, he was a man the Princeps could trust. He emerges quietly into history as a permanent official only at the end of Augustus' reign: the loyal and able L. Calpurnius Piso, *cos.* 15 BC, who was also a boon companion of Tiberius. Here perhaps was a distant successor of the controversial M. Valerius Messala Corvinus and T. Statilius Taurus (Ch. 2).[112]

Octavian experienced first-hand the rage of the people when food ran short at Rome in 40 and 38 BC (Ch. 1). Supplies were still likely to be disrupted by famine in the provinces, storms at sea, inadequate harbours and incompetence in distribution. In 33 the ex-consul Agrippa anomalously took on the aedileship to show how seriously the needs of the People were being taken. Ten years later the two aediles and the quaestor Ostiensis, who had been in charge, were helpless. That forced Augustus, who was in a position to command supplies from the provinces, to take over temporary responsibility (*cura annonae*); he provided twelve rations (a year's supply) for each recipient. Then he transferred the administration to ex-praetors, two a year, selected by lot. Then in 18 a board of four ex-praetors was appointed on an annual basis to supervise distribution in Rome, with the modest title 'Prefects put in charge of distributing grain' (*Praefecti frumenti dandi*). Again, that solution was unsatisfactory. There were food riots in AD 6, and Augustus appointed consular curators in 6 and 7. By AD 7 ex-consuls were in charge: the crisis was so severe that foreigners were evicted from Rome to save supplies. Augustus dedicated an altar to the plebeian deities Ceres and Ops (appropriately named Augusta) in AD 7. This was a characteristically double-barrelled approach to the problem; neither was successful. Suetonius tells us, implausibly, that in his vexation Augustus once thought of abolishing grain doles but realised that what he abolished someone else could easily revive. He had allowed increasingly senior members of the Senate to show that they were incapable of ensuring supplies, coming to the rescue himself when there were acute crises. Now the entrenched old Princeps made his final effort. Actual need and the length of time that these travails lasted allowed a decisive step, despite senatorial feelings: between 8 and 14 a permanent equestrian administrator (*Procurator Annonae*) was established; ex-praetors remained in charge of distribution (*Praefecti Frumenti Dandi*). Not surprisingly, Augustus' attention to the grain is strongly featured of the *Achievements*.[113]

Only a few knights enjoyed these posts, but dignity gratifyingly accrued to the entire order, down to the humblest freeborn possessor of *HS* 400,000 who laid claim to membership. Divided from the senate by taking over privileged functions and united with them by their separation from ordinary people, the coalescing *equites* could make themselves felt by sending representatives to Augustus or by informal demonstration in their privileged seats, as they did in AD 9. On happier occasions they had promoted Augustus' grandsons to their positions as *Principes Iuventutis* (Leaders of the Youth) and Augustus himself to that of Pater Patriae operating again from that same place of corporate assembly.[114] Whether the hesitancy of moves towards powerful equestrian posts shows that Augustus really wanted to try out the old Republican methods or simply to prove that they failed is a question.[115] The solutions of his last decades show more than anything his concern for the welfare – and good will – of the *plebs*.

The *plebs*, the *Magistri vici* and their master

Overall, the *plebs* seems to have trusted Augustus and enjoyed a less complex relationship with him than their betters. There was more to it than keeping the populace passively content, as Tacitus says he did at the opening of the *Annals*. The people were called upon to bring legislation on to the statute book, were the target of informal addresses (*contiones*), they still had their place at elections, and the accompanying tips. They were formidable on their own account in theatre and forum, and on behalf of their favourites, the Princeps, his daughter and her sons (Ch. 4).

Augustus' boasts of largesse were well founded.[116] The aim was to provide grain free to qualified citizens of Rome (the *plebs frumentaria*, a limited number, two hundred to two hundred and fifty thousand heads of household), and to secure a fair price for others. The limitation on numbers, which was not as low as he had originally hoped, gave the comfortably off a sense of control and a feeling that the resources of the Treasury were not being drained off. Given Augustus' vast wealth it was feasible for him to contribute to the donations. It was also easy to justify the allowance to his peers (who were not themselves excluded).

Flooding was another intractable cause of suffering to the people, lasting until modern times, but more limited in its effects than fire and famine. Flooding increased their discontent in 22 BC, and eventually Augustus or Tiberius set up a board of senatorial Curators of the Tiber Bank. Flooding nonetheless is recorded in AD 12 and 15 – and the inadequacy (or impertinence) of Asinius Gallus' advice in the Senate (to consult the Sibylline Books) is reported by Tacitus. This was not a sphere that Augustus had placed in equestrian hands.[117]

By this time even the good new moral and productive age that Horace's verses predicted in 17 BC was a future forgone. Once the final systems were in place the people had no one to blame for failure but the man at the top.[118] What had once seemed extraordinary had become the norm, and subject to criticism. Besides, Augustus, who had others to please, set limits on popular demands. Some concessions were readily made: it would not have been prohibitively expensive, but highly popular, when Augustus added three days to the Saturnalia.[119] There was discontent, some time after 21 BC, when the price of wine rose. Augustus was having none of it, as he told the people in an edict, when Agrippa had been at such pains to bring in plentiful supplies of water in his aqueducts.[120] That tone would have gone down well with the propertied classes, as it did with Suetonius, who said it showed a 'salubrious' Princeps, not one to curry favour with the people (*ambitiosus*). Augustus issued an equally stern edict when he heard complaints of his failure to deliver a special dole they claimed to have been promised. It would have been with an eye on upper-class opinion, too, that he reproved the people in another strongly worded edict when they rose at the games to applaud him when the words 'O fair and good-hearted master' (*dominum*) were spoken on the stage. Not the adulation, but the word 'Master' was unacceptable.[121]

Relations with the people of Rome were not confined to the matters of bread and circuses, and public safety; at least, the entertainment provided could be more valuable. It was part of Augustus' *popularis* appeal to the unprivileged masses to lay out splendid works in public spaces for their pleasure and edification. The disposition of works of art played a programmatic role by demonstrating the imperial role of the Roman People as managed by Augustus: the centre-piece of one scheme was an obelisk brought from Egypt (see Ch. 5). During his aedileship of 33 BC, his closest ally, Agrippa, announced that all Greek statues and works art should be displayed publicly. Wealthy collectors even before the Civil Wars ended need not fear for their property – unless they chose the side of Antony; after Actium there would be only the memory of those words to make owners uneasy about the disposition of their collections. The issue remained alive. Agrippa's own programme for improving Rome's water supply and beautifying the north-west sector, the Campus Martius, included the setting up of masterpieces such as the *Apoxyomenos* (a youth scraping oil and sand off his skin) of Lysippus. After it had been there for decades, the Emperor Tiberius, who cared little for the *plebs*, went against his one-time father-in-law's injunction, and carried it off to his bedroom. A public uproar changed his mind. Agrippa's pronouncement was approved by the elder Pliny, who wrote under an emperor who held the same views, Vespasian. Augustus and Agrippa had taken in better than Tiberius what Cicero said of the Roman People, that they did not mind luxury itself, but wanted money spent for the public good.[122] Augustus himself combined the assertion of Rome's centrality and supremacy by collecting curios from subject peoples. He took the tusk of the Caledonian boar from Tegea, leaving a decaying hide to the previous owners, and demonstrated the People's ownership (he displayed the tusk in a temple).[123]

Augustus needed the *plebs* for his own purposes. He admitted himself that popular interpretation of the comet of 44 BC forwarded the deification of Caesar, and he exploited astrology throughout his career,[124] but the period 23–19 is the most promising place to look. J. Crook scouts the idea that Augustus exploited, even provoked, the popular demonstrations that rocked the Senate those years, or even that his opponents were scheming to tempt him into a position that would justify tyrannicide. At most, on this view, he would have been working for a chance to refuse unacceptable offices.[125] It seems likely from the way he organised the *plebs* in later years that Augustus did exploit, and may have managed, such demonstrations to win himself freedom of choice in the way he would develop his Principate. His initial refusal of the People's offer of the title *Pater Patriae* does not show that their initiative was spontaneous.

In a fine illustration of the intertwining of Roman social and religious life, to the Princeps' benefit, Augustus reorganised the administration of the City of Rome in connexion with the re-establishment of the cult of the Lares. Domestic gods, but also cultivated at crossroads as *Lares Compitales*, they were transformed into the presiding deities of the districts into which Augustus divided the City in 7 BC. There were fourteen *regiones*, each subdivided into two and making up 265 *vici* (street communities).[126] The *vici* and responsibility for their orderliness were each under its four masters (*magistri vici*) with their own four assistants (*ministri*) and ceremonial dress. Traditional cults were re-established and indeed transformed, for the *Lares* came to be known as *Lares Augusti* (august Lares) and the cult of Augustus' genius was attached to theirs. Attention was paid to order in the City, much to the relief of the respectable. The *plebs*, freedmen and even slaves were given positions of gratifying privilege; for the upper classes these organisations were a welcome substitute for the unruly masses that populist politicians could hire for their own violent purposes; Augustus provided himself with an organised, ready-made rent-a-mob. Not only did grain distributions steady popular support, Augustus visited the districts (*regiones*) of Rome, and distributed tips to deserving children. However, the overall effect of the Augustan reforms has been traced by J. B. Lott and identified by him as 'bureaucratisation'. That was much to Augustus' advantage, as the man in charge.[127]

Other politicians who needed help on the streets or in the theatre, such as the supporters of Gaius Caesar in 6 BC and of his mother Julia in AD 2, had to improvise. They had slaves, freedmen and other clients to swell demonstrations. There were also precedents in P. Clodius, tribune in 58 BC, and his successor and rival T. Annius Milo, who killed him in a skirmish six years later, and they might have had something like Clodius' organised gangs at their disposal, members of *collegia*, associations of tradesmen, nominally religious and social. But those had been put under severe control by both Caesar and Augustus, who dissolved all those that were not licensed and of good standing.[128]

A high proportion of the inhabitants of Rome and Italy were slaves or freedmen, the former a potential danger to peace and security, the latter under-privileged and with a status that needed regulating. Augustus offered reassurance all round, by stabilising the condition of freedmen through the *Lex Junia* (17 BC), which created a stratum of men with 'Latin' rights (*Latium*) who through productive marriages and good behaviour could attain full Roman citizenship, and by restricting the numbers and ages of slaves to be emancipated (*Leges Fufia Caninia* of 2 BC and *Aelia Sentia* of AD 4).[129] Within western communities there was a place in governance for these men, if they had the money: debarred from city councils, they could form priestly associations – named after the Princeps Seviri Augustales.[130] Their sons, born free, had access to the gamut of service in the army and the cities. It was no hardship for the upper classes or Rome that such people had their own positions of honour, though they were resistant to the penetration of the equestrian and senatorial orders.

The feel-good factor

Clearly, the importance of the feel-good factor throughout the Roman world was fully understood by Augustus. The ill omens that had accompanied the formation of the Triumvirate were seized on, reinterpreted and incorporated into his *Autobiography*, and when the Tiber flooded in 27 BC, the night after he took the name Augustus, diviners (the *haruspices*) interpreted the portent as a sign of the Princeps' control of the city.[131] His benefactions to the *plebs*, to the soldiers in the form of donatives and of land bought for them in Italy and abroad, including his contribution to the Military Treasury, which paid discharge bounties, are naturally insisted on in the *Achievements*, he has nothing to say of the confiscations of land for his own and Antony's veterans that gave rise to the Perusine war of 41–40.[132]

Then there were the gladiatorial shows and wild-beast hunts, naval spectacles, theatrical performances and mimes, and the Secular Games. Assemblies were occasions for them to rise as one and salute the Princeps; to stay seated would be conspicuous.[133]

Augustus' gifts and privileges to Italy and throughout the Empire, directly and indirectly, and through his subvention of the State Treasury, were rewarded, as Nicolaus of Damascus noted, with homage and cult, in the form of statues, inscriptions, altars and temples. Italy was conspicuously favoured by its champion Octavian – only from the provinces did Octavian accept crown gold in recognition of his victories – and, if the documentation is taken at face value, effectively.[134] The census of Roman citizens taken in 29 BC, which had not been done since 70–69, would be a measure of success if we understood and trusted the figures (including women for the first time, or differently enrolled). At 4,063,000 it looks like a healthy increase over the previous 910,000, and later censuses showed further rises. Roman statesmen and thinking men had been concerned over the citizen population, and above all that of the Italian agricultural countryside and its manpower, potential legionaries. The effect on Italian agriculture that recruitment had was poignantly lamented by Virgil in the *Georgics*: 'The farmers have been carried off, the grain-fields are a wilderness.'[135]

Under Augustus a new picture of Italy emerged. Augustus divided the peninsula into fourteen regions, and the gazetteer of cities provided by Pliny the Elder in his *Natural History* seems to be based on his scheme (each area is headed by colonies that Augustus founded). But Pliny's list offers up to a hundred towns that cannot otherwise be identified. E. Bispham has suggested, very convincingly, that these ghosts, which are especially numerous in the less well-favoured heel and toe of Italy and in Samnium and the Sabine country, owe their life to Augustus' list, one that hovered between reality and wish-fulfilment, 'Italy as it was and as it should be', and so gave illusory body to the idea of the Italian revival.[136]

Men of standing in the country towns were courted by being allowed a voice in the selection of junior army officers, *Tribuni Militum*.[137] Some were given entry to the Senate, the men cited in Claudius' speech of 48 on the admission of Gallic nobles. Ovid of Sulmo (Sulmona) would have been the first senator from the Paeligni if he had chosen to pursue that career.[138] In the *Fasti*, his poem on the calendar, Ovid's aim was 'to sing of Caesar's altars' – the festal days celebrating him.[139] The hope of benefactions would be enough to prompt a community to take honorific action, spend some money, and make it known to the Princeps. The clearest instance of this mechanism at work is found in Asia Minor in 29 BC, when the communities of the Greek cities of the provinces of Asia and Bithynia-Pontus jointly offered him temples. Octavian was prudent: they were allowed temples to Julius Caesar and to Rome and Octavian, resident Romans only the first. He was not plunged into hopeless obligations to those communities, and Roman opinion was conciliated.[140]

Morality and religion

Augustus himself did not hide his gifts to the Roman people of all classes; they were presented in the magnificently adorned City itself, and magnificently described by Strabo.[141] But he came to be called the benefactor of the whole state, a claim implicit in the *Achievements* (Ch. 5). That included success abroad, notably in the field. It brought material benefits, as well as spectacular triumphs: booty and new sources of tax revenue. This combined to generate the feeling of well-being vital to the survival of an elected regime – the 'Falklands factor', as it was known after the islands were recovered by Britain in 1982 – and significant even in an autocracy. The number of festal days at Rome rose between 45 BC and AD 10 from 49 to 69; the name of Augustus itself was a guarantee of felicity, and it was only natural that in 12 BC the Senate allowed even the stigmatised unmarried to take part in his birthday festivities.[142] The significance of new or metamorphosing festal days with their wealth of associations has been brought out by M. Beard: the calendar provided 'a pageant of Romanness' available for Augustan productions.[143]

Roman success depended on the community's relations with the gods.[144] They had offended, and knew it, as Horace makes clear in odes written in the opening years of the Principate.[145] There were traditional ways towards restoration, and Augustus embraced them. In 29 the doors of the temple of Janus were closed for the first time since the end of the first Punic War: Rome was at peace. It was a cardinal rule for Augustus to associate himself with causes that were long cherished, reputable and tied to the security of the Roman People. Good relations with the gods were particularly carefully cultivated. In the same year Augustus undertook to seek the *Augurium Salutis*, a prayer and an enquiry as to the security of the state – which expected a favourable answer, displaying confidence – to be offered only in a year free of war.[146] The very length of the period since it had been sought (63 BC) signified the magnitude of the change that had taken place in Rome's prospects. The doors of Janus were soon to open again, but Augustus managed at least one other closure, in 25.[147] When in the *Achievements* Octavian claims in 28 to have restored eighty-two temples in Rome (at any rate he began the restoration, and he eventually constructed twelve new ones)[148] he is recording a brilliant stroke that repaired Romans' shattered relations with their gods, who had to be brought back to proper service of the Roman People, and demonstrated the victor's devotion towards them (*pietas*), besides providing contractors and workmen with lasting employment.[149] A smaller gesture also recorded in the *Achievements* combined modesty, devotion to the gods, and concern for Rome's permanent reserves of precious metal: eighty silver representations of Augustus, some equestrian, set up round the City were melted down and with the proceeds were acquired golden tripods as dedications for the temple of his patron Apollo.[150]

Along with the restoration of temples went the reconditioning of ancient but decayed religious colleges such as the *Fetiales*, whose functions included making sure that declarations of war were carried out in due form, and the twelve Arval Brethren, whose name shows their concern with the successful agriculture.[151] Individuals also benefited from these restorations: up and coming new men were proud, and presumably grateful, to be admitted even to the unprestigious priesthood of the *Fetiales*, now revived[152] and Arvals would enjoy celebrating (alongside members of the imperial family) the cult of Dea Dia outside Rome and the feasts that went with the meetings (the date of Dea Dia's festivals were made to coincide with dynastic anniversaries).[153] For under the *Lex Saenia* of 30 BC, Augustus enjoyed the privilege of appointing men to priesthoods.[154] Another venerable position was restored in 12 BC, to be occupied for the first time since 87, when the last holder was forced to kill himself. The *Flamen Dialis* served Jupiter Optimus Maximus and was subject to restrictions on dress and travel that made his post hard to fill; Augustus may have exerted pressure or offered inducements.[155]

Romans' consciousness of moral failure and the decline of traditional family values and religious practice, real or imagined, was addressed by Augustus, through the sense of moral well-being that he tried to inculcate. His claim in the *Achievements* that it was at the Senate's wish that he passed his social legislation was a claim that he and they shared common values. So it was to the common advantage that Augustus should put his views into practice. It is no coincidence that just after these enactments a festival celebrating Rome's birthday was held: the Secular Games of 17 marked the beginning of a new age – the age, it was to emerge, of Gaius and Lucius Caesars. The Games might have been due in 39 or might in more propitious political circumstances have been held in 23 or 22. Indeed, already in 44, according to Augustus' *Autobiography*, a haruspex had hailed the appearance of Caesar's comet as the sign of a new *saeculum*.[156] The placing rested on 'calculations' made by the loyal Augustan jurist C. Ateius Capito, who found that the *saeculum* should be a period of 110 years, not a mere century.[157] Such games should be held when no-one could be alive who had witnessed the preceding ones: the City's life began again in a new age, which this was, in Augustus' own estimation; and modern scholars have agreed.[158] Diviners now announced that the time had come and a comet was seen which was taken to be a reappearance of the star that had heralded the deification of Julius Caesar. Under the guidance of the board of priests (nominally fifteen) who were in charge of carrying out divine rituals, the *Quindecimviri Sacris Faciundis*, with Augustus and Agrippa at their head to instruct them, the whole population joined in the celebration, which lasted from the end of May until mid-June. Sacrifices were offered to the presiding deities Apollo and Diana, who were addressed by choirs of boys and girls singing Horace's poem composed for the occasion, the *Carmen saeculare*. Accounts of the proceedings were inscribed on a bronze and a marble pillar.[159] But the celebrations offered more popular attractions: performances in the theatre, circus games and wild-beast hunts.[160]

Five years later, Augustus was able to consolidate his connexion with Roman religion. He knew how to rally the people behind him, relying on their accumulated goodwill and on techniques learned early in his career: the oath taken to him in 32 BC. A similar demonstration of support was called for in 12 BC, when at last Augustus was elected to the Supreme Pontificate by Roman citizens divided according to their tribes (Ch 2). Lepidus was occasionally brought back from retirement, probably when his presence was required for official business, which might well show how inadequate the old man was for the post (he was at least 76 years old at his death). The election was the occasion on 6 March for a massive demonstration: people swarmed in (or were bussed) from all over Italy to show loyalty. This time no oath was required. The loyalists in charge, presumably leading men in each of the colonies and municipalities and prefectures of the peninsula, would have used their best endeavours to deliver the vote, but their own may have been all that was expected. Both the oath of 32 and the voting twenty years later shared the simple directness, and something of the brutal impressiveness of twentieth and twenty-first century totalitarian political rallies.

In the popular view the Supreme Pontificate had been Augustus' by rights since the death of his 'father', also in March: the story survives that the post had been made hereditary; nonsense, or he would have claimed it from the beginning. The use he made of it was more of an encroachment. His connexion with state religion became more intimate, more so than anything that earlier holders had enjoyed. They had been only the leading member of the most prestigious religious college and had charge of the Vestals and their sacred hearth. The Vestals, guardians of the sacred flame that represented Rome's life, were under Augustus' tutelage, and his wife

Figure 12 Augustus as Pontifex Maximus (akg-images Ltd. Photograph from Bildarchiv Steffens)

presided over a shrine of Vesta in his house on the Palatine, which as the official residence of the Pontifex he made over in part to become public property. For the new Pontifex Maximus chose not to live in the priestly *Domus Publica*, which Lepidus should have used as his Rome hotel. Instead that passed to the Vestals, and Augustus dedicated half his existing house on the Palatine (which as a rare privilege had been paid for by the State, as M. H. Dettenhofer points out) to public use; the rest followed in AD 3 after a fire and restoration. Ovid was able to write in the *Fasti* of Vesta, Apollo and Augustus 'sharing one house'. Even without the implications of that, the supreme pontificate enabled Augustus to behave in a sense as head of the state religion. That was how the post developed, as Princeps and Commonwealth became inextricably entwined.[161]

The last decade of the Augustan Principate shattered Roman confidence. Intrigue at Rome, shortage of cash for the soldiery, revolt in the provinces preceded the low-water mark: the destruction of Varus and his legions in Germany, AD 9.[162] Tiberius inherited political, military and economic problems that deprived it of any hope of the feel-good factor, no matter what was claimed in the senatorial decree of AD 20. The Senate's draftsmen spoke of the peace (*tranquillitas*) of the age; their unease was patent.[163]

Endnotes

1 I am particularly grateful to Professor Wardle for bibliographical help with this chapter.

2 Emperor and army: *HA Hadr.* 15. 12f. For an earlier intellectual dispute that ended with Tiberius invoking the military, see Suet. *Tib.* 11. 3 (I owe this reference to Dr Herbert-Brown).

3 Claudius' beneficence: Sen. *Cons. ad Pol.* 12. 3, with Wallace-Hadrill 1996, 196.

4 Patronage: von Premerstein 1937 was pioneering. R. Saller, *Personal Patronage under the early Empire* (Cambridge, 1982), made valuable modern comparisons; but cf. C. Eilers, *Roman Patrons of Greek Cities* (Oxford, 1999) 2–18, against conflating patronage with *patrocinium*. Bibliography: Dettenhofer 2000, 212.

5 Note material advantages for patrons: bequests from grateful friends, compulsory under some later *principes*: Suet. *Aug.* 101, 3, with Momigliano 1940, 76.

6 Caesar rightly killed: Suet. *Iul.* 76. 1. Augustus and Caesar: Strothmann 2000, 24–28; Kienast 2001, against distancing: the Senate contained many Caesarians; Augustan citizenship and German policies followed Caesar's; so did his building programme. These are diverse activities, not all carried out consistently (see below and Ch. 4); what Caesar had done was hardly a determining factor.

7 Buildings: *RG* 20. 3; vengeance: 2.

8 Comet: Pliny *NH* 2, 93f.

9 Caesar's *umbra*: Ovid, *Fasti* 3, 7–3f. Temple: Dio 51. 22. 4–9.

10 Caesar on Spanish coins, 19–18 BC: *RIC* 1², 44, nos. 37f. 17 and 12 BC: 48 no. 102; 66 no. 337–42; 74 no. 415, with Zanker 1988, 168, and Pollini 1990, 352f.

11 Gradel 2002, 265, argues that the deified Julius Caesar as *Divus* prevented Augustus being deified before his death, as Caesar had been: the *Divus* was associated with death; the deification was an embarrassment to Augustus' *moderatio* (263); Caesar in the *Fer. Dur.*: 340. For a more favourable interpretation of Caesar's status under Augustus, see Wardle 1997. P. Donié, *Untersuchungen zum Caesarbild in der römischen Kaiserzeit* (Hamburg, 1996) provides a thoroughgoing survey.

12 Caesar in Ovid, *Fasti* 4, 377–86, with Herbert-Brown 1994, 111–15.

13 Capitol: Dio 55. 1. 1; *RG* 20. 1, with Wardle 2005, 'Sponsors', 44.

14 Augustus at the games: Suet. *Aug.* 45. 1; lavish celebration: 75.

15 Caesar's conduct: Lucan 3. 108–68; slaves in charge of the mint: Suet. *Iul.* 76. 3. Triumviri monetales: *RRC* 2, 599, citing Suet. *Jul.* 41. 1; Dio 54. 26. 6.

16 Handover of revenues: Dio 53. 9. 6; *RIC* 1² 23 notes a similar claim made by Tiberius: Dio 56. 39. 4.

17 Accounts: Suet. *Aug.* 101. 4; Dio 53. 30. 2; 56. 33. 2.

18 Public and private funds conflated: Dio 53. 16. 1; 22. 2–4, with Rich 1990 *ad loc.*; cf. Tac. *Ann.* 6. 2. 1 (AD 32). *HS* 1400 m. inherited in Augustus' last twenty years: Suet. *Aug.* 101. 3; Dio 56. 40. 5. Gallus' property: 53. 23. 7.

19 Egypt's contribution: Vell. Pat. 2. 39. 2. Augustus supporting the Aerarium: *RG* 17. 1 (benefactions and income summarised by Brunt and Moore 1970, 57–59); Dio 53. 2. 1 (28 BC). Nero's claim (62) to be a contributor: Tac. *Ann.* 15. 18. 3.

20 Control of minting: *RIC* 1² (1984) 24; 32. The appearance on coins of the letters *SC* ('*Senatus consulto*', 'by decree of the Senate') has caused misunderstanding on that point: K. Kraft, '*S(enatus) C(onsulto)*', *JNG* 12 (1962) 7–49 = Schmitthenner 1969, 336–403; Talbert 1984, 380–83, with bibl.

21 Aerarium officials: Tac. *Ann.* 13. 29; Dio 53. 2. 1 (28 BC, cf. Vell. Pat. 2. 89.3); 32. 2 (23), with Rich 1990 *ad loc.*, 56. 29. 3. See M. Corbier, 'L'Aerarium Saturni et l'Aerarium militare', *Administration et prosopographie sénatoriale*, *CEFR* 24 (Rome, 1974), 637–50.

22 Fishermen seeking tax-relief: Strabo 10. 485f.

23 Pallas: *PIR*² A 858. Domitian's official: Statius, *Silvae* 3. 3. 86–8.

24 Resentment: e.g. Pliny, *Ep.* 7. 29; 8. 6.

25 Elections: Suet. *Aug.* 40. 2; 56. 1; Dio 53. 21. 6f., with Rich 1990 *ad loc.*; appointment: Dio *loc. cit.* and 54. 10. 2 (19 BC); 55. 34. 2 (AD 8). See Jones 1960, 27–50; Brunt 1961; Levick 1967; R. Frei-Stolba, *Untersuchungen zu den Wahlen in der röm. Kaiserzeit* (Zurich, 1967), 87–163; Holladay 1978. Caesar's misconduct: Suet. *Iul.* 76. 2f.; Triumvirs': Millar 1973, 52f.

26 Caesar's new men: Wiseman 1971, 183; R. Syme, *RP* 1 (1979), 31–41; 88–119. Gauls: Suet. *Iul.* 76. 3; 80. 2, cf. 41. 1f.

27 Three-year *praefectura morum* of 46 BC: Suet. *Iul.* 76. 1–3; Cic. *Fam.* 9. 15. 5;. 900 senators: Dio 43. 47. 3. One-day consul: Cic. *Fam.* 7. 30. 1; Dio 43. 46. 4. *Lex Antonia* on magistrates: Cic. *Phil.* 7. 16; Suet. *Iul.* 41. 2, with H. E. Butler and M. Cary (Oxford, 1927), *ad loc.* and Frei-Stolba (n. 25), 60–65 for other interventions; Dio 43. 51. 2f.; appointed ahead: Cic. *Att.* 14. 6. 2.

28 Thanks for consulship: Ovid, *Ex Ponto* 4. 4. 35–39; there is no proving an obligatory decree, as M. Durry, *Pline le Jeune, Panégyrique de Trajan* (Paris, 1938), 3–5, suggests.

29 Written canvassing: Dio 55. 34. 2 (the beginning of '*commendatio*': Levick 1967). Effectiveness: Tac. *Ann.* 1.15. 1. Right to reject candidatures: Eck 2007, 82; but cf. Levick 1967. Nero offered legionary commands to supernumerary candidates for the praetorship: Tac. *Ann.* 14. 28. 1 (60).

30 Recruitment of Augustan Senate: *ILS* 212; Wiseman 1971, 183.

31 Suffect consulships: Eck 2007, 84. Tiberius refusing advance designation: Tac. *Ann.* 2. 36.

32 Electoral practice: Lacey 1996, 219f. Law on bribery (?18 BC): Dio 54. 16. 1, with Ferrary 2001. Augustus' tip to his tribes: Suet. *Aug.* 40. 2. Problems of 8 BC: Dio 55. 5. 3; of AD 7: 55. 34. 2. *Lex Valeria Cornelia* of AD 5: Brunt 1961 and Rowe 2002 on *RS* 37f. See also Levick 1967; Crook 1996, 127. Eck 2007, 82, like Dettenhofer 2000, 186f. (bibl.), rightly regards the election of candidates approved by the centuries as a 'foregone conclusion'.

33 Elections transferred to Senate: Vell. Pat. 2. 124. 3; Tac. *Ann.* 1. 15. 1.

34 Praetorian elections of AD 14 and numbers of posts: Tac. *Ann.* 1. 14. 4.

35 Consular elections under Tiberius: Tac. *Ann.* 1. 81. Bargaining: Dio 59. 20. 4f. Quarrels under Trajan: Pliny, *Ep.* 4. 25. Discussion with Emperor: *Pan.* 69. 1; 71. 1.

36 Cicero humiliated: *Att.* 13. 27. 1; 31. 3; 14. 1. 2; 2. 3; *Fam.* 9. 15. 4. Matius: *OCD*[3] 397; Balbus' malign influence: Suet. *Iul.* 78. 1; Plut. *Caes.* 60. 2f.

37 Cicero's dislike of Matius and his like: *Att.* 15. 2. 3.

38 Advisers: Agrippa: Ch. 4. Maecenas: Dio 55. 7; Macr. *Sat.* 2. 4. Loss of influence: Tac. *Ann.* 3. 30. Their death: Sen. *Ben.* 6. 32. 2, with 4, cited by Griffin 2003, 159, for their difficulties. Sallustius Crispus: Tac. *Ann.* 1. 6. 3; 3. 30. Sejanus: apology in Vell. Pat. 2. 127f. Tiberius' freedmen: Jos. *AJ* 18. 145; Tac. *Ann.* 4. 70. 1; Claudius': 12. 53. 2 (initiating a senatorial resolution); Dio 60. 16. 4f. (in the House).

39 Use of friends: Dio 53. 2. 6; 11. 1.

40 Gaul and Spain: Schmitthenner 1962.

41 Absence from 16 to 13: Dio 54. 19. 1f.; 25. 1.

42 Pompey's 'refusals' might end in acceptance: Wallace-Hadrill 1982, 37. *Moderatio*: *ibid.* 41f. Professor Wardle has kindly drawn my attention to Hüttner 2004 (Octavian/Augustus 81–127).

43 Encroachment: Tac. *Ann*. 1. 2, 1, 'insurgere paulatim', with Lacey 1996, 3f., 210–32, but (12; 211) dating its beginning to 23 BC; encroachments in provinces: 97.

44 Senators' loss of self-representation: Galinsky 1996, 381.

45 Judicial matters: see E. S. Gruen, *Roman Politics and the Criminal Courts* (Cambridge, MA, 1968); A. H. M. Jones, *The Criminal Courts of the Roman Republic and Principate* (Oxford, 1972); adjustments under Augustus: Suet. *Aug*. 32. 3.

46 Caesar's reform of panels: Suet. *Jul.* 41. 2; Dio 43. 25. 1.

47 Augustus dispensing justice: Suet. *Aug.* 33.

48 Right to hear appeals: Dio 51. 19. 7, whether only criminal or also civil is unclear, and whether the decision of juries might also be vulnerable to appeal. See Professor Wardle's forthcoming commentary on Suet. *Aug.* 33, which he has kindly allowed me to read; Sherk, *RDGE* 341–45, no. 67 of 6 BC may be an instance.

49 Number of jury panels: Pliny, *NH* 33. 30 and 34, with Ramsey 2005.

50 Alteration of the voting system: Dio 54. 3. 6.

51 New jurymen: Suet. *Aug.* 32. 3, with Ramsey 2005 elucidating the stages of the reforms.

52 Senatorial court: Levick 1976 (1999), 184–88; operative by 4 BC (Fifth Cyrene Edict, EJ 311), perhaps by 9 BC (Malcovati 1969, 165, XXXIXn.).

53 *Maiestas*: Bauman 1969 and 1974; Rutledge 2001. Imperial voice: cf. *SCdPp*, *passim*.

54 Trials before the emperor: Tiberius: Tac. *Ann*. 3. 10 (mooted, AD 20); in Claudius' private quarters (*intra cubiculum*): Tac. *Ann*. 13. 4. 2.

55 Growth of jurisdiction: Ferrary 2001, 129f., rebutting the view of Jones 1960 that the grant of consular power in 19 was a turning point.

56 Religious programme: Lacey 1996, 83f.; 169–89.

57 Augustus' social legislation: *RG* 6. 2; with Brunt and Moore 1970, 46–48; Ridley 2003, 172; Tac. *Ann*. 3. 25–28 (failure); Suet. *Aug.* 34; 40. 4; cf. 89. 2; Gell. 2. 24. 14; Florus 2. 34. 65; Dio 54. 10. 6; 16. The idea that it was previously mooted, based on Prop. 2. 7. 1–3 (cf. Cic. *Att*. 13. 7. 1; *Fam*. 7. 26. 2; 9. 15. 5; *Marc*. 23; Prop. 2. 7. 1–3; Suet. *Iul*. 43; Dio 43. 25. 2) is rebutted by Badian 1985, who thinks that a triumviral tax on the unmarried was cancelled in 28 with other unacceptable measures; see also Edwards 1993, 41f.; Dettenhofer 2000, 133–44; Mantovani 2008, 40. Survival of adultery law: *CJ* 9. 9. 4.

58 Large family: Pliny, *NH* 7. 60. Motives for the social legislation: Dettenhofer 2000, 133; potential rivals 137; a curb on parents 139, citing Val. Max. 6.2. 12. Moral regeneration: Zanker 1988, 156–59. G. Williams *ad* Hor. *Odes* 3. 6 (Oxford, 1969), 65, points to the low ending of this Ode. See also P. A. Brunt, *Italian Manpower 225 BC–AD 14* (Oxford, 1971), 558–66; Treggiari 1996. Galinsky 1996, 128–40, arguing 128f. that not the birthrate but the State's concern with private life was the issue; moral superiority: 134f.; property: 136f.

Fragmentation of estates: rebutted by Wallace-Hadrill 1981, 60f.; rather the idea was to stabilise property by curbing bequests outside the family and so will-hunting.

59 'Obsession': Williams 1978, 56–60. Death of freedman: Suet. *Aug.* 67. 2.

60 Building height limits: Suet. *Aug.* 89. 2; Strabo 5. 235.

61 Interpretation of sumptuary laws: D. Daube, *Roman Law, Linguistic, Social, and Philosophical Aspects* (Edinburgh, 1967), 17–28.

62 Venus: Ovid, *Ars Amat.* 2, 566f.); dress: 1, 31–3, cited by Zanker 1988, 166. Tiberian methods: Suet. *Tib.* 35. 1; cf. Tac. *Ann.* 2. 50. 3. (I am indebted here to Dr Herbert-Brown.) Torture: Ch. 4.

63 Togas in Forum: Suet. *Aug.* 40. 5; Augustus' conventional dress: Nic. Dam. 11; Professor Wardle notes relaxation on Capri: Suet. *Aug.* 98. 3. Defining garb: Cic. *Pro Rab. Post.* 27.

64 Organisation of audiences at Rome: Suet. *Aug.* 44. 2f. including soldiers and exclusion of women from athletics, with Rawson 1987 (fundamental).

65 Slave 'friends': Sen. *Ep.* 47.

66 Augustus and freedmen: Suet. *Aug.* 74. Menodorus' *restitutio natalium*: Porph. and Ps.-Acro on Hor. *Epode* 4. 15. See DuQuesnay 1984, 45.

67 Poverty of information: Dio 53. 19. Punishment for disclosures: 67. 2. Gossip: Wallace-Hadrill 1996, 194f. Senate's *acta* and *acta diurna*: Baldwin 1979; White 1997 (sceptical of distribution under the Republic); Dettenhofer 2000, 131f., on Suet. *Jul.* 20. 1; *Aug.* 36; 64. 2; Tac. *Ann.* 5. 4. 1; 16. 22. 4 (evidently the *diurna* attracted little interest); Suet. *Cal.* 8. 2; 36. 2.

68 Augustan versions: Barchiesi 1997, 69.

69 Macedonicus: Livy, *Epit.* 59; Suet. *Aug.* 89. 2; cf. Gell. 1. 6 (Numidicus in 102). Gracchus' precedent: Plut. *Ti. Gracchus* 8. 1. Population increase should be a prime aim for Caesar: Cic. *Pro Marc.* 23.

70 Laws projecting the imperial image: Harries 2006, 132.

71 Augustus as legislator: Suet. *Aug.* 33.

72 Letters of 39/8: *Aphrodisias* 10–12. Seleucus: EJ 301, ll. 91–93 = *RDGE* 58, pp. 294–302 = Malcovati 1969, 32–38, LXI–LXIII; cited by Millar and Segal 1984 (1990), 37; letter to Mylasa: EJ 303 = *RDGE* 60, pp. 310–12 = Malcovati 1969, 39f., LXV; Cyrene Edicts: EJ 311 = *RDGE* 31, pp. 174–82 = Malcovati 1969, 32–38, LXI. Political importance: Momigliano 1940, 79f.

73 Samos refused: *Aphrodisias* 13. Date: G. W. Bowersock *Gnomon* 56 (1984) 48–53.

74 Greek and Gaul refused citizenship: Suet. *Aug.* 40. 3.

75 Livia rebuffed by Tiberius: Suet. *Tib.* 51. 1.

76 Demand for two colleagues: Suet. *Aug.* 37.

77 Collegiality: *RG* 6. 2, with Ridley 2003, 145 noting the moderation. Third consul: Suet. *Aug.* 37.

78 Nazi emblems: V. Klemperer, *The Language of the Third Reich* (tr. M. Brady, London and New York, 2000), 63–5; I owe the topic (and the book) to the kindness of Professor G. D. Rowe.

79 Capricorn: Keppie 1984, 139 and 229. Significance: Barton 1995. Professor D. Wardle has drawn my attention to Ramsey and Licht 1997, who at 147–53 (with star-map) link the rising of Caesar's comet on 23 July, 44 BC with the simultaneous rising of Capricorn: the comet was a sign of his own birth (he had recently changed his name), and Capricorn was the 'gate of souls' through which souls entered heaven in the Milky Way.

80 'Augustan' legions: Keppie 1984, 138; 142; 158f.: the title commemorated a particular success. Spanish legion: 205.

81 Towns named after Augustus: Suet. *Aug.* 60.

82 Months: Suet. *Aug.* 31. 2; Dio 55. 6. 6; Macr, *Sat.* 1. 12. 35.

83 Republican social relations: G. Alföldy, *Roman Social Relations* (London, 1985); freedmen: S. Treggiari, *Roman Freedmen during the Late Republic* (Oxford, 1969).

84 Instructions: Ch. 7. Bosworth 1999 (on Hellenistic tales of apotheosis) and Gradel 2002, 280–82, argue that the *Achievements* provided the justification. Deification: Tac. *Ann.* 1. 10. 8. First *imperium*: Ch. 1.

85 The Senate's role under the Principate: Talbert 1984. Rich 1998, 127 displays reciprocal processes. *Lares Compitales:* Gradel 2002, 116–39; Suet. *Aug.* 31. 4 says that it was Augustus who began the custom (*instituit*) of crowning the *Lares* with flowers. Offerings to Gratidianus: Cic. *Off.* 3. 80; Pliny *NH* 33. 132; 34. 27.

86 Senatorial *maiestas: JRS* 73 (1983), 101.

87 Antony's birthday: *Fasti Ver.; Opp.,* EJ p. 45.

88 Honorific proposals under Tiberius: Tac. *Ann.* 2. 35f.; 3. 47. 3; snubbed: 6. 2f. Accession' debate: 1. 12.

89 Antistius Labeo: Suet. *Aug.* 54; Dio 54. 15. 7.

90 Veto used: Tac. *Ann.* 4. 30. 1 (AD 24).

91 New offices: Suet. *Aug.* 37.

92 Senators palmed off with status: Wallace-Hadrill 1996, 301. New posts tabulated: Talbert 1996, 338f.

93 Request for Drusus Caesar: Tac. *Ann.* 3. 56.

94 Request for Marcellus: Dio 53. 28. 3.

95 'When they have earned it': Suet. *Aug.* 56. 2; cf. Dio 54. 27. 1 (13 BC). The question is posed by Dr Herbert-Brown.

96 Marcellus' marriage: Dio 53. 27. 5.

97 Claudiae Marcellae: *PIR*[2] C 1102f.

98 Iullus Antonius: *PIR*[2] A 800.

99 Consuls of 16 BC: Crook 1996, 94.

100 Silani: Syme 1986, Table XII f.

101 Drusus Caesar: Tac. *Ann.* 2. 43. 6.

102 Census qualification and gifts: *RG* App.; Suet. 41.1; Dio 53. 2. 1; 54. 17. 3 (28 and 18 BC). Pensioners: Tac. *Ann.* 2. 37f. (Hortalus); Pliny, *NH* 18. 37. See Talbert 1984, 52f.

103 Equestrian roles in the early Principate: S. Demougin, 'L'ordre equestre sous les Julio-Claudiens,' *CÉFR* 108 (Rome, 1988); Dettenhofer 2000, 208f.

104 Scrutiny and parade: Suet. *Aug.* 38f. Eighteen centuries: P. S. Derow in *OCD*[3] 310. Voting assemblies: *RS* (*Tabula Hebana*) ll. 6–16.

105 Pilate's title: EJ 369.

106 Praefectus Vehiculorum: *CIL* 3. 4802.

107 Procurators: P. A. Brunt, 'Procuratorial Jurisdiction', *Lat.* 25 (1966) 461–87 = *Roman Imperial Themes* (Oxford, 1990) 163–87.

108 Senators' loss of credit for grain supply: Eck 1984, 154 n. 16.

109 Equestrian service preferred: e.g. Tac. *Ann.* 16. 17. 3.

110 Development of fire brigade: Dio 53. 24. 6 (Egnatius Rufus; aediles; 26 or 22 BC); 55. 8. 6f. (*magistri vici*; 7 BC), with Rich 1990 *ad loc.* Praefectus vigilum: Strabo 5. 235; Suet. *Aug.* 25. 2; 30. 1; Dio 55. 26. 4f.; 27. 1; *Dig.* 1. 15. 1–3. See Dettenhofer 2000, 193. The figure 3,500 assumes 500 men in a cohort, with R. Sablyrolles, 'Libertinus Miles: les Cohortes de Vigiles', *CÉFR* 224 (Rome, 1996), 33; it might just have been 1,000.

111 Praetorian Guard: Dio 53. 11. 5 (27 BC), with Rich 1990 *ad loc.*

112 Piso Prefect of the City: Tac. *Ann.* 6. 10. 3; predecessors: Ch. 2.

113 Grain for the people: Rickman 1980, 61–66. Agrippa aedile: Dio 49. 43. 1–5. Measures of 23 BC and 18: *RG* 5. 2; 15. 1; 18; Suet. *Aug.* 37; Dio 54. 1. 3f. (two ex-praetors to supervise distribution); 17. 1 (four ex-praetors in succession); Crisis of AD 5–7: with Herbert-Brown 1994, 223–26; war and want going together: Ovid, *Fasti* 4, 405–08; Pliny *NH* 7. 149; Suet. *Aug.* 42. 3; Dio 55. 26. 1–3; 31. 4 (consulars in charge). Ops: EJ p. 50, *Fasti Val.*; *Amit.*; *Ant.* The restoration of the temple of Ceres, Liber and Libera, destroyed in 31 BC (Dio 50. 10. 3), had been a slow business (Tac. *Ann.* 2. 49). B. Spaeth, *The Roman Goddess Ceres* (Austin, TX, 1996) 23 with fig. 9 (Vat. Inv. 715) mentions a bust of Augustus wearing the Wheat crown (*Corona spicea*) associated with the Arvals.

114 Principes Iuventutis: *RG* 14. 2, with Rowe 2002, 71.

115 *Vigiles:* Suet. *Aug.* 30. 1. Old methods tried out: Brunt and Moore 1970, on *RG* 5 1f.

116 Festivities and gifts to people: *RG* 15. 1; Dio 51. 21.1–22. 9 (29 BC, 400 *HS* each); 53. 28. 1 (24 BC; 400 *HS* each).

117 Floods: G. S. Aldrete, *Floods of the Tiber in Ancient Rome* (Baltimore, MD, 2007) 23–22 BC, drawn to my attention by Professor Wardle: Dio 53.33. 5; 54.1.1; 12: 54. 25. 2; AD 5: 55. 22. 3; 12: Dio 56. 27. 4; 15: Tac. *Ann.* 1. 76. 1–3. Date: O. F. Robinson, *Ancient Rome: City Planning and Administration* (London and New York, 1992), 87f. *Curatores* and chronological problem: Suet. *Aug.* 37. 1, with J. Carter (1982), *ad loc.*, Aldrete (2007), 198–202, and Professor Wardle's forthcoming commentary; *ILS* 5923d; 5924 (Gallus himself fixing *termini* as consul in 8 BC).

118 New age: Hor. *Carm. Saec.* 57–60; see Barker 1996 for a rebuttal of the idea that this was a 'golden' age (Ch. 6). Popular complaints: Suet. *Aug.* 42. 1; cf. 3 (abolishing corn doles altogether).

119 Saturnalia extended: Macr. *Sat.* 1. 10. 23.

120 Augustus' rebuke: Suet. *Aug.* 42. 1; Dio 54. 11. 7 misses the point.

121 *Dominus*: Suet. *Aug.* 53. 1; Domitian's demand to be addressed by this title caused offence: Suet. *Dom.* 13. 2.

122 Agrippa as *popularis*: Roddaz 1980. His building programme and the *Apoxyomenos* anecdote: Zanker 1988, 139–43; Agrippa's pronouncement: Pliny *NH* 35. 26; Tiberius' mistake: 34. 62. Cicero on luxury: *Mur.* 76.

123 Tusk: Paus. 8. 46. 1 and 5 (for this story see M. Beagon in Bispham 2007, 37).

124 Astrology exploited: Herbert-Brown 2002, 113–21, also noting the horoscope, published in AD 11 (Dio 56. 25. 5), and the Pantheon.

125 Scheming for positions: Crook 1996, 88.

126 *Vici* and *regiones*: Suet. *Aug.* 30. 1; 31. 4; Pliny *NH* 3. 66: Dio 55. 8. 6f., with Rich 1990 *ad loc. Lares Compitales*: Galinsky 1996, 300–309; Lott 2004; Rea 2007, 72–76. Temple rebuilt: *RG* 19.2. *Lares Augusti*: *CIL*² 753. Cult and implications of 'genius': Gradel 2002, 7f.; 36–44 ('life force'); 116–28. Genius: Ovid, *Fasti* 5, 143–6. See also Zanker 1988, 129–35; Lacey 1996, 182–86.

127 Tips to children: Suet. *Aug.* 46. Augustan reforms and bureaucratisation: Lott 2004, 81–127.

128 Abolition of *collegia*: Suet. *Aug.* 32. 1.

129 *Lex Iunia*; *Aelia Sentia*; *Fufia Caninia*: *LPPR* 463 (Tiberian), 454f., 455f., respectively. Survey of terms: Southern 1998, 151.

130 Augustales: Ostrow 1990.

131 Triumviral omens: Appian *BC* 4. 1. Flood: Dio 53. 20. 1.

132 Benefactions to *plebs* and soldiery: *RG* 3. 3; 15–18; *App.* 1. Purchase of land: 16. 1. Dio 53. 28. 1 (24 BC) with Rich 1990 *ad loc.*; Van Berchem 1939, 122–24; 142–44.

133 Shows and Secular Games: *RG* 22f.; *App.* 4. See Brunt and Moore 1970, 64; they find the games attested on seven occasions between 28 BC and AD 6, and note Augustus' enthusiasm for them (Suet. *Aug.* 45). See also Favro 1996, 114f. Salutation: Tac. *Dial.* 13. See also *RG* 22f; Vell. Pat. 2. 100. 2, with Zanker 1988, 147–53.

134 Subvention of Aerarium: *RG* 17. 1. Remission of gifts from Italy: 21. 3, with Brunt and Moore 1970, 63; Dio 51. 24. 1.

135 Census results: *RG* 8. 2–4; interpretation: Brunt and Moore *ad loc.*, with reference to Brunt 1971; Canali 1973, 167 n. 45; Kienast 1982, 70. Concern: Virg. *Georg.* 1. 505–08.

136 Pliny's list (*NH* 3. 46): Bispham 2007, 62f.

137 Vote on officers: Suet. *Aug.* 46. 1.

138 Ovid as potential senator: *Tr.* 4. 10. 28f. First Paelignian senator: *ILS* 932. Claudius' speech: Smallwood *Docs. Gaius-Nero* 369, col. 2, ll. 1–5.

139 Ovid's celebration of *feriae*: *Fasti* 1, 13f.

140 Benefactions and cult: Nic. Dam. 1; Philo, *Leg.* 149–51, cited by Zanker 1988, 297. He also notes (307f., fig. 240), the cornucopiae flanking his portrait on a

posthumous altar of Praeneste. Temples in Asia Minor: Dio 51. 20. 7. The distinction between Roman citizens and aliens could not survive: in the oath taken at Gangra (Çankiri), Paphlagonia, in 3 BC (EJ 315) all took part, swearing by Olympian deities and Augustus himself.

141 Rome: Strabo 5. 235. Suet. *Aug.* 28. 3; Dio 56. 30. 3.

142 *Feriae*: see Herbert-Brown 1994, 24f. 'Augustus': Ch. 2. Birthday feasts: Dio 54. 30. 5.

143 Festivals: Beard 1987.

144 Religion in the Augustan Age: Galinsky 1996, 288–331.

145 Romans and gods: e.g., Hor. *Odes* 1. 2f.; 14; 35.

146 *Augurium salutis*: Cic. *Div.* 1. 105; *ILS* 9337; Suet. *Aug.* 31. 4; Dio 37. 24. 1f.; 51. 20. 5.

147 Temple of Janus: *RG* 13; Dio 51. 20. 4. Suet. *Aug.* 22. 1 records three closures. A second closure was ordered in 25: Dio 56. 23. 5; Oros. 6. 20–22. See Syme 1979 and 1989, 450.

148 Restoration of temples: Hor. *Odes* 3. 6. 1–8; *RG* 20. 4; Livy 4. 20. 7; Suet. *Aug.* 30. 2; Dio 53. 2. 4f. Zanker 1988, 108f. Beginning: Ridley 2003, 182f.

149 Employment: P. A. Brunt, *JRS* 70 (1980), 81–100.

150 Dedications to Apollo: *RG* 24. 2; Pliny, *NH* 36. 34f.; Suet. *Aug.* 52, with Galinsky 1996, 297–99; Dio 53. 22. 3, with Rich 1990 *ad loc.* suggesting that the silver contributed to issues made in Italy down to 26 BC.

151 Arvals: Galinsky 1996, 292f., noting that the priests were *brothers*. Membership: J. Scheid, *Les Frères Arvales: Recrutement et Origine sociale sous les Empereurs Julio-Claudiens* (Paris, 1975), 13–108.

152 A grateful *Fetialis* may be postulated in e.g., EJ 197.

153 Rescheduling of anniversaries: Herz 1978, 1147–51 (January 1; August 1, 13; September 1, 23).

154 Appointment of priests, including supernumerary: Dio 51. 20. 3 (29 or 28 BC).

155 *Flamen Dialis*: Tac. *Ann.* 3. 58. 2–59. 1; 71. 2; Dio 54. 36. 1. Bowersock 1990, 391–3 (cf. Rüpke and Glock 2005, 916), arguing against Dio that the post was filled in 14; if the frieze of the *Ara Pacis* represents an event before Lepidus' death he has been airbrushd out of it. (I owe this observation to the kindness of Professor Wardle).

156 Caesar's comet and the *saeculum*: Augustus *ap.* Serv. *Ecl.* 9. 46. C. and L. Caesars: I owe this point to Dr Herbert-Brown.

157 Games due in 39 BC, contemplated for 23: Virg. *Aen.* 6, 61–70; 791–94; Syme 1939, 218 n. 2; 339. Price 1996, 837 argues that the 'puzzling' choice of 17 BC was due to disagreement over the date of the foundation of Rome. See T. Cornell *et al.*, eds in *FRH* (Oxford, forthcoming), no. 75: *Ti. Claudius Augustus. Saeculum* of 110 years: Zosimus 2. 4, with Taylor 1934, 105f., noting the useful contribution of the loyalist Ateius Capito.

158 17 as turning point: Dettenhofer 2000, 18.

159 Documenting games: Schnegg-Kohler 2002; EJ 30–33; instructions: Malcovati 1969, 44f., LXXI; Zanker 1988, 167–72; Price 1996, 834–37.
160 Lavish entertainments: Suet. *Aug.* 43. 1–4.
161 Hereditary right to be Pontifex Maximus: Ch, 2, with Simpson 2007, connecting the date of Augustus' and Tiberius' assumption of the post with the date of the assassination of Julius Caesar. Implications of post: Eck 2007, 74 and 139f.; development of it: Herbert-Brown 1994, 63–73; 80; 99. Augustus' house: Dio 49. 15. 5f.; gifts of building or site: Asc. on Cic. *In Pis.* 12f. (Clark), with Weinstock 1971, 276–81. Decoration: Galinsky 1996, 187–97. Public and private on the Palatine: Suet. *Aug.* 57. 2; Dio 54. 27.3 (13 BC); 55. 12. 5 (AD 3). Statue and altar of Vesta: Ovid, *Fasti* 4, 949–54; *Met.* 15. 864; Gradel 2002, 115f., denies that the presence of Vesta and Apollo made Augustus' household cult public; Augustus became Vesta's priest, like Julius Caesar, whom he avenged (Ovid, *Fasti* 3, 699f; 5. 573–78), and so the protector under her of the Roman People's hearth and home; Aeneas had brought her from Troy, establishing the link. See also Dettenhofer 2000, 161.
162 Varian defeat: Suet. *Aug.* 23. 2.
163 *SCdPp* l. 13.

Chapter 4

Opposition and Discontent

Opposition?

It was once taken for granted that the development of Augustus' power met 'opposition'; indeed, the existence of a persistent body of constantly threatening opponents of one man's continued and hereditary dominance, '*the* opposition' or 'the Opposition', was taken for granted for the whole Julio-Claudian period as well. This view, partly based on the claims of Suetonius and Dio, especially on reports of conspiracies that make a standard list,[1] has lost ground. Not surprisingly: one strand in the meaning of the word, that of an organised and officially accepted body of politicians hostile to a government in power, derived from modern democratic politics, could never be expected to hold for the Principate. Nor could any scheme for reversion to the system of the second century BC, annual consuls obedient to the Senate's wishes. Augustus had too close a hold on the affections of classes below the senatorial, for one thing; and many remembered the period that followed Caesar's death. What came to be in question was not the system but the individual seen controlling it – with which imperial writers were concerned.[2]

As the word has lost credit, an effort has been made to present Augustus' supremacy itself in less dramatic terms. In particular, his changes of constitutional position have been seen not as the reaction to efforts of opponents to shake or unseat him but as the product of mundane factors, including ill health, or even as planned events (Ch. 2).[3] Seven years after Actium, it has been said, there were signs of stability, and Augustus was able to step down from the consulship.[4] How far Augustus was in control of events is important. If he was not, it will involve accepting the unpalatable view that 'he founded the Principate by lurching from crisis to crisis, with the main decisions merely *ad hoc* responses to emergencies'.[5] It is entertaining, then, to notice the melodramatic performance that took place in the Senate House already in 27, when a tribune of the people vowed loyalty to the death to the Princeps, in the Spanish manner. What need of such a show if the House was not torn with hostile factions, with violence in the air?[6] Reviewing recent interpretations of the Augustan Principate tempts one to believe that the Princeps is still exercising his influence in an age when current politicians have lost most of theirs.

The idea of 'opposition' has met with a much more radical scepticism, that of D. C. Feeney, who notes how Augustus changed from one time to another and even could present himself simultaneously and contradictorily as a champion of war and peace, magnificence and frugality. Ideology is misguidedly reified, and, like the very figure of Augustus himself, dissolves on inspection.[7] This is a serious criticism, but there was still one kernel in the Augustan Principate that did not change: that was Augustus' determination to be master of the Roman world, whether or not he was concealing that aim, and that determination was always there to arouse hostility, even to stimulate assassins, as Caesar found.

The most comprehensive essay on the capacious notion of an 'opposition' to Augustus, that of K. A. Raaflaub and L. J. Samons II,[8] divides the material on 'opposition' into political and intellectual, goes through cases one by one, and comes to balanced conclusions: there was a small amount of opposition, of low intensity, and only one organised conspiracy against Augustus, that of Fannius Caepio and Murena in the late 20s. The others they dismiss, and their interpretations may be considered as we come to each. As they concede, in the latter part of Augustus' Principate there was intrigue in plenty, but then we are dealing not with conspiracy against Augustus himself but with infighting between rival members of his family and their supporters. Altogether, it is claimed, there is nothing in the reign of Augustus to compare with the 'conspiracies' alleged and brutally repressed by any one of his Julio-Claudian successors. On the contrary, Augustus was met with resentment intermittently but throughout, and expressed in a number of ways, from irony through open opposition in the House, anonymous pamphlets and graffiti, and popular demonstrations, to assassination attempts.

The reasons that inhibited possible 'conspirators' are listed by Raaflaub and Samons, and they are indeed thoughts that ought to have passed through the minds of critics. Though diminished in powers under Augustus (and in some ways, as in jurisdiction and legislation, its role was enhanced), the Senate acquired additional distinction, even *maiestas* (majesty) (Ch. 2). Next, Augustus solved problems that the Republic had found insoluble especially under the general headings of getting things done and putting a stop to marches on Rome. Third, discord among senators would make a united stand impracticable. Last and least, there was Augustus' winning *humanitas* (considerateness). But those reflections would be secondary for those who cared for liberty and the old Commonwealth; the prime fact for the senatorial order was that they were lost. The Senate had never put the solving of mundane problems first, not even urgent ones, such as the need to provide for protection against disorder by ensuring the security and grain supply of Rome; they were second to the immediate interest of the Senate as a whole: that is, to the curbing of ambitious individuals who would gain by solving such problems. As to *humanitas*, the good qualities of an autocrat are secondary to his main offence: Caesar's *clementia* (forbearance), made possible by his supremacy, was an insult to his peers. As time went on and the Augustan regime established itself ever more firmly, the possibility of civil war – not excluded in 23 BC when Horace published his first three books of *Odes*[9] – was extinguished. There could be no mass movement without the support of a substantial army, and, as we have seen, Augustus had firm control of that. Blind assassination, leading to the accession of a new autocrat, or the milder forms of dissidence were the alternatives. There could be no 'Antonian' party, no active 'Republicans', no programmatic 'Opposition'. It was a question of individuals reacting differently, by class, history and individual temperament, to the realities of the political world in which they found themselves.

A plethora of opinions

Moves against Augustus are not to all to be brushed out in attempts to sanitise his regime, any more than we should accept stories of conspiracy because they emanate from him or his successors; but it is worth remembering the Emperor Domitian's complaint that nobody believed in conspiracies until an emperor was assassinated.[10] Augustus himself was acutely aware of his critics and had a sense of danger: he told Tiberius in a letter that they were lucky to get away with criticism and escape physical assault; we do not know the date of it, but since Augustus alludes to Tiberius' youth, he was presumably less than forty years old, putting the letter earlier than 2 BC.[11] Conventional anecdotes about assassination attempts, serving as pegs for discourses about mercy, need not detain us. Dio uses the consulship of Cn. Cornelius Cinna Magnus in AD 5 to introduce a flimsy story of his previously planning to assassinate Augustus, and being saved by Livia's pillow talk.[12]

The response then to those who have argued for a smooth political trajectory for Augustus rather than a series of forced improvisations may lie in refining inquiries into what contemporary politicians were trying to do, instead of compelling one English word to do all the work. There is a whole spectrum of conduct, to be discussed in Roman terms. At the extreme Velleius Paterculus, dealing with notorious 'conspirators', had a word for those who were against the new dispensation, like Caepio and Murena: there is little room in Velleius' view for programmes or even principles; these are men who 'hated the present most fortunate state of affairs', a phrase which surely echoes one used by Cicero in 56 when he berated those 'who hate the Commonwealth itself and the present condition of good men' simply as 'utterly bad' (*pessimi*); those who acquiesced were *boni* ('good').[13] The Ciceronian parallel suggests that these words had political content as well as moral; and, although Caepio had always been deplorable, Murena, according to Velleius, underwent a change for the worse. If their own story had survived, the conspirators might have been heard appealing for 'freedom' (*libertas*). But the accepted extremists may be approached after men who looked to change Augustus' course without drastic action.

Constitutional methods

Regular constitutional means could hardly swing issues, such as grants of *imperium* and tribunician power to Augustus and his heirs, which were vital for the preservation of the regime. Augustus had enough of a following in the Senate, to get it to vote for what he wanted. His periods of power could not be brought to an end. If persuasion failed he had demonstrated in 43 and 32 what force could do. All the same, the advancement of Augustus'

nephew Marcellus in 24–23 BC, approved by the Senate, most likely without a formal vote, gave rise to signs of resentment. Paradoxically, Augustus'
authority was only reinforced by the chaos of 23–19, when the Senate's efforts to govern were defeated; 19 is a good place for the definitive 'start' of
the Principate, when relations settled into a stable pattern.[14]

The 'resistance' of the Senate as a whole has not been found to amount
to much, though Augustus was subject to oral interruption and dissent, like
a schoolmaster with an unruly class whose numbers gave it some protection:
'I couldn't understand!' Or 'I'd speak against you, if I had the chance!' Or,
as Augustus left the House in anger, 'It's only right for senators to be allowed to speak their mind on politics!'[15] In the preceding chapter, individuals figured who helped the Princeps by promoting or supporting his
proposals and points of view in the Senate. Others did their best to embar-
rass him and sometimes are expressly said to have succeeded. It was most
prudent to play this as a team game. In 18 BC, according to Dio, senators
denounced (women's) immorality as a reason for slowness in the marriage
market, and urged Augustus to put an end to it, inescapably calling to mind
his own promiscuity (though his name was particularly linked with that of
one particular woman, Terentia, Maecenas' wife). At first he denied that
legal regulation would be useful, then he told his peers to admonish their
wives as he did. That only gave his tormentors more leverage: they wanted
to know precisely what he said to Livia, and he came out with bland remarks
about clothing, jewellery and grooming, about going out and decorum,
without any regard, as Dio reports from a hostile source, for the fact that
they had no relation at all to the reality of Livia's way of life.[16] Cornered,
Augustus bluffed his way out. Some bold individuals too, if harassed, were
ready with tart responses to Augustus. When the Senate censured Cornelius
Sisenna for his wife's unseemly behaviour, his defence was that he had married her on Augustus' advice. Augustus was so put out that he rushed out of
the Senate – a technique he used when in 12 the Senate pressed unwanted
honours on him in addition to the supreme pontificate.[17] Even in much
later reigns a determined senator, exceptionally engaged in a serious issue
such as the imperial succession, could make himself felt. A story from the
reign of Vespasian has him too leaving the House after an altercation on that
subject.[18]

All the same, any serious dispute involving the interests of the whole
Senate that emerged from time to time must be given its proper weight.

The purges of 29 and 18 BC caused resentment among those excluded, though there is no trace in the sources of any joint political aim; Augustus himself in 18 had to finish work on vetting its membership that the Senate had begun. Avoiding exceptional offices himself, Augustus soon set up posts that violated the regular senatorial *cursus*, most obviously the Prefecture of the City that M. Messala Corvinus quickly resigned in 26 or 25. Corvinus described it as inappropriate for the Commonwealth, but there will have been others ready to put that idea into his head. Senatorial resistance and pressure from grandees and envious peers may have been at the back of his resignation. In spite of this, Augustus tried the experiment again, appointing a close friend, T. Statilius Taurus, to the charge of Rome and Italy when he left in 16. Another appointment that went wrong was that of the censors of 22. Again, senatorial hostility may have been involved. The office was traditional enough, though often controversial, but L. Munatius Plancus had enemies, and they would have resented the control over membership of the Senate that the office conferred. It was never held again by a pair of private individuals, and not by an emperor until Claudius took it in 47 (Ch. 2).[19]

Then there was obvious distaste for the social legislation (Ch. 3), perhaps mooted and successfully resisted in 28 BC, imposed in 18. In AD 9 the *Lex Julia* imposing penalties on celibacy and childlessness was modified by a consular law, the *Lex Papia Poppaea*, whether to clarify, sharpen or soften it in response to the protests. Perhaps this was the occasion when Augustus told a restive audience to listen to him, old as he was: it was sinister for him to point out in that connexion that as a young man he had been heard by his elders. While the Senate had its proper House for debate, the knights had nothing of the sort. Members of the equestrian order, using a lower-class model, organised a demonstration in its seats at the games. The aged Augustus' response was a harangue in the Forum against childlessness. Protests continued into the principate of Tiberius, who in AD 20 set up a fifteen-man commission of senators to sort out anomalies and injustices caused by attempts to evade the legislation and by the denunciation of offenders.[20]

Dio offers an elaborate account of the trouble that the Senate caused Augustus when he introduced the Military Treasury – and the taxes it would require. For the problem of providing bounties to discharged soldiers he proposed, during the years 5–7, to set up a new treasury, for that sole purpose, and it was to be funded, after an initial endowment of *HS* 170 million from Augustus (using property of his adopted sons Tiberius and Agrippa Postumus), by new taxes, first a 1 per cent sales tax on items sold in Rome and even more offensively a 5 per cent tax on inheritances when the beneficiaries were not close relatives. It had been unheard of for more than a century and a half that tax should be paid on Italian property. The Senate, feeling its own pockets affected, jibbed for once. Augustus invited written alternative proposals, but accepted none and told his peers that the scheme did have a precedent. Not for the first time, he was able to produce documentary evidence, a memorandum of Julius Caesar's. At the mention of Caesar and his schemes, the Senate's resistance collapsed, but the tax remained unpopular. It survived further protests in AD 13 – Augustus could not give way, faced with the demands from the troops – and it continued to be tinkered with for the next century.[21] Infringements of individual freedom through the social legislation and threats to their purses gave the upper classes courage, but not enough for the Senate to reject these unwelcome proposals outright.

Refuseniks

The opposite of confrontation was turning away altogether. Some senators or potential senators voted with their feet by declining to take part in public life or refusing office, with or without making a plea of poverty: Cn. Piso was the best known. Significantly in 23 BC we find him and another convinced Republican, L. Sestius, who had portraits of Brutus in his house, in consulships, Piso as Augustus' colleague, Sestius as his successor (Ch. 2). It was an extraordinary *volte face* on Piso's part, hardly to be explained unless he was taken in at last by protestations on the part of Augustus, who is said actually to have canvassed Piso to stand. A more plausible explanation, given the notorious toughness of this Piso and his son, is that they thought that Augustus' position had been so weakened that they might achieve something for the Commonwealth.[22] They accepted the challenge – and played into his hands.

Even undistinguished senators could make themselves felt by staying away from the House, especially if enough were involved. Absenteeism is noticed in 17 and 9 BC, and Augustus tried to deal with it by fining defaulters increasingly heavily. In 11 BC, according to Dio, he had to compromise by ordaining that its decrees should now be valid even if fewer than four hundred were present out of the notional six hundred enrolled in 19.[23] Two years later a complex measure on meetings of the Senate, the *Lex Julia de senatu habendo*, Augustus' own work, passed into law. He introduced requirements for Senate sittings on fixed dates, with members excused (virtually banned) from paying him their morning respects on those days. The fact that senators considered themselves obliged to perform this ceremony at all shows how far they had sunk from being peers of the Princeps. The new regulations were put up on whiteboards in the House and the six hundred odd senators sent through two by two to peruse them. Ignorance was to be no excuse.[24] Augustus knew how to wear down his colleagues with boredom, as he showed in the discussions on the social legislation, when he read them Metellus Macedonicus' speech 'On increasing the birth rate' (Ch. 3).

In the decade after 19 Dio records problems with filling the lower offices. To start with the lowest, pre-senatorial post, young men who should have embarked on the senatorial career were declaring themselves ineligible, and the Senate itself ordered that posts in those preliminary magistracies (the *Vigintivirate*, reduced to twenty men from the previous *Vigintisexvirate*) should be appointed from the knights. This was a bold gesture, taken in the absence of the Princeps, and the Senate followed it up with another: a shortage of candidates for the tribunate of the *plebs* induced them to force ex-quaestors of less than forty years of age to draw lots for the vacancies. They were looking to the prestige of the House – but tacitly bringing it home that service in the Augustan Principate could seem unrewarding.The quaestorship, tribunate and aedileship were especially unpopular: there had already been a shortage of quaestors to serve in the provinces in 24 BC, and the tribunate had become virtually redundant when Augustus took tribunician power. In 8 BC, Augustus himself had to open it to knights, allowing them to retire after their year of office or to stay on as senators. This revived an old route to senatorial status, though Sulla's specification of the quaestorship as the regular qualifying position had long been established.[25]

The shortage can be explained by appealing to poverty or a fall in the numbers of well-born young men available due to losses during the Civil Wars. Augustus imposed a senatorial property qualification for the first time, originally *HS* 400,000, which was less than the property qualification of knights under the Republic (*HS* 500,000), but reached a million *HS* in 13 BC.[26] Nonetheless, the timing of the problems, the decade after Augustus' political triumph in 19, suggests that political factors were involved as well.[27]

Augustus' own reaction to the shortage of junior senators on his return to Rome in 13 was severe: he examined qualified young men under thirty-five years of age, presumably the sons of senators, and took affidavits as to their property. All those – presumably ex-quaestors – not physically or financially disqualified he forced to take their seats, and in 11 BC another formal revision of the list of senators was undertaken. The focus of attention was on the young. That suggests that they were at the heart of the political strike.[28] Men who had already held the quaestorship might be willing to go forward and invest still further effort and money in winning the prestigious praetorship and its *imperium*, or they might be content with their senatorial status, but it was uninviting to have to embark on three unrewarding offices before the chance of the praetorship arose.

This was not the end of unrest among the upper class, or of Augustus' fears. Under 8 BC, Dio records Augustus' discontent with the power that the law allowed him to deal with 'treason' – attacks on himself and the magistrates. It was forbidden to extract information from an accused person's slaves or freedmen by torturing them. This ban was bypassed, to some disapproval, by providing for the slaves' sale to the State 'when necessary'; later it was also to be set aside in a trial for adultery, as we shall see. As M. Dettenhofer points out, as Triumvir, Augustus had already undermined the loyalty of slaves to their masters by offering rewards and freedom to those who betrayed anyone proscribed.[29]

It was the nobility who were unwilling to serve under the new regime: there would be plenty of new men from the country towns of Italy who would count themselves lucky to enter the Senate at all. Celebrating the Secular Games was a triumphalist act, a declaration of success, and so in itself a provocation to dissent. Augustus encouraged the nobility with the carrot of the consulship as well as forcing it into service: no 'new' men reached the office between 19 and 4 BC. Another mitigation was the retirement age introduced in 9 BC. Presumably he learned from the boycott. An accommodation was reached after the shocks that Augustus delivered in 23 and 19 and in the decade that followed. From 9 BC he had trouble from his family to preoccupy him, and that went on to the end of his life.[30]

Tittle-tattle

Refined as the analysis of Raaflaub and Samons is, more allowance could be made for fluctuations of opinion under pressure of internal and external events, for the shock of the new, for tedium as the novelty wore off, or for the re-emergence of buried resentments. Organised conspiracies rarely came to fruition, but they were sensational when they did, or were alleged. We also hear of pamphlets and graffiti, the oral tactics of undermining and in particular of irony employed in Senate and courts. What does not emerge as part of distinct and traceable events is the unremitting subversive dinner-party talk, gossip, ridicule and minor disobedience. It came to the surface at times of crisis. Some of this will have been blatant, intended to reach the ears of the Princeps, even calculated to influence him. We have seen that Augustus was aware of some of it at least, and mentioned it to Tiberius. Tacitus more than once makes a point of telling his reader that even the reclusive Tiberius was also abreast of what was being said and done. His friends and confidential servants will have given him what they knew; it is likely that there were also professional spies and informers, paid piecemeal or on a retainer.[31] All this was risky to the participants in dissent. In a society that is under surveillance or, at a later stage, no longer free to speak openly, it was (and remains) unclear where mocking or dissenting talk, or even thought, ends and subversion begins. The distinction is not made objectively on a graph, but depends subjectively on the ruler's sense of security. Attempts to discomfit or shame a ruler in possession of autocratic power could be taken as 'disloyalty' and under Augustus' successors often were. Even in-fighting between factions might be represented by the winning side as a failed assault by the defeated on the Princeps himself.[32]

Conspiracy

Conspiracies against Augustus, the main basis of the idea of the Augustan Principate as controversial and hazardous, have very largely been scouted, with the exception of that of Caepio and Murena. It will be convenient to take them in chronological order.

The defeat of Antony and Cleopatra meant the end of civil war. Resentments still smouldered on, as did fears on the part of the victors: Dio speaks of them under the year 29.[33] That Octavian's claim to have burnt Antony's papers was disingenuous did not matter: the claim constituted a reassuring promise. The previous year Lepidus, son of the Triumvir, was alleged to have plotted a coup at Rome. It was detected by Maecenas, Octavian's chargé d'affaires. Lepidus was brought before the Senate, sent to Actium and executed. This was handled as matter of urgency, like the case of

Salvidienus Rufus ten years previously (see Ch. 1): the accused was treated as the Catilinarian conspirators were in 63 instead of being tried in a regular court. What form this emergency could have taken in the absence of Octavian is uncertain. A civil coup in the City at that point, possibly in favour of the deposed and discredited Triumvir, now relegated to Circeii, would have been futile and crushable as soon as the victor returned at the head of legions. To hazard a guess, we may be at most dealing with virulent dinnerparty talk, the notion of an assassination when Octavian was back in Rome, as Velleius suggests. In that case, the evidence may have been thin, fierce talk, daggers pawed over dessert and the whole scene reported by a faithless slave. That thinness does not matter any more than it did in later years of tension under Tiberius and his successors.[34] At any rate, as Raaflaub and Samons note, this was an isolated act, the plan of a man who might well have thought that under the new dispensation he would never reach the heights that his ancestry and Republican and Antonian connexions earned him. It seems unlikely that Maecenas alone simply framed him, causing unnecessary perturbation amongst other members of the nobility. Either there was something in the 'plot' or Octavian blatantly caused Maecenas to rid him of an inconvenient young aristocrat, a redundant pawn or hostage, as R. Syme baldly called him. This was the year in which the sons of Cleopatra by Caesar and M. Antony were put to death.

No conspiracy at all can be alleged against Cornelius Gallus, the celebrated poet and the commander who distinguished himself in Octavian's invasion of Egypt and became its first Prefect. Gallus was driven to suicide in 27 or 26. In a province where senators who outranked him and even other knights were not allowed to set foot without the Princeps' permission he had merely made too much of his successes in the south, testing the limits of a governor's power beyond what was now acceptable. That offence is provable from the inscription he set up. His subjects too lacked the sense of hierarchy that placed their direct ruler so far below the Princeps: they put up statues to him. Perhaps too he had been guilty of extortion; Roman treatment of Egypt, ex-enemy, source of grain and gold, continued to be reprehensible, despite governors who promised reform. Augustus banned Gallus from his house and the provinces he governed; the Senate, probably with some pleasure, for, as W. Schmitthenner notes, all this took place in the absence of Augustus and enemies had some play against one another, took cognisance of Gallus' behaviour too, and apparently decreed that it should be dealt with in the courts (only senatorial governors had been liable to charges of extortion). That decree was necessary, for men of equestrian rank had frustrated prosecution under the extortion law. With that in mind, the Senate was probably chary of taking the case entirely on its own in the absence of the Princeps. When Gallus died, Augustus lamented that he alone was not free to choose and reject his own friends.[35] The hounding of Gallus left a bad taste in the mouths of some members of the upper class: C. Proculeius was also an equestrian friend of Augustus, of sufficient standing later to be considered as a bridegroom for his daughter; he made clear his disgust at what had happened. Whenever the accuser Valerius Largus came into his presence he would hold his nose and mouth.[36] It looks as if Augustus felt that he had to say something about his treatment of Gallus in his *Autobiography*: it was one of his chief complaints that Gallus had taken in a freedman tutor of Pomponius Atticus who had been suspected of tampering with his pupil, Atticus' daughter; and she was married to Agrippa.[37]

A counterpoint to this story of Gallus and his protégé is the anecdote told of Augustus' restraint towards Timagenes, a Greek historian, but one who involved himself in Roman politics.[38] Timagenes was a constant critic of the Princeps, Livia and the whole imperial family. He evidently flourished on the notoriety and, after being denied Augustus' house, went to live with C. Asinius Pollio. All Augustus did was to tell Pollio that he was keeping a zoo. The Princeps realised that taking out small fry such as Timagenes would only make him look vengeful; Pollio himself was too big to touch. Perhaps Augustus had learnt from the repercussions of the Gallus affair. Augustus did not allow himself to be drawn into the trap laid by Pollio, who challenged the Princeps to order him to have Timagenes ejected. Augustus' reported reply was a question: 'Do you expect that kind of order from me?'

It is a relief to come to the one conspiracy that is both labelled as such and plausibly attested and is acknowledged by Raaflaub and Samons, however problematical its details (see Ch. 2, Appendix). Paradoxically, however, this most fully documented conspiracy of the regime is best interpreted as the work of the Princeps himself. When 'Marcus Primus', who had come back from his governorship of Macedonia, was accused of diminishing the majesty of the Roman People (*maiestas*) by attacking the Odrysae, a contributory root of the imminent crisis may have been rivalry between Augustus and Crassus for the patronage of powerful Balkan tribes, going back to

Crassus' own command in Macedonia and the success for which Augustus had denied him the *spolia opima*, and even to the campaign of Augustus' father. There was a social aspect to the trial of 'Primus': Augustus was occupying a pre-eminent position in the system of patronage that guaranteed the security of subjects and little men in the Roman Empire and added to the grandeur of the great. The tribe that 'Primus' was accused of attacking was part of the Bessi, previously defeated by M. Crassus. He had brought the Odrysae under his protection in the course of his campaigns, which had not been sufficiently rewarded by a mere triumph and the grant of the title 'Imperator' (Ch. 2). Henceforward it would be his duty to protect them. It may be that this was exactly what he was doing in the trial. There is no concrete evidence that Crassus was behind the prosecution of 'Primus': only this association and a suspicion rebutted by some scholars.[39] Augustus' 'friend', for that was what Dio implies 'Primus' was, attacked the tribe. Crassus had a strong motive for reasserting his patronage and discrediting the friend. We do not know the name of the prosecutor; it was probably a young man. Winning spurs by tackling seniors was traditionally permissible, but it was courageous to challenge a man who claimed to have been acting under Augustus' orders.

Augustus came of his own accord into the court, in spite of a challenge from 'Primus'' counsel: 'What brings you here?' 'The public good' (*to demosion*), was the reply, and the humiliation of counsel will have given Augustus a bitter enemy. Equally, Augustus had a motive for silencing an eloquent and courageous opponent. 'Primus'' counsel unforgivably exposed Augustus to political attack by denying him formal access to a court in which he could, truthfully or not, flatly have denied infringing *maiestas*, and he had also betrayed the existing good relationship between himself and the Princeps.

After that, according to Dio, Fannius Caepio and 'Primus'' counsel (but even Dio is not sure of his guilt) conspired against Augustus (Ch. 2, with Appendix). Their death in flight is attested by a later item in Dio's narrative, which has Caepio's father parading and executing a slave who had betrayed his master, while he freed another who stood up for him when the soldiers came. A fourth-century source, Macrobius, has a persuasive account, which has Caepio killed at Naples after conviction (Murena was taken along with the philosopher Athenaeus, brought back to Rome and executed). The trial had gone on in their absence, with the heavyweight job of prosecuting

Caepio assigned to Augustus' stepson Tiberius, who was young and ambitious and, as the son of a former adherent of Antony who had fought on the wrong side in the Perusine war, a coming politician who needed to be confirmed as a loyalist. According to Dio the guilty verdict was brought in because the court believed that the accused would be allowed to go into exile (*eremen men hos kai feuxomenoi helosan*), *but* not long afterwards they were killed; jurors who went so far as to vote for acquittal did not believe that there had been a conspiracy at all.[40] Dio is using at least one source that is highly favourable to Augustus; he has to acknowledge that 'he would have allayed the blame of all who were discontented with what had been done if he had not allowed victory celebrations for it'.[41]

Again, the two men fled because they were tipped off about Augustus' plans for dealing with them (before any charges were brought, then, or when Augustus let slip that he did not mean to let them live) and the information allegedly came from Maecenas through his wife Terentia, the sister of Murena (and allegedly the mistress of Augustus). It was claimed too that this episode led to a cooling off of relations between Augustus and Maecenas. Hence, perhaps, the story of Augustus' complaint that Maecenas talked too much. That cooling has convincingly been denied in modern times; it does not discredit the rest of the story.[42] Strangely, another one of the defendants did not long survive the trial. Athenaeus of Seleucia (Silifke) in Cilicia compared his accusation and pardon on the charge of involvement in Murena's conspiracy with death and rebirth – an unfortunate comparison. He was killed in an accident at Seleucia when his house collapsed after his return home.

Another man did better out of the alleged conspiracy. Augustus showed his gratitude for the evidence that was supplied against the perpetrators. The chief informant was a person called Castricius. Later Augustus saved him from a conviction by appealing to his prosecutor in court, Suetonius reveals.[43]

Fannius Caepio, as we have seen, was already 'utterly bad' and his name suggests that from Augustus' point of view this is right: he had Republicanism in his bones. Caepio was a *cognomen* of the Servilii and so was used by Brutus, the assassin of Caesar. Fannii may be found amongst stout defenders of the Republic through the last century of its life, beginning with the consul of 122 BC, the C. Fannius who had opposed Gaius Gracchus' plans to enfranchise the Italians.[44] The last of them was a praetor of 55 or 50 BC who served under Sex. Pompeius. But Murena the conspirator should have been the half-brother of the C. Proculeius who been holding his nose in the presence of Valerius Largus, if both had Terentia as a sister. A series of events that had begun as a moderate attempt to curb Augustus' increasing high-handedness, though perhaps it was motivated by personal rancour, ended by splintering the core of Augustus' supporters.

In the disorder that followed Augustus' renunciation of the consulship, and in his absence overseas, there were opportunities for men to make their way by unorthodox methods: the Senate was not in control. Egnatius Rufus, the ambitious creator of a fire-brigade who stood for the consulship out of turn in 19, was trying to take advantage of his own popularity in the absence of Augustus. The story in Velleius Paterculus is that it was when he ran out of money that he began plotting against Augustus; but the same difficulty arises as in the case of young Lepidus: how, in the absence of the intended victim? Perhaps this was becoming a standard charge in troubled times, and unlikely to be questioned. He was forbidden to stand by the one consul in office, C. Sentius Saturninus, subsequently brought before the Senate, and taken to the Tullianum for execution. If this was also Saturninus' work he was modelling himself on the consul Cicero and his treatment of the 'Catilinarian conspirators' of 63. At any rate, Saturninus' hardihood is highly commended by Velleius Paterculus. It looks as if Egnatius had lost his head and mistaken his chances of holding office irregularly in the absence of the Princeps; he may even have calculated that an addition to the Senate's discomfiture would not displease him.[45]

The period after Augustus' political triumph of 19 has Dio convincingly reporting conspiracies against both him and Agrippa. They were both in Rome from 19 until the celebration of the Secular Games of 17, and enhancing their powers (Ch. 2). Raaflaub and Samons are unwilling to accept Dio's testimony, but have little to say against it, except that no details are provided.[46] It may be that no prosecutions were actually brought, when Augustus had fared so badly in the courts; rather, rumours of conspiracy could have flown round at a time of natural resentment and agitation after the events of 23–18; all the same, Dio does report actual executions. The victims might not have been men of distinction, even if they were even senators.

During a scrutiny of the Senate's membership, whether in 29 or in 18, Augustus allegedly presided with the protection of a breastplate under his garments and a sword at his side, with ten of the sturdiest members of the senatorial order who were friends of his surrounding his chair of state. The contemporary historian A. Cremutius Cordus wrote that none of the senators was even allowed near the Princeps unless he were on his own and had the folds of his clothing searched. Cicero sported a breastplate when he was consul, but he was intent on proving the existence of a conspiracy led by Catiline – which he had detected and deterred. Augustus had no such specific motive; either he was genuinely trying to protect himself or he was vaunting his courage in undertaking the work at all.[47]

Weariness: the 'second term'

Dio tells us that Augustus went abroad in 16 BC to avoid criticism. We can hardly rely on his or his source's knowledge of Augustus' motives, but we can be sure that the Princeps was unpopular enough by then to make the guess plausible. In particular, Dio points out that Augustus had been in Rome for a long period – three years![48] The same factor has affected modern politicians, however adroit. Even party members in late twentieth and early twenty-first century Britain have become used to tiring of leaders that have been a decade or more in office ('ten years is enough for anyone' became the accepted view);[49] Romans had been conditioned to the annual magistracy. Caesar's supremacy had lasted five years. Mistakes and mishaps (interpreted as mistakes) aggravate an underlying boredom. Even in the flux of fifth-century BC Athenian politics, a man allegedly voted for the ostracism of Aristides because he was tired of hearing him called 'the just'. The fates of Margaret Thatcher and Tony Blair awake respect for the US presidency, tenable for no more than eight years.[50] By 16 Augustus was well into a 'second term', the Principate was set, and subjects knew what to expect.

Agrippa as Augustus' colleague

It is significant that Dio mentions Agrippa as one target of the alleged conspirators. He seems to have been a focus of resentment, not only in himself but as the unworthy means of ensuring that power continued within the family of Augustus. The Princeps' friend, son-in-law since 21, now since 18 his colleague in the tribunician power and a holder of *imperium*, whether independent or delegated between 23 and 19, then certainly independent since 18 and enhanced again in 13, Agrippa would be left supreme by default if Augustus died; that had been the case, *de facto* at least, since he left for the East in 23 BC. Besides, his marriage to Augustus' only child Julia had made him the father of two sons, who in 17 were both adopted by Augustus as Gaius and Lucius (Julii) Caesares. Nor is it surprising if dislike focused on him for personal reasons for his ostentatious populism. In 33 BC (Ch. 3), managing the City of Rome in a way that left successors little hope of shining, and advocating the nationalisation of works of art in private hands. In fact, Pliny describes Agrippa as in the highest sense a 'friend of the people'; but the word *popularis* has unpleasant connotations and needed excuse. This was the man who had refused the triumphs that the Senate would have allowed him, making it difficult for other men to apply (Ch. 2). In the event it was Agrippa who died before Augustus, in 12 BC, just after his power had been renewed and enhanced to near-equality with that of the Princeps. According to Dio, after he died the nobility were encouraged by Augustus to attend the games that began on 4 April and ended a month later, the *Megalensian, Cereales* and *Florales*, in spite of their reluctance. How he knew that they were reluctant is a question; nothing is specifically said of cancellation mooted in the Senate, or a plan to give up such trivial amusements in their grief at his loss. This initiative may have come from Augustus, anticipating and so concealing upper-class reluctance to make voluntary demonstrations of grief.[51]

The struggle for the succession

Agrippa and his marriage take us to a new phase of discontent. Struggles for Republican privileges and freedoms – a possible return to a lost past – were over by the time he died. Augustus' relationship to Julius Caesar faded as a subject, to be superseded by his position as *paterfamilias* in the 'Domus Augusta'.[52] Henceforward, we are dealing in the main with on-going conflicts over the future. Rooted within the palace, they were re-interpreted when they entered the public and legal domains as involving anti-Augustan plotting. That is not to deny that the parties involved did adopt a particular stance as part of their movement, exploiting and even believing in old principles and slogans. When the events of 12 BC to AD 14 are surveyed, the salient feature is Augustus' single-minded ruthlessness in disposing through marriage and divorce, not only of womenfolk, who had nothing better to expect from their *paterfamilias*, whatever their station in life, but of men out of paternal control and of an age to know their own mind. It was not new: dynastic marriages arranged by Augustus went back to the Triumviral period. Most significant, however, had been the marriage of Agrippa to the widowed Julia in 21 BC: it was through her, evidently, that the line of succession was to pass. What was new was the unswerving determination of the Princeps to achieve his plans of the moment, and the pitiless measures he was prepared to take against his own kin to achieve them. It was a stimulus for intrigue and rebellion amongst those who lost out in the schemes.

After the death of Agrippa, and especially after that of Nero Drusus on campaign in 9 BC, Augustus' luck began to run out. His immediate reaction in 11 was to take action to ensure continuity of power for his dynasty by marrying his now twice widowed daughter to his stepson Tiberius. Augustus himself might survive to ensure that her sons Gaius and Lucius Caesar were assured of power through grants of wide-ranging *imperium*. If he did not he still had two adjutants in strong military commands on hand in the Balkans and Germany, Tiberius and his younger brother Nero Drusus. This scheme was not perfect. First, though Julia was said to welcome her new match, Tiberius divorced his wife Vipsania, a daughter of Agrippa, only reluctantly. He was thirty years old and an experienced general, and he chose the political advancement that went with Julia's hand over his existing marriage and the obscurity that keeping to it would have meant. Marriage to Julia was something different. Tears were seen in his eyes when he saw Vipsania again, and he had to be manoeuvred out of her way.[53] Moreover, the two young Claudii would have to be trusted to ensure the advancement of Gaius and Lucius if Augustus did not survive: both had sons of their own. That was a problem quite apart from the Republican sympathies that Nero Drusus in particular allegedly harboured.[54] But Tiberius' marriage to the mother of Agrippa's sons would strengthen the obligations that the two young men felt to their stepfather.

The death of Nero Drusus in 9 BC made adjustments necessary. Augustus would have to trust Tiberius still more: he himself was now three years older and his legate Tiberius' subordinate authority[55] was not sufficient to sustain the current regime. A new collegiality would have to be constructed, with Tiberius raised to a position comparable with that of Agrippa between 18 and 13. Less than a year after Drusus' death he was elected to a second consulship, for 7 BC. In 6 Augustus took the decisive step, giving Tiberius the tribunician power. It was an integrated plan: the progress from consulship to tribunician power followed the pattern of 23 BC. Now Augustus, in a stroke of genius, was turning the humiliating sequence that involved loss of his consulship into a dignified ceremony. With the tribunician power there had to go a military command: Tiberius was to go east, for the second time, and settle affairs with Parthia and Armenia, with an *imperium* that was presumably superior to that of governors in the area. With exaggeration, Velleius speaks of Tiberius as being put almost on a level with Augustus.[56]

Livy did not take his history beyond 9 BC, perhaps because the brilliant feat of Drusus in crossing the Elbe made a good closing point, while his death was too grievous to describe. There is a simpler explanation. Court politics now became contentious: a historian could not mention leading figures without committing himself to one dangerous position or another. Tiberius' advancement was intolerable to those who had attached themselves to the rising stars of Gaius and Lucius Caesars and who mistrusted his willingness to allow them their share of power after Augustus' death. That may have been true of the *plebs*: Tiberius, whom nobody thought affable, unlike his dead brother, who was very popular, seems to have had more of a sense of duty towards them than any affection. Moreover, his marriage to Augustus' daughter, mother of the people's favourites, turned out badly, and she too may have shared the mistrust and feared that Augustus' inheritance would not after all pass through her.[57] Her hopes of continued position for herself rested on the supremacy of her sons (as did that of Livia, as historians never tire of pointing out). In 6 BC, the very year of Tiberius' advancement, there was a popular demonstration in the theatre in favour of Gaius and at the consular elections votes were cast for him, fourteen-year-old that he was. This was a serious, and probably orchestrated, protest against Augustus' new plans for the succession. The clear will of the Princeps was being challenged, perhaps by some of his advisers, by his daughter and by sections of the populace primed by them. A more subtle interpretation is that the demonstration was orchestrated by Augustus himself in a divide and conquer strategy, to keep Tiberius on his toes. It was in his interests that Gaius should be popular, because that was endorsement of hereditary monarchy. If that were the case, the idea backfired catastrophically, and Augustus could have guessed that it might. For that reason it seems implausible.[58]

In the face of the disorder Augustus compromised, after rebuking the people. He told them that it was a bad time if consuls had to be elected so young (this from the man who had held his own first consulship at nineteen).

Gaius was designated for AD 1, and for the moment became, with his brother, Leader of the Youth (*Princeps Iuventutis*). As for Tiberius, he too moved into action that was in defiance of the Princeps' wishes. Either the compromise was a slight to his new prominence that was too much for him to bear, or he could not accept the unpopularity that the demonstration showed, or (perhaps the best guess) he felt that his good intentions towards his stepsons were being questioned, and that Augustus was granting that the questioning might be valid. Instead of braving the commotion, Tiberius allowed himself the luxury of going into a huff and removing himself to the island of Rhodes, after opening his will in fine Augustan style, evidently to show Augustus and Livia its propriety, even generosity towards his step-sons. Both sides went to the edge to gain their end: Tiberius went on hunger-strike, Augustus fell ill, the last time we find him incapacitated in a crisis.[59] If this surrender of position on the part of an ambitious *triumphator*, twice consul, seems too un-Roman to be credible, one may still invoke other factors: his wife's contempt and, above all, his awareness that he had been left alone by his brother's death to take on a position that, contrary to his own principles, was increasingly monarchical.

Tiberius' period of 'study' on Rhodes turned into virtual exile when his powers expired in 1 BC. He was in no position to have them renewed: only Augustus could do that. He spent the last two years of the seven in terror when his *imperium* had expired and Gaius Caesar came east in 1 BC clad in the power that he himself had had. In AD 2 Gaius consented to Tiberius' recall – to a life of retirement in Rome. Both young Caesars died on their duties abroad, Lucius on his way to Spain in AD 2, Gaius in Lycia in AD 4, from a wound received in Armenia. Their distance from Rome did not prevent the story going about that they had been poisoned by Livia; that would have been by agents of hers in their entourages. The story is worth repeating only because it shows the depth of the hatred between various members of the imperial house and their partisans, as well as their vulnerability. (Foul play is never attributed to Julia and her followers; they were the losers, the popular side, descended from the Princeps.)

This is the place to consider three oaths taken to Augustus and his kin, on Samos, 6–5 BC and at Conobaria, an unidentified site in Baetican Spain, in 5 BC, and at Gangra (Çangırı) in Paphlagonia in 3 BC.[60] They are taken to represent a surge of loyalty towards the Julian house (as opposed to the Domus Augusta, to which Tiberius belonged) at the time of Gaius' taking of the toga of manhood, precisely in 5. That is not enough. There were indeed other displays of loyalty. Sardis (Sart) ordained an annual celebration of the occasion, and informed Augustus of it. In reply, he thanked the city for showing itself appreciative to himself 'and all his own' of his benefactions.[61] The bellicose wording of the oaths, and the specific inclusion in the Conobarian of a member of the household who had not yet been taken into the Julian *gens* (Agrippa Postumus), suggest as well that there was something else in mind: an enemy, the departed Tiberius, who had manifestly abandoned his Princeps and was still in possession of *imperium* and enough support amongst his former troops – legions he had conducted in Armenia or commanded in Germany – to make him a credible threat. Oath-taking last featured in the crisis year of 32 BC (Ch. 1). The boys' position might be challenged by their step-father. What is in question is the predominance of the male blood-line of Augustus.

It is not necessarily helpful to enquire into the ancestry of these oaths, when they were promoted by a master of improvisation and adaptability. But how they came to be taken is a good question. J. González believes that Augustus 'required' the oath of Conobaria. Instead, a sensitive and zealous governor may have been responsible for exacting it; or it may not have been required at all, but produced voluntarily as evidence of unshaken loyalty, and with a clear echo of the oath exacted from the West in 32. It is worth remembering that Nemausus (Nîmes), where the colony had been founded by Ti. Nero, Tiberius' father, tore down the statues of the 'exile' towards the end of his stay. The council purged itself of the stain: Nemausus is the site of the temple inscribed with the names of Gaius and Lucius Caesar, the Maison Carrée. Local enterprise, then, or pressure from a governor, could account for differences between the oaths. There was no real threat from Tiberius, only a cultivated image of one, thrown into high relief by the golden notions of the sons of Agrippa whose advancement he menaced by his mere existence (which he was effacing in the interior of Rhodes). Cultivating this loyalist fantasy gave cities the opportunity for oaths and conspicuous iconoclasm.

In AD 4 Augustus, not deterred from his main purpose, the continuation of supremacy for the dynasty after his death, called on Tiberius to resume his tribunician power and partnership with the Princeps, this time as his adoptive son. With him Tiberius brought two more boys from the next generation into the Julii Caesares: his own son Drusus and his nephew,

Nero Drusus' son who, having been adopted by Tiberius, became Germanicus Caesar. Both Velleius and Suetonius note that when Augustus brought forward his proposals he declared that he was adopting Tiberius 'for the sake of the Commonwealth', but Suetonius notes that he made some remarks excusing Tiberius' demeanour and way of life. This is supposed to show his reluctance to undertake the adoption. It rather shows the savagery of hostility to Tiberius amongst the populace and echoed in the tradition, no doubt whipped up by his enemies in the family.[62]

Feuding had continued in Tiberius' absence. In 2 BC, precisely the year in which Augustus had been declared Father of his Country, his inability to control his own daughter was ironically exposed.[63] It was no friend of Augustus or even of Tiberius who achieved Julia's fall. Augustus himself did not altogether shun publicity in disgracing his daughter: he had her denounced in the Senate. That will at least have gratified some members of the aristocracy chafing under his social legislation, even if it was not by one of them that the offences were brought to light. It was an appalling blow to the Princeps, and M. Dettenhofer's suggestion that he knew of the offences and kept them quiet until he was installed as *Pater Patriae* and ready to strike is surely wide of the mark. It was the least convenient moment for the scandal to break. 2 BC saw Julia exiled, and the death or exile of her highly aristocratic paramours, T. Quinctius Crispinus Sulpicianus, consul 9 BC, a patrician with philosophical pretensions, Sempronius Gracchus, descendant of a renowned political family. One of them, Iullus Antonius, consul 10 BC, a man whose paternity made him dangerous, for he was Antony's younger son by Fulvia, certainly died, executed or more probably as a suicide. These were certainly men worthy of Julia's attention; allegedly she considered her husband, now four years away and about to lose his official powers, beneath her – which Tacitus gives as the real reason for his original departure.[64] In spite of his denunciations Augustus avoided the public trial in the courts that the offence now demanded, and it does not sound as if Julia was tried in the Senate. It is even suggested that he used his authority as a father against her, despite the fact that she was a mother of five and so exempt from *patria potestas*; his consular *imperium* is the likely weapon. Augustus was putting a high premium on preventing open debate on whatever had happened; the debate that followed his denunciation in the Senate, if there was one at all, would have been, if not short, certainly short in content, and cautious.

Tacitus insists that Augustus exceeded his own legislation by treating adultery as if it were treason (*maiestas minuta*); but such dealings with Augustus' daughter and the wife of the exiled Tiberius were not far off it. Hence, even if there was no conspiracy against himself, Augustus, as J. Ginsburg claimed, treated such adulterous relationships with his daughter as subversive in themselves.[65] This was not simply a matter of loose morals: what was revealed about Julia weakened her sons' claim to legitimacy, for one thing, however careful she claimed to be. Augustus also exceeded his authority as a father-in-law by sending Julia notice of divorce on behalf of Tiberius.[66] A husband was obliged to divorce his wife if she was proved adulterous, or, if he failed to act within a certain length of time, suffer the legal penalty for pimping. On Rhodes Tiberius might not have heard of Julia's fall for a month or even six weeks after it occurred.[67] A similar length of time would have been necessary for the divorce order to reach Rome, even if Tiberius sent it at once: he is said to have pleaded for lenient treatment, for his loss of position as her husband made him even more useless

Figure 13 Agrippa Postumus (Ancient Art & Architecture. Photograph by Ronald Sheridan @ Ancient Art & Architecture Collection)

and vulnerable in 2 BC than he had been before. Augustus may have feared that delay caused by the weather or Tiberius' scruples would lay him open to the 'pimping' charge. More likely Augustus wanted the affair settled and past as soon as possible; Tiberius' absence would serve as an excuse.

Whether Julia and the men round her were politically motivated or simply enjoyed illicit freedoms is in dispute. Antonius may have hoped to replace the apparently ruined Tiberius as stepfather to the young princes. Julia's fall did not help her husband, and Livia, surprisingly, has not been associated with it. The informant or informants remain unidentified, their motives, hatred of Julia, of Augustus, of Antonius, unclear. It is possible that they were frightened by Julia's behaviour into laying information for Augustus' own sake. Julia had her supporters, who demonstrated in her favour. Whether those demonstrations were spontaneous or orchestrated, as it is tempting to believe, we also have no means of knowing. Augustus tried to be firm. He would no more take her back than fire would mix with water. They threw firebrands into the Tiber (were they implying that they could be thrown into buildings?). In the end Augustus partially gave way: Julia was brought back to the mainland from Pandateria (Ventotene) to Rhegium (Reggio di Calabria).[68]

After Tiberius' return the prospects before Julia's surviving son Agrippa Postumus, born in 12 BC, were weak, though his adoption was achieved alongside that of Tiberius and required no explanation: he was Augustus' surviving grandson, and it was the adoption of a second son, Tiberius, an adult with his own son, that required excuse. Postumus was sixteen and had held no office; no *imperium* or tribunician power accompanied the adoption, not even the title 'Leader of the Youth'. This was not enough for Postumus, and there were politicians who agreed with him, especially if they were former followers of Gaius and Lucius Caesar who had let it be seen that they did not favour the return of Tiberius, still less his elevation to a higher position than before. Over the following years Postumus was disgraced, expelled from the Julian family, and exiled, at first only to the agreeable town of Surrentum (Sorrento) on the coast of Italy (probably in AD 6), then, firmly by senatorial decree as the family feuding grew more intense, to the island of Planasia (Pianosa), thirteen kilometres south-west of Elba.[69]

Augustus, his purpose firmly in mind, went on to arrange marriages between the two branches of the family, trying to bring them together and show them their future role. Julia's daughter Vipsania Agrippina married

Germanicus Julius Caesar in a spectacularly successful and productive match, and Nero Drusus' daughter Claudia Livia Julia, or Livilla, wed Tiberius' son Drusus Julius Caesar. Both branches then were to have a share of power. After that Augustus' new partner might have expected a clear run.

But in 8–9 there was another 'adultery' scandal, involving Postumus' sister the younger Julia, more distinguished politicians, and the poet Ovid. She and another batch went into exile, though the aristocratic D. Silanus merely lost the friendship of Augustus and saw that as a signal that he should go on his travels; the view that her husband L. Aemilius Paullus was executed cannot be maintained: he seems to have been replaced as an Arval Brother in May, AD 14. The less highly placed Ovid went, solely on the Princeps' say-so, specifically to Tomis (Constanţa), right out of the way on the Black Sea. Ovid on trial, whether in a jury court or in the Senate, might have proved embarrassingly eloquent. Slaves were tortured, a measure that Augustus in an edict of this very year (evidently in the face of existing or expected criticism) pronounced necessary in capital and serious cases.[70]

Ovid learned of his sentence on Elba, close to Postumus' last home – a striking coincidence. At least one letter, extremely bitter, according to Suetonius, purporting to come from the youth was circulated amongst the people, by a person called Junius Novatus, who was let off with a fine. Linked with him in Suetonius' catalogue, though not dated, is Cassius of Patavium (Padua; but his name may have been Patavinus), who might have been of higher status: he announced at a dinner that he was resolved on the death of Augustus and had the courage to knife him too. Even this met only with exile.[71] Evidently Augustus, having shown his severity against popular rebels in the imperial family, did not wish to aggravate any reaction. As soon as Augustus died in August 14 Postumus was put to death. Responsibility for his execution has been assigned to the late Princeps, who, as Tacitus points out, had never killed any of his relatives, or alternatively to Tiberius, Livia, and the imperial confidant Sallustius Crispus, separately or in collusion.[72] Aggravating the charges against them was the tale that before he died Augustus had sailed to Planasia and been reconciled with Agrippa. There was also talk of a rescue attempt: Postumus was to be rushed to the armies and saluted as *imperator*, that is, proclaimed Emperor; the elder Julia was included in a scheme attributed to L. Audasius and Q. Asinius Epicadus. Four lesser men were associated with 'conspiracies' against Augustus at this time: Epicadus' name suggests that he was a dependent of the family of Asinius Pollio.[73] There was enough plausibility and attraction in the 'rescue' plan (or fantasy) for a slave impostor, Clemens, who it was said had carefully stolen Postumus' ashes when he failed to arrive in time to save the youth himself, to travel round Italy two years later, with great success in the country towns until he was captured and made away with in Tiberius' palace. Possession of an urn of ashes proved nothing about Postumus' death – or survival; the masquerade was an effective way of rousing a sentimental populace.[74] Postumus was seen, rightly, as a real threat to Augustus' settled plans.

A whiff of social rebellion comes from the two Julias. Augustus had presented himself as a restorer of old-fashioned morality. The Senate had been purged and given stability and dignity and in return had to set a reassuring example to the rest of society, so that it would stay quiet in its ranks. But such measures for regeneration were also about the legitimacy of the dynasty's claim to power.[75] A younger generation, of which Ovid was the most eloquent spokesman, found these expectations restrictive. The elder Julia and her paramours were supposed to have danced on the very *rostra* (speakers' platform) from which Augustus had promulgated his social legislation, and she sold her favours every day at the statue of Marsyas in the Forum. So Seneca reports, claiming to give the content of Augustus' complaint to the Senate. As Dr Herbert-Brown remarks, it would not make sense for Julia publicly to flout her father's laws; that would have damaged her sons' legitimacy. Seneca's version might be a literal-minded misinterpretation and elaboration, fuelled by male fantasy, of a metaphorical way of speaking, but it is still significant, especially the variant allegation that Julia garlanded the statue of Marsyas; that monument was associated with *libertas*, at any rate that of communities. One should not make anything of his being a personage who competed on the reed-pipe against Augustus' patron deity and was skinned for his pains.[76]

The struggles for power within the imperial family that came to a crisis in 8 continued on the same inherited lines long after the reign of Augustus, as long as the dynasty lasted, or rather until Nero killed the only other surviving male descendant of Augustus. Relatives and their associates whose schemes for their own advancement misfired, or who were brought down by the intrigues of rivals, went on being variously punished, by death, imprisonment or exile.

Slander and libel in the succession struggle

It is in connexion with these dynastic struggles that a new and blatantly re-
pressive tendency can be seen in the techniques that the ageing Augustus
used against discontent. At the same time techniques of opposition seem to
change and to become more covert. Augustus had a reputation for tolerance, reported by Suetonius, and when pamphlets attacking him were found
distributed in the Senate House, probably in AD 6, he merely took pains to
rebut the charges. He did, however, propose that pamphleteers who published libels against anyone pseudonymously should come to trial; that limited the secondary damage of recriminations between senators perhaps
already at loggerheads.[77] Aemilius Aelianus, a native of the Roman colony
Corduba (Córdoba), which produced the distinguished literary family of
the Annaei, including the Senecas father and son, was accused of habitually
expressing unfavourable opinions of the Princeps; Augustus at the inquiry
said he would say something about Aelianus too.[78] There was an inquiry,
then; unfortunately we know nothing about it.

Without excluding all intellectual dissidents,[79] it is legitimate with
Raaflaub and Samons to pass over poets, unless like Ovid they became ac-
tively entangled with politics, and even to send historians to join them in a
literary niche in Ch. 6. We are concerned with active politicians. Orators
could prove immediately confrontational. T. Labienus is the first known to
have suffered.[80] He would be kin to the officer who, in spite of being Caesar's legate in Gaul and distinguishing himself there, had rejoined Pompey
when the Civil War broke out, and to Q. Labienus who led Parthian troops
into the eastern Empire against the Second Triumvirate. Labienus, who was
given the nickname Rabienus ('Rabid'), was as independently minded as his
kinsmen, probably self-consciously so. He may have made his living as an
orator after his family property had been confiscated by the Triumvirs. Now
in the *annus horribilis* AD 6 came the senatorial enactment making slander
of eminent persons an offence under the *maiestas* statute. (Augustus passed
no substantive law on the offence: the *Lex Julia* in force under the Empire
was Caesar's.) Labienus refused to survive the burning of his books and had
himself taken to the family tomb and walled up. These developments were
new in the history of the law, says Tacitus. The initiative against him did not
come from Augustus himself, but there would have been eager accusers in
the charged atmosphere and impoverishment of Augustus' last years. The
reinterpretation of the statute to include verbal abuse is itself evidence of

feuding amongst politicians over their place in the second generation of the Principate and of Augustus' determination – and perhaps Tiberius' – not to allow men he favoured to succumb to slander.

Another man of the same bold stamp as Labienus was the orator Cassius Severus.[81] An upstart, Severus' fate was merely exile. He went in for prosecutions of Augustus' associates, and in 9 BC had brought L. Nonius Asprenas, a close friend of the Princeps, to trial on a charge of mass poisoning, after a dinner party had ended fatally for some of the guests. When Severus was arraigned for his pamphlets it was because the successful – 'distinguished men and women', as Tacitus calls them – were becoming targets for the losers. Cassius Severus described the Vitellii, one of the most distinguished of the rising families connected with the incoming Princeps Tiberius, as being of slave descent.[82] L. Vitellius operated in the East at the end of Tiberius' life, as members of the imperial once had, Agrippa, Gaius Caesar and Germanicus, though his powers were not so wide. One of Vitellius's sons was three times consul and censor as the colleague of Claudius, and his grandson was briefly emperor in 69. There were many who would take advantage of the pride and fear of thin-skinned emperors and their coteries to accuse their detractors and win property and rank by a successful prosecution. Under Domitian the charge of insulting the Emperor and those close to him became a scourge for which he was never forgiven. Some emperors renounced this use of the law, though only to deal with verbal or implicit abuse, and it looks as if Domitian's confident successors were able to discourage prosecutions.[83]

Vilification came in written as well as oral form, and so from anonymous or pseudonymous sources. Tiberius himself and his mother Livia were pilloried in graffiti, slander and pamphleteering.[84] Anonymous pamphlets were found in the Senate House itself, the work, presumably, of its members, but it is uncertain whether the malicious allegations that prompted Augustus to reply in an edict belong to this episode; he made no effort to find out the perpetrators, but spoke for holding to account the authors of pseudonymous libels uttered against anyone. That is, he claimed to be preventing irresponsible feuding.

The *plebs*

So far we have concentrated on the upper class and its increasing resignation; but members of the *plebs*, from a variety of levels and geographical centres, have been seen joining their betters in subversive schemes. As a mass the Roman *plebs* burst in only from time to time when its physical conditions became markedly worse, in the period 23–19, or in (perhaps paid) political demonstrations, such as those run by Clodius in the 50s BC. The upper class stood to lose in any social or economic change, for the Republic had been run for their benefit. Lower social strata with little to lose were particularly likely to look forward to improvements, especially those in Rome, where they could make themselves felt. They had no golden age to look back to; instead they looked to the future, in particular for help from the younger members of the imperial family. Conditions of life in Rome had improved under Augustus in important ways (see Ch. 3), but not enough: something more could always be demanded. Any hopes the *plebs* had of Caesar were dashed when he was assassinated. Now, after two decades, Augustus' regime had become stable and routine, the *plebs* might think static. Augustus' control had a negative side for them: on becoming Supreme Pontiff, one of his first acts was to purge the accumulated Sibylline oracles of more than two thousand prophetic items that might be used unofficially, even subversively. Spontaneous events of religious significance, such as the appearance of vultures when Octavian took his first consulship, could be dangerous if they presented themselves to the wrong people. Augury and prodigies were allowed less prominence than they had had before the Augustan age. Only when he was at death's door was Augustus unable to inhibit dire signs; in the years preceding his death he took measures to curb the astrology to which he, like Tiberius, was devoted.[85]

Augustus' heirs, who needed support, might do better. In particular, the affable Nero Drusus and later his son Germanicus won the people's love; they pinned their hopes on them, and evidently on Augustus' grandsons Gaius and Lucius; if they ever did anything to earn affection it remains hidden. It seems not to have been necessary: they still commanded support in theatres and voting enclosures. At any rate they were young and had not shattered any illusions; one of them even bore the prestigious name of Gaius Julius Caesar. The Roman people had their favourites, ill-starred, as Tacitus remarks, bringing the fate of Princess Diana and its effect on the British public irresistibly to mind. In the later years of Augustus the people can be seen in a new role: in the background of dynastic tussles, spontaneously or as hired extras, backing the premature election to the consulate of Gaius Caesar (6 BC) and the impeccable appointment of Augustus as Pater Patriae in 2, and marching in protest against the island exile of the elder Julia (*c.* AD 3).

The people had specific grievances to display while they waited for over-all improvement. First, simple shortage of money, connected with shortage of work for quarrymen, waggoners, builders and decorators. The great building programme at Rome was slowing down, though it did not cease after it received its 'final seal' in 7 BC. One construction of the last two decades was the evocative temple of Concord, dedicated in AD 10 by Tiberius in his own name and that of his dead brother. Equally significantly, at about the same time came the restoration of the shrines of Ceres Mater and Ops Augusta on 10 August, AD 7.[86] Many projects had been completed, and there was less cash available for new ones. Yet as Dr Herbert-Brown points out, suddenly Augustus was impelled at this late stage to restore the Aventine (and so quintessentially plebeian temples) that he had left out of his original programme.

In flood, fire and shortage of grain, the plebeian electorate were simply victims, and we have followed Augustus' efforts to cope with these problems, none wholly successful (Ch. 3). Significantly, his watchmen, the *Vigiles*, had other duties besides fire-fighting: the maintenance of order. Augustus' reaction to popular agitation was moderate, for it usually had only nuisance value. There were rebukes, but he was prepared to make compromises, and to improve administrative structures where they were obviously inadequate. But he also took considered measures to hinder gratuitous and unwelcome expressions of the popular will in the future. By AD 23 Tiberius had gathered the cohorts of the Praetorian Guard into a barracks on the walls of the City. He had a particular fear of popular agitation, as the precautions that were taken at Augustus' funeral show.[87] But Augustus had had praetorian cohorts available since the 30s. In 2 BC, the issue of command of the guard surfaces: Dio tells us that it was conferred on two men, but not who had commanded it before. A change from one man to two might be significant and show lack of confidence in a year of crisis; but if Augustus simply relinquished direct command himself to a pair of subordinates it would be due simply to the burden of administration on a man now over sixty, and facing civil unrest.[88] It was very near the end of his life, probably in AD 13, and in his virtual absence through infirmity, that Augustus saw to the appointment of a permanent official, the Prefect of the City: L. Piso, a consular of great seniority and tried loyalty, but importantly one who was also a close friend of Tiberius.[89] Piso, the first in a regular series of appointments, commanded troops of his own, the three Urban Cohorts.

The military threat

There was a less specific cause for discontent among the people, but one that Augustus could do nothing to allay. The advance of Roman arms, which had seemed unstoppable, was ended. Nero Drusus' campaigns in Germany were carried on by Tiberius and then by lesser generals. When Tiberius returned to service in AD 4 tracts of Germany east of the Rhine were set to become a regular province.[90] Two years later, the Pannonian revolt drew Tiberius away, and in AD 9 Roman hopes of the province were shattered beyond any chance of substantial restoration before Augustus' death. Vicarious success, excitement and the hope of a share in the proceeds buoyed up the *plebs*, just as they buoyed up the Victorian and Edwardian working class in England ('Wider yet and wider may thy bounds be set'), and they joined up in 1914 to defend them. The same was not true in late Augustan Italy: slaves had to be freed and enlisted; men were recruited from the city of Rome itself. Emergency measures had to be taken again after the Varian losses of AD 9.[91] A decade and a half later Tiberius was lamenting the state of recruiting in Italy: the legions were attracting only 'beggars with no fixed address'.[92]

Trouble in the army itself is a woe signalled again in the last two decades of Augustus' Principate. The trouble had the old causes. The soldiers were being kept on beyond the time that Augustus had conceded in 13 BC, when men recruited before the Actian campaign, and who may have been still active in the recent successful conquest of the Alps by Nero Drusus and Tiberius, were demanding discharge and land. Augustus had promised a definite term, twenty years for legionaries, sixteen for praetorian guardsmen; and on that occasion at least, since satisfactory enemy territory was not available, he promised a monetary bounty of *HS* 12,000.[93] The limits were exceeded, and unrest began again in AD 2. By 6 Augustus knew that he had to act. Dio's claim that in these last years Augustus was softer and anxious not to offend his peers may have been true in theory, but we have noticed signs of impatience and lack of consideration. On the issue of the Military Treasury he was and had to be resolute. He demonstrated integrity and serious purpose to all classes, civilian and military, by contributing funds from his own property and from that of Tiberius and Agrippa Postumus. For now Tiberius' property belonged to his adoptive father Augustus; so did Postumus' even after he was expelled from the family.[94] This donation served a second purpose: of mitigating anger against Augustus for his treatment of Postumus. Again Augustus' efforts were insufficient. The mutinies of 14 showed how dissatisfied with pay, conditions and discharge bounties the soldiery remained.[95]

It was the provinces that supported the expenses of the Empire, notably the army. But in the last years of Augustus' reign resources were short there too, as requests for remissions of tax and changes of governor, and, in some places, rebellions, showed, and that in turn meant more bad news and expense for Rome.[96] The sober, even joyless, principate of Tiberius was anticipated a decade before he was left in sole power.

Conclusion

Scholars have successfully reinterpreted much, though not all, of what ancient writers, and sometimes the Augustan sources that fed them, treated as conspiracies. Their success has led to a devaluation of a less dramatic phenomenon: mundane discontent, especially during the last two decades of Augustus' Principate.[97] The regime was secure, machinery for its continuance was in place; there were still functions, honour and profit for the senatorial and equestrian orders. For the latter they were enhanced: Egypt would never have had an equestrian governor under the Republic. The courts continued with their mixed juries of senators and knights; in AD 5 the two ranks were put side by side in places of honour as members of the voting centuries of Gaius and Lucius Caesar. Yet eruptions of discontent came from within the imperial family, from senators and knights, the people, the provinces and the army, and Augustus' freedom to deal with them was severely limited by individual interests, traditional attitudes, natural forces and shortage of cash. The problems were passed on to the next Princeps, and aggravated by his unpopularity.

Endnotes

1 Conspiracies: Vell. Pat. 2. 88. 3f., 91. 2–4; Pliny, *NH* 7. 149; Sen. *De Brev. Vit.* 4. 5; *De Clem.* 1. 9. 6 (Caepio following Murena: Seneca must have misunderstood his list); Tac. *Ann.* 1. 10. 4; Suet. *Aug.* 19. 1; Williams 1978, 91, takes Ovid, *Met.* 1. 200–06, to refer obliquely to conspiracies. List of 'conspiracies'

with sources, in Raaflaub and Samons 1990, 422–33. Crook 1996, taking a moderate position, 73, demands sobriety of judgment, 102f. 'Opposition' among the poets is taken for granted by Woodman and West 1985, vii.

2 Individuals not systems preoccupying the ancients: I owe this point to Dr Herbert-Brown.

3 See especially Badian 1982 (repudiated by Dettenhofer 2000, 113 n. 136); Raaflaub and Samons 1990; Rich 1996; Crook 1996, 104–44; Lacey 1985 (a bland view of the change to tribunician power in 23 BC).

4 Stability: Rea 2007, 125.

5 Lurching from crisis to crisis: Badian 1982, 37.

6 Vow to Augustus: Dio 53. 20. 2–4, with Rich *ad loc.*, and interpreted by Schmitthenner 1969, 417–19.

7 Conceptual problems: Feeney 1992.

8 Scepticism on 'opposition': Badian 1982; Raaflaub and Samons 1990; conclusion 448; factors militating against opposition 451f.

9 Civil war possible in 23: Putnam 1990, 236.

10 Dettenhofer 2000, 130 n. 15, notes that Raaflaub and Samons 427, treating conspiracies in too isolated a manner, are unable to cope with Dio 54. 15. 1f. and 4 (18 BC and later) and 55. 4. 3 (under 9 BC); they discard the first as too general. Domitian: Suet. *Dom.* 21.

11 Slander and assault: Suet. *Aug.* 51. 3.

12 Cinna's conspiracy: Dio 55. 14– 22. 1; cf. Sen. *De Clem.* 1. 9, suggesting a date of 16–13 BC; see Dettenhofer 2000, 159, n. 70.

13 'Bad men': Vell. Pat. 2. 91. 2; cf. Cic. *Sest.* 46.

14 19 the start: Badian 1982, 36, suggests 23.

15 Opposition by Senate: Raaflaub and Samons 1990, 433–35. Interruption and dissent: Suet. *Aug.* 54.

16 Augustus cornered on immorality: Dio 54. 16. 3–5 (18 BC). Alleged liaison with Terentia: 19. 3; Suet. *Aug.* 69. 2 (*c.* 32 BC).

17 Sisenna's wife: Dio 54. 27. 4 (13 BC); unwanted honours: 27. 2. Cf. Hortalus' technique in Tac. *Ann.* 2. 37. Altercation: Suet. *Aug.* 54.

18 Vespasian quitting the Senate: Dio 65. 12. 1.

19 Taurus prefect: Dio 54. 19. 6, with Rich 1990 *ad loc.* Hostility to Plancus: Watkins 1997, 141; Wright 2002.

20 *Lex Papia Poppaea*: Tac. *Ann.* 3. 25–8; Suet. *Aug.* 34; Gaius, *Inst.* 2. 111; 286; Dio 56. 1–10, with knights' demonstration and speech in forum, with Wiedemann 1975, 265, for mitigation and Dettenhofen 2000, 201 for sharpening: lack of children now brought down penalties by limiting the right to inherit. Wallace-Hadrill 1981, 76 suggests rather that the law provided exceptions, within families, to the penalities of the *Lex Julia*. AD 20: Tac. *Ann.* 3. 28. 4. Professor Wardle points out that Dio and Suetonius may be describing two demonstrations, one early in 9 at celebratory games for Tiberius, the other at the passing of the law by the suffect consuls; see his forthcoming commentary

on Suet. *Aug*. Augustus' restive audience ('young men of rank', which suggests the equestrian sons of senators): Plut. *Mor*. 207F (*Sayings of Aug*. 12). Tiberius' remedy: Tac. *Ann*. 3. 28. 4.

21 Concise accounts of Augustus' problems with financing the army: Lacey 1996, 213–15; Eck 2003, 115–20; *Aerarium militare* and taxes supporting it: *RG* 17. 2; Suet. *Aug*. 49. 2; Dio 55. 24. 9–25. 6; 56. 28. 4–6. Resistance: Dio 55. 24; 56. 28; Tiberius' adjustment: Tac. *Ann*. 3. 28. 4; continued unpopularity: Pliny, *Pan*. 5. 4f.

22 Cn. Piso: *PIR²* C286, esp. Tac. *Ann*. 2. 43. 2. Won over: Badian 1982, 30. Sestius: *PIR* S 436.

23 Absenteeism: Dio 54. 18. 3; 55. 3. 2f.; remedies: Suet. *Aug*. 35. 3. Validity of decrees: Dio 54. 35. 1f., with Rich 1990 *ad loc*.; he suggests that Dio's reference to a revision of the senatorial list and to the quorum (cf. 55. 3. 2) are references, misplaced because linked in Dio's notes with a census, to the law on senatorial attendance passed in 9 BC (55. 3).

24 *Lex Julia de senatu habendo*: Suet. *Aug*. 35. 3; Gell. 4. 10. 1; Pliny, *Ep*. 5. 13. 5; 8. 14. 19f.; Dio 55. 3f., with Rich 1990 *ad loc*.; Dettenhofer 2000, 153 n. 44. Morning greeting: Suet. *Aug*. 53. 3; Dio 54. 30. 1; 56. 26. 2f. New regulations: Dio 55. 4. 1.

25 Declarations of ineligibility: Dio 54. 26. 3–7. *Vigintiviri*: 26. 5 (13 BC); quaestors: 53. 28. 4 (24 BC); tribunes: 54. 26. 7, with shortages in general 3–9 (13 BC); 30. 2 (12 BC), all with Rich 1990 *ad loc*.; 56. 27. 1 (AD 12); Suet. *Aug*. 40. 1; aediles: Dio 48. 53. 4; 49. 16. 2 (36 BC); 54. 11. 1 (19); 55. 24. 9 (AD 5 and on other occasions). See Dettenhofer 2000, 150–58.

26 Property qualification: Dio 54. 17. 3; 26. 3; cf. Suet. *Aug*. 41. 1.

27 Quorum: Suet. *Aug*. 35. 3.

28 Encouraging young senators: Suet. *Aug*. 38. 2; inspection: Dio 54. 26. 8f., with Rich's interpretation, 1990 *ad loc*. Role of the young: Dettenhofer 2000, 152; at 164f. she invokes Nero Drusus and Tiberius.

29 Slave evidence: Dettenhofer 2000, 159, on Dio 55. 5. 4; Tac. *Ann*. 2. 30. 3; 3. 67. 3.

30 Strains after Agrippa's death: Dettenhofer 2000, 160–66.

31 Tiberius informed: e.g. Tac. *Ann*. 3. 6. 1.

32 Dramas on sensitive subjects could at least be offered as subsidiary evidence, witness the *Atreus* of Mam. Scaurus in AD 34 (Tac. *Ann*. 6. 29. 3).

33 Octavian's fears: Dio 52. 42. 8.

34 Lepidus' conspiracy: Livy *Epit*. 133; Vell. Pat. 2. 88; Dio 54. 15. 4; Suet. *Aug*. 19.1. Lepidus as pawn: Syme 1986, 35.

35 Fate of Cornelius Gallus: Suet. *Aug*. 66. 1f.; *Gram*. 16. 1f.; Dio 53. 23. 5–24. 3, with Schmitthenner 1969, 470f. and Rich 1990 *ad loc*., preferring 27, the date given by Eus.-Jer., *Chron*. 164 Helm; Augustus' opponents in play: 420–22. Gallus could not keep his mouth shut in drink: Ovid *Tr*. 2. 445f. Inscriptions: Flower 2006, 125–29; Gallus' monument: EJ 21.

36 Proculeius: Tac. *Ann.* 4. 40. 6; Dio 53. 24. 2f.; 54. 3. 5; he was the uterine brother of Maecenas' wife Terentia but no help to Murena: Bastomsky 1977. Political 'friendships': Dettenhofer 2000, 95.

37 Augustus' complaint against Gallus: Suet. *Gram.* 16; in the *Autobiography:* Malcovati 1969, 97, XXIIn.

38 Timagenes: Sen. *Ira* 3. 23. 4–8.

39 Crassus' campaigns: R. Batty, *Rome and the Nomads. The Pontic-Danubian Area in Antiquity* (Oxford, 1976), 402. Crassus and the Odrysae: Dio 51. 25. 5. Behind the trial of 'Primus': Levick 1975; but cf. Badian 1982.

40 This interpretation of Dio 54. 3. 5 is a modification of that proposed by Daly 1983, 260. The Loeb translation of E. Cary neglects the adversative sense of '*de*'.

41 'Victory celebrations' (*supplicationes?*): Dio 54. 3. 8; cf. 53. 3. 1.

42 Antecedents of Murena and Caepio: Vell. Pat. 2. 91. 2. Absence from court and flight after conviction: Macr., *Sat.* 1. 11. 21, and Dio 54. 3. 4–8, with Daly 1983. Terentia: Suet. *Aug.* 69. 2; Maecenas 'talking' to Terentia: 66. 3. Capture of Murena and Athenaeus, and the latter's subsequent death: Strabo 14, 670.

43 Castricius: Suet. *Aug.* 66. 4; *ILS* 2676 tells that before 16 BC a Castricius son of Myriotalentus ('Millionaire') obtained one of the preliminary magistracies, the *Vigintisexvirate*, before becoming an officer in the navy. He came from Lanuvium (Lanuvio), ancestral seat of the Licinii Murenae (Cic. *Mur.* 90). These points would be made in tutorials by C. E. Stevens, using the word 'blackmail': B. Levick, *The Ancient Historian and his Materials* (Farnborough, 1976), 2. It goes too far to ask if the fortunes of P. Sulpicius Quirinius (*PIR*[2] S 1018), another loyal native of Lanuvium (Tac. *Ann.* 3. 48. 1), also began in 23 BC.

44 C. Fannius, *cos.* 122: Broughton, MRR 2, 516; see Birley 2000, 743–45.

45 Egnatius Rufus: Vell. Pat. 2. 91. 2; 93. 4 (Galinsky 1996, 70, uses the phrase 'found guilty', implying procedural correctness); Dio 53. 24. 4–6, with Rich 1990 *ad loc.* on Dio 's discrepant dating; 54. 10. 1f. and for the events of 19, Phillips 1997, noting the unexplained abdication of Saturninus. Augustus may not have cared for a consul in his absence who was worthy of the post. Birley 2000, 719f., notes that punitive action by Sentius is not attested.

46 Conspiracies of 18–17: Dio 54. 15. 1–4, with Rich 1990 *ad loc.* unnecessarily associating this with the Egnatius case.

47 Augustus' breastplate: Suet. *Aug.* 35. 1 (two purges, breastplate and searches in the second); Dio 54. 12. 3 (18), worn 'often', but perhaps he means during a single episode. Tränkle 1980 argues for 18 and is followed by Professor Wardle (the continuation in Suetonius has material that belongs to 18) *ad loc.*); Suetonius mentions his first occasion 'when one individual selected another' again in 54; Dio deals with the selections of 29 (52.42) and 18 BC (54.13f.). See also Jones 1960, 19–26, Brunt and Moore 1970, *ad RG* 8. 2 (three purges), and

Rich on Dio 54.13; Manuwald 1979; T. J. Cornell *et al.*, eds., *FRH* no. 82 (Cremutius Cordus; forthcoming).

48 Augustus' departure for Gaul: Dio 54. 19. 2; Rich 1990 *ad loc.* regards this as part of a considered pattern.

49 'Tiring' politicians: Tony Blair in *The Times* Magazine (23 June 2007) 38: 'They get tired of the face and tired of the voice. Past a certain point it almost doesn't matter whether you're doing the right thing or the wrong thing. People get tired and say "Time to move on".'

50 Popular discontent: Lacey 1996, 230f.

51 Agrippa's funeral: Dio 29. 6, with Rich 1980 and 1990 *ad loc.* refuting the idea that his funeral games were boycotted; cf. 55. 8. 5; his aedileship: Dio 49. 43. 1–5; art collections: Pliny NH 35. 26, cf. 10 (Pollio). (Pliny, *Ep.* 6. 31. 3, calls an Ephesian politician *innoxie popularis*.)

52 The Domus Augusta: Corbier 1995; Wardle 2000. I owe the idea of the shift from *Divi filius* (son of the deified Caesar) to patriarch to Dr Herbert-Brown.

53 Tiberius' reluctance to divorce Vipsania: Suet. *Tib.* 7. 2f.

54 Nero Drusus' republicanism: Suet. *Tib.* 50. 1.

55 Tiberius a legate: *RG* 30. 1; that authority would expire on Augustus' death.

56 Tiberius advanced, 7 BC: *RG* 6. 2; Vell. Pat. 2. 99. 1; Suet. *Tib.* 9. 3; 55. 9. 4, with Rich 1990 *ad loc.*

57 Tiberius and Julia: Sattler 1969 ('Julia').

58 Elections of 6 BC and progress of Gaius and Lucius: Dio 55. 9.

59 Tiberius's retirement: Vell. Pat. 2. 99; Tac. *Ann.* 1. 53. 1; 6. 51. 2; Suet. *Tib.* 10–13; Dio 55. 9. 5–8.

60 Samos oath: P. Herrmann, *MDAI(A)* 75 (1960), 70–89, arguing for date and doubting spontaneity; Herrmann 1968, 125f.; Conobaria: González 1988 = *AE* 1988, 723; Gangra: EJ 315. Military language: González 125; Osgood 2006, 357–60. Rowe 2002, 135–39, sees the Tiberian reference. Nemausus: Suet. *Tib.* 13. 1. Maison Carrée: P. Gros in *PD s.v. Nemausus*.

61 Letter to Sardis: EJ 99 II (drawn to my attention by Dr Herbert-Brown). 'All his own' is inaccurate: honours only to Gaius were in question. The phrase may be intended as a rebuke for failure to mention Lucius. It certainly implies the exclusion of Tiberius. (C. E. Stevens considered it a rebuke for that failure.)

62 Tiberius' adoption: Vell. Pat. 2. 103. 3; Suet. *Tib.* 20. 3; 68. 3, with Levick 1976 (1999), 49f.

63 Fall of the elder Julia: Sen. *Brev. Vit.* 4. 5; Tac. *Ann.* 3. 24. 2; 4. 44. 3; Suet. *Aug.* 65. 1f.; Dio 55. 10. 12–16; 13. 1, with Dettenhofer 2000, 176–79. Iullus Antonius' suicide: Vell. Pat. 2. 100. 4; see Sattler 1969 ['Julia'], 516–18; Syme 1986, 90–92, with reference to earlier work. It is piquant to remember the consular Fulvius who had been allied with Gaius Gracchus in 121 (Ch. 2).

64 Tiberius beneath Julia: Tac. *Ann.* 1. 51. 1.

65 Adultery subversive: Ginsburg 2006, 126, based on Tac. *Ann.* 3. 24. 2.

66 Tiberius' divorce: Suet. *Tib.* 10. 4. Perhaps instead Augustus sent Tiberius notice of divorce on behalf of Julia; that was permissible.

67 Time for news to travel between W. Asia Minor and Italy: EJ 69 (early spring).

68 Demonstration for Julia: Suet. *Aug.* 65. 3; Dio 55. 13. 1. Her status at Regium: Linderski 1988; cf. J. F. Gardner, 'Julia's freedmen: questions of law and status', *BICS* 35 (1988) 94–100, and Linderski, *Roman Questions* II. Selected Papers. Habes 44 (2007) 630f.

69 Fate of Agrippa Postumus: Vell. Pat. 2. 112. 7; Tac. *Ann.* 1. 6; Suet. *Aug.* 65. 1. and 4; Tib. 22; Dio 55. 32. 1f., with Dettenhofer 2000, 195f. (bibl.).

70 Fall of the Younger Julia: Levick 1976; Syme 1978, 206–11; Crook 1996, 108f.; Survey: Southern 1998 185f.; Dettenhofer 2000, 195–97. Fate of Ovid: *PIR*[2] O 180 at p. 475f.: Silanus' recall: Tac. *Ann.* 3. 24. L. Aemilius Paullus: Suet. *Aug.* 19. 1: Scheid 1975, 91f. Torture of slaves: *Dig.* 48. 18. 8 (from Paul's Book 2 on adultery).

71 Novatus and Cassius: Suet. *Aug.* 61. 1.

72 Augustus' forbearance with relatives: Tac. *Ann.* 1. 6. 2.

73 Conspiracy of Audasius and Epicadus: Suet. *Aug.* 19. 1. Pollio had triumphed over the Parthini in 39 BC (Stein *ad PIR*[2] A 1227; Dio 48. 41. 7).

74 Death of Postumus: Tac. *Ann.* 1. 6. Campaign of Clemens: 2. 39f.

75 Morality and the legitimacy of power: Edwards 1993, 47.

76 Dancing on the Rostra, and Marsyas: Sen. *Ben.* 6. 32. 1; Pliny, *NH* 21. 9; Sattler 1969 ('Julia'), 520f. Crawford, *RRC* 378 rejects Republican associations with *libertas*, allowing the later symbolism of Serv. *ad* Virg. *Aen.* 3, 20; see F. Coarelli, *LTUR* 4, 364f.

77 Tolerance, and reaction to pamphlets: Suet. *Aug.* 55f., with Carter 1982 *ad loc.*; Dio 55. 27. 1.

78 Aelianus of Corduba: Suet. *Aug.* 51. 2f.

79 Intellectual opposition: Raaflaub and Samons 1990, 436–47, with a bibliography of Augustan poetry to 1989: 436 n. 86.

80 Labienus and his kin: *PIR*[2] L 19; Raaflaub and Samons 1990, 439f, with n. 97. 'Rabienus' and his poverty: Sen. *Contr.* 10, *Pr.* 4. Syme 1978, 212–14, followed by Lacey 1996, 230, couples him with his rival Cassius Severus as indicating that freedom of speech was 'curbed and subverted under pretext of social harmony'. Developments in *maiestas*: Tac. *Ann.* 1. 72. 2–4.

81 Cassius Severus: Tac. *Ann.* 1. 72. 3; 4. 21. 3; Suet. *Aug.* 56. Trial of Asprenas: Pliny *NH* 35. 16 4; Quint. 10. 1. 22; 11. 1. 57; Suet. *Aug.* 56. 2; cf. Dio 55. 4. 3; Macr. *Sat.* 2. 4. 9; further refs.: Malcovati 1969, 165, XXXIX n.

82 Attack on Vitellii: Suet. *Vit.* 2. 1. Rise of the family: Syme 1939 and 1986, indexes.

83 Prosecutions: Rutledge 2001. Domitian: e.g. Tac. *Agr.* 44. 5–45. 2. Renunciation of *maiestas*: P. A. Brunt, 'Did emperors ever suspend the Law of "Maiestas"?', in *Sodalitas* 1. *Scritti in Onore di A. Guarino* (Naples, 1984), 469–80.

84 Slanders: Tac. *Ann.* 1. 72. 4; Suet. *Tib.* 51.

85 Auguries: Galinsky 1996, 293. Destruction of prophecies: Suet. *Aug* . 31. 1. Omens before Augustus' death: Dio 56. 29. Restrictions on astrology: 56. 25. 5.

86 Temple of Ops: *Fasti Val., Amit., Ant.* (EJ p. 50). Continued building: Haselberger 2007, 192–221, citing aqueducts, Naumachia pool, temples of Mars Ultor and Magna Mater; 'final seal' 220f. It may be coincidence that no compital dedications are attested for the years 5–6 to 9–10 (Lott 2004, 124, table 2).

87 Precautions at Augustus' funeral: Tac. *Ann.* 1. 8. 6.

88 Command of Praetorian Guard: Dio 55. 10. 10.

89 L. Piso as City Prefect: Tac. *Ann.* 6. 10. 3, with Syme 1986, 341–44.

90 Archaeological evidence for occupation: von Schnurbein 2003.

91 Recruitment: EJ 368 (freeborn men at Rome); AD 7 and 9: Dio 55. 31. 1; 56. 23. 1–3.

92 Beggarly recruits: Tac. *Ann.* 4. 4. 2.

93 Discharge arrangements of 13 BC: Dio 54. 25. 5f.

94 Donations to Aerarium Militare: Dio 55. 25. 2; 32. 2; Suet. *Aug.* 49. 2. Tiberius' and Postumus' property: Levick 1972.

95 Mutinies of AD 14: Tac. *Ann.* 1. 16–49.

96 Provincial unrest: Dio 55. 28. 1–4; 29. 1f.

97 E.g., in the carefully documented narrative of Crook 1996, 100–12.

Chapter 5

The Self-Presentation
of a Monarch

Human and divine

The 'self' that Augustus presented was polymorphous: the evolution of Triumvirate and Principate shows that it depended on circumstances, on medium, above all on audience. He was avenger of Caesar, military victor, restorer of the Commonwealth (during the Triumvirate his troops heard themselves addressed as 'Comrades!', afterwards only as 'Soldiers!'[1]), popular leader, reformer, elder statesman – and a personage more than human who was moving towards the supreme honour of state cult. The public played its part in creating these personalities, but this chapter is concerned with Octavian/Augustus' own efforts and guidance. Architecture has its place here, and sculpture, but not poetry or history, the media of individuals often of high status and theoretically independent.

The distance that lay between the scion of an equestrian family and the deified Princeps should not astonish, for two reasons. First was the Graeco-Roman idea of a continuum between gods and men, passable and bridged by demi-gods such as Hercules, the viable and fertile offspring of one divine and one human parent; men and gods were of one species. Every Roman male was entitled to claim his own spark of divinity, his *genius*, and by his 'adoption' Octavian was already son of a god. A man of *virtus* (merit, especially military prowess) could hope for protection from the gods, or from one in particular, as Sulla the Dictator did from Venus.[2] From favour it was easy to move to relationship or even, with male deities, to identification. Extraordinary merit brought quasi-divine status. At the beginning of the second century BC a Roman general, T. Quinctius Flamininus, referred to himself in his dedication to Apollo as 'godlike'.[3] Merit and success served Caesar well, though he claimed descent from Venus Genetrix. Second, such connexions, above all acquired divine status, made a man more effective and better able to protect his followers. Like all political leaders, the Princeps needed to convince his men that they were on the winning side, that is that the gods (after Constantine's vision God) were for them. It would be something they already wanted to believe; there would be complicity between the two parties involved.

Octavian's Triumviral rivals went at least as far as he did in associating themselves with established divinities. In the East from 41 BC Antony was identified with the powerful and normally beneficent Dionysus, conqueror of the Orient and patron of Alexander, and he enjoyed divine ancestry through Anton, son of Hercules. Sex. Pompeius had it that he was the son of Neptune, as was only right for the last heir of Pompey the Great and one whose source of power, like his father's, lay in his ships.[4] Octavian took over other men's deities, notably from Brutus and Cassius, and Antony's Hercules after Actium, with a festival held on 12 August 29. That was the day before his triple Triumph, when he waited outside the City gates at the spot where Aeneas found the Arcadian king Evander sacrificing to the hero.[5]

Such identifications with the gods, notably the ebullient Dionysus, look unseemly, but Roman tradition allowed aristocratic families openly to associate themselves with eroticism and lewd gods: G. Herbert-Brown cites coinage of the Vibii Pansae, the Iunii Silani and the Marcii, advertising their connections with Pan, Silenus and Marsyas. This puts Octavian/Augustus' association with Venus and Mars in an acceptable context. The Romans lacked our boundaries between the sublime and the ridiculous.[6]

Octavian and his friends played at identification when they feasted as the twelve Olympian deities, with Octavian as Apollo. The anecdote is placed in a food shortage, so 39–37 BC – and that makes it sound apocryphal Antonian propaganda. Already in that decade the story spread that Octavian's mother, like those of Alexander the Great and P. Scipio Africanus, had been impregnated by a snake, the creature of Apollo.[7] A relation with Apollo was confirmed when lightning struck near Octavian's house on the Palatine. Over the site he built the white marble temple of the god, focus of the Secular Games in 17 and later a place where the Senate met.[8] Octavian had had his own statue, with the features and attributes of Apollo, placed in the Palatine Library.[9] His very house now lay between his new Temple of Apollo and the small Temple of Victory – with that of the Great Mother, now a reputable Trojan deity – just to the north.[10] There was a change in 28 BC, when the avenging Apollo who had presided over his victory at Actium was transformed into the lyre-playing deity of the Palatine temple, and, in Horace's words, laid down his arms for peaceful choruses: at the same time blatant assimilation ended.[11] Later, Augustus established a privileged relationship with Mars Ultor, as we can see from the coins, but there was an ever-widening variety of backgrounds, religious, military and political, against which he could present himself.

He could not neglect the King of the gods, especially as his father had dreamt of seeing him with the attributes of Jupiter Optimus Maximus. Jupiter under more than one aspect played an important part in the religious programme, and Octavian took an interest in Feretrius' temple when it was restored in 31 BC – claiming it, indeed, as his own in the *Achievements*.[12] Some years later, in fulfilment of a vow taken in Spain when he escaped a lightning bolt, Augustus constructed a temple of Jupiter Tonans, dedicated and celebrated on 1 September 22.[13] His election to the post of Pontifex Maximus in 12 made it possible for him to develop that position into the headship of Roman religion (Ch. 3). As K. Milnor has it, the imperial house itself was not a private space but a performance of privacy, by the Princeps, for the Roman people. A politician who thrived on ambiguity was also putting in concrete terms a representation of his own political life and ambitions: his path from private individual to public institution.[14]

The title 'Father of his Country' (Ch. 2), refused over the previous quarter of a century, was one that, in this or variant forms, had been bestowed unofficially on statesmen before, even briefly on Cicero. Augustus might well consider that he had merited it. Psychologically, without conferring the formal *potestas* of a father, it put Augustus into a parental relationship with all his fellow-citizens no matter how eminent. The conferment of the title is the last item in the *Achievements*, and it balances the opening claim about Octavian's first political act, performed without official sanction and now in retrospect perfectly justified.[15] It is hard to believe that at this late stage of Augustus' principate the Senate had anything other than flattery and congratulation in mind. The entrenched and elderly ruler was beyond influence, and subjects were indeed dependent on his paternal benevolence; we are only two decades away from the sycophancy of the *Senatorial Decree on Cn. Piso the Elder*, in which that body of elders (*patres*) has nothing to teach its rulers; on the contrary, they are its teachers.[16]

Theatricality

Augustus' attention to men's minds was that of an actor. His last words show that (Ch. 7), as does his awareness of his place in the public view when he was seated at a show, as much part of it as the performers below him. State and religious events involved pageantry and spectacle. He could star at a triumph, but after those of 29 BC he was too sensitive to the danger of devaluing the performance to give way to the 'desire to be seen'[17] by celebrating another. Different genres came into play, in sculpture as in life: sacrificial processions, vows, dedications, reviews. Augustus provided and regulated entertainments that allowed the people to forget their difficulties or suffering.[18] He understood the etiquette of relations between a ruler and his subjects. Unlike Julius Caesar, who worked on state papers in the imperial box, and Tiberius after him, who did even worse by absenting himself from it to avoid being accosted and harassed, and eventually left Rome altogether, he knew the value of being seen, especially in pursuits that ordinary men enjoyed. He would have observed or heard of popular reaction to Caesar's indifference. Augustus 'thought it civil to mingle in the pleasures of the populace'.[19] With an eye to the future of the dynasty, he displayed his grandsons Gaius and Lucius in the imperial box: and later kept out the disabled boy Claudius.[20] Theatricality in politics came ever closer to the surface with succeeding generations (not all of his direct descent: this was acquired behaviour), notably in Germanicus Caesar, Gaius. Caligula and Nero.

Augustus knew how to organise others in his own productions. His simple and well-tried methods have survived until the present day. The crowd in action ('mob'), which offers its members a collective sense of power and removes individual responsibility and danger, was particularly useful.[21] Octavian rallied Italy against Cleopatra and her satellite Mark Antony with the oath taken by *tota Italia*, which 'demanded' him (as he said in the *Achievements*, borrowing a word of Cicero's)[22] as commander against her; another rally swept him into the post of Pontifex Maximus.

Verbal performance

Augustus' use of language, varied as it was, remained moderate. It could not match the multifarious ways he was presented to his subjects in sculpture and architecture or seen by them. He never spoke as a deity, even to those who were offering cult in Asia and Bithynia. Romans in their turn called him 'Imperator' or 'Caesar'; Tiberius was equally careful not to overplay his position.[23] In the 30s Octavian had friends to win, especially in the East, and roughness should be avoided; even when he was firmly urging Ephesus to return a statue of Eros looted from the favoured city, Aphrodisias (Geyre), he diplomatically pointed out that it was hardly a suitable offering to Artemis.[24]

The utterances of the Princeps preserved on stone or papyrus, or copied by interested reporters, make a meagre harvest, subject to the accidents of time, to the selection of individuals, or to both.[25] (The large-scale *Achievements* are to be taken separately.) The recipients are diverse: they range from the Senate to provincial cities and individuals. Common features survive in inscriptions set up in provinces and addressed to subjects: self-justification and a claim to care for the welfare of the addressees (Ch. 3). Preambles, even the core text of measures often passed in response to per-ceived shortcomings or abuse, gave a chance to project the imperial image.[26] What he said was preserved, and the opinion of subjects was signif-icant to him, even when he was unwilling to grant a request. Augustus was a well-trained orator, attached great importance to speaking, and worked at it assiduously, even practising (as Antony was also doing) during the Mutina campaign in 43.[27] In Seneca's *Apocolocyntosis*, written in AD 54, Augustus is made to discourse with 'supreme eloquence'.[28] Yet he was not a man of many or fancy words; a connoisseur of language and rhetoric, he displayed a studied simplicity in his taste and expressions; he paid attention to clarity and could be home-spun in Latin.[29]

A Triumvir or Princeps did not normally have to encounter organised opposition or take part in the cut and thrust of Republican debate carried out on equal terms in court or in the Senate House. Exceptions are noted in the sources (see Ch. 4). Neat replies to the People are recorded, perhaps from informal assemblies (*contiones*). But Augustus was a supreme master of considered verbal spin. In the pivotal year 35, he had delivered and circulated written versions of speeches explaining to Senate and People his policies and achievements since the death of Caesar.[30] His very choice of the name Augustus (Ch. 2) shows the ingenuity he inspired in his clique, or his own skill. He was, above all, a master of the political vocabulary.

In the edict, its date uncertain, in which he claimed that he wanted to be known as the promoter of the best form that the Commonwealth could take (*optimi status*), he proclaims thoroughly consistently that he hoped likewise to be a salubrious (*salutaris*) Princeps. This is the nearest approach by Augustus that we have to the figure of speech beloved of 'conservative' politicians, which likens the state to a body. The useful word was also deployed by Tiberius early in his principate in his own definition of what a ruler should be.[31] It forwards the healthy condition of an entire body, that of an individual or a community, and is available for various causes. In Hitler's Germany 'a healthy sense of justice' meant one that accorded with the will and interest of the National Socialist Party.[32] Augustus' wish implied his intention of bringing health, however he defined it, to the entire Roman People. The body metaphor was used by Livy, who at the beginning of the 20s BC, when he was writing the Preface to his history of Rome, saw a sickness that his contemporaries were unwilling to cure.[33] Co-operation (*concordia*) was the remedy, invoked by Augustus in his speech of acceptance for the title *Pater Patriae* in 2 BC, when the three orders acted together, the people taking the initiative. Cicero had made it famous in 63 BC – when he had crushed a popular movement.[34]

For Augustus even poached the phraseology of the man in whose murder he had connived. In 43 he was granted *imperium* as a pro-praetor 'to ensure that the Commonwealth takes no harm'. In the *Achievements* he picked up the expression used by conservative politicians when they were about to launch a violent attack on radicals such as C. Gracchus in 121 BC, Appuleius Saturninus in 100, and the followers of Catiline in 63.[35] After Actium, Octavian was in complete control, 'by the agreement of every group of men' this is an echo of the phrase that Cicero used of his return from exile in 57 BC: it had come about 'by agreement of all good men' (*consensu omnium bonorum*). 'The whole of Italy' (*tota Italia*) poured into Rome to elect Augustus Pontifex Maximus.[36]

A master of verbal techniques, Augustus could command virtuosi in other skills. In Chapter 6 we shall see him presented by literary men and artists. At the Empire's centre, the material they worked on could be based on their own observations, modified by the front that Augustus consciously presented. Outside Rome visual artists worked on approved official models. The expenditure of private and public money on highly embellished architecture and works of art at Rome and elsewhere was well-judged and rewarded by the alacrity with which communities and individual men and women in Italy and the provinces took up the subjects and styles in vogue at the centre, right down to imperial hairstyles. This phenomenon, which P. Zanker has compared with the spread of the 'Empire style' under Napoleon I,[37] was the product of the Princeps' success and prestige.

Coinage[38]

The evidence of coinage begins with Octavian's earliest steps in politics, celebrating the young Caesar as Consul and Triumvir.[39] It is immediate, virtually complete, and widespread, if sometimes resistant to interpretation. Augustus was interested in coins,[40] and would have been sensitive to the images and legends they bore. They began to carry the portrait of a living person – signalling his authority over the mint – only under Caesar, but the Liberators followed suit, and Augustus' bust and those of his successors was rarely away from obverses, except when replaced by that of members of the dynasty. This saturation of the coinage with Augustus' portrait was the more significant because in his time the Roman became a world coinage.[41]

The significance of coinage as a means of presenting the ideology of the ruler, even as 'propaganda', is a matter of debate,[42] but certainly nothing appeared that did not suit him, whether he instructed the moneyers (*Triumviri monetales*) and mint officials on what was to appear, or approved it, or even simply accepted what they chose, or something in between and varying from one occasion to another. The elected moneyers were aristocratic young men in their late teens who were looking forward to a senatorial career. Their types celebrated Augustus in the last two decades BC and they may have gone on proposing them even when their names disappeared from the coinage;[43] it was a tribute worth having from Rome's future élite legislators. Augustan types, some often selected, others unique, were diverse and eloquent, eclipsed in those respects only by the coinage of Hadrian. They are characterised by bold but vague claims punctuated by references to concrete achievements, such as of the provision of grain and the construction of roads. Concern for the people's welfare was proclaimed in the reverses that displayed corn ears, whether in a wagon or simply bunched together.[44] Altogether the themes make an intelligible whole, and some are so strained in favour of the Princeps as to compel the view that they were initiated by him or by men sensitive to his wishes: they might be used as illustrations for an edition of his *Achievements*, but the coins also exhibited deities with whom Augustus particularly associated himself, and they went beyond the *Achievements* by presenting third-party 'narratives'.

A coinage of world-wide significance must mention achievements in war and diplomacy. Coins celebrated occasions that were particularly important to Augustus, the defeat and annexation of Egypt (*AEGYPTO CAPTA*) and the recovery of the province of Asia in 30 (*ASIA RECEPTA*).[45] A decade later came the peaceful settlement with the Parthians, the claimed annexation of Armenia, and the recovery of the standards lost with M. Crassus and Mark Antony: *SIGNIS RECEPTIS*.[46] That justified representations of *MARS ULTOR*, in whose temple, specially constructed for the purpose, the standards were to be deposited.[47] One reverse was insidiously deceitful – *ARMENIA CAPTA*[48]; Tiberius had been present in the country with an army in 20 BC, ratifying the new pro-Roman regime established by the Armenians themselves.

The Princeps' achievements in the civil sphere were also celebrated: victory in civil war had given Octavian an opportunity to demonstrate his merits in relation to fellow-citizens whose lives he had saved, earning him his oak-wreath; but coins inscribed *OB CIVES SERVATOS*[49] would have been put unceremoniously aside by relatives of men who had died. Then, in his sixth consulship, of 28 BC, Octavian was champion of the freedom of the Roman People (*LIBERTATIS POPULI ROMANI VINDEX*).[50] In the *Achievements*, Augustus claims at the very beginning of his career to have saved Rome from the tyranny of a 'faction'. In truth, factionalism was the essence of *libertas* as it had been known under the Republic; Augustus was offering controlled *libertas*. It went with security, though *SECURITAS AUGUSTI* was to appear on the coinage only under Nero. So when the Romans in AD 70 offered their rebellious subjects in Gaul *securitas* it went with *obsequium* (obedience to Rome).[51] The award in 27 of the *Clipeus Virtutis* is as pervasive on the coinage as it is prominent in the *Achievements* (see below).[52]

After the crisis of 23–19 one moneyer invoked *FORTUNA REDUX* (Fortune who brings about homecomings), the deity to whom the Senate raised altars when Augustus came back from the East to restore order in 19 BC.[53] In 16, the year after the new age had been inaugurated and in which it was still being celebrated,[54] we have a record of the vows offered in Augustus' honour to Jupiter Best and Greatest because he had brought the Roman People into a grander and more peaceful state of affairs – *IN AMPLIOREM ET TRANQUILLIOREM STATUM* – than they had previously enjoyed.[55] Another design, of 13 BC, exhibits shocking candour and arrogance on the part of Augustus, or (better) blatant servility on the part of those ostensibly responsible for the design, notably the moneyer Cossus Lentulus: the Commonwealth, *RES PUBLICA*, kneels at the feet of *AUGUSTUS*, who extends his hand to her.[56] A more personal and even touching note, struck in 16, with a call from Senate and Roman People 'for Caesar's good health' (*PRO VALETUDINE CAESARIS SPQR*), suggests that here officials were divining for themselves what would go down well with the Princeps.[57]

It is noteworthy that later achievements, such as those in Germany, were not directly celebrated; in any case, they were the work of subordinates. Augustus had been fêted adequately and to do more than continue him as an obverse bust would be repetitious. However, this impression is artificially strengthened by the fact that the mint at Rome closed for precious metals in about 12 BC, and for base metals in 4 BC, opening again only in about AD 10.[58] Again, in the Triumviral Period, Octavian's status as *Divi filius* had been prominent on his coinage from 38 BC; there was less room for it after he became 'Augustus' and when dating by tribunician power began. The supreme pontificate and the title of 'Father of his Country' simply took their place in the legend, when there was space. The coinage began to focus on Augustus' plans for the future: in 13 BC it showed him and his political partner Agrippa, their heads back to back on obverses and on reverses seated together on the tribunician bench; Julia appeared on another reverse between her sons Gaius and Lucius. In 8 BC the boys graduated to a military context as *equites*; finally came Tiberius, bareheaded or in his triumphal chariot.[59]

Buildings restored and new

The architect Vitruvius, evidently writing before the settlement of 27, already commented on Octavian's concern to ensure that the majesty of the Empire might find effective and distinguished expression in suitable public buildings.[60] There was much that Augustus could do to stabilise his position, that is by remedying interrelated failings – religious, social and so moral, and military – that were the commonplace complaints of poets and historians.[61] The reconstruction of the face of Rome was the manifest sign that these changes were being carried through. As the year-long Dictatorship of Sulla had shown, and later the manifest incompleteness of Caesar's projects, there were no instant remedies. In 28 BC eighty-two temples at Rome needed restoration; several were dedicated on Augustus' birthday.[62] He claimed in his *Achievements*, as we have seen, to have allowed some buildings (the Portico of Octavius, and less surprisingly the Capitol and the Temple of Saturn and the Theatre of Pompey), to credit their originators, without inscribing his own name on them.[63] But Augustus used his wealth to rebuild Rome far beyond that restoration. Construction went on almost until the end of his life, and had begun in the Triumviral period. It must be set against the works of earlier politicians, notably their temple buildings, culminating in those of Pompey and Caesar. The most lavish expenditure went on temples that were particularly associated with Augustus, after Apollo on the Palatine and Jupiter Tonans, Mars Ultor.[64] A great Roman had to build to acquire prestige and influence (*auctoritas*). By that token Augustus was the greatest Roman since Romulus.[65]

Augustan architectural schemes in Rome were inspired in part by Caesar's plans, though it was Agrippa who achieved the *Saepta Julia*. The Senate House, *Curia Julia*, burnt in 44, was rededicated in 29, and the *Basilica Julia* were their realisation. The Julian name, with all its dynastic implications, was imprinted on the city.[66] Augustus completed Caesar's forum before going on to build his own. Then the Temple of the Deified Julius was erected in the Roman Forum between two triumphal arches of the Princeps himself. There were some abstentions. It is worth noting projected buildings of Caesar that are not known ever to have been constructed: the temples of Clementia Caesaris, Libertas and (Caesar's outrageous usurpation of the optimate slogan) Concordia Nova.[67]

Augustus had his own designs to follow: the temple of Mars Ultor in his forum, Jupiter Tonans on the Capitol, and the Temple of Apollo attached to the Theatre of Marcellus, which had first been dedicated by Cn. Iulius, consul in 431 BC. Augustus' own family were brought into service, in what D. Favro dubs a 'sham', since the credit redounded on Augustus. They could connect with or take over buildings such as the Temple of Castor and Pollux, recalling Augustus' grandsons, and two shrines of Concord (one, to Concordia Augusta, built by Tiberius, with reference to his brother Nero Drusus, the other by Livia). Augustus paid for porticos named after his sister and his wife.[68]

The Princeps enumerates the structures he initiated or improved and notoriously claimed to have left a brick-built city one of marble. Suetonius implies a motive that chimes in with the words of Vitruvius: Rome had not been adorned as the majesty of the empire demanded.[69] The buildings were practical amenities, and their very construction generated prosperity for all those involved, architects, developers, tradesmen, quarriers, carriers, builders, scaffoldmen, carpenters. They also looked magnificent, did demonstrate the greatness of Rome's Empire, and, importantly, made Romans feel good (Ch. 3). More than any earlier dynast, even Sulla, Augustus was also in a position to adorn the city with Greek works of art, and did so with a sense of purpose that has engaged modern scholars as well. Romans were to view their city, notably the ancient centre, the Palatine and Capitoline, through Augustus' eyes and with his perspective of the past. Their view was also conditioned by the common sense of history and identity that he fostered: they were 'seeing socially'. Romans possessed that sense to a high degree, and could 'read the environment' as well; that made it easier for the Princeps to guide their view.[70] To take one minor example, Romulus's hut on the Palatine was devotedly preserved under the Augustan regime. But the fact that it had survived until Augustus took it over suggests that Augustus himself was buying into Roman sentiment.[71]

A negative side to Augustan building at Rome is worth noticing at once: the diminution of public construction by other individuals, apart from Agrippa and, on a smaller scale, Livia and Tiberius; they had nothing to compare with Agrippa's *Saepta Julia*, aqueducts, baths and Pantheon. Significantly, the axis of this north-facing building was aligned with that of the Mausoleum, and, according to Dio, Agrippa originally planned to place a statue of Augustus among those of the gods it housed, and to name the building after him. When Augustus refused such honours he put a statue of Caesar in the building and those of Augustus and himself in the antechamber.[72] Building was traditionally paid for from the war booty of triumphing generals, and the triumphs ended in 19 BC. Two years later Augustus reminded those who had held triumphs to undertake public work, and Cornelius Balbus did build a theatre.[73] Already in the Triumviral years there had been friction between Octavian and Cn. Domitius Calvinus, who was reconstructing the Regia, over sculptures that Octavian had lent during the rebuilding; and the temple of Apollo that the Antonian Sosius was building to celebrate his success against the Jews was taken over and the decoration altered to fit Octavian's triumph over the Balkan tribes.[74] There was to be no blazoning of lesser men's successes in later 'Augustan' Rome, though those who won the triumphal decorations (*ornamenta triumphalia*) that were substituted for the triumph proper were allowed their own statues.[75] Nothing was forbidden, but men were unwilling to compete with the Princeps in such popular activities; road-building too, and certainly the less popular road repairing, became imperial monopolies, and only the name of the Princeps was found on Italian milestones after the early 20s BC (some legates in the provinces added that the work had been done *through* them).[76] There was a stir in AD 22, when M. Aemilius Lepidus asked permission even to restore the Basilica of Paullus. Tiberius took over the cost, but refrained from putting his name on the building. This was a replay of Augustus' restoration of the theatre of Pompey, which Pompey's family, not surprisingly, could not afford.[77]

Apollo, Nicopolis and the Mausoleum, with the Ara Pacis and the Meridian

Two schemes planned in the Triumviral period were already devoted to 'self-aggrandising display', in P. Zanker's words: 'propaganda for an ambitious general, with no regard for the traditions of the Republic'.[78] These monuments were the Temple of Apollo on the Palatine, where Romulus had his hut, and the Mausoleum on the Campus Martius (outside the Pomerium, as a tomb must be), worthy successors to the Theatre of Pompey the Great and the Forum of Julius Caesar. The Temple of Apollo was vowed after the victory at Naulochus in 36 and dedicated on 9 October 28 BC, the anniversary of a religious triad, including Venus, which was connected with Victory.[79] Augustus was able to buy out private owners in a residential area and a providential thunderbolt justified the consecration of Apollo.[80]

In Greece, Apollo also presided over the complex that Octavian constructed to commemorate his defeat of Cleopatra and the forces of the East. The victory monument itself consisted in an altar with three-sided stoa dedicated to Mars and Neptune. The wall of the base carried a Latin inscription above a row of thirty-six ships' rams. It tells that the monument was on the site of the camp from which Octavian had issued forth against the (anonymous) enemy to his victory for the Commonwealth, securing peace on land and sea (a reference to the closure of the Temple of Janus on 11 January 29). Just to the south on the Preveza peninsula rose the 'free' city of Nicopolis, created from an enforced synoecism of neighbouring peoples and with materials from existing settlements. Actian Apollo was on the promontory over the water from Preveza, facing north.[81] The altar and the new city were a permanent reminder to the Greek world of the authority and power of Rome and its new master.

The massive Mausoleum in the Campus Martius was perhaps begun in 32 BC as an answer to Antony's domestication in Alexandria; it was a visual reminder of the greatness of Caesar Augustus and all his dynasty, and the whole transformation of the Campus was 'the most novel and exciting part of a newly-defined Rome'. Eventually fronted by bronze tables bearing the record of his *Achievements*, the Mausoleum held the remains and presented the careers of M. Claudius Marcellus, M. Agrippa and C. and L. Caesar; it was a dynastic monument that proclaimed the greatness of the leading family.[82] Around it developed an extraordinary scheme of architecture and landscaping.

To the park adorned with statues, trophies and inscriptions was added the Altar of the Augustan Peace, decreed by the Senate on 4 July 13 BC, on Augustus' return from Gaul, and dedicated in 9. Along the outer precinct walls of the Altar processed on the north side magistrates and priests, on the south the equipollent family of the Princeps. Now the dynastic plans were laid out to view – and with the Senate's sanction. Anniversary sacrifices at the Altar enabled the Princeps to experience, and senators and people to see him experiencing, the beginning of Rome and the Julii, represented by Aeneas and Romulus. In the ideology of the regime – which has also captured the imagination of modern scholars – the City and family could turn again to the perfection of a new age. A less positive exposition has been put forward by J. Elsner, who stresses the role of participation in a sacrificial ritual – a death to obviate death – in constructing the meaning of a monument that had no cult

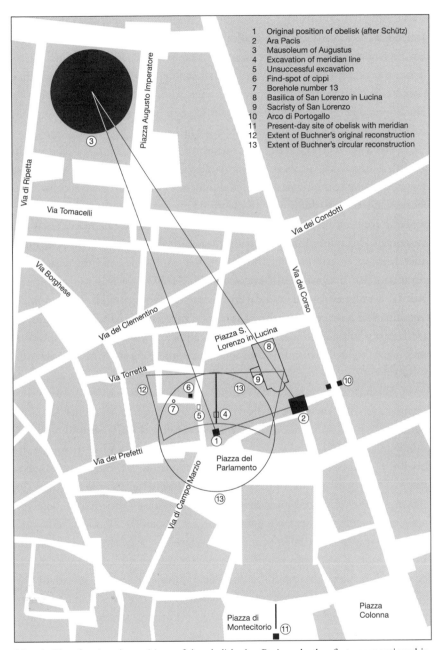

1   Original position of obelisk (after Schütz)
2   Ara Pacis
3   Mausoleum of Augustus
4   Excavation of meridian line
5   Unsuccessful excavation
6   Find-spot of cippi
7   Borehole number 13
8   Basilica of San Lorenzo in Lucina
9   Sacristy of San Lorenzo
10 Arco di Portogallo
11 Present-day site of obelisk with meridian
12 Extent of Buchner's original reconstruction
13 Extent of Buchner's circular reconstruction

Map 4   Plan showing the positions of the obelisk, Ara Pacis and other features mentioned in the text (after Heslin, 2007)

statue and invited creative interpretation, evoking ambiguity and uncertainty. Indeed, Elsner considers the ideology of the Principate less dominant than has been supposed; the gaps between procession and sacrifice, between sacrifices past, present and future, and ambivalences implicit in Roman sacrifice potentially undermined the imperial image from within. That is going too far. Imperial ceremonies were enfolded in, and developed from, an ancient tradition and should have been able to profit from it.[83]

It was long accepted that to the south of the Mausoleum was laid out in 10 BC a huge sundial, its thirty-metre-high gnomon an obelisk, loot from Egypt. On the spring and autumnal equinoxes (the latter almost coinciding with Augustus' birthday on 23 September) the shadow of the gnomon would have pointed along the axis of the Altar's enclosure and ended at the entrance. The symbolism would be manifold: Augustus' horoscope, birth and death were engraved in the topography of Rome, and the peace that Augustus had imposed on the world from 31 BC onwards was manifestly part of destiny ordained by heaven.[84] Further thought and archaeological investigation have reduced the sundial to a mere solar meridian: it indicates the shortest and longest days of the year, and can be used to check the congruence of the solar year and civil calendar, something that was corrected in 9 BC.[85]

P. Heslin's careful study of the site and the alignment of Mausoleum, obelisk and Ara Pacis shows how closely the three monuments are connected. The sides of the obelisk are not oriented north–south with the meridian itself, but parallel with the Via Flaminia, and a line through the obelisk and perpendicular to the road will pass through the centre of the Ara Pacis. The obelisk is the right-angled corner of a right-angle triangle. On this formation Heslin builds symbolic possibilities. The obelisk, erected after the death of the unworthy Pontifex Maximus Lepidus, tells how Augustus was the right man to manage his father's calendar; the Mausoleum stresses Augustus' commitment to Rome, as opposed to Antony's wish to be buried in Alexandria; and the Ara Pacis alludes to the 'bloodstained Octavian who was transformed into Augustus, bringer of peace'. The inscription on the obelisk implicitly refers to all three triumvirs: Augustus, Lepidus' successor in the priesthood, looks back to his youthful usurpation of Antony's dominions in the East ('having brought Egypt into the power of the Roman People'). The meridian measured the dedicator's progress from Triumvir to Princeps, from man of war to man of peace.

Much of this, notably the significance of the Mausoleum, is indisputable; but there is no actual reference to Lepidus in the inscription, only the title 'Pontifex Maximus'; and the claim of the victor is to have conquered Egypt, the source of the obelisk, that is Cleopatra, not Antony. Certainly, Augustus was a bringer of peace; that does not mean that he did not want his years of war recalled; nor does the meridian itself point to either of the two monuments linked to the obelisk. Doubts on these points make it difficult to go further with Heslin in reading each pair of the monuments together: the obelisk as marking the lingering end of the Triumvirate and suggesting, with the Mausoleum, the opposition between East and West; the Mausoleum, a building for death, facing the altar that celebrates peace; while the obelisk celebrates the pacification of the East and the altar that of the West. Then, each of the three is seen as a family monument for the Julii – though the altar was dedicated on Livia's birthday,[86] while the meridian commemorates the forbearance of Augustus in taking the priesthood late in life (aged 51), which his father had occupied in youth (37) as a token of his unprecedented ambition. These are constructions that an ingenious poet of the time, like a modern scholar, might well have elaborated when he came to celebrate the complete scheme; but aesthetic considerations may have been what told with Augustus when he was considering the alignment of the obelisk. What remains certain is Pliny's point that the pavement stopped where the shadow reached at midday on the winter solstice, where Augustus' Capricorn sign was, marking the imminent return of the sun. Nonetheless, there is justice in P. Rehak's formulation: the complex in the northern Campus Martius 'serves as an eschatological "museum" of Augusus' life and accomplishments'.[87]

The temple of Mars Ultor

In his *Achievements*, Augustus presented a 'factual' view of himself in close-up. It might be juxtaposed to the scheme of adornment in the shrine of Mars Ultor in his new Forum, which some have thought was vowed before the battle of Philippi, with Caesar's assassination in mind.[88] There within the walls, on private ground, and in proximity to the shrine of Venus, he offered a fresh version of Roman history from the beginning, and of his own family's place in it, with Augustus the culmination of both lines, those of the Julian family and of the Roman heroes; in front was a four-horse chariot carrying a statue of the Princeps. The complex showed an advance in his self-representation, as W. K. Lacey has remarked, dynastic in intent. In one extreme and unacceptable formulation it is combined with the grant of the title of *Pater Patriae* to bring the Principate to the state of an absolute monarchy comparable with the Hellenistic kingdoms; such a conception could not be allowed to rise over the Roman mental horizon.[89] The Forum was the embodiment of Vitruvius' view of the function of public architecture, to enhance the grandeur of empire through its influence.[90] Fittingly, it used materials from all over the Empire. The historical references went back beyond Rome's supremacy: as K. Galinsky points out, it recalled Greek achievements with the Caryatids in the porticoes of the upper storey, just as the sea-battle that Augustus held in 2 BC represented the Greek victory of 480 BC over Persia at Salamis. In the shrine were figures of Venus, Mars and the Deified Julius Caesar, and on its pediment those of Venus and Mars again, but flanked by Romulus, Fortune and Rome. However, the long sides of the colonnaded Forum contained niches to the right, north side, in which Augustus' Julian ancestry was represented, obscure under the Republic, but leading from Aeneas and the kings of Alba Longa (in the exedra) down to Marcellus. Those on the left presented other great figures of Roman history (*summi viri*), including Sulla and Pompey. Such a parade of Roman heroes was already familiar in literature from the sixth and eighth books of Virgil's *Aeneid*, where Augustus can be seen laying claim to the past,[91] and the military theme recalls Horace's fourth book of Odes. By embedding himself in Roman history, Augustus guaranteed his own position as a figure who would be seen alongside the greatest. In including a statue and *elogium* for Pompey – the latter-day Republican – in his Forum Augustus was going beyond controversy – but he was also putting Pompey in a mass of heroes beneath himself.[92]

Augustus himself composed the prose commemorations of the heroes, or supervised their composition. Elsewhere, in the portico of Octavia, he seems to have statues of revered matrons erected: Cornelia, mother of the Gracchi, provided a niche for his wife Livia to occupy. More radically, in 35 BC, he had allowed his wife and sister to have statues erected to them. That was a novelty, and E. Hemelrijk has plausibly suggested that previous examples of female statues, including that of Cornelia, were in fact representations of goddesses or boys that were redesigned to show women and so provide precedents; it was a wilful refashioning of *mos*.[93]

The commandeering of time

Augustus, then, commandeered the past, which led up to his achievements. The solar meridian laid down in 9 BC in connexion with the corrections made to the calendar showed him the master of current time, and his position in the new Forum showed him as an *exemplum* outdoing the old heroes who themselves had set him an example. It was his purpose for the Roman people to judge him and future *principes* by the standards of the men commemorated in his Forum, says Suetonius, citing the words of his edict. That was also a leading theme of his *Achievements*, set up outside the Mausoleum and elsewhere in the Empire. It was accepted by the Senate: the statue of Augustus in a four-horse chariot was raised in front of the Temple of Mars Ultor by their order. At the same time, Augustus was winning authority for his own activities and setting a new standard for the future. His view of history and his own achievements was to be accepted as a model for generations of Romans to come. The propagation of this idea offers spectacular instances of his skill with language and of his manipulation of Roman conventions about old and new: the *exempla* were conveyed 'by the passing of new laws at my instance'. The word 'new' (*novus*) has unfavourable connotations; Augustus makes his innovations salutarily traditional, and reminds readers that his own achievements will acquire the same status as those of their ancestors. His work is poised between old and new, to be taken for either. Command of the past extended even to details, as Livy noticed, when he related the story of Augustus' interpretation of the inscription on the corselet of Lentulus. The expertise of an autocrat in any field invariably wins respect; Stalin the opera critic is a striking example. So Augustus commandeered the future as well as present time and the past. [94]

Even more audacious was Augustus' 'turning of all Roman time into Augustan time', as A. Wallace-Hadrill has persuasively termed it.[95] Augustus controlled the *Fasti*, and on the *Fasti* inscribed after 19 within the 'Parthian' arch that crossed the Sacred Way the last triumph to be recorded is that of Cornelius Balbus, at the bottom of a plaque; after that triumphs belonged solely to the imperial family – having originated under the monarchy. That accords roughly with the production of important monuments in Rome, apart from those commemorating imperial success, which went on at least until the teens: L. Aelius Lamia, governor of Spain 22 BC, and, with a funerary monument at Gaeta (Caieta) that was modelled on that of the

Princeps himself, L. Munatius Plancus, censor in the same year, M. Licinius Crassus Frugi, consul 14 BC, and a man with the cognomen Rufus, were all grandly commemorated.[96] Again, in the surviving fragments of the *Fasti* Augustus is shown from AD 2 to be counting years by those of his tribunician power, and the doings of the imperial family were inscribed in them.[97] For the Asian province, in 9 BC, an idea suggested by the alert governor Paullus Fabius Maximus (consul 11 BC) was enthusiastically accepted by the provincial assembly: the beginning of the year was to be reckoned as Augustus' birthday, which had given a new look to the cosmos.[98] Such a change to the calendar could not take place at Rome, although in 8 BC the eighth month, Sextilis, came to be 'August', as the seventh, Quintilis, had become 'July',[99] but Augustan celebrations were interspersed among ancient days of note, creating a new 'pageant of the Roman past' and hence a new understanding of what it meant to be a Roman. Unwilling to be left behind, individual cities made the date he visited them the first day of their year.[100] It went far beyond Mussolini's modest attachment of his own regnal years (in Roman numerals) to those of the Christian Church, still to be seen in books published under his regime.[101]

The autobiography

Augustus naturally did not deal with his own origins and earliest years in the *Achievements*, but they would have figured in the thirteen-book autobiography that he composed in the 20s BC, taking his career down to the end of his Cantabrian campaigns and the closing of the temple of Janus. We have only references and a few surviving citations. He made no attempt to deceive anyone (certainly not his dedicatees Maecenas and Agrippa) about his equestrian ancestry (see Introduction).[102] It is likely that positive items written up in the *Achievements* already featured in the autobiography, notably the award in 27 of the Clipeus Virtutis (Shield of Merit).[103] The work was probably intended largely as a defence of his past, although the fact that nearly half the citations from it are apologetic may tell as much about the selectors' preoccupations as about the author.[104] Certainly cowardice was a charge he is often found rebutting.[105] He admitted that he had needed Cicero's oratory to legitimise his early military successes, which went along with shifting the guilt of Cicero's murder on to the shoulders of Antony; so he had the face to praise Cicero as a man of literature, and patriotic.[106]

The *Achievements* [107]

The *Achievements of the Deified Augustus* (*Res Gestae Divi Augusti*), are a substantial survival from Augustus' hand, and, as G. Rowe remarks,[108] a reason why we tend to see the whole period through Augustus' eyes. He wrote that he completed the work in his seventy-sixth year, in 13–14, but it culminates in the grant of the title 'Father of his Country' in 2 BC. Many have held that it was composed over a considerable period, reaching definitive form in that year, with some later revision; four Appendices were added after his death.[109] There were few achievements to add after the grant of the title; Augustus could have kept his memoir by him for years, titivating it until he knew he was near the end. The document was brought into the Senate early in September 14 along with his will of 3 April 13,[110] instructions for his funeral, and a summary of the state of the Empire that incorporated advice on how it should be run. The themes of this ultimate work are consonant with numismatic and architectural material, already considered, that comes from Augustus' entire career.

The *Achievements* deserves close inspection. It represents Augustus' final and considered statement about himself, an elaborated equivalent of the *elogia* he had provided for the republican worthies in his Forum – and outdoing them.[111] By the time Augustus composed even a first draft of his own memorial, he was a master of the art of bending minds to his own purposes. Its virtuosity in misrepresentation (omission and implication rather than assertion of checkable untruths) signals the genius of the author. For historians, whose purpose should be to discover the truth, this is dismaying:[112]

> *The ideology behind the text is laid bare: Augustus' selflessness in every action, his observance of tradition, his generosity, the stimulus provided not by his own ambition but by the offers of senate or people, his moderation, his sense of duty. . . . So much for the ideology: what of the historical trustworthiness of the* Res Gestae?

The fact is, first, that Romans used to the conventions of political and forensic oratory would not be taken in, but would find it convenient to accept what was said, second, that the work, considered as a whole, precisely because of its historical untrustworthiness, illuminatingly reveals its author and his milieu. Indignation is misplaced, for the aim, tone and content are still instructive in their own way.[113]

Attempts to classify the work as a literary production have not succeeded. The style aims at the impersonal and objective, as Julius Caesar's
third-person narrative had done in his *Commentaries*, but R. T. Ridley
claims with some justice that 'there has never been a more personal or contrived piece of piece of self-aggrandisement'.[114] The view of E. S. Ramage[115] that the primary purpose was explication, and that Augustus was
describing a new form of government, with a detailed idea of how the Principate was to function, is not correct. Ramage juxtaposes the work to Cicero's *De Republica*, which provided the theory of kingship, while the
Achievements provides a theory of Principate. But the work is not a prescrip-
tive treatise, nor can those who have treated it with scepticism be dismissed.
The view argued by A. B. Bosworth convincingly holds that, with its insistence on world conquest and benefaction and its kinship with Euhemerus'
story of the apotheosis of Zeus, translated by Ennius, it justified Augustus'
deification, but that does not rule out other and wider functions, and the

Figure 14 Ara Pacis Augustae (akg-images Ltd. Photograph by Andrea Jemolo)

Figure 15 Ara Pacis processions. (a) North side: L. Caesar; Julia; Iullus Antonius; Marcella Maior (b) South side: Agrippa; C. Caesar; Livia; Tiberius; Antonia Minor; Nero Drusus (c) South side: *Flamines*; Agrippa, veiled. (akg-images Ltd. Photographs by Pirozzi and Andrea Jemolo)

Figure 16 Mausoleum of Augustus, Rome (Bridgeman Art Library Ltd. Photograph from Private Collection/Ken Welsh)

work is grittily prosaic. It needed interpretation for that purpose, perhaps provided by those who drafted the dactylic preamble.[116] In genre the work is closest to a private funerary inscription written in the first person; its ego-ridden prose was to impinge on every passer-by.[117]

As the document was inscribed on two bronze pillars outside the Mausoleum, there is a facile answer to the question for whom it was intended, but that takes no account of how far down in society it might reach, or of the fact that the existing preamble was designed for a provincial audience and the three surviving versions come from the Province of Galatia, one in Augustus' Latin, one in a Greek version, one bilingual, all perhaps procured by a single loyal governor.[118] It is a good question[119] why it was set here, rather than in the central Forum with the other *elogia* that it so grandly outstripped, where it would have been more easily read. The obvious answer is formal: the *elogium* belonged with the funerary building. But beyond that, the contrast in length between the other inscriptions and the *Achievements* would have been glaring. The deified Princeps was best removed from the company of lesser worthies.

The question is part of the larger one, often asked: how far down in society Augustus was concerned to reach, not only with the rest of his self-representation, but with his social legislation. Augustus, who favoured the broad brush of such phrases as 'the whole of Italy',[120] would have given the enquirer a wholesome, all-inclusive answer, regardless of practicalities: the entire Roman People. For the *Achievements*, modern answers have been significantly diverse: the Senate was a target, because the document was first read to them; the *equites*, a well-to-do section of society which, having been outside politics, had fewer preconceptions about their role in directing the state; the people of Rome, because of the document's stress on Augustus' benefactions; the young, for whom Augustus' achievements were to form a model. Of course there are objections. The Senate was a body of sophisticated sceptics; the *plebs*, partly illiterate, would hardly put itself to the trouble of tracing out the inscription.[121] The touching picture of an ambitious equestrian bringing his promising son to the Mausoleum so as to be seen standing in front of it reading the revered words with him, has attractions, but the strip of society that this pair represents is too narrow for it to be worth the Princeps' effort. Rather, the facile answer subsists: the document was salutary reading for any inhabitant of Rome that it reached, at whatever level of society, and then for any Italian who was in the City. The provincials beyond were not excluded, as the author of the preamble saw (in spite of the aggressive imperialism of the opening sections and 25–33). Otherwise the governor of Galatia would not have seen the prudence of getting copies inscribed in his administrative centre, Ancyra (Ankara) and in Augustus' leading colony in the province, Pisidian Antioch (Yalvaç), whose Greek neighbour, Apollonia Pisidiae (Uluborlu), was graced with the Greek version, with an introduction that had nothing about world conquest. The governor's role is not attested, but seems probable: in Baetica, six years later, the proconsul was explicitly responsible for setting up copies of the senatorial decree on Cn. Piso. In short, Augustus was addressing Romans at home and abroad, but not excluding subjects, even the world at large. Presenting commitments and activities welcome to participants of every class was one of Augustus' chief concerns. In the view of Z. Yavetz, the main theme was *humanitas*, human feeling, the art of endearing oneself to the lowly while winning the affection of the eminent.[122]

Certainly, the work purported to be an educational document, showing, as the Latin preamble blatantly put it, the achievements by which he brought the world under the *imperium* of the Roman People and the costs he incurred in doing so.[123] History was doctored on the spot for the benefit of the coming generation. The implicit overall message was that Augustus was the first or the best in a given field, *the* model for future young men (he did not boast of his unprecedented change of name (Ch. 2)).[124] 'I brought back into use many exemplary practices of our ancestors which were disappearing in our time, and in many ways I myself transmitted exemplary practices to posterity for their imitation.' The education of the young was a well-founded preoccupation of Roman aristocratic circles: in the opinion of the second century BC historian Polybius, the purpose of the Roman funeral procession was to teach the young about valour and the reputation that it brought.[125] The opening and closing sections tell the same story: the Princeps' enterprise as a private individual of nineteen in 44 BC in section 1 leads to the grant of 2 BC, with the suggestion of a father's traditional power (*patria potestas*) that it conveyed. All that Octavian/Augustus did outside the framework of law is thus justified. The whole work accordingly presents a smooth and bland surface, its bald and disingenuous treatment of traumatic events between 23 and 19 BC an example.[126] The first four sections record military successes, 5–8 offices held or offered and the use made of them, 9–14 honours and religious celebrations; sections 15–24 celebrate money gifts, buildings and games, 25–33 Augustus' extensions of the Empire and the compliance of powers beyond it; in 34 comes the achievements of 28–27 and the awards that they brought, leading without a break to that of 'Father of his Country'.[127] It is an entertaining antidote to the *Achievements* to read the passage of Pliny's *Natural History* that records a piteous tale of the woes that befell the Princeps, a list designed to counter the story of Augustus' *felicitas* (good fortune), or the relentless successes of the *Achievements* itself.[128]

Whatever the tone, the leading theme is service to the Commonwealth. That is how the work opens, with its rescue from a tyrannical clique, and near the end comes its transfer to the discretion of Senate and People.[129] He records that it was in recognition of service to the state and restoration of constitutional government that the Senate, in 27, voted him the *Clipeus Virtutis*. Augustus embraced the tribute; it was noted on coinage, as we have seen, and replicated in the provinces.[130] The individual merits of the Shield were celebrated in the *Achievements*. *Virtus* represents his personal military successes, specifically in having defeated Caesar's assassins and Antony and Cleopatra.[131]

There were doubts about valour (Ch. 1), but *clementia* was even more controversial,[132] a virtue, it has been claimed, of the gods and of autocrats such as Caesar.[133] Certainly it was the virtue of the man in the more exalted station, as Seneca wrote, addressing Nero; and the younger Cato had won his greatest glory by refusing Julius Caesar's.[134] Augustus claims to have spared defeated citizens, if they asked him, and foreign enemies who could safely be pardoned, where there is an unmistakable reference to Virgil's line, surely already famous, that the Roman should spare those who submit, and beat down the arrogant (*parcere subiectis et debellare superbos*). It showed to best advantage when it was granted to defeated foreign enemies, as on the Boscoreale cups. It was a lame point in the *Autobiography* that he had the bodies of men executed on capital charges returned to their relatives.[135] An anecdote concerning the Princeps' clemency could have embarrassing strings attached. Once, adding a gift to an act of clemency, and so giving the act the widest publicity, Augustus said to the recipient that he would try never to be angry with him again – for his own sake (that is, his pocket's).[136]

The historical record is patchy. There were notorious exceptions to his clemency,[137] and the claim to have burnt Antony's correspondence was false.[138] Into the historical tradition, probably from the *Autobiography*, has crept the assertion that he would have spared Sex. Pompeius had he had the chance, and L. Du Quesnay has detected a change of behaviour after the battle of Naulochus in 36 from ruthlessness against the proscribed and those defeated at Philippi: Appian says that he spared the Pompeian generals, but Dio mentions exceptions.[139] Individual cases were determined by the balance between rage and prudence, perhaps increasingly by the impression the victor wanted to make.

Nonetheless, after two decades of civil strife, professions of clemency were now accepted by grateful subjects, who hoped that they would justify themselves by restraining the ruler. The professions were duly reflected in another published document: in the 'Eulogy of Turia' the widower shows Octavian displaying his *clementia* and by contrast brands the insolent cruelty (*crudelitas*) of Lepidus.[140] Again, three sources have stories of a proscribed person popping out of a chest in the theatre and being pardoned, probably in 39 BC. G. Sumi plausibly suggests that Octavian was in on the ruse: it is hardly credible otherwise.[141] The Senate put *clementia* in second place, suggesting how much they still feared their master in 27. It seems then that senators had something else in mind in 27 than simply doing

Augustus honour: they expected him to demonstrate all the qualities specified on the shield. This interpretation of tributes paid to the virtues of supreme rulers as a form of pressure is satisfying; self-representation comes with a price attached, that of living up to the claims put forward.

The third virtue, *iustitia*, was hard to weigh up, though it afforded a daily series of tests; in some circumstances it could be seen as in conflict with *clementia*.[142] It was a quality that Virgil lamented in the *Georgics* as having left the earth; now Augustus brought it back, permanently.[143] His routine performances may have been satisfactory, as Suetonius suggests, but there were failures such as the show trial of Caepio and Murena and the ensuing tampering with the jury's voting system (Ch. 4): 'Rise, murderer!', said the tablet thrown into Augustus' lap as he sat in judgment, implying not one misjudgment but a whole climate of dissatisfaction.[144] Two Plutarchan anecdotes show Augustus being warned by a friendly philosopher to recite the alphabet before doing or saying anything in anger and just being saved from hitting one of the men accused of adultery with the elder Julia by being reminded that he had passed a law on the subject.

The polyvalent *pietas*, devotion towards gods, family, Commonwealth and People, was less controversial and was exemplified over the years in Augustus' ostensible devotion to the memory of Julius Caesar and in the list of temples he constructed or rebuilt, in the priesthoods he held and the offerings he made.[145] It was superbly evoked by Virgil's Aeneas, whose devotion to his family and his cause, the preservation of the people of Troy, the foundation of Rome, anticipated Augustus' own single-minded preoccupation, as it seemed.

It was in response to the Senate's dedication of 27 that Augustus brought the Clipeus into his *Achievements*. *Virtus* Augustus obviously believed that he possessed – his campaigning showed it, but the burdens that *clementia, iustitia* and *pietas* imposed were worth bearing for the recognition they gained, and by mentioning them in the *Achievements* he was asserting that he had succeeded in carrying it. A reciprocal relationship had been established, and Augustus was claiming to have met the challenge presented to him in 27. Nonetheless, at the end of his principate an exiled poet appealed to one of the qualities that Augustus claimed, but in vain.[146]

The virtues of the Clipeus do not belong to a philosophical canon and they are naturally not exclusive.[147] Crediting the Emperor Julian (AD 332–63) with the philosopher's virtues of moderation, wisdom, justice and courage, his admirer Ammianus Marcellinus adds a penumbra of 'external' merits: knowledge of the art of war, authority, good fortune and liberality.[148] Liberality too is displayed in Augustus' *Achievements*, for its supreme importance to the *plebs*, though without being named. It was played down in explicit verbal advertising precisely for its disturbingly populist associations; the word *largitio* (largesse) could be used to expose the unfavourable connotations that *liberalitas* (open-handedness) disguised. Such merits came into vogue only after the end of the Julio-Claudian dynasty, with *liberalitas* first on the coinage of Hadrian.[149] To Augustus' four publicly proclaimed intrinsic merits others have cavalierly been added in modern times: *victoria, pax, fortuna redux*, making for a misleading mixture of categories. These last three are independent deities – *fortuna* certainly had a mind of her own; or else they are external blessings conferred on men with the requisite qualities. They are nothing like the merits of the shield, or even the four characteristics that Cicero claimed belonged to the successful general such as Pompey, and Ammianus for Julian.[150]

As to what was discreditable, right from the start of the *Achievements* spin is put on illegal acts, turning them into resounding claims to be acting in defence of freedom:[151] Octavian's stand against the consul Mark Antony in 44 BC becomes freeing the state from a *factio*. The ostensible end justifies the illegal means. To designate Antony Augustus exploits a word with a built-in bad sense: *factio*, a cabal with a reprehensible plan of action (*facere*, to act).[152] On the other hand, Augustus flaunts his private status, which might have debarred him from public action but for the principle pronounced by Cicero that it was the place of private persons to take action in emergencies.[153] Even the claim that Augustus financed his own political debut privately is not quite true, for he purloined funds earmarked for Caesar's campaigns against the Parthians. The *Achievements* makes adroit use of literary precedents that have political resonance, and yet are not altogether consonant. Indeed, the language of the first chapter exploits both that of the radical and *popularis* Caesar in the opening of the *Civil Wars*, where he denounces an earlier *factio*, at the same time as citing the passage from Cicero's third *Philippic* that commended Octavian's efforts against the radical Antony.[154]

It is not surprising that discussion of the *Achievements* has focused on the reliability of a main source of information for the Principate of Augustus. These details have to be considered, but they are not everything. G. D. Rowe

Figure 17   Temple of Mars Ultor and part of Forum Augustum (akg-images Ltd)

adopts a broad and illuminating approach to the *Achievements* and its ability to mislead;[155] he stresses not individual statements but the structure of the work. It is largely thematic, rather than chronological, and that detaches Augustus' deeds from their historical context and makes them appear as manifestations of his overmastering will. Similarly, Rowe stresses the pervasive logic of exchange that Augustus adopted: I performed deeds and made expenditures on behalf of the Roman people, and the Roman people rewarded me with honours, offices and powers – which supposes that the Roman people were free actors.

   The document does indeed trumpet the honours, religious and political, that Senate and Roman People conferred on Augustus[156] – both are responsible for bringing him on after his first private initiative. The chapter records Octavian's election to the consulship, the grant of *imperium*, and his appointment as Triumvir (omitting the circumstances). Yet Augustus is aiming at an effect of restraint – neglecting to mention that the accumulation of powers that he held since 19 BC was unheard of (Ch. 2). The broadest claim is that he 'accepted no magistracy that was not sanctioned by custom'.[157] This restraint, in the context of Rowe's concept of exchange, makes good

sense. So it does in the provincial context: when Octavian/Augustus was offered cult he refused anything extreme; the services he could be expected to
perform in return were similarly restricted. His successors usually followed
his example: it left leeway in their obligations to citizens and subjects.[158]

The refusal of unique powers features strongly for another reason. Sole
power, with its tyrannical connotations, recalled the Dictatorship, the only
Republican magistracy held without a colleague and abolished after Caesar's
death. It has a positive counterpart in the *Achievements*. Augustus tells how
he 'actually' (*ultro*) asked five times for a colleague in the tribunician power
(Agrippa in 18 and 13 BC, Tiberius in 6, BC, AD 4 and 13). Clearly there
was merit to be won in taking a colleague, or so Augustus was making out.
The truth was that that very manoeuvre confirmed the regime in power by
ensuring its survival on the death of the Princeps;[159] and Augustus' own
position overall remained unique.

Such moderation had other uses, carefully deployed. Moderation in the
use of *auctoritas* enhanced it. So when Augustus adroitly consulted the Senate about his proposed behaviour at the trial involving Cassius Severus and
Augustus' friend Nonius Asprenas: he was afraid of seeming either to bring
undue influence to bear on the court by appearing as a witness or to fail a
friend by refusing his help. In the end, he sat out some hours of the trial as
a silent presence on the public benches, having done more than any witness
statement would have done for Asprenas as well as laying a justifiable claim
to civility.[160] And his pointing out in the *Achievements* that he had refrained
from putting his name on monuments he had restored put his name on
them more gloriously, redoubling the credit. (It has also been suggested,
not altogether plausibly, given the resources at his disposal, that it saved
Augustus from becoming permanently responsible for their upkeep.[161])

We are dealing with something more subtle than the 'lies' that have been
enumerated – a tone and a way of describing events, a constant spin – as well
as with something on a larger scale and more structural. Blatant lying on
what is in the public sphere is dangerous. Omissions and misleading com-
pression need further consideration.

Laying claim to the past, Augustus also took the right to obliterate what
did not suit him. What has been silenced is easily detected by comparing the
text with literary accounts of the Principate. The Perusine War is an obvious
and understandable absentee. It has been a complaint of scholars that after a
brief mention of the original *imperium* taken at the beginning of 43 in

dubious circumstances, Augustus has nothing to say of its survival in one form or another for the rest of his life as the basis of his control of the military and his command of Romans and aliens throughout the Empire, nor of its renewal for different periods of time in 18, 13 and 8 BC, AD 3 and 13.[162] Certainly mention of those renewals could have caused offence to readers forced to see what a mockery the five- or ten-year limit was; for later emperors the *decennalia* and *vicennalia* were mere celebrations of decades in power. However, this complaint does not hold. First, tenure of *imperium* is implicit in what Augustus says of many of his actions at Rome and especially in the field. Second, the *imperium* acknowledged came originally in undistinguished pro-praetorian form. Renewals did not constitute acceptance of one of those concrete powers – a magistracy, a *cura*, a priesthood – that in a narrow view made up the Commonwealth and so figure on senatorial funerary monuments. Third, the renewals lacked the *éclat* that might have come with an original grant; not only did they become routine, but, more importantly for the commemorative *Achievements*, mention of them would have detracted from the actual successes that were to be the focus of the reader's attention. For R. Syme, there was still some duplicity involved in Augustus' reticence,[163] but the real duplicity lies in the form taken by the document as a whole: smooth, monumental ashlar that conceals the strains and tensions that the building had to undergo, and the changes that took place as it shook and settled.

In a different and familiar style of omission, Augustus declined to name his opponents, removing their humanity and eliminating past relations. Pompey's son Sextus is a pirate;[164] the Mark Antony of 44 BC is represented by a tyrannical clique, from which Octavian liberated Rome. There is certainly nothing about the rapprochement with Antony in 43; he is 'the man I fought'. As for the campaign of Actium, neither opponent is named: it is only the gender of a common noun used by Augustus that, in contrast with the stress laid on Cleopatra by contemporary and later writers, gives away the fact that the main enemy was male.[165] Brutus and Cassius and their allies, who make war on the Commonwealth, are identified as 'those who slaughtered my father'. Their double defeat at Philippi is Octavian's achievement, with no mention of the true victor.[166] The men he was discussing had become enemies of the state and liable to have their memories erased from its records. Roman citizens spared by Octavian when they asked for pardon are naturally not named either. Why recall the humiliation of great families?

But even the name of Julius Caesar, for all its resonance, is avoided in the *Achievements*: he is consigned a particular role to play, apart from that of victim, precisely that of Augustus' parent. Augustus also fails to mention any of his later commanders in the field, bit-part players in his drama of conquest, except Gaius Caesar and Tiberius, expressly described as his stepson and legate.[167] Mentioning a person by name brings them vividly before the eye of the reader; Augustus wanted others away. Ironically, when Appian came to write of the Triumviral proscriptions he studiously avoided using Octavian's name.[168] It was for a very different reason that poets never named women of Augustus' household, though Ovid celebrated the mother of Augustus' heir: respect for the convention of womanly modesty.

Augustus' presentation in the *Achievements* of his position at the end of the Triumvirate, of its duration and of the oath of loyalty that he exacted have been discussed in Ch. 1 (Appendix).[169] It is the gross misrepresentations that mark Augustus' account of the settlement of 28–27 and what followed it that have justly attracted most discussion. They display the Princeps at his most disingenuous and his most skilful. First, Augustus claims that he 'transferred the Commonwealth to the discretion of the Senate and People of Rome', just as if the Senate (they were the men with the initiative) would have the hardihood to accept the gift and wave farewell to Octavian as they had once done to Sulla upon his genuine resignation of all formal power. Then he says that 'after that time I had powers equal to those of my colleagues in each magistracy, but my *auctoritas* excelled that of everyone else.' Strictly true as both parts of that statement were, the first was trivial and veiled the fact that after that time the only magistracies proper that Augustus had held were seven more consulships: he stopped holding real magistracies precisely because they were collegiate and limited in time. The second part, with its use of the fair-sounding word *auctoritas*, masks all that happened afterwards when Augustus misused it (Ch. 2). A suggestion of P. Brunt and J. Moore mitigates the deceit: it is that the passage belongs to an early draft, perhaps as early as 23 BC, before the adoption of tribunician power and global *imperium*, when it could still have seemed suitable, but was allowed to remain. Its survival, though, cannot have been due to oversight. Augustus was too careful for that. By the time the *Achievements* was completed the over-use of *auctoritas* had become accepted, the *de facto* monarchy too; parity in an occasional magistracy was a gracious concession. But the statement, poised between truth and falsehood, at once vapid and revealing, and by 2 BC quite anodyne, may even have come from the *Autobiography*, it proved too precious a formulation to relinquish.[170]

Then there is gloss put on the way the controversial social legislation and the Military Treasury came into being (Chs. 3 and 4). Augustus claims in the *Achievements* that the legislation was something that the Senate 'wanted him to carry through', and it is true that the enactment followed denunciations in the Senate of the disorderly behaviour of women and young men. The Senate got more than it bargained for in return for its conventional complaints, and Augustus' remark in the *Achievements* may invoke that fact. Only in particular senses, that they were what everyone 'knew' should be carried through, or that the Senate voted on them before they were taken to the public assembly, is Augustus' claim true.[171] But this was part of the point of the refusal of offices that would put the responsibility for imposing reforms squarely on the Princeps; Senate and People were to be involved and committed. The Military Treasury, according to Augustus, resulted from his advice (*ex consilio meo*). The easy phrase veils the dramatic resistance that met the proposal, and the continuing resentment.[172]

Augustus put up a magnificent show both in his array of salutations as *imperator* and in the *Achievements* of his success as a military leader and the enhancement of Rome's Empire that it had won. It was all embodied in the dress and decorations he was authorised to wear: laurel crown in 36 BC, gold crown at festivals in 29, and New Year's Day (with triumphal dress) in 25.[173] But in the central section of the *Achievements*, the language is equivocal in its very exactness. Referring to his extension of Roman power beyond the existing provinces and the creation of new dependent kingdoms, Augustus avoided mention of any 'provinces', and in alluding to the short-lived successes in Germany (12 BC – AD 9), which did almost reach provincial status, he used the word *pacavi* ('I pacified') instead of *vici* ('I conquered'), with its implication of permanence. Lack of substance was masked by emotive language: Augustus' fleet, passing from Ocean to the regions of the East (that is, Jutland), penetrated where no Roman had reached before, even to the Cimbri (who had threatened Italy at the end of the second century); they and other barbarously named peoples had sought the friendship of Augustus and the Roman People.[174]

Augustus had indeed 'pacified' the coast of Europe from southernmost Spain (his own Spanish campaigns, for all his claims, had to be followed up by Agrippa[175]) to the mouth of the Elbe, but how far inland did Roman rule go, and how long did it last? It was once fashionable to play down Augustus the conqueror, regardless of the increase in size of the Empire during his supremacy. For Augustus claimed in the *Achievements* that during his conquest of the Alps he attacked no tribe without provocation, and Suetonius in Hadrian's time made an even stronger claim: Augustus never invaded any country nor felt tempted to increase the Empire's boundaries or enhance his military glory. The right to indefinite expansion, promised to Aeneas' descendants by Jupiter in Virgil's epic, is not easily reconcilable with the claim that Rome's wars were defensive.[176] A more robust view then took over: Augustus was the heir of Roman Republican generals out to make their mark; he bore a seal ring with the portrait of Alexander the Great. Augustus was no Alexander, but could make up for that with the claim that he did more than conquer: the Romans continued to rule the Empire they had won. Augustus kept Alexander in mind as someone in the same world class as himself, and accordingly he made himself a master of world geography. His signet ring bore, originally, an image of the Sphinx, then one of Alexander, finally his own.[177] Then, in 1990, E. Gruen put forward a subtle analysis, one supported by the cagey formulation of the *Achievements*. Augustus made himself out to be a glorious imperialist, but his actual achievements were modest; proponents of this view can survey the areas of conflict one by one, Parthia and Armenia, Spain, the Balkans, the Alps, Germany.[178]

E. Gruen's formulation suits the theme of this book, but it does not allow for changes over time in what Augustus needed to do, or to seem to be doing. Augustus may have been even more responsive to public opinion than the formulation allows. A young politician needs valour successfully displayed, even if he is not a brilliant general, and a young ruler needs a justification for holding on to power. In the 30s BC, Octavian fought in the Balkans, an ancient theatre of war for Rome, and was twice wounded. The main provinces he was charged with governing in 27, Spain, Gaul and Syria, were those that required 'defending' and, coincidentally, those that the first Triumvirs had allocated to themselves in 55 BC, regions inviting Caesar, Pompey and Crassus to further conquest. Augustus needed them as a means of prolonging his tenure of power beyond the ten years he was allowed, and had the choice of enemy to subject. Parthia, Britain and Germany were attractive options, allowing for the wars of expansion that would demand renewal of Augustus' powers, all areas where Julius Caesar had been active, or had intended action.[179] The unsuccessful expedition into the Arabian peninsula in the mid-20s and the ensuing advance into Ethiopia, given up after two years, only helped to damage Augustus' credit (Ch. 2).[180] When senators saw through the scheme for perpetuating the Princeps' control, and their discontent ended in the crisis of 24–23 BC, Augustus had to change his plans: the easy conquest of Britain, for example, mooted in the late 30s and 20s, was silently given up and the excuse later offered that customs dues outweighed the profit to be gained from an island garrisoned by a legion and some cavalry.[181]

Augustus' more significant dealings with Parthia became a public relations exercise in which the enemy under threat were 'compelled', as Augustus writes in the *Achievements*, to return the Roman standards they had won from Crassus and Antony, and allowed Augustus to send Tiberius to crown a Roman puppet in Armenia. Both sides accepted détente on those terms. Augustus' implication that the Parthians were 'suppliants' for the friendship of Rome, and so effectively a dependency, was far from true, and his claim to have received all the sons of the Parthian monarch as hostages surely exaggerated, given the number of concubines that the monarch had. We have already noted the excessive claim on the coinage: '*ARMENIA CAPTA*'. The Parthians had been in no hurry to return the standards and the two powers reached an agreement on co-existence, with an end to expansion on each other's ground. After the deal was struck the Princeps actually sent a letter to the Senate lecturing them on the unnecessary acquisition of new territory. Inconsistently, he treated his success at once as a military triumph and a diplomatic settlement. That renunciation in 20–19 BC of what J. Griffin has called Horace's 'cheap fantasies' may well have given satisfaction to senatorial critics, paving the way, with the Armenian success that it accompanied, to Augustus' triumphal return in 19. The settlement was not permanent, and was liable to be upset every time an Armenian dependant died or was deposed, at a substantial cost to Rome in men and materials; but it was never to be expected that Augustus would recite the later vicissitudes of his puppets.[182] In 6 BC Tiberius, who had recognised the dependent kingdom of Armenia in 20, was given *imperium* and a commission to settle Armenia once again. When he retired to Rhodes the task fell to Augustus' adopted son Gaius Caesar, who was hailed in Athens as a 'new Ares'. War with the Parthians seemed imminent, but Gaius' meeting with their monarch in mid-Euphrates apparently averted it and was a source of renewed celebration. This happy outcome has given rise to the suspicion that it was staged, and that an agreement had already been reached in AD 2; 'one of the greatest hoaxes of the Augustan regime'.[183] That may be so, but Augustus cannot be blamed here for putting a glorious front on a mundane but solid achievement, nor for keeping his son from an unnecessarily dangerous encounter. It was a cheaper but almost as prestigious a success, worth recording for Nicolaus of Damascus and in the *Achievements*, when embassies from India approached Augustus, first in Spain, then in Syria: Augustan magnetism was felt in the farthest reaches of the world.[184]

The settlement with the Parthians in 20 BC had been an outstanding diplomatic coup for Augustus in his dealings with the Senate, but there were real military problems that Rome had to face: to complete the pacification of Spain and the Balkans and the conquest of the Alps, and to secure a restive Gaul against invasion from over the Rhine (there was a reverse suffered by M. Lollius in 17, involving the loss of an eagle to the Usipetes, and further incursions in 13). In 19 and the following years Agrippa and Augustus' stepsons Tiberius and Drusus tackled these problems. They came to the conclusion that trouble in Gaul would be brought to an end only if Roman rule were extended between Rhine and Elbe and north from the new sub-Alpine provinces of Raetia and Noricum. Not seriously contemplated by Julius Caesar, this move eastward was nonetheless within the Roman programme of world conquest, the empire without end that Virgil makes Jupiter promise in the *Aeneid*; Virgil's identification of *cosmos* and *imperium* is finally realised, according to P. Hardie, in the Shield of Aeneas.[185] A series of campaigns was launched under Nero Drusus and, after his death during his consulship of 9 BC, Tiberius. This serious effort at conquest, dictated by military need, went on even during Tiberius' absence on Rhodes and he resumed it in AD 4. A 'final' two-pronged assault over the Rhine and northwards through Bohemia, scheduled for AD 6, had to be broken off when the Balkan tribes revolted. As soon as Tiberius had subdued them, in AD 9, Arminius dealt a deadly blow against Roman military power and Roman settlement in Germany.[186] Consolidation in Gaul, restive again and vulnerable to German penetration, and on the Rhine was all that could be hoped for now and for some years to come, at least by Augustus and Tiberius, although the claim on Germany remained; the younger and highly ambitious Germanicus, son of Drusus, was thinking in the years after Augustus' death of recovering his father's conquests.[187]

The disaster of AD 9 came at a time of political conflict at Rome and financial difficulty in the Empire. Even the earlier, comparatively minor reverses, such as that M. Lollius, were not items that could be presented as virtual triumphs, as the diplomatic settlement with the Parthians could in 20 BC. The question for Augustus was how to handle them in public. After he assumed *imperium* over the whole Empire, all wars were conducted under his auspices.[188] It was *his* legions that he demanded back from Quinctilius Varus in AD 9. Augustus' link with the gods would not have failed; disasters were the responsibility of incompetent generals. In a record of his achievements their failures were passed over.

Augustus was a self-proclaimed hero of war, and hence a bringer of peace, both to the Roman state, broken by civil strife, and to the outside world that had submitted to him. He was able to claim that in accordance with what the ancestors had willed when victories had established peace by land and sea throughout the Roman Empire, the Senate voted three times for the closure of the doors of the Temple of Janus, signifying that Rome was at peace. R. Ridley has pointed out that Augustus does not say that the proposal was carried out: once it was ineffective. Nor does he give the dates, for the closures stood against a background of continuous Augustan warfare. G. Herbert-Brown convincingly suggests that he was developing the concept throughout his Principate right up to the completion of the *Achievements*.[189]

What appears in the *Achievements* is a straightforward record of universal military success, with traces of its ephemeral nature, as in Germany and in Arabia and Ethiopia, brushed out. Boldly Augustus runs together the Arabian excursion fiasco and the Ethiopian adventure – and includes them in a list of conquests won on his orders and under his auspices. A recital of diplomatic triumphs follows.[190]

As to areas governed by dependent rulers, Augustus' view of them was inconsistent and opportunist. According to Suetonius, he treated such 'client kingdoms' as integral parts of the Empire. In the *Achievements*, however, he presents himself as recovering for the Roman people tracts of country that had been lost to their control: Antony had entrusted them to dependent monarchs. The tally would have included Cilicia, Cyprus, Cyrene, part of Syria and Armenia. In fact, Augustus left six major Antonian protégés in control, and later reinstated some of those he had deposed.[191] Client kings could always be seen as aliens who had submitted.

The publication of the *Achievements* was one aspect of being 'seen', as Augustus was also seen in person in Senate, Forum and theatres. As O. J. Hekster remarks, 'The more this figure [the emperor's] became clearly defined, the more the individual who occupied the position became the incarnation of the position, rather than an individual.'[192] Augustus stood at the beginning of this process, and helped to start it while still presenting a multifarious personality to his contemporaries. Two related points are being made, the disappearance of the emperor into the institution and the significance to his power of being 'seen', or not. The institution was created by an extraordinary individual, the cynosure of all eyes. Augustus came to believe about this exchange of gazes that in real life his own glance had a peculiar power: men could not meet it.[193]

The funeral

Along with the *Achievements* and the other documents brought into the Senate in September 14 were instructions for Augustus' funeral, probably in an appendix to the will. Like other eminent men, Winston Churchill among them, Augustus gave thought to his own funeral and interment. We have seen the significance of the Mausoleum from 32 BC onwards. He planned his funeral with equal care.[194] He died at Nola on 19 August, it was said in the very room in which his father, the man of praetorian rank, had died. The funeral procession moved by night from one town to another, escorted by knights and council members from the cities they passed; Italy was still his support. It arrived in Rome probably on 3 September. And the body, or rather a wax effigy, since the body itself must at any time of the Italian year have been in a sealed coffin, lay in state for five days. The Senate had been summoned at once to discuss detailed arrangements, but ordinary people of Rome, Italy, and even some provincials, did not need to be summoned, but came together in the last of the Augustan demonstrations of support to mourn and to attend the cremation in the Campus Martius. The bier was carried by magistrates designated for the following year (his creations) down to the Rostra in the Forum Romanum. There two eulogies were delivered, one by Tiberius, the other by his son Drusus Caesar, for the elder boy, Germanicus, was away in Gaul; they were all the Princeps' political heirs. It was through the Porta Triumphalis that the bier was then taken to the Campus Martius, and as the smoke rose from the pyre, an eagle was seen to rise with it; one senator (as he later swore) saw Augustus' spirit going up to heaven. It was a clear sign that he had been received among the gods, and Livia rewarded the witness with a million sesterces, so it was said. Livia herself, however, attended by men of equestrian rank, stayed by the pyre for five days, then gathered the bones and placed them in the central chamber of the nearby Mausoleum, which was now to be surmounted with Augustus' statue. When the Senate met again on 17 September it was to vote Augustus a state temple and priests, the *Sodales Augustales*, to hear his will and political testament, and to welcome his son as the new Princeps. They hoped he would take the title of Augustus that his predecessor had borne and now, in an echo of Caesar's will, wished on Tiberius, who had already been a Julius Caesar since his adoption in AD 4. Tiberius demurred, but came to allow the designation. There was no problem with Livia, who under the terms of her husband's will took the names Julia Augusta.[195] Through the funeral and his political testament Augustus had done everything he could not only to glorify his own memory but to put his family into the way of all that he could bequeath them of his own prestige.

Endnotes

1 'Comrades': Suet. *Aug.* 25. 1; contrast *Caes.* 67. 2.

2 Favour of deities: Sulla: A. Keaveney, *Sulla the Last Republican* (2nd edn, London, 2005), 33–35.

3 Flamininus '*theios*': Plut. *Flam.* 12. 7. Divine assimilation: Pollini 1990.

4 Sex. Pompeius and Neptune: Gowing 1992, 309f.

5 Appropriation of gods: Galinsky 1996, 222–24, Hercules and Dionysus (from Actium): EJ 12; Nisbet 1984, 31 (bibl. n. 55); Bosworth 1999, 7f.; Hekster 2004 ('Constraints' and 'Omphale', denying Hercules as an Antonian deity); Neptune: Suet. *Aug.* 18.2, cf. 16. 2 and a cameo invoked by Galinsky, 20–23, along with Virg. *Aen.* 1, 148–56; Hercules: Livy 1. 7. 3–15; Prop. 4. 9; Virg. *Aen.* 8, 102–04; 190–305, with Grimal 1951; Rea 2007, 120.

6 I owe this point to Dr Herbert-Brown. Coinage of Vibii Pansae: *RRC* 342 (90 BC), 449 and 451 (48); Iunii Silani: 337 (91); Marcii: 363 (82).

7 Banquet: Suet. *Aug.* 70, 1f., with Osgood 2006, 237f.; Hekster and Rich 2006, 161, are sceptical, and stressing that Octavian's connexion with Apollo cannot be demonstrated before 36; their discussion of Apollo (Palatine and Actian), covers 160–68. Apollinian snake: Suet. *Aug.* 94. 4; cf. Dio 45. 1. 1; Zanker 1988, 50–53. Scipio: Gell. 6. 1. 1–5. Lorsch Wildfang 2000 sees such stories and dreams, with their eastern antecedents, directed at the Greek-speaking provinces between the Treaty of Brundisium and Actium.

8 Apollo temple: Vell. Pat. 2. 81, 3; Suet. *Aug.* 29. 3. Begun 38 BC, dedicated 28: *Fasti Ant.*, EJ p. 53; Dio 49 15. 5f.; 53. 1. 3.

9 Relations with Apollo: Galinsky 1996, 215–19. Palatine Library statue: Ps.-Acron *ad* Hor. *Epist.* 1, 3, 17; Serv. *ad* Virg. *Ecl.* 4. 10, with Hekster and Rich 2006, 166.

10 Augustus' house: Suet. *Aug.* 72. 1f., with Royo 1999, 119–71. Neighbours and their literary and ideological connotations: Wiseman 1984, 124–28; Hekster and Rich 2006, 151f.; Rea 2007, 30–35.

11 The Palatine deity is firmly linked to Actium by Hekster and Rich 2006, 163–65. Apollo at peace: Prop. 4. 6. 69f., cited by Galinsky 1996, 218; Prop. 4. 6, 67–70, interpreted by Welch 2005, 100 and L. B. T. Houghton *JRS* 95 (2005), 312. Apollo Citharoedus: *RIC* 1², 52 no. 170–71ab (15–13 BC); 54 no.190a–193b (11–10 BC).

12 Octavius seen as Jupiter: Suet. *Aug.* 94. 6. See Hekster and Rich 2006, 167, on *RIC* 1², Aug. 269ab. They also draw attention to Mercury: Hor. *Odes* 1. 2. 41–44. Feretrius: Dion. Hal. *Ant. Rom.* 2. 34; Nep. *Att.* 20. 3; Livy 4. 20. 3; *RG* 19. 2. See Favro 1996, 107, drawing attention to Augustus' claims to Quirinus and Minerva, and Rea 2007, 44–63. Similarly Ovid, *Fasti* 4, 347–49, notes the shrine of the Magna Mater, once credited to Marcellus, now to Augustus.

13 Tonans (P. Gros in *LTUR* 3 (1996), 159f.): *RG* 19. 2; Suet. *Aug.* 29. 3; 91. 2; Dio 54. 4. 2f.

14 Palatine 'privacy': Milnor 2005, 43; see also Dettenhofer 2000, 199.

15 Balance of beginning and end of *RG*: Ridley 2003, 232, but stressing the mention of Augustus' age at both.

16 *SC de Pisone patre*: Eck *et al.* 1996, 44 l. 92.

17 'Desire to be seen' in a triumph: Cic. *Pis.* 60.

18 Funding of shows: Ovid, *Tr.* 2. 497–518; Dio 54. 2. 4.

19 Augustus in the theatre: Suet. *Aug.* 45. 1; (and Tiberius): Tac. *Ann.* 1. 54. 2; cf. Dio 57. 11. 5.

20 Grandson in box: Dio 54. 27.1; Claudius kept out: Suet. *Claud.* 4. 3.

21 Crowds: E. Canetti, *Crowds and Power* (tr. C. Stewart, rev. edn, London, 1976); P. A. Brunt, 'The Roman Mob', *P&P* 35 (1966), 4–27.

22 Ciceronian language: Cic. *De Imp. Cn. Pomp.* 44, with De Visscher 1969, 215–17 (examples).

23 Modes of address: Tiberius: Dio 57. 8. 1; 11. 2; cf. the individual handing Augustus a petition, like a bun to an elephant: Suet. *Aug.* 53. 2.

24 Statue of Eros: *Aphrodisias* 12.

25 Augustus speaks: Malcovati 1969, 32–48, LXI–LXXVI. See Ch. 3. Also worth noting: EJ 366: funeral oration over Agrippa.

26 Image in legislation: J. Harries, *Cicero and the Jurists: from Citizen's Law to the Lawful State* (London, 2006), 132.

27 Practice of oratory: Suet. *Rhet.* 25.5; [Epit.] *Caes.* 1. 17. Education in speaking: Dio 45. 2. 8.

28 Augustus' eloquence: *Sen. Apocol.* 10. 1f., where the editor P. T. Eden speaks of 'a cleverly contrived specimen of Augustus' oratorical powers'.

29 Augustus (and Aeneas') taciturnity: West 1998, 313f., citing Suet. *Aug.* 54. Augustus and rhetoric: Milnor 2005, 85f. (letters); she cites Millar 1977, 203f. and 217, and specimens of homeliness; note Suet. *Aug.* 72–74; 76; 86. 1 (striving for clarity); 87; Gell. 10. 24. 1; Quint. 1. 6. 19.

30 Octavian's speeches circulated: App. *BC* 5. 527.

31 Optimum condition: Suet. *Aug.* 28. 2, with Canali 1973; Wardle 2005 ['Edict']; cf. Cic. *De re publ.* 2. 33 (Scipio Aemilianus); 'salubris princeps', 42. 1; cf. Suet. *Tib.* 29. 1; Dio 56. 39. 2.

32 V. Klemperer, *The Language of the Third Reich. LTI – Lingua Tertii Imperii. A Philologist's Notebook* (tr. M. Brady, London and New York, 2006), 222. (I am much indebted to Professor G. D. Rowe for the gift of this book.)

33 Sickness: Livy, *Pr.* 9.

34 *Concordia* in 'Pater Patriae' speech: Suet. *Aug.* 58. 2; see Levick 1978.

35 'To prevent the Commonwealth taking any harm': *RG* 1. 3; cf. Cic. *Ad Fam.* 16. 11. 2 (49 BC).

36 'Per consensum universorum': *RG* 34. 1, with Brunt and Moore 1970, 76 inclined to accept the claim. 'Cuncta ex Italia': 10. 2; cf. Cic. *De Har. resp.* 5; *Pro Sest.* 38.

37 Transmission of models empire-wide: Smith 1996; Augustan style in private life and in Italy and the provinces: Zanker 1988, 265–333, with Napoleonic comparison, 291.

38 Sutherland 1951 remains fundamental.

39 Earliest: *RRC* 499, no. 409.1–4.

40 Augustus as coin collector: Suet. *Aug.* 75.

41 World coinage: Crook 1996, 138.

42 Minting authority and propaganda: Rich and Williams 1999, 186, n. 58, citing Levick 1982 and Wallace-Hadrill 1986.

43 *Monetales:* Dio 54 26. 6; types chosen by them: Noreña 2001, 160 n. 75.

44 Grain: *RIC* 1², 63 no. 303 (19 BC); 80 no. 478 (Ephesus, *c.* 25 BC). Roads: 50 no. 140–44; 68 no. 360 (18–16 BC).

45 Egypt and Asia: *RIC* 1², 61 nos. 275a and 276 (29–27 BC), etc.

46 *Signis receptis: RIC* 1², 44 no. 41 (with Mars, 19–18 BC), etc.

47 Mars Ultor: *RIC* 1², 43 no. 28 (19–18 BC), etc.

48 *Armenia Capta: RIC* 1², 62 no. 290–2.

49 *Ob cives servatos: RIC* 1², 43 nos. 29a–30b (19–18), etc.

50 *Libertatis vindex: RIC* 1², 79 no. 476 (Ephesus, 28–*c.* 20 BC), with Welwei 2004. Cf. Cic. *Phil.* 8. 12.

51 *Securitas Augusti: RIC* 1², 160 no. 112–14. Gauls: Tac. *Hist.* 4. 74.

52 *Clipeus Virtutis: RIC* 1², 43 no. 30a–32 (25–23 BC), etc.

53 *Fortuna Redux: RIC* 1², 45 no. 53a–56b (19–18 BC), etc.; cf. Prop. 4. 3. 71; *RG* 11; Dio 54.10. 3.

54 *Ludi Saeculares*: *RIC* 1², 68 no. 354 (16 BC).

55 *Amplior status*: *RIC* 1², 68 no. 358.

56 *Res Publica* at Augustus' feet: *RIC* 1², 73 no. 413, citing *Numismatica* NS 1 (1960) 5–11.

57 Good health: *RIC* 1², 69 no. 369.

58 Closure of the Rome mint: *RIC* 1² , 34.

59 *Divi filius*: *RRC* 535 no. 534f., etc.; Agrippa: *PIR* 1² 51f., 154–61 (heads, *c.* 20 BC–AD 14); 73 no. 406f. (with Augustus on bench, 13 BC); no. 408f., 412; 414; Julia: 72 no. 404f.; C. and L. Caesars: 54f. no. 198f. no. 205–15 (Lugdunum, 8–7 BC down to AD 5); Tiberius: 56–58 nos. 221–23, in chariot; 224–26, bareheaded; 230–48b, obverse heads (Lugdunum, *c.* 9–14).

60 Buildings: Vitruv. *De arch.* 1. 2.

61 Known failings: Zanker 1988, 102.

62 Temple restoration: *RG* 20. 4. Dedication on 23 September: Favro 1996, 107.

63 Name not inscribed on restored buildings: *RG* 19f. Capitol and Saturn: 20. 1. Powell, '*Aeneid*' 144, compares appearances of Augustus in the *Aeneid* with these sparing mentions.

64 Temples and other buildings: *RG Appendix* 2f.; Ovid, *Fasti* 2. 55–66. Expenditure on temples associated with Augustus: Zanker 1988, 108–10.

65 Building and *auctoritas*: Purcell 1996, 785. Building programme: Strabo 5, 235f, with Zanker 1988, 154–56.

66 Caesar's plans: Favro 1996, 60–78; 95–97. Carrying them out and imposition of the Julian name: *RG* 20. 3; Torelli 1996, 934–6; cf. Suet. *Jul.* 30. 2; 44. 1, with the Theatre of Marcellus; Dio 44. 5. 2; 47. 19. 1; 51, 22, 1 (Curia and Basilica).

67 Failure to build *Clementia*: Weinstock 1971, 309.

68 Augustan construction at Rome: Suet. *Aug.* 29; 31. 2. Porticus Octaviae and its library, built by Augustus' sister near the Theatre of Marcellus, and restoration of the Porticus Octavia constructed by fellow-clansman in the second century: A. Viscogliosi, *LTUR* 4 (1999), 139–45, with Festus 188L, Favro 1996, 91 and 117; ('sham': 107). Tiberius' Temple of Castor and Pollux, dedicated AD 6: Dio 55. 27. 4; Temple of Concord, dedicated 10 January, AD 10: *Fasti Ver.* and *Praen.*, EJ p. 45; Ovid, *Fasti* 1, 637–50; Suet. *Tib.* 20; Dio 55. 8. 2; 56. 25. 1. Livia and Tiberius' Porticus on the Esquiline, containing her shrine of Concord, begun 15 BC, dedicated 7: Dio 54. 23. 6, and 55. 8. 2, with Rich 1990, *ad loc.* Dio also notes that Tiberius was responsible for the Temple of Concord at the foot of the Capitol. Payment: Suet. *Aug.* 29. 4.

69 Brick into marble: Suet. *Aug.* 28. 3; Dio 56. 30. 3; Augustus' own list and building and decorations: *RG* 19–21.3. See Favro 1996, 79–106; succinct account: Eck 2007, 137–47. Feel-good factor associated with abundance and victory: Zanker 1988, 172–92. See *RG* 4, 1–3 for the celebration of military success.

70 A 'moral museum': Walker 2000. Seeing socially: Rea 2007, 67–84; reading the environment: Favro 1996, 6f.

71 Romulus' hut(s): Dion. Hal. 1. 79. 11; fires: Dio 48. 43. 4; 54. 29. 8,

72 Agrippa's buildings: Schmitthenner 1969, 461f. Saepta: Dio 53. 23. 1–4 (26 BC); Portico of Neptune, with frieze of Argonauts, baths, Pantheon: 27. 1–4 (25 BC), aqueducts: 54. 11. 7; all with Rich 1990 *ad loc.* Others' buildings: Suet. *Aug.* 29. 4f.

73 Augustus' order and Balbus' theatre: Dio 54. 18. 2; 25. 2, with Rich 1990 *ad loc.*; cf. 53. 22. 1 (27 BC).

74 Dispute with Calvinus: Dio 48. 42. 4–6; Sosius' temple: Favro 1996, 91.

75 Statues with *ornamenta triumphalia:* Tac. *Ann.* 4. 23. 1.

76 Road-construction by senators: Suet. *Aug.* 30. 1; Dio 54. 22. 1, with Rich 1990 *ad loc.* Cessation of building activity: Eck 1984, 140–42 (an exception, 146–48). Milestones: 140 with n. 92, citing e.g. *ILS* 889.

77 Restoration of Basilica Paulli: Tac. *Ann.* 3. 72. 1 (cf. Dio 54. 24. 2f., with Rich *ad loc.*); Pompey's theatre: 72. 2.

78 Temple of Apollo and Mausoleum: Zanker 1988, 24; foot on a globe: 41; Favro 1996, 117f. Globe as symbol: Hardie 1986, 367f.

79 Dedication of Apollo Temple: *Fasti Amit.* and *Ant.*, with triad of Genius Publicus, Fausta Felicitas, and Venus Victrix: EJ p. 53.

80 Palatine Apollo: Galinsky 1996, 213–24.

81 Actian commemoration: Strabo 7, p. 325; Plut. *Ant.* 65.3. Suet. *Aug.* 18. 2; with Zachos 2003 and Osgood 2006, 377–80; inscription (EJ 12) at 76.

82 Mausoleum: H. von Hesberg and M. Macciocca, *LTUR* 3, 234–33 Suet. *Aug.* 100. 4 (completed 28 BC); Dio 53. 30. 5 (Marcellus, 23 BC), with Rich 1990 *ad loc.* Begun 27?: Torelli 1996, 934. Transformation of Campus: Haselberger 2007, 220f.; 238f.

83 Dio 54. 25. 3; with Rich 1990, *ad loc.*; Simon 1967; M. Torelli, *LTUR* 4 (1999) 70–74, and 1996, 943–47 (eloquent description); see also Galinsky 1996, 141–55. Elsner's interpretation: 1991.

84 Mausoleum and 'sundial': Pliny, *NH* 36. 72f.; inscriptions: EJ 14; succinctly described by Eck 2007, 161f.; Crook 1996, 96; Zanker 1988, 72–77 (diagrams), stresses the power it represented, with its size and monarchical name, and the un-Republican message it conveyed; Augustus in the topography of Rome: Nicolet 1990, 16f. Date of procession 6 March 12 BC: Bowersock 1990, 393, when Augustus was elected Pontifex Maximus. 'Sundial': Buchner 1982; Bowersock 1990, 385–87; Torelli 1992, 33f.

85 Heslin 2007: bibl. 1–3; Barton 1995, 44–6 (Augustus' horoscope 41), use of meridian: 5; correcting the calendar: 5f., with Suet. *Aug.* 31. 2; Macr. 1. 14. 13–15; Solinus 1. 45–47; plan: 7; symbolism: 16.

86 Livia's birthday: Suerbaum 1980, 335–37.

87 Pliny, *NH* 36. 72, with Barton 1995, 46. Rehak's formulation, 2006, 146.

88 Vow: Ovid, *Fasti* 5, 569–95; *RG* 29. 2; Suet. *Aug.* 29. 2 (Philippi), with the scepticism of Weinstock 1971, 130–32, backed by Herbert-Brown 1994, 96–108; Hekster and Rich 2006, 153f. are doubtful; see also Rich 1998, 88. 20 BC, and temple on Capitol: Dio 54. 8. 3, with Rich 1990 *ad loc.* and Simpson 1977.

89 Stated functions of Forum: Suet. *Aug.* 29. 1f.; Dio 55. 10. 1ª–5. Dynastic intent of Temple and Forum: Lacey 1996, 198, with following description and citing Ovid *Ars Am.* 1, 177–228; Hellenistic monarchy: Dettenhofer 2000, 183. See also Galinsky 1996, 197–213. Greek references: 203. The Forum spared public and private ground: *RG* 21.1; Suet. *Aug.* 56. 2.

90 Function of architecture: Vitr. *Arch.* 1, pr., cited by Galinsky 1996, 197.

91 Laying claim to the past in Virg. *Aen.* 8: Rea 2007, 85–93.

92 Pompey in the Forum: Frisch 1980, 97f.

93 Statues of 35 BC: Dio 49. 38. 1. Cornelia: *ILS* 68; Pliny, *NH* 34. 31. Augustus' forgeries: Hemelrijk 2005.

94 Forum of Augustus and Temple of Mars Ultor: Zanker 1988, 194 (with plan) 215, recalling Anchises' prediction to Aeneas in Virg. *Aen.* 6. 792, and noting that Augustus' funeral procession (Dio 56. 34) also commandeered the past. Augustus' authorship of *elogia*: Pliny, *NH* 22. 13, with Frisch 1980. Luce 1990 disjoins Livy's view of the past from that presented in the Forum. Setting standard: Suet. *Aug.* 31. 5. *Quadriga*: *RG* 35. 1. Augustus as exemplary: Herbert-Brown 1994, 55–59, comparing *RG* 8. 5; Ridley 2003, 109–12. The idea was familiar: Pol. 6. 54. 2f.; Caes. *BG* 7. 77. 13. Corselet: Livy 4. 20; see Ch. 2.

95 Time: Wallace-Hadrill 1987, quotation 226, referring to Beard 1987. Calendar: Barchiesi 1997, 69–73. *Fasti*: Feeney 2007, 172–93. Asian calendar EJ 98. Month of August: Ovid, *Fasti* 5, 147; Suet. *Aug.* 31; Dio 55. 6. 6f.; Cens. *De Die Natali* 22; Macr., *Sat.* 1. 12. 35.

96 Commemoration of private individuals: Flower 2006, 122, with nn. 17–22. Watkins 1997, xiii, and Osgood 2006, 176–86, discussing Plancus, illustrates his tomb. Dio 54. 12. 1 (19–18 BC) boasts of triumphs for ordinary senators.

97 Insertion of family: Ovid, *Fasti* 1, 7–12; 2, 15f.

98 Asian calendar: EJ 98.

99 August: Macr. *Sat.* 1. 12. 35 (EJ 37); Suet. *Aug.* 31. 2; Dio 55. 6. 6f.

100 Date of visit to open year: Suet. *Aug.* 59.

101 Mussolini's regnal years: e.g., Arangio-Ruiz *et al.* 1938–XVI.

102 Autobiography: Suet. *Aug.* 85. 1; *Suda* 1. 1. 410 Adler, with Malcovati 1969, xlvi–l; 84–97, I–XXIII. Yavetz 1984, 1f., plausibly regards it as a defence of his family, easy success and past conduct, notably concerning Q. Gallius (Ch. 4). Closing date and publication: Schmitthenner 1969, 455–57.

103 Difference of approach between Autobiography and *Achievements*: Yavetz 1984, 4f.

104 Powell, '*Aeneid*' 140f., analyses Malcovati's 23 items and finds 10 apologetic.

105 Narrow escapes and wounds: Suet. *Aug.* 20; 91.1; Plut. *Brut.* 41. 7; App. *BC* 4. 463.

106 Cicero's oratory: Plut. *Comp. Cic. and Dem.* 3. 1. Praise: *Cic.* 49. 3. Octavian was exonerated: Vell. Pat. 2. 66. 1. For another shifting of blame, see below on Lepidus in the '*Laudatio Turiae*'.

107 *RG*: Text: Malcovati 1969, lii–lxv, 105–49; Brunt and Moore 1970 (Latin, with tr.); Drew-Bear and Scheid 2002. See Eck 2007, 1–3 with translation

169–86. History of document: Ridley 2003, 1–50. Classification: Syme 1939, 523; Yavetz 1984, 31 n. 100.

108 Influence of *RG*: Rowe 2007.

109 Augustus' date for completion: *RG* 35. 2. Period of composition: Ensslin 1932, 362 puts the final redaction in AD 11; Weber 1936, 102–240 argues for a work of art created in the summer of 14; Brunt and Moore 1970, 6, provide a list of references to events later than 2 BC, n. 1; Yavetz 1984, 5f.; Ramage 1988 is uncompromisingly for the summer of 14: six references to 13–14 are clear indications of its date.

110 *Achievements* in Senate: Suet. *Aug.* 101. 4; Dio 56. 33. 1. Date of will: Suet. *Aug.* 101. 1.

111 *Elogia* of Mars Ultor complex: Suet. *Aug.* 31. 5. Augustus as the author, and parallels with *RG*, the *summi viri* outdone: Frisch 1980, esp. 96f.

112 Historian's functions: Ridley 2003, 39, criticised W. Weber's 1936 discussion of the *RG* published in Nazi Germany. Weaving of unreliable material into the *RG*: Rowe 2007, drawing attention to Heuss 1975.

113 Hoffmann 1969, 27–33, traces the origins of Roman problems in relating their present to their history. As Dr Herbert-Brown reminds me, *RG* offered instruction to Augustus' successors – not accepted.

114 Genre puzzle: Bosworth 1999, 1. Self-aggrandisement: Ridley 2003, 34. His examination is acute, but cf. Rowe 2007 for his treatment of 'lies'. Aware of the need not to expect what such a document cannot deliver, he nonetheless complains (75) of the bare recital of offices in 1. 4 'making nonsense of history'. Nor can the omitted crucifixion of six thousand slaves after the victory over Sex. Pompeius in 36 BC (80; recorded by Orosius 6. 18. 33) have been as significant to a Roman commander as the restoration of thousands of others to their masters (*RG* 25. 1).

115 Augustus and Cicero: Ramage 1987, 112–14.

116 Justification for deification: Bosworth 1999, esp. 12 f., with earlier history of the view; Euhemerus: H. J. Rose and S. Hornblower *OCD*[3] *s.v.*; Gradel 2002, 280f.

117 Ego-ridden prose: Canali 1973, 151f.

118 *RG* ('*index*', catalogue) mentioned in Suet. *Aug.* 101. 4. See Brunt and Moore 1970, 1f. for the adaptation of *RG* for provincial readers, and the three existing texts, at Ancyra (bilingual), Pisidian Apollonia (Greek) and Antioch (Latin). Consumption by Romans: *ibid.* 4; but cf. Yavetz 1984, 8–13, arguing for the more educated classes: what did the only partially literate *plebs* care for long-winded inscriptions? Summed up: Syme 1954, 522f.

119 Siting of *RG*: the question was put to me by Dr Herbert-Brown.

120 'Cuncta ex Italia': *RG* 10. 2.

121 Cf. Ridley 2003, 231f., favouring the *equites*: 'Length and complexity . . . rule out any but the educated'. Crude divisions by class should be avoided; status dissonance bedevils them. Treggiari 1996, 902, cites the patriotism of a freed-man who declared himself from the heart of the plebeians: *CIL* 6. 33960 = 10097; though this man emerged from the imperial *familia*.

122 *Humanitas*: Yavetz 1984 and 1990, 39, citing Pliny, *Ep.* 9. 5. Acts of the earlier phase were presented as 'miscalculation', according to Milnor 2005, 189, citing Sen. *De Clem.* 1. 9. 3, Plut. *Cic.* 45. 5 and *Brut.* 27. 2 for fear of the tyrannicides as a motivating force; so in App. *BC* 5. 43.

123 Augustus' expenditure: *RG* 15–24, with Brunt and Moore 1970, 57–66.

124 *Exempla*: *RG* 8. 5; Suet. *Aug.* 89. 2. 'First' and 'greatest': Yavetz 1984, 29 n. 66, citing Reinhold 1980, 36. Mid-third century claims to primacy: *ILS* 65, the *Elogium Duilii*.

125 Funeral processions: Pol. 6. 53–54. 3.

126 Dictatorship: Ch. 2 n. 77 for sources cited by Dettenhofer 2000, 115, nn. 5–7. Vell. Pat. 2. 89. 5 is equally bland. For the disingenuous account of the embassies, see Ridley 2003, 180–82.

127 Analysis of *RG*: Nicolet 1990, 17f.

128 Augustus' woes: Pliny, *NH* 7. 147–50. *Felicitas*: Eutropius 8.5.

129 'Republican' stress in *RG*: Eder 1990, 86.

130 *Clipeus Virtutis*: *RG* 34. 2; Zanker 1988, 95–97, showing the representation from Arelate (Arles), EJ 22.

131 *Virtus*: *RG* 1–4 (personal achievements).

132 'Clemency': *RG* 3. 1f.; Vell. Pat. 2. 71. 1 (Messala Corvinus); 86. 2, claiming that after Actium only those were exiled who refused to plead, and that Octavian would have been equally merciful in the proscriptions and after Philippi. Cf. Suet. *Vit. Hor.* and *Aug.* 17. 5; with Dio 51. 2. 4–6; 15. 5; 53. 7. 2; 56. 38. 2; App. *BC* 4. 175–8. Shield: Griffin 2003, 165f. Foreign peoples: *RG* 3. 2; Virg. *Aen.* 6. 853. Boscoreale cups: Galinsky 1996, 66f., figs. 32f.

133 *Clementia* the virtue of the divine: Cic. *pro Marc.* 8. Bad taste: Z. Yavetz, *Julius Caesar and his Public Image* (London, 1983), 174f.; Syme 1939, 299f.; Weinstock 1971, 233–43; Lacey 1996, 132, n. 3. Griffin 2003, 160, however, defends its repute.

134 The more exalted station (*maior . . . fortuna*): Sen. *Clem.* 1. 21. 1. Cato: Augustine, *City of God* 1. 23.

135 Bodies returned: Ulpian in *Dig.* 48. 24. 1.

136 Clemency with generosity: Sen. *Ben.* 3. 27. 4, cited by Griffin 2003, 179.

137 Exceptions to clemency: Plut. *Ant.* 81. 1f.; 87. 1; Sen. *De Clem.* 1. 11. 1; Suet. *Aug.* 13–15; 17. 5; 27; Dio 51. 2. 4–6 (mixed conduct); 6. 2.

138 Burning of letters: Dio 52. 42. 8.

139 Development: Du Quesnay 1984, 35, citing App. *BC* 5. 127 and Dio 49. 3. 6; 49. 12. 4f.

140 '*Laudatio Turiae*': EJ 254 ii. 29 = Wistrand 1976, 24–27, ll. 19–21a.

141 Victim in a chest: Suet. *Aug.* 27. 2; App. *BC* 4. 487; Dio 47. 2. 4, with Sumi 2004, 203f., for date and Octavian's collusion.

142 *Iustitia v. Clementia*: Noreña 2001, 157, with bibl. and notice of the infrequency of these virtues on coinage. *Iustitia* was extended to foreign peoples (*RG* 26. 3; Suet. *Aug.* 21. 2) but primarily concerned the citizen body.

143 Departure of *Iustitia*: Virg. *Georg.* 2, 473f. Statues of Iustitia Augusta, 8 January AD 13: *Fasti Praen.*, EJ p. 44.

144 Routine leniency: Suet. *Aug.* 33. 1f. Warnings: Plut. *Apophth.* 7 and 9, *Mor.* 207E.

145 *Pietas* in *RG* 10–21; it was the second commonest virtue displayed on coinage: Noreña 2001, 158.

146 *Clementia* invoked: Ovid, *Tr.* 2, 43f.; 141–60.

147 Virtues of the Clipeus uncanonical: Noreña 2001, 152 n. 32; 157.

148 Ammianus on Julian: 25. 4. 1.

149 *Liberalitas*: Noreña 2001, 158f.

150 Ramage 1987, 228. Pompey's gifts: Cic. *Pro leg. Man.* 28.

151 Illegality: Brunt and Moore 1970, 38 on *RG* 1. 1, citing Cic. *Phil.* 11, 28, and Syme 1939, 154f.

152 *Factio*: see R. Seager, *JRS* 62 (1972) 53–58.

153 Milnor 2005, 12, draws attention to Augustus' arrogation of the word 'privatus' (*privato consilio et privata impensa*): he flaunts the strict illegality of the act, justified by the end: cf. Béranger 1958 14f. (Vespasian); Yavetz 1984, 8: Cic. *Phil.* 3. 3; 5; 5. 28.

154 The relationship between *RG* 1 and Cic. *Phil.* 3. 3–5 is noted by Galinsky 1996, 45, drawing attention to the way the paragraph recalls the acitivities of young Pompey and the claims of Caesar, *BC* 1. 22. 5.

155 How the *RG* is misleading: Rowe 2007.

156 Priesthoods listed, e.g., at *RG* 6. 2–7; supreme pontificate: 10. 2; altar of Fortuna Redux: 11; altar of Pax Augusta: 12, with Brunt and Moore 1970, 53f.; other religious honours: 9–10. 1. Secular honours: Senatorial embassy to greet him in 19: 12. 1.

157 Refusal of unwonted posts: *RG* 6. 1; documented, with the Pompeian precedent, by Dettenhofer 2000, 117.

158 For this aspect of the 'imperial cult', see B. Levick, *The Government of the Roman Empire* (2nd edn, London, New York, 2000), 125–46.

159 Colleague in tribunician power: *RG* 6. 2.

160 Asprenas affair: Ch. 4; Augustus in court: Dio 54. 3. 2f.; 30. 4.

161 Name on restored monuments: *RG* 20. 1. See Ch. 3. Upkeep: Favro 1996, 304 n. 67.

162 *Imperium*: *RG* 1. 2; Brunt and Moore 1970, 40 deny any concealment; so Yavetz 1984, 10 (it is implicit in what Augustus writes of his own achievements); inclusion of *imperium*: Ridley 2003, 90. Renewals: Dettenhofer 2000, 27 n. 78; *contra*, Lacey 1996, 73. Consul and Triumvir: 1. 4.

163 Syme 1946, 156 = *RP* 1, 191.

164 Omission of names: Brunt and Moore 1970, 3 (it is possible that the *factio* is that of the supporters of Caesar's assassins: Ridley 2003, 96); other omissions: 4f. Antony: *RG* 1. 1; 24. 1; Brutus and Cassius 3; Sex. Pompey: 25. 1, with mention of a 'slave war' at 27. 3.

165 Male gender used in *RG* 24. 1: Ridley 2003, 125. Stress on Cleopatra: Virg. *Aen.* 8. 671–713; Hor. *Odes* 1. 37; Plut. *Ant.* 60; Dio 50. 6. 1. Nonetheless, Cleopatra's name is suppressed in the poets (Hor. *Epode* 9; Prop. 3. 11; 4. 6).

166 Philippi: an Augustan story in Suet. *Aug.* 91. 1. Ridley 2003, 167f., citing *Fasti Praen.* in *Inscr. Ital.* 1. 3. 2. 135, 522 for the second battle only. *Epit. Liv.* 124; Vell. Pat. 2. 70. 1; Pliny *NH* 7. 148 (flight; illness; three days in a marsh; using Agrippa and Maecenas); Suet. *Aug.* 13. 1; Plut. *Ant.* 22; App. *BC* 4. 463 (from the autobiography).

167 Suppression of Caesar's name: *RG* 2; of the names of 18 commanders: Ridley 2003, 126. Tiberius as legate: *RG* 30. 1.

168 Octavian and proscriptions: Gowing 1992 ('Narratives'), 57f. on App. *BC* 4. 16. 62.

169 Duration of triumvirate: *RG* 7. 1. Octavian's supporters in 31: *RG* 25. 2f., with Brunt and Moore 1970, 68. Oath: *RG* 25. 2, with Brunt and Moore 1970, 67f., citing Suet. *Aug.* 17. 2.

170 Augustus' 'transfer of the Commonwealth' and his powers as a magistrate: *RG* 34. 3, with Brunt and Moore 1970, 6 and 78–80.

171 Social legislation: *RG* 6. 2, with Brunt and Moore 1970, 46–8 (Ch. 3).

172 Military Treasury: 17. 2, with Brunt and Moore 1970, 60 (Ch. 4).

173 For Augustus' salutations as *imperator* (IX to XXI, after 25 BC, earned by family members), see Barnes 1974. For the globe on coin types see Nicolet 1990, 41, and *RIC* 1², 210f., no. 81, 84f., 90 and 97. Dress: Dio 51. 20. 2; 53. 28. 5.

174 Military successes and expansion: *RG* 3; 14–33, echoed in Suet. *Aug.* 21, discussed by Nicolet 1990, 19–24. Triumphs, etc., 4. 1–3, with Brunt and Moore 1970, 43 and 69f., and Ridley 2003, 196–213, for the details. 'Pacavi' and emotive language: 26. 2–4, with Ridley 192–6. Near-provincial status of Germany beyond the Rhine: Vell. Pat. 2. 97. 1; see Rich 1990 on Dio 55. 6.2f.

175 Augustus' claims to have completed the conquest of Spain: *RG* 26. 2; Vell. Pat. 2. 90. 3f. Subsequent campaigns: Dio 53; 29. 1f. (24 BC); 54. 5. 1–3 (22); 11. 2–5 (19).

176 Justified military action: *RG* 26. 3; Suet. *Aug.* 21. 2; A. M. Riggsby, *Caesar in Gaul and Rome: War in Words* (Austin, TX, 2006), 157–60. Jupiter's promise: Virg. *Aen.* 1, 279.

177 Augustan imperialism: Brunt 1963. Augustus and Alexander: Plut. *Sayings of Aug.* 3, cf. 8, *Mor.* 207D. Seal: Suet. *Aug.* 50; Pliny *NH* 37. 10. Attention to geography: Malcovati 1969, 81–83, I–VII.

178 Augustan claims not substantiated: Gruen 1990; unsatisfactory treatment of Pannonia and Dacia in *RG* 30. 1f: Ridley 2003, 217f. Strabo 7, p. 305, is hesitant.

179 Areas allowing expansion: Eder 1990, 106, but propounded long before by C.E. Stevens.

180 Arabian and Ethiopian expeditions of 25–22: *RG* 26. 5, with Brunt and Moore 1970 *ad loc.* (25–4, 24–22 BC); Strabo 16, pp. 780–82; 820f.; Dio 53. 29. 3–8;

54. 5. 4–6, with Rich 1990 *ad loc.* (25–24, 24 and 21 BC); Jameson 1968 (26–25; 24–22); Marek 1993 (link with Parthian policy).

181 Britain: Dio 49. 38. 2; 53. 22. 5, with Rich 1990 *ad loc.* (bibl.); 25. 2: invasion mooted 34, 27, and 26 BC; cf. Virg. *Georg.* 1, 30 ('ultima Thule'); 3, 25; Hor. *Epod.* 7. 7; excuse: Strabo 4, p. 200.

182 Parthia 'subjected': *RG* 29. 2; compelled to return standards 30. 2; cf. the cuirass of the Prima Porta statue of Augustus; Dio 54. 8. 1–5, with Rich 1990 *ad loc.* (bibl.). Critical assessment: Ridley 2003, 205–08. Number of hostages: *RG* 32. 2, with Ridley 218–20. '*ARMENIA CAPTA*': *RIC* 1^2 (1984) 82f., nos. 513–15; 519. Détente: Herbert-Brown 1994, 100f.; Armenian puppet: *RG* 27. 2; Vell. Pat. 2. 94. 4; Suet. *Aug.* 21. 3; *Tib.* 9. 1; Dio 54. 9. 4f., with Rich 1990 *ad loc.* (bibl.). Letter to the Senate: Dio 54. 9. 1. 'Fantasies': Griffin 1984, 198.

183 Tiberius' commission: Dio 55. 9. 4. Gaius' expedition: 10. 17–21; 10a. 4–9; Syme 1978, 11 n. 6; Bowersock 1984; Herbert-Brown 1994, 105f.; hoax: 108.

184 Indian embassies: *RG* 31. 1; Hor. *Carm. Saec.* 55f.; Strabo 15, 686; 719f.; Suet. *Aug.* 21. 3; Dio 54. 9. 8–10, with Rich 1990 *ad loc.* (bibl.). Suet. *Aug.* 21. 3 notes the embassies that reached him; cf. *RG* 26. 3; 31–33, with Ridley 2003, 218f.

185 Cosmos and *imperium*: Hardie 1986, 339.

186 Roman penetration of Germany by 9: Schnurbein 2003.

187 Gaul vulnerability: *Tabula Siarensis*, RS 1, p. 515 l.13f; Vell. Pat. 2. 121. 1, Claim on Germany: Strabo 7, p. 291. Germanicus: Tac. *Ann.* 1. 58. 5; 2. 26.1.

188 A proconsul's leadership balanced by Augustus' auspices: EJ 43 (AD 6–7).

189 Three closures of Janus ordered: *RG* 13; see Brunt and Moore 1970, 54f.; Syme 1979; Rich 1990 *ad* Dio 53. 26. 5 (25 BC) and 54. 36. 2 (10 BC, abortive) with 35. 2; Herbert-Brown 1994, 185–96; Ridley 2003, 114f. Dr Herbert-Brown has suggested to me that Orosius 6. 21f. may after all be right to claim the third closure for 2 BC: there was no war.

190 Military successes: *RG* 26–30: invasions of Arabia and Ethiopia 26. 5, stressing the distance advanced; see Brunt and Moore 1970, 71, for an assessment of their effectiveness, and Ridley 2003, 203–05 for the chronological obfuscation; diplomatic successes: 31–33. Augustus as bringer of peace: Virg. *Aen.* 1. 291; *RIC* 1^2 79 no. 476 (Ephesus, '28 – *c.* 20 BC').

191 Client kingdoms part of empire: Suet. *Aug.* 48, with kingdoms restored. Provinces recovered: *RG* 27. 3, with Ridley 2003, 208–13, distinguishing Antony's handling of client kings from the two 'Donations of Alexandria' of 37 and 34 (37: Jos. *BJ* 1. 361f.; Plut. *Ant.* 36. 1f.; Dio 49. 32. 3f.; 34: Plut. *Ant.* 54. 34; Dio 49. 41).

192 Hekster 2005, 175f.

193 Augustus' gaze: Suet. *Aug.* 79. 2.

194 Augustus' plan for his own funeral: Dio 56. 33. 1. Course it followed: Suet. *Aug.* 100. 2–4; Tac. *Ann.* 1. 8. 3–6; Dio 56. 34–46.

195 For these transactions, see Levick 1976 (=1999), 68–81.

Chapter 6

Augustus in Art and Literature

A Golden Age?

The Second Triumvirate and the Principate of Augustus is famously a Golden Age in literature and art, emulated in later epochs in which classical dignity and grace were valued, earning them too the title 'Augustan'. This burgeoning of literature and art rested on a basis of enhanced prosperity, and that in turn not just on the access of wealth that came into Rome when Egypt was made into a province, or even on the steady income from the taxes of an Empire at peace, but on an upsurge of confidence and gratitude that marked the end of the Civil Wars. That was not mere hindsight, but something dwelt on in the Augustan age itself.[1]

Yet literature was given additional force and edge by residual fears of fresh civil disturbance. The second *Ode* of Horace's first book conveys the sense of risk, and the sixth of his third book calls for the restoration of temples, which Augustus promptly undertook. What poets wrote was related to their own experiences and observations, and they were heard. Some work, such as the *Aeneid*, could be appreciated by men in the street, but poets also offered a multiplicity of meanings on several levels, and *cognoscenti* appreciated their complex allusiveness. So in art: a reduction in the number of literary motifs was compensated for by multiple associations and meanings.[2] In this chapter we consider, not Augustus' representation of himself, but the figure that he cut in the work of contemporary artists and writers.

Three obvious and related questions are raised: first, how much he was able to influence this figure (for, with all the attention he gave to self-representation, there can be no doubt of his wish to do so); second, the varied responses of his contemporaries towards the man and his wish; third, what our own judgement of the artists should be. Class, financial circumstances, awareness of history and political conviction will have played their part in shaping their attitudes, and it is hard to draw common threads when so many artists and literary men are involved, and in such diverse media. Only a few themes can be traced.

A cultivated Princeps

Augustus was a well educated and highly cultivated Roman aristocrat, with a keen ear for language, a verse and prose *litterateur*, though he did not speak Greek fluently. He wrote an unfinished Greek drama of which he said in reply to an enquirer that his *Ajax* had thrown himself on his sponge, a hexameter *Sicilia*, and equally slight elegies. His political ambitions excluded any hope of literary immortality. He also had wide-ranging, or variable, tastes. The Triumvir could write Latin verse (the licentious Fescennine) when an opponent asked for it; the Princeps professed a taste for morally improving works and would send excerpts to his household and even to magistrates and army commanders. Augustus was a connoisseur, critical of others' verbal skills: he can be found discussing the authenticity of a couple of Caesar's speeches; certainly he criticised the style of his stepson Tiberius, who was notoriously arcane and obscure, and he once recalled a governor who misspelled a word in a dispatch. (It hardly matters that this may have been a pretext.) An admirer of Apelles, his exacting taste as a patron of art is attested by Suetonius: he would allow nothing to be associated with him but serious work by the best artists.[3]

Augustus' resources enabled him to pay generous salaries and make generous gifts to individual practitioners. He had the pick of artists and writers and could afford to be selective.[4] As an arbiter of taste Augustus made himself into a precursor of Louis XIV, not of Hitler, Stalin or even Mussolini. A light touch and an undeveloped apparatus of control granted him that. Art

Figure 18   Belvedere Altar (Deutsches Archäologisches Institut)

and literature were not harnessed to a developed populist ideology, Communist or Fascist, that aimed at maximum comprehension and was fuelled by on-going hatred, against Jews, bourgeoisie or both. The tyrannicides and Antony and Cleopatra, once defeated, were gone, leaving little in the way of an inheritance to constrain Augustus when he set the Commonwealth working again.

Art and architecture

Relationship between themes in literature and the plastic arts was only to be expected and is not necessarily a sign of clear direction from above. Alert writers and artists understood the resonances of what was being done and echoed them again: the Belvedere altar and Ovid both celebrate the election of Augustus to the supreme pontificate.[5] But distinctions must be drawn here between one art or craft and another. For one thing, relations between the Princeps and artists of various kinds varied with their social status and so the medium in which they worked, with a sharp divide between the plastic arts and literature; there were more refined distinctions between Roman poets and historians, and between one poet and another: the freedman's son Horace, conservative, and the *eques* Ovid, more popularly inclined.[6] Sculptors and architects would normally be Greeks, without the Roman citizenship, or freedmen. To complete their work they needed an allocation of space and, in the case of architecture, huge sums for materials and manpower, which Augustus and the state could command. Strabo gives a good idea of the stunning effect of the work done at Rome in his time, vindicating Augustus' own claims[7] to have transformed Rome from a brick-built to a marble city, with the specific operations he mentions in the *Achievements*. Architects, monumental masons and sculptors, men paid by Augustus, were under the tightest control. Their commissions were carried out at the bidding of a master whose specifications may have been closely or loosely defined, and who was able to scrutinise plans at every stage. Architecture on the grand scale, then, has been taken as part of Augustus' self-presentation (Ch. 5).

At the other end of the scale we can be sure that, whatever view we take of the authorship of Roman coin types (Ch. 5), nothing was put on a coin of which Augustus would have disapproved, and that when a bust of Augustus close to that of the Prima Porta statue came to be used on the coinage of the Asian province it was because Augustus particularly approved that image.[8] As for the detailed work of an individual sculptor, still more when a small-scale work of art such as a cameo was in question, the Princeps lacked the means of conveying his own full conception in words, however vivid it was to him, beyond specifying the subject, the individuals to be portrayed and the impression that it was intended to create. Besides, the influence was mutual. What contemporary architects, artists, poets and historians made of Augustus was intimately connected with his own view of himself, but at the same time the image was refracted through their own experience and perceptions, and varied from one medium to another. Their own creative input will have varied. There was a series of mirrors: Augustus' own conception was picked up, re-presented and packaged, and picked up again by the Princeps. The possible gradations are illustrated by the differing opinions that scholars have offered of Augustus' role in the creation of Augustan art. Addressing from close quarters the question of how tight a control Augustus may have been able to exercise, A. Bonanno has concluded that it was comparatively limited and general; power lay in the hands of the artist, and he was conditioned by his own upbringing and by contemporary fashion.

P. Zanker on the other hand stresses that it was the artist's job to fulfil someone else's desires.[9] It can be maintained at least that with sculpture as with coinage, the patron retained control of any message that could be interpreted in words.[10] One marked and simple change brings the point home: after the Triumviral Period we find no statues of Augustus in heroic and charismatic nudity (Ch. 1): he is always in the conventional old toga or the cuirass. Two other factors may have played a part: the extent to which the Princeps on the one hand already shared the taste of his contemporaries; and the extent to which an artist could both divine the precise vision of his employer and respond to it. None of this can be quantified, but the input of the Princeps was certainly prime at the outset of a project and remained considerable throughout the execution of a design. It was magnified by employees' need to please.

One complex instance is that of the Boscoreale cups, which represent respectively the present Princeps Augustus as ruler of the world in the company

Figure 19 Prima Porta statue (akg-images Ltd. Photograph by Erich Lessing)

of the gods and personified provinces, and recipient of the children of a barbarian tribe, and the future Princeps Tiberius sacrificing before a campaign and returning in triumph, probably in 7 BC.[11] They are miniature works, designed for an eminent person, evidently an admirer of the Claudian brothers – but probably based on a large-scale sculpture in Rome. Both artists were constrained in their choice of subject-matter by the wishes of the patron in each case, with the second enjoying the privilege of selecting, if he wished, from the original design. The iconography of the cups went back to the Republic.

When in 29 BC Octavian removed silver statues of himself and used the coin to pay for golden tripods in the Palatine temple of Apollo (a significant upgrading of the metal, perhaps) (see Ch. 3), he was making room, as P. Zanker notes, for a more modest, less overbearing, style in representations of himself, and in other sculptures, despite the emergence of the elaborate Corinthian capital. The new style was couched in a limited number of Archaic and Classical images.[12] Certainly by the time of the definitive settlement in 19 BC style was becoming more classical, more austere and more modest, in political terms even 'democratic', and in the literary terms of the day, less 'Asiatic' and floridly magnificent, more 'Attic'. To illustrate this point, the association of stylistic change with political, N. Purcell cites the Temple of Mars Ultor, completed in 2 BC, the most beautiful temple in the world, it was said. The temple and its adornments were works of art, and they were described by Ovid in the medium of words, giving an impression of how it would strike the visitor.[13] However, as Dr Herbert-Brown remarks, Ovid strikingly leaves out all connection between the two neighbouring *fora* of Caesar and Augustus, and the deities Venus and Mars, which, it could be argued, was the raison d'être of the temple's location and meaning. For him, Vesta has replaced Venus.

Statuary: the Augustus of Prima Porta

When Augustus is shown on reliefs alongside other men, he is naturally given the most prominent position by the sculptors, who use their technique to afford him a majestic pose and exalted stature, and particularly high relief. When he is shown with men of a lower social status, they are markedly shorter, in spite of the fact that he was not very tall and wore high-heeled shoes (Ch. 7). In real life too he needed to be imposing.[14]

Individual portraiture, especially sculpture from Rome itself, is the best witness for the spin that Augustus wanted on artists' work, down to details of dress. Suetonius does not stress any beauty of feature in the Princeps, though he says that he made up for it in grace, but it is conspicuous in his portraits, notably in the statue from Prima Porta, one of the most moving works of art of the age.

This monument[15] illustrates the complexity of relations between subject and artist. The dress and accoutrements could have been specified down to the smallest detail; style and expression had to be left to the artist, who has shown the spectators how they are to view the Princeps – and the Princeps what he has to live up to. The statue we have is a marble copy of a bronze original, and post-dates the Parthians' return of captured military standards to the Romans in 20 BC. But the type had taken the place of the more expressive Triumviral representations, displaying the classical calm and majestic equilibrium that scholars have taken go back to Polyclitus' masterpiece, the 'Doryphorus', 'a man of integrity and weight', fitting to go with the name 'Augustus'. The statue does not dramatise the Princeps or browbeat the viewer. This man is grave and self-controlled. The cuirass he wears represents and celebrates the diplomatic success over the Parthians for which he declined a triumph, his spear denotes the *imperium* he wielded, but recalls representations of Alexander. He is bareheaded, but also barefoot like a deity, and he wears a hip-mantle after the fashion of the deified Caesar. As M. Torelli puts it, the statue in its heroic pose both conforms to and infringes tradition (*mos*). Such an infringement looks forward to the time when the Princeps could become a *divus*. Like all the portraits, the Prima Porta statue, representing a man in his early forties, shows no sign of ageing. W. Eck remarks that there is no portrait of Augustus as an old man, though there are marks of wear and tear on the fifty year-old Augustus of the Ara Pacis.[16] The Princeps of the Prima Porta statue is youthful and vigorous, and capable of sustaining the cares of responsibility that his expression calls upon the viewer to recognise. The work set the style for Julio-Claudian portraiture.

Links between art and literature

Despite the distinction between the origin and rank of men who were engaged in architecture and the plastic arts and poets and above all historians, there are links between the subject-matter and treatment of their material, and that suggests that their preoccupations were also related, that their audiences also shared them, and, likewise the Princeps, with stronger or weaker influence on the product. There were descriptions in the poets, naturally, of the new wonders of Rome, not always in a serious spirit: Ovid alluded in the *Art of Love* to the Portico of Octavia – as a place to pick up girls.[17] For the subtle resonances of detail one example, expounded by S. Harrison, will suffice.[18] The story of the Danaids, who killed their bridegrooms on the wedding night, figured both in the architectural decor of Augustan Rome, as statues in the portico before the Temple of Palatine Apollo, and on the baldric in Virgil's *Aeneid*, snatched from the body of young Pallas by Aeneas' enemy Turnus, who was to die in the last lines of the poem at the hands of the enraged hero when he saw Turnus wearing it. The significance of this story for Augustus' contemporaries, and the way it was handled by sculptor and poet, are interpreted as reflecting the demands of public politics at a time of propagandistic triumph, and a more thoughtful and measured view of war and its consequences in the slightly later literary context. The house of Augustus and the Temple of Apollo figure in another rich nexus of associations that Augustus created: he was to live next to the Temple of Victoria, in whose precinct the shrine of the Great Mother had been constructed in 191 BC, after the aid she had given in defeating Hannibal. The rehabilitation of Cybele as a Trojan rather than a Phrygian deity has been traced by T. P. Wiseman in passages of the *Aeneid*, notably where she immediately precedes the Julii and Augustus, in the catalogue of Roman heroes in Book 6.[19]

Beyond this, there were echoes of great themes from Classical Greece and the Hellenistic kingdoms, notably from the Attalid monarchy of Pergamum (Bergama) in western Asia Minor.[20] The battle between gods and giants (Gigantomachy), with its cosmic mythological and historical connotations, is the subject of a fruitful examination by P. Hardie, along with its exploitation in Triumviral and Augustan literature.[21] It appears in Horace, Tibullus and Ovid, and is hinted at in several places in Virgil's *Aeneid*, notably in the passage describing the shield of Aeneas and dealing with the Gauls on the Capitol, just before the battle of Actium. The Gauls, it seems, were depicted on the door of Apollo's Palatine temple. At Virgil's Actium the divine participants include not only the decisive bowman Apollo, but also Minerva, the goddess of wisdom; rationality had prevailed. Hardie cautions against drawing too close a parallel between sculpture and literature – Virgil himself calls the shield of Aeneas a fabric not to be described.[22] Augustan sculpture shows the enemy defeated after the battle; Virgil displays the huge struggle – to bring the Roman People into being – on-going, manifestly so in the second half of the *Aeneid*. The ensuing repose was safer ground for Augustus, but, as we shall see, not available to the poet.

Propaganda, ideology and patronage

In the Introduction anachronistic concepts such as 'propaganda' and even 'ideology' were questioned. 'Propaganda' certainly must be avoided,[23] except when it is demanded for the particular circumstances of war and systematic political campaigning. Students of the Augustan age are now very circumspect: so J. Rea aims to avoid the Scylla and Charybdis of propaganda and pessimism: dealing with a distant past that had been grim as well as triumphantly successful, the poets created a dialogue that navigated the area between praise and polemic.[24]

Augustus was a 'patron' of several of the poets, Horace, Virgil and L. Varius Rufus, in the literary sense that he gave them encouragement, even material help. He did not enjoy the technical right of patronage (*patrocinium*) over them, as he would have over his freed slaves, and the language used between and of them would have been that of friendship, not that of *patronus* and *cliens*.[25] 'Mentor' might be a better term, but suggests help of a professional kind. The artists were indebted to Augustus to varying extents, and etiquette alone was enough to ensure that his policies and actions were presented in a favourable light, though epics on military exploits might be avoided.[26] A sincere friend of the Princeps, even one with good cause for gratitude, such as the poet Horace had, might feel free to offer criticism – though for him to say that was itself to offer praise. He knew too that Augustus could extort it.[27]

In Augustan Rome, the main patron was inevitably Augustus himself, although at first it was his close friend Maecenas who encouraged Virgil, Horace, for whom Maecenas cared a great deal, and Sextus Propertius; Horace was introduced to the potent Maecenas by his friend since 39 BC, Virgil, and the epic poet Varius Rufus – whom he suggested to Agrippa in the *Odes* as the poet to treat his achievements.[28] Some months after an interview Maecenas *ordered* Horace to be included in his troop of friends.[29] The first two attended Maecenas when he went to Brundisium in 37 to meet

Antony's agents, so that they would be aware of his achievement, and perhaps celebrate it. As J. Osgood puts it, Horace was loyal to Maecenas and Maecenas to Augustus.[30] Both also owed personal debts of gratitude to the Princeps and his friend: plots of land. Virgil is generally thought on the basis of *Eclogues* 1 and 9 to have lost his estate near Mantua (Mantova)[31] and came to the attention of Maecenas after enjoying the support of C. Asinius Pollio. Horace, born at Venusia (Venosa) in 65 BC – a city that figured in the first eighteen to be colonised after Philippi, the son of a freedman and a soldier on the wrong side at Philippi[32] – dedicated the *Satires* to Maecenas, and was given a small country property and a flat in Rome. R. Nisbet is firm about the immediate effect of Horace's relations with Maecenas, beginning in 38, on the triumviral *Epodes*: it trivialised his treatment of war and politics. All the same, in *Epode* 16 he significantly envisaged an island utopia, perhaps a response to Virgil's elevated fourth *Eclogue*.[33] Some of his targets in the *Satires* are opponents of the Triumvirs. The poet who had begun the work as a follower of the scathing seventh-century poet Archilochus of Paros ended as a committed devotee of Octavian, even if he was not actually in his suite at the battle of Actium.[34] Nonetheless, the poets were poised between Antony and Octavian for the greater part of the Triumvirate.[35] Horace gave up his appointment as a clerk in government service (*scriba quaestorius*) and was able to refuse Augustus' offer of a secretaryship without damaging their good relations.[36]

The part played by the poets in Octavian's struggles of the 30s is modest: any greater and more focused role was, as yet, undeveloped. The poets shared the hopes of all Romans and Italians for peace and stability. Octavian shared them too, on his own terms. After 30 BC, they all knew that such hopes were dependent on the new Princeps, and Horace for one was ready to celebrate his success in defeating Cleopatra, to share in building a new age, in 17 to hymn the later achievements of the regime, when a 'better age' (*melius aeuum*) had indeed been achieved, and finally in the mid-teens to celebrate the military successes of Augustus' stepsons. These last two works Horace's demanding friend 'compelled' him to write and 'imposed' on him (*coegerit, iniunxerit*); but these are the interpretative words of Suetonius. Otherwise he was entitled to follow his own concerns. After a reading of some *Satires* Augustus twitted Horace with leaving him. Such letters tease; did Horace's to the Princeps do the same?[37]

By the teens it is agreed that Maecenas was fading from his prominence as a patron, and Augustus himself was taking over,[38] with Horace's *Carmen Saeculare* and the first poem of *Epistles* Book 2 the earliest products of the change, then *Odes* Book 4. The fourth book of Propertius' *Elegies* also belongs to this period. Political weakening, even the disgrace, of Maecenas has been taken to be the cause of the change, and denied. It would be rash to accept the political explanation unsupported. We might think rather of enhanced assertiveness on the part of the Princeps after his political success in 19.[39]

Tibullus (born between 55 and 48 BC) died in that year. He does not mention Augustus but had another patron, M. Messala Corvinus, who had fought on the Liberators' side at Philippi, and on Octavian's at Actium. Tibullus was the literary successor of the prematurely dead Cornelius Gallus and, like his close contemporary Propertius, a precursor of Ovid. All of them were of equestrian rank and so not in Augustus' debt, apart from the fact that membership of the equestrian order was conditional upon Augustus' favourable scrutiny.[40] Tibullus rejects but does not disdain soldiering. He has done it and does not consider his current pursuits inferior: he uses military metaphor for his own activities. The financially independent Propertius of Asisium (Assisi) was not indebted to Augustus, far from it: his family property had suffered from the confiscations and his sympathies were with the losers in the Perusine war: he knew 'the graveyard of our country' but his brother lay unburied.[41] He has been thought insidious and subversive in his distaste for a public and approved subject – 'non-conformist'. He explicitly declined to glorify Augustus in an epic and left writing something greater than the *Iliad* to Virgil; he even on occasion likened himself to Antony. Hence in part unfavourable modern criticism of his ultimate hymn on the victory at Actium, written in about 16 BC.[42] That poem came late: Varius Rufus had written his drama *Thyestes* for Octavian's triumphal games of 29 BC and been well rewarded for it.[43] The standpoint taken in this chapter presents a panorama of writers aware of the blessings that Augustus' victory had brought, mainly that of peace and all that stemmed from it. They were realists and knew that, barring accidents, the new regime was permanent. Accepting it, they reacted individually, according to (and with conscious regard for) their gifts and talents: magisterially, festively, playfully. Some too were aware of their own power in shaping the behaviour of a Princeps who at first at any rate needed their sanction (see below).

Virgil and the limits of patronage

Augustus' reputation for a light touch in his dealings with literary artists remains unshaken despite the closeness to the greatest of the poets, Virgil and Horace, and despite Cornelius Gallus' death (for reasons that had nothing to do with poetry) and Ovid's eventual exile. That is due in part to the disparity between the known work of those poets and those of the 'Silver Age' that lasted from Augustus' immediate successors until the end of the first century AD, even of those as gifted as Lucan and Statius. That in turn is connected with the ever-deepening entrenchment in power of successive rulers.[44]

The greatest of the Golden Age poets, Virgil, offers a test case, both of the likely impact of contemporary affairs on a poet's life and of his vision of his own age; the *Aeneid* has been interpreted as a panegyric of Rome and Augustus and as a tragedy of an individual caught up in the processes of history.[45] The surviving work is copious, and evidence for the poet's life plentiful; much else can be conjectured from the well-documented history of his time. Already accepted by his fellows as a 'seer' (*uates*) in the last of the *Eclogues*, the weighty themes of the *Georgics* and *Aeneid* confirmed him in that position, above his lesser peers.[46] Born in 70 BC, he would have remembered the fighting in northern Italy that ended Catiline's conspiracy against the Roman state. It was only four years afterwards that government began to be paralysed when three ambitious politicians took power from the corrupt ruling Senate: it was the end of the Republic, some said.[47] And when Virgil was 21 Julius Caesar crossed the River Rubicon and invaded Italy from Gaul to hold sole power until his assassination.

No wonder the young poet is said to have taken refuge from these horrors in Naples and with a philosophy that preached non-intervention in politics and the indifference of the gods to men and their sufferings: Epicureanism.[48] But it is dangerous to accept the biographies of poets constructed in ancient times and continually repeated: they are often made up from reinterpreted snippets of the poet's own works. (Modern biographers are still found treating the work of their subjects in the same way.) We only need to know the work to realise that Virgil was soon writing verse that his contemporary Horace described as 'tender and charming'.[49]

Certainly Virgil's earliest poems were in part a kind of escape: the *Eclogues*, rustic idylls written some time before 39–38 and set in a shepherd's never-never-land, but one also populated by real people and affected by the violence of the proscriptions, the Philippi campaign, and the civil war in northern and central Italy that centred on the siege of Perusia. The first and ninth echo the feelings of men who had lost their farmlands in the confiscations, some of them graciously returned by Octavian to the thankful owners: 'That man will be my god'. In a subtle analysis J. Osgood has shown how, in a poem that presents Octavian as confiscator and benefactor, the grateful Tityrus sees him as a full god, demonstrating the power of his image.[50] Virgil was not the only poet to treat this theme. Horace, like Propertius, was a loser in the confiscations; his father's farm went, but he did well later; such losses, and how they should be borne, figure in the second *Epistle* of Book 2.[51] The quarrel between Antony and Octavian was patched up in 40 and Virgil's fourth *Eclogue* looks forward to the birth of a child who would preside over a new age, not the Christ Child, as some once supposed; probably a child of Antony and Octavian's sister – who turned out to be a daughter, the elder Antonia, born in 39.

In the decade that followed, Virgil made friends that linked him with the party of Octavian who was in control in the West. While Antony occupied himself with building up his supremacy over the Greek-speaking half of the Empire he left behind other problems in the West, longer-standing ones that had helped to cause the political unrest of the past hundred years and were a constant source of worry to concerned Romans. One symptom was acute grain shortages in Rome and the rioting they provoked when they were aggravated by the activities at sea of Sex. Pompeius. Could Italy feed itself? What would happen if farmers were all taken away to serve in the swollen armies of the Second Triumvirate? Were current farming methods as productive as they might be? Varro published his treatise *On Agriculture* in 37 BC, and Virgil was celebrating the beauty and fertility of Italy in his four books on rural life, the *Georgics*. He complained there of depopulated countryside, fields left rough and uncultivated;[52] if peace held, men could turn back to their proper work on the land, and there would be a constant supply of young recruits to keep Rome's empire expanding. Nonetheless, the *Georgics* were far from being propaganda for an officially inspired revival of agriculture (in any case, Virgil's past Golden Age in the second *Georgic* preceded that of rustic Sabine virtue).[53] Of the divergent interpretations of the poem on offer, pessimistic, hopeful or something between, the cool view of C. Nappa, that Golden Ages in the poem are all flawed, and another was not to be looked forward to, only the hard work (*labor*) that does offer some reward, is the most plausible.[54] Anything 'golden' raises suspicion and, in any case, we cannot assume that all Golden Ages are the same, even to a single writer. Horace's model would be different from Virgil's, more down to earth, and he noticeably omits any mention of it from the *Carmen Saeculare*.[55] The contrast with the Triumviral fourth *Eclogue* of Virgil is poignant. There the Golden Age is imminent, even if it is premature to claim that it has arrived.[56] The birth of the boy, the hoped for son of Antony and Octavia, is already associated with the rule of one man, and further expansion abroad, a theme of the *Aeneid*.

The *Georgics* also refer to the victories in which Octavian saw off Antony and Cleopatra. The hope of peace was now sure and rested entirely with Octavian, whose future task was to rebuild the shattered community. Already Virgil was displaying Octavian's achievements in an imaginary temple, and he was promising a modern political epic on those achievements, something very different from the *Aeneid* we have.[57] In 27 BC, when Octavian restored constitutional government and took on his grand new name, a new and happier age began under his benevolent and restrained guidance.

So it was hoped, and so Virgil evidently believed. He did embark on an epic, but not a modern one: his prospective survey of Roman history in *Aeneid* 1 culminates ambiguously with 'Caesar Julius' – but can hardly exclude the younger man. Augustus is fulsomely praised in the *Aeneid*, by Jupiter, by Aeneas' father, and by the poet directly in the description of Aeneas' shield.[58] Augustus is going to found a new Golden Age.[59] But the three great prophecies of Roman success in the *Aeneid*, those of Jupiter and Anchises, and the depictions on the shield of Aeneas, which even signals the processional route of Octavian's triple triumph of 29,[60] are still set in a background of struggle, loss and cruelty. As K. Galinsky stressed, Virgil's perspective on Roman history starts from the beginning: the summit is not yet achieved. So on coins *FELICITAS PUBLICA* was of necessity to be a slogan for later emperors, beginning with Galba and the Flavians (although Ovid offers *felicia saecula* after his exile); endeavour rather than success was what was stressed, the creation of order and the effort that was needed to bring the Roman people into being.[61]

Virgil had to believe what Augustus promised, because there was nothing else left. And the restoration of the commonwealth of Rome in its ancient and original form (Ch. 2) was to be echoed in the creation of an epic poem about the heroic origins of the Roman people greater than anything that Virgil had ever attempted before, something to rival even what Homer had achieved. Virgil's epic looked forwards from the heroic age and celebrated Roman history in Books 6 and 8, which included the Battle of Actium, as well as the Trojans who were the Romans' ancestors. And this Roman history culminated in the pre-eminence of Augustus and his family. As D. F. Kennedy sums it up, bringing in Livy as well as Virgil, 'ideology tends to assume a narrative form: stories are told which glorify those in power. History is the most important of those associations.' It lays claim to truth.

But again, after 27 BC, many politically conscious Romans were disappointed. Achieving the great goal of civil peace did not after all mean the end of discord. Other leaders have had to make fresh starts: Lenin with his Five-Year Plan, Mao with the 'Great Leap Forward'. Whatever he had promised in the early twenties, Augustus continued to rule and dominate every aspect of government. There were scandals, culminating in the crisis of 24–23 BC.[62] Perhaps the turbulence, involving 'conspiracies' and deaths, most notoriously of Virgil's friend and fellow-poet Cornelius Gallus (Ch. 4) is also reflected in the work of Horace, whose twelfth *Ode* in his first book wrestles precisely with the place of Augustus in the scheme of things, and ends with Augustus ruling as the vice-gerent of Jupiter. Yet he includes an awkward reference to the 'noble death' of the Younger Cato, a martyr of the Republic, worthy of honour if only for his suicide.[63] A figure like Cato had an honoured place in the settlement of 28–27, if only it had lasted; it was only towards the end of Augustus' principate, apparently, that Cato's life was to be honoured (Ch. 2). But Augustus was bent on consolidating his own predominance. When Horace opens the *Ode* he asks in conventional terms what man or what hero or god he is to sing. It was a real question, who was to govern the Roman Empire, and how.

By the time this problem was resolved, Virgil was dead. His death in 19 BC coincided with the final establishment of Augustus' Principate, his informal leadership of the Roman state. Virgil never finished his epic – or so it seems from its ending with the merciless slaughter of the Italian warrior Turnus by Aeneas. Virgil knew only the years of struggle. It is transition that his poems reflect, and uncertainty. The context of Virgil's work, violence and deferred hopes, provides a clue to the tone and depth of what he wrote: forward-looking and celebratory, yet tragic. K. Galinsky has rightly characterised the Augustan Golden Age as one involving labour; that being so, it necessarily involved disappointment too, political and social.[64]

Virgil's poetry made him a classic in his lifetime: when he entered the theatre people rose from their seats.[65] What gave him honour like that may well have been the grandeur of the Rome that he celebrated – it was the Roman people assembled together in their proper ranks in the theatre that saluted him. But it may have been his depiction of the sufferings of individuals, Dido and Turnus as well as Aeneas, the losers as well as the winners, that made him loved. Virgil presents Aeneas' fatal outburst of anger with Turnus, 'frightful in his wrath', knowing of Augustus' equally fatal outbursts.[66] Scholars have argued about the outlook of the *Aeneid*, 'positive' or 'pessimistic'. It is a misleading dichotomy: like his contemporaries, Virgil did not know.[67] Even Augustus knew only what he wanted.

It is one of the more positive interpretations of the relation of Virgil's epic to the Augustan regime, that it seeks to ground the Augustan interpretation of Rome. Troy is equated with Rome of the civil wars, and its fall is a precondition for the rise of (Augustan) Rome. And Aeneas is the ancestor of the Roman race, or of the line of Augustus; the two are elided. 'The Augustan regime was rewriting history to its own design.' Yet the fall of Troy precedes the main action of the *Aeneid*, and that ends in an act of vengeance. Certainly, Rome was a military society, and, as Dr Herbert-Brown points out, vengeance was integral to the value system; not to take revenge was to lack *virtus* and *pietas*. Octavian had to avenge Caesar to attain credibility with his veterans. Poetic empathy with those caught up in it did not cancel out or even necessarily criticise this heroic value-system.

All the same, it does not look quite like an (ultimately) triumphant narrative of simple success.[68] So saturated is the poetry with awareness of what human beings go through in their successes and failures, whether they are winners or losers, and what they have to sacrifice even if they are winners, as Aeneas and the Roman people and Augustus did, that it must embrace the whole gamut. In the eulogy of Augustus delivered by Aeneas' father Anchises,[69] Augustus, offspring of a god (*divi genus*) *is going to* found a Golden Age of peace (*aurea condet saecula*) in Latium where Saturn once ruled; we cannot be told when. And he will advance Rome's *imperium* into Africa and India; the journeyings of Hercules on his labours did not cover as much of the earth, nor those of Bacchus as he drove his tiger-yoked chariot from distant Nysa. The future tense of the verb, and the nimbus of divinity accorded the ruler, are proper not only for the prophecy delivered in the heroic age but for Virgil's own time. That is why the *Aeneid* can have no proper closure, and the ending it has is a just one.[70]

Lyric, elegy and the limits of freedom

That was the long view. But Augustus was sensitive to the needs of his contemporaries, and learned to present himself as the man of the moment. As K. Galinsky puts it in connexion with Horace's *Satires* (second decade BC), Horace had a sense of shared direction; the destiny of Augustus was clear, elaboration was left to the creativity of individuals. So Horace is multi-referential rather than ambiguous. In one of the most famous *Odes* he promises Augustus that he would be *praesens divus*, an immanent deity. K. Galinsky offers no fewer than three interpretations of those lines; and in the earlier poem mentioned above Horace presents a less exalted picture of Augustus' destiny: he is to rule Latium 'under Jove'. But the future can fulfil both visions.[71]

Ovid, like Propertius, was in a more difficult position than his predecessors. Rank made its demands on him, and it was not offset by benefits that put him under an acknowledged obligation to Augustus. Born into an equestrian family at Sulmo (Sulmona) among the Paeligni in about 43,[72] he had no experience of the Republic, though he lived through its last years, but came to manhood when young men of rank were expected to take part in the renewed public life and, with Augustus' support, could look for successful careers. Ovid not only declined that opportunity, but moved in circles that were defiantly independent, even frivolous, and hence vulnerable. A. Wallace-Hadrill has no hope for Ovid: 'All that was most delightful about Ovid, his wit, irreverence, perceptiveness, ambiguity, made him an unsuitable vehicle for publicizing Augustus.'[73]

Ovid claims that he had been Augustus', but in the only way he knew – as an intellectual.[74] He was already aware of charges against himself, even of danger, in the *Art of Love*, of which the first and second books belong to 2–1 BC. There was no ground for legal action against the love elegists: after the murderous upheaval of the civil wars there were widows and divorcées available and no legislation forbade their love affairs. It could even be argued that Augustus could afford to take love elegies lightly: they exemplified the freedom that had existed before the Republic fell. So Ovid protests early on that the affairs he is describing are perfectly lawful: they involve call-girls and cultivated young women who recited poetry and were skilled singers, dancers and actresses; besides, elegiac poetry owes as much to him as epic does to Virgil.[75]

Yet there was a change. Ovid's older contemporaries died young; even Horace was dead in 8 BC, Propertius by 2 BC, with nothing heard from him after 16. The tension between Ovid's earlier poems and what the Princeps might hope to read has been neatly set out by D. F. Kennedy: Augustus was to be inscribed within the most potent charter myths of Rome;[76] Ovid re-inscribed those very myths within his own frivolous discourse. Suetonius' remark that Augustus would take offence if anything were written about him other than by the most eminent authors, and in a serious spirit, was a point that Ovid eventually countered in a poem addressed to Augustus from exile: Jupiter himself was delighted to be treated in Ovid's poetry.[77] In any case, during the last, harsh, decade of Augustus' Principate, Ovid took on the writing of the calendrical *Fasti*, a hard task, but one that did not prove too much for his talent: he did indeed succeed in creating, in G. Herbert-Brown's words, 'a new mythology in literature'. In this it is not Romulus but Augustus who is the paradigm.[78] The work was dedicated to Augustus, the Pontifex Maximus.[79]

It was not enough. After his involvement with the younger Julia and her circle, and his exile in AD 8 Ovid's verses were taken off the public shelves.[80] From slanderous pamphlets and Ovid's inappropriate *Ars Amatoria*, intolerance spread to representations of the past, to historical works, as we shall see (cf. Ch. 4). It was unsafe, not just to cast aspersions on successful figures of the present but to write anything to revise the accepted view of the past. Precedents were set for the worst that was to happen under Tiberius, new weapons made available for those powerful at court – while lampoons had to preserve the anonymity of critics.[81]

When Ovid fell foul of Augustus, it was not for abusing him, rather, if the poem that caused offence was the *Ars Amatoria*, for flouting new moral standards.[82] Yet the penalty of exile (in its mildest form, relegation) has lent some plausibility to an extreme view, that a thoroughly subversive Ovid was systematically attacking Augustus in his epic poem, the *Metamorphoses*, written just before the exile. One relentless exposition of this view, that of S. Lundström, allows it to be thoroughly assessed.[83] Ovid belonged to the opposition to Augustus and showed it in the *Metamorphoses*, while Augustus realised that the irresponsible individualist of the *Art of Love* had not changed. One item after another in the poem provides a key to Ovid's thinking: the story of Iphis, the replacement of Apollo's mother Leto by Isis, an act of opposition to Augustan policy. As for Byblis, that led to *exempla magna deorum*, to Augustus' predecessor on the throne of the Pharaohs, and to Caesarion. The mighty example of the gods is not edifying either: they are vicious or helpless, with Augustus' patron Apollo the worst offender in his savagery to Marsyas and Niobe: he is flayed and she deprived of her brood of children; even kindly Ceres punishes Sicily for the rape of her child by Pluto as the Triumvirs punished it after the victory of Naulochus: prayer is useless and altars protect the guilty. Kings are no better, and they can be old and feeble too. Lundström finds Ovid's war heroes equally unimpressive: lapiths and centaurs, there is nothing to choose between them. As for Ulysses' preposterous claim to Achilles' deeds on the ground that he brought Achilles to the war, that recalls Augustus, the proxy victor. Then there is the good-humoured idyll of the serpentine tourist Aesculapius: it was not clever of Ovid to treat Augustus' half-brother with such levity. References to Caesar's triumphs contrive to bring them into disrepute, while his 'grotesque' apotheosis becomes only one of the series of transformations; and would the aged Augustus have appreciated Ovid's two pointed references to his own demise?

There could be something in all this; anything that Lundström notices Augustus too could have divined. But did he choose to adopt those interpretations? The question is how one particular reader – reading before or after the exile? – took the allusions. Nor does Lundström distinguish between different grades of offence: attacks on Augustan sacred cows from attacks on the achievements of the Princeps himself. And denigration of Caesar would not have displeased him. Proponents of this kind of view may have missed the point. For the poet of the stories of Iphis and Byblis, of the piteous tale of Ceyx and Alcyone, Augustan Rome was irrelevant; that in truth may have been offence enough. Augustus had done his work, but Ovid laid claim to his own immortality as an artist and an entertainer. It was Augustus who perpetrated the greater *error*.[84]

It is better to return to the *Ars Amatoria*. In AD 8 Augustus took advantage of Ovid's association with discontented members of the aristocracy who went into exile, Julia the Younger and her husband. Once in exile,

Ovid shows up, for R. Syme at least, as a man of stature, a courageous and dedicated artist still. By contrast, the men ranged over against him as recipients of his poems are specimens of the aristocracy, ambitious, unscrupulous and obsequious for the most part; their failings and failures are known mostly from Tacitus.[85] But the exile without a bargaining counter makes a sorry sight. Horace had explicitly offered the Princeps what he earnestly desired and had to earn: immortality. Ovid himself was too late to proffer that reward. At the end of his Principate Augustus was sure of his immortality; then it was confirmed by the state. Ovid had to turn elsewhere for any hope of a return to Rome, to Germanicus Caesar and lesser men able to intercede with Augustus or, after 14, an implacable Tiberius. (Tiberius was implacable not because he disapproved of frivolous and risqué verse – he himself wrote poetry that the younger Pliny thought needed an apology[86] – but because of Ovid's association with his ex-wife's daughter, both of them hostile to his own advancement.) We have to remember that Romans do not seem to have thought that exile demanded a stiff upper lip. Three examples bring that to mind: Cicero, pleading for help in 58–57 BC; more surprisingly Tiberius, whose mother intervened on his behalf and who, soon after his return from virtual exile on Rhodes in 2 BC, but still thoroughly marginalised, had composed an elegy on the death of one his young rivals, Lucius Caesar; and the younger Seneca, who wrote an obsequious work, the *Consolatio* addressed to Claudius' freedman Polybius, while he was stranded on Corsica between 41 and 49.[87]

The subversive poet?

Modern scholars long since became disaffected with the idea of literary men in thrall. In response, they have offered them more than one way out: they have cast Virgil and Ovid as ambivalent in their attitude towards the Princeps, even subversives peddling veiled criticism and irony, sceptics undermining 'official' lines. There is something to be said for this view – irony and the playfulness so effectively deployed by Ovid pervade Roman poetry, and that would be a way of avoiding censure – but the tone will vary from poem to poem, as we have seen with Ovid. Recent exponents of such views are A. Eich and J. Elsner: the political system is absent from the poets, Ovid was subversive, and Virgil unfavourable to Augustus. Critics need not be extreme: A. Barchiesi, hedging his bets, urges a double interpretation of the

Fasti: 'The poet picks out the weak points in Augustan discourse'; but 'The *Fasti* is *also* a poem of praise.'[88] None of this will do: 'The poet himself claimed that the *Fasti* was his gift to the Augustan state.'[89]

Alternatively the poets are seen as totally apolitical, self-contained and concerned only with their art. This second suggestion has little to recommend it: the severance of literature and politics has met sharp criticism.[90] Literature is political, even when it turns away from political life, which at Rome was in any case grounded directly in moral language. The very rejection of a committed point of view is itself a political act; poets are embedded in society. To deprive the work of Roman poets of its social and political context is to diminish it. Their writing was polyphonic and multifocal.[91] But there is another way of evading the unwelcome conception of poets in thrall.

The poet as compelling seer

The promotion of Augustus' name and fame in architecture and sculpture, paid for by him, was only to be expected. But the favourable presentation of him in the very different field of literature, even by men who chose genres and material unsuitable for adulation, who were sufficiently well enough off to do without Augustus' financial support, and who did not intend to go into politics, still needs explaining. If we leave aside the dark aspects of the *Aeneid*, supremely intelligent and sensitive writers, some close to the heart of the ruling clique, passed over what was going on in political life. They were aware of all the encroachments, even crimes, for which Octavian/Augustus was responsible, and later in his principate of the sordid jostling for power behind the scenes, and yet subscribed apparently without question to his predominance, sometimes, as with Propertius and his Actian *Ode*, producing as a result what has been denounced as bad poetry.

There is a further, twofold answer, which puts that matter in a different light. The first, minor, part of it lies in the background of some of the poems. So with Propertius' choric hymn, the Actian poem, which is itself a performance, and Horace's hieratic first Roman *Ode*, which attacks an impious building developer because he represents behaviour that Augustus wished to eradicate.[92] The second consideration and the more cogent as an overall interpretation is that after Actium it was obvious that there was no other option in government than Augustus, except continuing chaos ending in blatant tyranny. So with Virgil, whose deep and pervasive political feeling is urged by A. Powell.[93] The new regime was a given and intellectuals literally had to make the best of it. That is far from dynamic as an exposition of their thinking. It went further: they may have thought of using their power as writers, above all as poets, to alter things for the better. Latin poets were not just makers of poetry, *poetae*, but in the Augustan period also *vates*, inspired prophets with (in P. Hardie's words) serious things to say about religion and the gods and with privileged access to eternal truths. As we have seen, Virgil makes one of the shepherds in his ninth *Eclogue* say: 'The Muses have made me too a poet . . . the shepherds call me a *vates*.'[94] Moreover, he was a seer of a particular kind. When an Augustan poet speaks of what will happen he is not just making predictions about the future; he is helping to bring it about, for he also had privileged access to the Princeps, as well as a public following limited only by its literacy. A man who is told by a great poet that he is good will have to live up to the praise; and if he does live up to it he will achieve immortality through his great deeds – at any rate the immortality of fame, more if that was what was in his mind. Hence the power of literature, with which practitioners and rulers were and are deeply concerned.[95]

It is an Augustan historian, Livy, who near the beginning of his work, and so writing in the early 20s BC, tells the story of the founder of Rome, Romulus, with whom Augustus had commonly been associated, putting up an altar to an earlier hero, Hercules, and so acknowledging the immortality that Hercules' merit (*virtus*) has won him: Hercules was the already half divine hero who in his twelve labours had ranged from one end of the world to the other in the service of humanity.[96] Livy, according to Pliny, said that he went on writing out of a restless spirit (*inquies animus*); Augustus was equally indefatigable.[97] That shared characteristic helps to explain why Augustus' regime proved so acceptable. Cicero noted 'the darkness that saw nature carrying Romulus away to his death also, it is said, saw his *virtus* carrying him up to heaven'. Romulus had tried to make himself *augustior*, more impressive – or more like Augustus, the end towards which the Roman enterprise was evidently striving.[98] Even autocratic rulers have to earn their supremacy by winning hearts and minds, especially rulers without guns, explosives and gas, who know that their coercive powers are limited. Augustus did hope for immortality: fame and deification. According to Tacitus this was something that people claimed made Augustus better regarded, and really better, than his successor Tiberius: precisely because he entertained those ambitious hopes. The very fact that Augustus wanted to provide *exempla* for future generations (Ch. 5) made him vulnerable. Tiberius, on the contrary, arrogantly and short-sightedly spurned what other men thought and relied on his own self-righteousness, thus adding to it and increasing his own ill-repute amongst those he ignored. Augustus' hope of glory did him more credit than Tiberius' ostentatious modesty, for public opinion, according to Tacitus, held that a man who despises what people say about him (*fama*) necessarily despises good behaviour (*virtutes*). So, in DuQuesnay's words, the poets 'may have helped to shape the way in which Octavian progressed from the bloody and ruthless pursuit of power . . . to the enlightened self-interest of the Principate'.[99]

The *virtutes* of the Shield of Merit that Augustus was awarded in 27 were sung by Horace in his *Odes*, and he prophesied in the 20s that Augustus would sit drinking nectar among the gods, when he had conquered the Parthians or the wild Britons.[100] In the view of R. Seager, the only major question on which Horace and Augustus may not have seen eye to eye is the desirability of imperial expansion.[101] Horace's exhortations belong to the period before 23, when expansion was politically desirable for Augustus, but it was always creditable. After the renunciation of easy conquests in 20 BC (Ch. 3) there was little to be said of Britain and Parthia. Scholars have called the 'sincerity' of the poets into question, but that perspective is inappropriate. It is more profitable to think of them, perhaps from their conscious point of view, in terms of something more active when they were dealing directly with the Princeps: effectiveness in shaming Augustus into good behaviour. They could never be sure of success, and in any case it might not be something measurable or particular. But the more highly respected the writer, the more effective his expectations would be. Even in the Triumviral period, Octavian and Antony paid attention to public opinion – their intense propaganda, and their twists and turns of policy show it. Incidents in which women played a prominent part – the plea of 'Turia', the demonstration against taxation led by Hortensia – illustrate their vulnerability to being shamed.[102]

There was something similar about Augustus' dealings with provincials (Ch. 3). One might almost speak of a similar mechanism, except that the poets did not yet – as they were to do under Domitian – ask for favours for themselves, but for exemplary behaviour towards the gods and the Roman

People and their traditions. In the provinces the apparently all-powerful ruler was readily offered cult or other forms of homage, in return for benefits hoped for or actually requested: so when he accepted those honours he knew that he would have to provide something in return if asked for it. The clearest instance of this is to be found in two documents. One is a letter from Tiberius to the people of Aezani (Çavdarhisar) in Phrygia written at Bononia (Boulogne-sur-Mer) soon after he was elevated to the position of heir in AD 4. It acknowledges the devotion that the city has shown him right from the beginning and promises (in quite general terms) that he will do what he can to help them. The second, more specific, is the famous letter of Claudius to the Alexandrians, containing a list of honours offered Claudius in AD 41, some accepted, others refused, which is followed by a second list of the Alexandrians' own requests, some accepted, others denied. Claudius did not deny himself some freedom of speech in addressing his audience. After all, he had not accepted all their honours and had even shown disapproval of some of them.[103] That was why Augustus was notoriously so cautious about accepting; his caution was not due so much to sheer modesty nor to sensitivity about the way such honours might be seen in Rome (they were commonplace) as to a wish to avoid excessive obligations to his subjects.[104] Augustus' paradigm performance was his reaction to the offer of temples from the provincial assemblies of Asia and Bithynia in 29 BC: Romans were allowed to worship Julius Caesar at Nicaea and Ephesus (Iznik, Efes), non-Romans Augustus at Nicomedia and Pergamum (Izmit, Bergama), but only in combination with the goddess Roma.

Although Virgil adumbrated Augustus' future divinity, he died before Augustus, through bringing peace to Rome and the Empire, was seen to have done enough to justify his power and his formal deification. Another poet, Ovid, outlived Augustus for three years and survived long enough to sum the matter up succinctly: 'his merit (*virtus*) had indeed carried him to the stars and made him one of them'.[105]

The decline of influential literature

The influence of the poets inevitably declined. Augustus and still more his successors became entrenched in an accepted system, one that, in the crises that followed the assassination of Gaius Caligula in AD 41 and the enforced suicide of Nero in 68, proved indispensable. About eulogy something mechanical could easily develop, but at the earliest stage of the Principate there need be little that was routine, and that remained the case for any princeps who felt that his title to rule was vulnerable. Hence conflicting views on the freedom and outspokenness of Augustan writers, and on their actual views. Each writer made his own way, as divergent presentations of Augustus' wars demonstrate.[106] Allowance must be made for the genuine efforts of Augustus' contemporaries, those at least outside the ranks of senators jealous for the old constitution, who wanted to believe in one who brought peace and with it prosperity, and strove to immortalise his merits. But already in the latter part of the Augustan Principate, blight, as it has been called, descended even on Horace.[107] After Augustus there developed inflation of language and imagery, as poets such as Statius and Martial tried not to be outdone by or to repeat their predecessors and contemporaries, and as emperors such as Domitian demanded or at least hoped for ingenious novelties (for which they paid money). They were confident in the permanency of the Principate, which had survived the civil wars of 68–69, and in their own position. There was less of a need to earn it.

The poets' influence should not be over-estimated. Ovid's work on the *Fasti* did not save him from a penalty inflicted at Augustus' personal command (his eloquence could not be allowed free play during a senatorial trial). The fate of Cornelius Gallus three and a half decades earlier showed what verse, and friendship, counted for in politics. His surviving lines, written probably in 30 BC, tell how sweet his destiny will seem to him when Octavian becomes the greatest theme in Roman history and he reads of temples hung with Octavian's spoils.[108] He did not live to do it, but his vision was fulfilled: according to Ovid in the *Fasti* the calendar consisted entirely in records of Augustus.[109] We are free to make of that what we will.

Freedom of speech: history and politics

Freedom of speech did not come to an end with Augustus, even though slander and libel began to be prosecuted in AD 6 under the existing law against diminishing the majesty of the Roman People (see Ch. 4).[110] Later ages looked back on his Principate as a time of free speech and writing. In Latin poetry, conventions had not yet been established in any new panegyrical genre, and writers went their own ways. History, for obvious reasons and because it had always been written by judgemental politicians, usually with axes to grind, was a real test of imperial nonchalance. History would be recited at soirées and read in Rome by the entire political class, by the alert municipal notables of Italy and all the cities of the provinces that had pretensions to Latin culture. Again, there was evidently a period of tolerance. Tacitus relates that in the earlier part of the Augustan Principate there was no lack of distinguished talents in his field, but sycophancy took over: candour (*veritas*) deserted historians who curried favour with the incumbent, and afterwards vented their spleen on him.[111] As to the most distinguished of all, Livy, his patriotic history, begun in the earliest years of the Principate, was fully consonant with the declared aims of the regime as Augustus expressed them in the *Achievements* and with the Princeps' own evaluation of what he had done: it offered specimens from Roman history of exemplary conduct for later generations to emulate.[112] Yet there was an inbuilt conflict here. The great heroes of the Republic were necessarily republicans, and some of the greatest, such as the younger Cato, had died defending the Republic against Caesar. Livy was an admirer of Pompey ('Pompeianus').

Figure 20 Cup from Boscoreale: Augustus receiving homage (akg-images Ltd. Photograph by Erich Lessing)

Augustus knew his leanings and yet did not prevent him encouraging a young relative and would-be historian, the later Emperor Claudius.[113] All the same, the studious Claudius, grandson of Mark Antony, was effectively prevented, by his mother Antonia and grandmother Livia, it was said, from undertaking a work that would have stretched from the assassination of Caesar through the Triumviral Period. Livy himself is reported to have held back the last two decades of his history, which in any case terminated in 9 BC, until after Augustus' death. The terminal date coincided with Nero Drusus' victorious campaign in Germany and with his untimely death. By the same token it preceded the contentious years of Tiberius' voluntary exile on Rhodes and the disgrace of Augustus' daughter and grandchildren. It was impossible to write without offending one clique or another, and Augustus too, if he favoured the clique that took offence. Whether Livy completed the account of earlier controversial years of Augustus is unclear: no *Epitome* survives of Books 136 and 137, for events between the conquest of the Salassi in 24 BC and that of Raetia in 15.

To go further down in history beyond Pompey the Great was to reach Brutus and Cassius, Augustus' own opponents, and at first sight that was more dangerous. Pollio had taken part at a high level in the events from 60 BC onwards that he described, and his high authority could not be silenced, even though Horace warned him that he was walking over fires still burning under treacherous ash.[114] Pollio got away with his history, as well as with opening his house to harbour Augustus' (indeed, Rome's) bitter critic the historian Timagenes (Ch. 4).

A. Cremutius Cordus, who was born in about 35 BC, recited part of his history to Augustus, with or without its praise of Brutus and Cassius, and apparently met with approval. Only under Tiberius in AD 25, when Augustus had been deified, was his history used against him, fatally. Cordus was tried in the Senate and forced to suicide; the Senate ordered his work to be burned. What exactly being a 'Pompeian' meant, or 'praising' Brutus and Cassius, could vary. A rhetorical expression such as calling them 'the last of the Romans' could escape notice where there was no pre-existing tension; a reasoned defence of the assassination of Caesar would be quite another matter at any time. There was a range of freedoms open to historical writers, especially those who were too eminent to touch, such as Pollio, or whose views, like those of Cremutius Cordus, might not prove influential. It is hard to make firm pronouncements, for the limits were arbitrary, the boundaries unclear and fluctuating; but they narrowed towards the end of Augustus' Principate.[115] The case of the ferocious polemicist Labienus (Ch. 4) is paradigmatic. Not only his scurrilous writings were burnt when he was condemned, but his histories too.[116] What they contained is a matter of guesswork, but there may have been a vindication of his kinsman Q. Labienus, who had enlisted Parthian help when he resisted the Triumvirs in the East. Another outspoken polemicist, Cassius Severus, made a neat double comment on the state of affairs: talent was scarce – and it was being repressed (Ch. 4).

Anecdotally, Augustus is presented as a defender of free speech, and we have seen him harassed in the Senate House (Ch. 4).[117] There were certainly rewards for men who said the right thing (writing of the victorious Caesar would be sure to win rewards, says Horace[118]) and words were adaptable. The owner of the talking crow that hailed Octavian as 'Caesar, victorious, commander' – but had in reserve another bird trained to hail 'Victorious, commander, Antony' – knew that.[119] From the eastern fringe of the Empire came the apparatchik of Herod the Great, Nicolaus of Damascus, who was a contemporary of Augustus and wrote his biography, a panegyric with a philosophical veneer.[120] Unsurprisingly, in his Preface he announced that fine rewards were to be had for competing in festivals extolling the virtues of the ruler. Evidently rewards might come not directly from the ruler but from those who wanted to please for the sake of their political positions, and who enlisted the support of lesser men to that end. The wishes of the ruler, real or supposed, permeated through society and were fulfilled sometimes without his knowledge.

How did Augustus deal with those who said the wrong thing? Suetonius' famous story of Augustus warning Tiberius against taking action against offenders does no favours to Tiberius, who turned out notoriously rancorous and vengeful; it may have been quoted (or invented, though a letter is cited) for that reason, as much as to favour Augustus. Much would depend on whether Augustus considered himself in serious danger; evidently not in the case that Suetonius noticed.[121] Moreover, freedom of speech had a value of its own in building up a favourable picture of the Princeps. Early in Octavian's ascendancy Pollio said that a man could not be expected to write freely about someone who could write him up on the proscription lists. The acute danger posed by those lists did not last;[122] with the overthrow of Antony and Cleopatra the sole surviving dynast was secure, and normality could be restored.

Censorship

Nonetheless, caution, that is to say, self-censorship, developed, not only in what historians wrote, for all the routine declarations of impartiality and regard for truth, but in the art of declamation, whether academic (in the choice of subject) or partisan and pamphleteering, which was often subversive and covert (anonymous or pseudonymous). Not only Augustus' sensitivities were in question. Friends of the Princeps are significantly mentioned as taking the initiative in two episodes: Tiberius, noticed above, and Agrippa. The declaimer Porcius Latro was signalled by Agrippa to bring his performance before Augustus to a speedy end when he touched on the subject of the adoption of a low-class child into an aristocratic family (Agrippa's sons would be the parallel).[123]

A distinct turning point came in AD 6 and we have seen (Ch. 4) that it was not the regime as such that had come under criticism but (again) leading men and women, whom powerful politicians wanted to protect.[124] These people were part of the structure that Augustus had established; and, if Ovid was exiled in AD 8 partly for his verses that was because Augustus saw them too as undermining the society he had been trying to reconstruct.[125] Cassius Severus' work was already known to Augustus at the turn of the millennium: so persistent (and unsuccessful) was Severus that his activities prompted Augustus to wish that he would 'prosecute' his slow-growing Forum, in which the Temple of Mars stood (dedicated in 2 BC). Once the law of *maiestas* had encompassed pamphleteering and insult, the law could not let it go and accusers keen to profit from the rewards of successful prosecutions certainly would not, however much Augustus' successor discouraged them when first he came to power.[126] It may be no coincidence that in Tacitus' *Dialogue on Oratory* Cassius Severus, whose books were burnt, seems to form a turning point in the history of oratory.[127] It was only fear of public opinion that helped to keep critics safe under the Principate. In the view of the younger Seneca, words were not dangerous to a man under Augustus, but they could cause him trouble, as he illustrates with an anecdote about a senator called 'Rufus' who got drunk and wished ill on the Princeps. On the advice of a slave he went straight off next morning to denounce himself.[128]

As the struggle over the succession developed in the last two decades of Augustus' Principate and throughout Tiberius' reign, and accusers grew bolder from their predecessors' successes, the subjects and genres of offending material became wider, and enquiry as to what statute had been infringed was neglected. In AD 21 the knight Clutorius Priscus died for his premature elegy on the death of Drusus Caesar; in 34 it was a serious charge against Mam. Aemilius Scaurus, an aristocratic advocate, that he had written a play containing verses that could be interpreted as an attack on Tiberius. If it was an *Atreus*, as Dio suggests, that makes it an ironical counterpoint to Varius' lauded *Thyestes* of 29 BC. The dramatist committed suicide.[129]

Augustus chose not to continue Caesar's practice of publishing the proceedings of the Senate, and Dio, occupied with the serious business of writing history, complains of the difficulty in obtaining material when decisions were taken behind closed doors, while information was circulated that was not true.[130]

It was awareness of such attempts at control and the connivance of a powerful section of the upper class that benefited from the regime that gave rise to unofficial methods of transmitting information and changing public opinion. Limits on the availability of information often forced the urban *plebs* to make do with rumour: news from abroad was brought by imperial messengers and conveyed to the Princeps by the system that he had developed. Travellers, returning soldiers and merchants could provide unofficial information; the less the material available, the keener the appetite to obtain it. Street-corner oratory, pamphleteering, placarding and rumour-mongering, the sphere of a lower class of politician, were seen differently from the cultivated expression of members of the propertied classes. They came close to the ad libbing and gestures of common theatre players, and they could not easily be repressed. The attacks on Tiberius that circulated when he returned from exile and came to power (Ch. 4)[131] could even be considered a form of literature. Sentiments expressed in verse put in a claim for that dignity, and certainly made it easier for readers to remember them.

Endnotes

1 Golden Age: Galinsky 1996, 90–121. Art, architecture and literature: 141–287. He stresses experimentation (234–37) and the taking of new directions on the initiative of authors (Hor. *Ep.* 1. 1. 3 and Prop. 4. 1). Upsurge of prosperity denied, 119–221.
2 Virgil's popularity: Tac. *Dial.* 13. 3. Allusiveness in art: Galinsky 1996, 149.

3 Augustus' education, compositions, language and orthography: Malcovati 1969, xf.; Suet. *Aug.* 84f.; Tac. *Ann.* 13. 3. 2; Dio 45. 2. 7; as admirer of Apelles: Pliny, *NH* 35. 91; Suet. *Aug.* 89. 1, with Williams 1978, 137f. Fescennine attack on Asinius Pollio: Macr. *Sat.* 2. 4. 21. (Pollio as a friend of Augustus: Bosworth 1972; (more nuanced) Morgan 2000, 61 and 65f.) Augustus and Caesar's speeches: Suet. *Caes.* 55. 3f. Critical of Tiberius' speech and the spelling of a governor: Suet. *Aug.* 86. 2. On 'seriousness' Dr Herbert-Brown notes 'holidays for pimps and prostitutes in Flaccus' religious calendar, obscene pantomimes and satyr plays performed in the theatre under Augustus' patronage, and cupids, semi-naked women and famous adulterers in Augustan iconography'. Tradition conferred respectability.

4 For Augustus' use of writers and artists see Wallace-Hadrill 1987, most famously the *Fasti* of Praeneste, the work of Verrius Flaccus (AD 6–10).

5 Ovid, *Fasti* 3, 415–28, with Galinsky 1996, 320f. Dr Herbert-Brown points out a distinction between the Belvedere iconography and the theme in the *Fasti* which Galinsky misses: in the latter, Vesta (the people's goddess) replaces Venus. This would seem important for demonstrating independence of the artist and flexibility within a certain framework.

6 Horace and Ovid: I owe this point to Dr Herbert-Brown; it is less paradoxical than it appears at first sight.

7 Strabo on construction at Rome: 5. 235f.

8 Prima Porta bust ('the standard Augustan portrait') on coins: *RIC* 1^2, 12. For the Roman response to portraits and images, see Gregory 1994. Copies of imperial portraits were made for distribution throughout the Roman world: Fronto, *ad Caes.* 4. 12. 4. Galinsky 1996, 164–79, distinguishes four Augustan types, the 'Actian' (before 31), the 'Prima Porta', the more individualised 'veiled priest' type, and the 'Forbes', a further adaptation of a less abstract and life-like type, intended in Galinsky's view to present the '*civilis princeps*', which appears on the Ara Pacis. Meanwhile, as he also points out, private individuals might adopt the same style, or, like M. Agrippa, keep to the more rugged Hellenistic depictions. Smith 1996, in a different approach, stresses a balance of 'ideal' and 'portrait' (46).

9 The Princeps' influence: Bonanno 1976, 176; Zanker 1988, 107f. Contribution of poets from their own experience: Galinsky 1996, 165; 225.

10 Patron's control: Rea 2007, 122.

11 Boscoreale cups: Kuttner 1995, with Lobur 2007, 25.

12 Statues melted: *RG* 24. 2; cf. Suet. *Aug.* 52, with Zanker 1988, 86f. See Ch. 3. Corinthian capital: Osgood 2006. 5.

13 Classicism in the 20s BC: Torelli 1996, 931–34, 938. Temple of Mars Ultor: Purcell 1996, 789f.; beauty: Pliny *NH* 36.102. Temple in art and literature: Zanker 1988, 113, quotes Ovid *Fasti* 5, 553–68.

14 Augustus' treatment by sculptors (on the Altar of Peace): Bonanno 1976, 24f. With plebeians: Zanker 1988, 133 and 135, figs. 109 and 111.

15 Prima Porta statue: Zanker 1988, 98–100; Torelli 1996, 931; Galinsky 1996, 24–8. The head designed, according to Smith 1996, 38, for the 'settlement' of 27 BC; model: 47. Doryphorus: Quint. 5. 12. 20–22 (*vir gravis et sanctus*), with Yavetz 1984, 7; critique of this theory: Smith 1996, 41–45. Cuirass: Galinsky 1996, 155–64, admitting (410 n. 35) that if the central figure represents the young Tiberius, it suggests a Tiberian date for the statue. For hip-mantle and the bare feet: 161, noting that an original may have been shod; spear: 163. Derivatives of the type: Hausmann 1981, 565–95.

16 Youthfulness of Augustus' statues: Eck 2007, 163; so Smith 1996, 47.

17 Portico of Octavia: A. Viscogliosi, *LTUR* 4 (1999) 141–45. Ovid, *Ars Amat.* 1. 69f. Ovid's Rome surveyed: Boyle 2003.

18 Danaids: Harrison 1998; Putnam 1998, 15f., 189–209, sees a difference of opinion between Augustus and the poets.

19 Wiseman 1984, on *Aen*. 6, 776–95.

20 Pergamene influence: Hardie 1986, 125–43.

21 *Gigantomachy*: Hardie 1986, 85–120, alluding to Hor. *Odes* 3. 4; Ovid, *Met*. 1, 151–62; shield: Virg. *Aen*. 8. 625–731, Gauls at 655–62 (cf. Prop. 2. 31. 13).

22 Differences between sculpture and literature: Hardie 1986, 135. Struggle: Virg. *Aen*. 1. 33. However, as Dr Herbert-Brown notes, sculpture may convey more than a bald description of the subject implies. *Non enarrabile textum*: Virg. *Aen*. 6. 825, with Putnam 1998, 187f.

23 'Propaganda' to be avoided: Galinsky 1996, 39–41; cf. above, Introduction.

24 Aims of poets: Rea 2007, 15.

25 Patronage: Lyne 1995, 15; see C. F. Eilers, *Roman Patrons of Greek Cities* (Oxford, 2002). Horace may have had help from Asinius Pollio or M. Valerius Messala as well as from Maecenas: Osgood 2006, 214. Poets' material gains : Lyne 1995, 9–11 ('paid more like stars than academics').

26 *Recusatio*: Lyne 1995, 31–9 (Virg. *Ecl*. 6. 5–9; Hor. *Odes* 4. 15; *Epist*. 2. 1. 250–9; *Sat*. 1. 10).

27 Criticism from Horace: Hor. *Ep*. 2. 1. Forced eulogy. Hor. *Sat*. 1. 3. 4; Suet. Hor. 41–48 (p. 116 Rostagni).

28 Propertius refused both Maecenas and Augustus: 2. 1. 17–26; 2.10; 3. 9. 3f.; Maecenas' affection for Horace: Suet. *Hor*. 9–16 (p. 112 Rostagni); Hor. *Sat*. 1. 5f.; 2. 6. Varius to write on Agrippa: Hor. *Odes* 1. 6.

29 *Iubesque esse in amicorum numero*: Hor. *Sat*. 1. 6. 61f.

30 Journey to Brundisium: Hor. *Sat*. 1. 5. On the poets' presence, see Osgood 2006, 246 n. 163, and on Horace's loyalties 362f., on *Epode* 1. 1–4.

31 For caution on Virgil's loss see Osgood's vivid interpretation 2006, 125f.

32 Horace's hard early life: Osgood 2006, 213f.

33 Hor. *Epode* 16: see Osgood 2006, 233–36.

34 Horace and Maecenas: Nisbet 1984, 9f.; DuQuesnay 1984, 57f. Targets: 53–57; Lyne 1995, 139–57. Horace at Actium: Watson 1987, on the strenuous propaganda of Hor. *Epode* 9, at 121.

35 Poets and Triumvirs: Osgood 2006, 250.

36 Secretaryship refused: Suet. *Hor.* 18–25 (113f. Rostagni).

37 Poets' detachment from Civil Wars: Townend 1996, 909f. Sharing in construction of ideology: Santirocco 1995; Shumate 2005, with Horace as a proto-nationalist. *Melius aeuum*: Hor. *Carm. Saec.* 67f. Augustus' letters to Horace: Malcovati 1969, 22–24, XXXVII–XLI. Refusal (*recusatio*) is a recurrent theme: Virg. *Ecl.* 6. 5–9; Hor. *Odes* 4. 15; *Epist.* 2. 1. 250–9; *Sat.* 1. 10.

38 Fading of Maecenas' patronage: Williams 1978, 56–58. Any suggestion that the transfer of patronage from Maecenas was prearranged with Augustus to the time when the Princeps was securely established is too schematic. Disgrace: Tac. *Ann.* 3. 30. 4; *contra* Williams 1990, but Lyne 1995, 136–38, accepts a decline in his influence in the 20s and especially after the Murena affair (Ch. 2). He also connects retirement from a public role for Horace, 23–19 BC, with this affair (186–92).

39 19 BC: M. Morford, *ANRW* 2. 32. 3 (1985), 2005 thinks of a turn for the worse in that year.

40 Succession of poets: Ovid, *Trist.* 4. 10. 43–54.

41 Perusine burial places: Prop. 1. 22. 3–5.

42 Propertius the nonconformist: Schmitthenner 1969, 409, citing 2. 15. 45f.; Stahl 1985, 3; cf. 99–129; 'human stand in the face of authoritarian rule', 150; refusal of epic: 139–71; Virgil: 172–88. So Welch 2005, with 25–27 (on Rome); 104–11 (Apollo); 162–64 (the triumphs); 168–70 (transient cities) on the exaltation of poetry; cf. the review by L. B. T. Houghton, *JRS* 95 (2005), 311–3. Antony: Griffin 1977. Dr Herbert-Brown suggests that Propertius' elegy on Cornelia (4. 11) and his praise of her as *univira*, a one-man woman, was a criticism of Augustus' forcing her half-sister Julia into three marriages for his own political aims. Cairns 1984 defends Prop. 4. 6 against critics as a choric hymn, sung perhaps in 16 BC in connexion with the annual celebration of Apollo's Palatine temple.

43 Varius: see E. Courtney in *OCD*³ 1581 *s.v.*; A. Hollis, *CQ* NS 27 (1977), 187–90.

44 Williams 1978, 292f., tabulates factors of decline.

45 Two interpretations of *Aeneid*: Hardie 1986, 1, with n. 2.

46 For Virgil: Galinsky 1996, 246–53; Virgilian scholarship: Stahl 1998, xv–xxxiii. Poet as prophet, see below.

47 Republic ending in 60 BC: the politician and historian Asinius Pollio began his history then. Horace, *Odes* 2. 1. 1: 'Civil War since Metellus was consul'.

48 Virgil's flight? [Virg.] *Catalepton* 5 and 8. Delights of Naples: *Georg.* 4. 563–66.

49 Virgil's *Eclogues* offer what is *molle et facetum* in Hor. *Sat.* 1.10. 44f.

50 *Ecl.* 1 analysed by Osgood 2006, 117 and 122.

51 Hor. *Epistle* 2. 2, with Osgood 2006, 212.

52 Agriculture neglected: *Georg.* 1. 506–8. Famine: App. *BC* 5. 60.

53 *Georgics* not propaganda for official policy: Townend 1996, 910; a Triumviral programme *followed* by Augustus: Galinsky 1996, 121–23, citing *Georg.* 1, 121–46. Place of Virgil's Golden Age in *Georg.* 2, 532–40: Osgood 2006, 313.

54 Interpreting the *Georgics*: Nappa 2005, reviewed by K. Volk, *JRS* 96 (2006), 252f.

55 Horace and the flawed Golden Age: Barker 1996, against Zanker 1988, 167 (bibl. 435); he compares Hor. *Epist.* 1. 12. 25–29, and cites Ovid's joke at *Ars Amat.* 2. 277f.

56 *Ecl.* 4 is so expounded by Osgood 2006, 193–200, at 195; but it will take time, 198; the verbs 'is being born', 'are returning' make that clear enough. One-man rule and expansion 199, comparing with *Aen.* 6. 791–95.

57 Defeat of Cleopatra in Virg. *Georg.* 3. 28f.; achievements in an imaginary temple: 26–39; political epic promised: 46–48.

58 'Caesar . . . Julius' as the culmination of Roman history: Jupiter in Virg. *Aen.* 1. 286–88 (see Bosworth 1999, 6, with bibl. n. 38); praised by Anchises: 6. 789–95; on Aeneas' shield: 8. 678–81.

59 '*Augustus* . . . *aurea condet saecula*', *Aen.* 6. 792f.

60 The shield and the triumph: McKay 1998.

61 Virgil's perspective: Galinsky 1996, 125; cf. 140; *FELICITAS PUBLICA*: *RIC* 1^2, p. 251; *RIC* 2 *passim*. Augustus' Capricorn, however, was associated with the quality: Barton 1995, 46, and Ovid proclaims '*felicia saecula*': *Tr.* 1. 2. 103f. Creation of Rome: Virg. *Aen.* 1. 33: '*Tantae molis erat Romanam condere gentem*'.

62 Gallus' friendship with Virgil: *Ecl.* 10.

63 Hor. *Odes* 1. 12: see La Penna 1963, 257–62. Cato at 35f.: '*Catonis nobile letum*'.

64 Golden Age involving labour: Galinsky 1996, 118; cf. also Putnam 1998, 211–14.

65 Virgil a national treasure: Tac. *Dial.* 13. 1–3.

66 Aeneas' anger: *Aeneid* 12. 946f.: '*ira terribilis*'; Augustus: Ch. 7.

67 'Much of menace in the prospects for Roman civilization': Powell 1992, ('*Aeneid*'), 143.

68 Morgan 2000, 69, citing P. Hardie, *The Epic Successors of Virgil. A Study in the Dynamics of a Tradition* (Cambridge, 1993), 1.

69 Eulogy of Augustus: Virg. *Aen.* 6, 791–805; placed by Hardie 1986, 257, in his 'hyperbole' section.

70 Virgil and Augustus: Parry, 1963, 66–80, stressing suffering and emptiness; Powell, 1992; Stahl 1998; Thomas 2001, on 'attempts to put Virgilian poetry back into a constructed Augustan box' (xix); essays in Woodman and West 1984.

71 Horace's multi-referentiality: Galinsky 1996, 258f. citing Hor. *Odes* 3. 5. 1–4 and (318) 1. 12. 49–60.

72 Ovid's rank: *Trist.* 4. 10. 27–36.

73 Ovid's unsuitability: Wallace-Hadrill 1987, 228.

74 Tibullus and the army: 1. 1. 75–8, with Galinsky 1996, 271.

75 Protest in the *Ars Amat.* 1. 31–34; cf. 3. 315ff. esp. 351–2; 611–13; his eminence: 383–98 (quoted by Williams 1978, 70–73).

76 Death of Horace: Eus.-Jer. p. 167 Helm. Ovid's offence: Kennedy 1992, 42, referring to Wallace-Hadrill 1982 ('Sin').

77 Augustus as subject for literature: Suet. *Aug.* 89. 3; cf. Ovid, *Trist.* 2. 55–74. For the context of this poem, see Wiedemann 1975.

78 New mythology: Herbert-Brown 1994, 52. McKeown 1984, 187, regards the *Fasti* as a failure for Ovid's inability to accommodate eulogies of Augustus into the general spirit of the poem.

79 Dedication of *Fasti* to Augustus: *Trist.* 2. 550f.

80 Ovid's works taken from libraries: *Trist.* 3. 1. 59–82; 3. 14. 5–18, cited by Williams 1978, 81.

81 Freedom of expression: see Crook 1996, 111; Tac. *Ann.* 1. 72; Suet. *Aug.* 51.

82 *Ars Amatoria* a pretext: Syme 1978, 222.

83 Ovid subverting abusive power: Boyle 2003, rev. K. Galinsky, *JRS* 95 (2005), 288. *Metamorphoses:* Lundström 1980, reviewed by B. Levick, *Lat.* 40 (1981), 413f.; cf. Barchiesi 1997. Critics of this approach: Barsby 1978, 35f. with n. 8; review by K. Galinsky, *Bryn Mawr Class. Rev.* 98. 1. 26, citing Galinsky 1967 on the Cipus episode as an example of the ease with which 'anti-Augustanism' can be read into Ovid, *Met.* Galinsky 1967, 181, regards the apotheosis of Caesar as 'grotesque'. For an attack on empiricist definitions of 'Augustanism', see Phillips 1983, 780–83, who also argues (801f.) that Ovid's problem lay crucially in a 'religious outlook antithetical to acceptable norms'; he 'affirmed meaninglessness' (815).

84 Augustus' 'error': Syme 1978, 215–29.

85 Ovid's stature contrasted with that of the aristocrats: Syme 1978, 228.

86 Tiberius' verse: Pliny, *Ep.* 5. 3. 5.

87 Cicero in exile: *Ad Q. Fr.* 1. 3 and 1. 4; *Ad Att.* 3. 7–20 are cited by D. L. Stockton, *Cicero, A Political Biography* (Oxford, 1971), 190 n. 43; Tiberius' *Conquestio de morte L. Caesaris:* Suet. Tib. 70. 2.

88 Double interpretation: Barchiesi 1997, 252, cf. 256.

89 Rebuttal of this approach: G. Herbert-Brown, *Bryn Mawr Class. Rev.* 10. (1997) 1. 1: 'It has become the fashion of much literary criticism of Ovid's *Fasti* (represented by e.g., Barchiesi, Hardie, Feeney, Harries, Hinds) to judge the poem a cynical, ambivalent defiant, or even subversive Ovidian stance vis-à-vis the Augustan regime'; see Elsner 1991, 51 (against 'naturalism'): Eich 2003, 52 n. 45; 82 n. 148; Maleuvre 1995, seeing Horace 'figé . . . dans le rôle de thuriféraire d'un regime profondément pervers' (53). The alternative view: Herbert-Brown 1994.

90 Apolitical poets: White 1993, 96: 'The political interpretation of Augustan poetry' . . . is a habit 'to be combated head-on'. Attempted divorce of literature and politics: Feeney 1992, 5f., with n. 23 on Galinsky 1975, 210–61; Williams 1978, 93–96; McKeown 1984.

91 Polyphonic way of writing: Stahl 1998, xxiif.

92 Significance of literary form: Woodman and West 1984, 189f., dealing with the problem of good poetry and political commitment.

93 Virgil's political feeling: Powell, '*Aeneid*' 142.

94 Origin and nature of *vates*: Hardie 1986, 16f., with n. 33 (bibl.). 'Lycidas' in *Eclogue* 9, 33f.: '*Et me fecere poetam Pierides, . . . me quoque vatem dicunt pastores*'. See Lyne 1995, 184f.

95 Self-interest of poets and others in literary society: Hardie 1986, 11.

96 Livy 1. 7. 15: '*immortalitas virtute parta*'.

97 Livy's spirit: Pliny, *NH* Pr. 16.

98 Romulus seeking to be 'more august': Livy 1. 8. 2, with Kennedy 1992, 43.

99 Augustus' seeking immortality: Tac. *Ann*. 4. 38. 5; role of poets: DuQuesnay 1984, 58.

100 *Virtutes*: Hor. *Odes* 3. 3–6, with Putnam 1990, 215, on 'conditionality': at Hor. 3. 3. 12 (despite conflict in the *MSS*) Augustus *will drink* nectar among the immortals. Similarly Virg. *Georg*. 4, 560–62 has Caesar fulminating over the Euphrates and making his way to Olympus ('*viam adfectat Olympo*').

101 Expansion: Seager 1993, 38f., with Horace disgruntled and subversive.

102 Women's demonstrations: Sumi 2004.

103 Letter to Aezani: EJ 319; to the Alexandrians: Smallwood, *Docs. Gaius-Nero*, 370, with B. Levick, *The Government of the Roman Empire* (2nd edn, London, 2000), 119 and 124.

104 Paradigm story of Augustus being offered temples in Asia Minor in 29 BC and modifying the plan: Dio, 51. 20. 6–8. See Levick 2000, 130f.

105 Virgil's claim: Bosworth 1999, 2–9. Augustus a god '*quem virtus addidit astris*', Ovid, *Ex Ponto* 4. 8. 63. *Exempla*: Osgood 2006, 346.

106 Augustus' wars: Gruen 1996, 190–2, with nn.

107 'Blight': Woodman and West 1984, 194f.

108 Gallus' verses, published by R. D. Anderson, P. J. Parsons and R. G. M. Nisbet, *JRS* 69 (1979), 125–55 interpreted and redated by Woodman and West 1984, 193f.

109 Augustus filling the calendar: Ovid, *Fasti* 2. 15f.

110 Libel as diminishing majesty: Tac. *Ann*. 1. 72, 3; Raaflaub and Samons 1990, 441, denying heightened political censorship towards the end of his Principate (445f.)

111 Increasing sycophancy under Augustus: Tac. *Ann*. 1. 1. 2.

112 See J. D. Chaplin, *Livy's Exemplary History* (Oxford, 2000).

113 Livy's views: Tac. *Ann*. 4. 34. 3. Encouragement for Claudius: Suet. *Claud*. 41.1. Galinsky 1996, 286 remarks that Livy got away with denying the authority of historical evidence useful to Augustus (4. 20. 5–11).

114 Asinius Pollio: Raaflaub and Samons 1990, 442 , following Bosworth 1972; his authority: Morgan 2000. Horace's warning: *Odes* 2. 1. 1–8.

115 Cremutius Cordus: Tac. *Ann.* 4. 34f. Arbitrary limits on freedom of speech: Feeney 1992.

116 Labienus, including Severus' comment: Sen. *Contr.* 10 pr. 4–7. Later restored: Suet. *Cal.* 16. 1 (with Cordus and Severus).

117 Free speech: Suet. *Aug.* 54–56. 1; Dio 54. 27. 4.

118 Rewards: Hor. *Epistles* 2. 1. 10–12.

119 Alternative crows (and another tale): Macr. 2. 4. 29f. Cf. the parrot training other birds to hail Caesar: *AP* 9, 562, cited by Yavetz 1984, 21 n. 166.

120 Nic. Dam. 2. 2 with A. Momigliano, *The Development of Greek Biography* (Cambridge, MA, 1993), 86 and L. M. Yarrow, *Historiography at the End of the Republic: Provincial Perspectives on Roman Rule* (Oxford, 2005), 74.

121 Clemency: Suet. *Aug.* 51. 2. On this passage, see Morgan 2000, 68: the regime tried to draw a line between the public and the literary – a line in the sand.

122 'Writing and proscribing' ('*scribere/proscribere*'): Macr. 2. 4. 21 (Triumviral).

123 Porcius Latro silenced: Sen. *Contr.* 2. 4. 12f.

124 Libel diminishing majesty: Tac. *Ann.* 1. 72. 3; Raaflaub and Samons 1990, 441; they deny heightened political censorship towards the end of Augustus' Principate (445f.)

125 Ovid's exile: Raaflaub and Samons 1990, 445f. ('a singular event').

126 Tiberius' discouragement of prosecutions for *maiestas*: Tac. *Ann.* 1. 74, etc.

127 Turning point: Tac. *Dial.* 19. 1; 26. 4.

128 Freedom of speech: Yavetz 1990, 34, has a nuanced account, with Sen. *Ira* 3. 23. 4 (Timagenes); *Ben.* 3. 27 ('Rufus'' denunciation of himself); Suet. *Aug.* 54. Development of *maiestas*: Tac. *Ann.* 1. 72f.

129 Priscus: Tac. *Ann.* 3. 49–51.1; Scaurus: 6. 29. 3; cf. Suet. *Tib.* 61. 3; Dio 58. 24. 4, citing Euripides, *Phoenissae* 394.

130 Senatorial acts: Suet. *Aug.* 36; decisions made behind closed doors: Dio 53. 19. 3f.; cf. 56. 31. 1.

131 Verses against Tiberius: Suet. *Tib.* 59.

Chapter 7

Unmasking a God

Making Augustus a God

> *Vesta has been received over the threshold of her kinsman, so have the right-eous senators decreed. Apollo has one share; another part has been given up to Vesta; what remains from them Augustus himself occupies as a third . . . a single house holds three immortal gods.*

So wrote Ovid late in Augustus' Principate, in response to his self-presentation (Ch. 5).[1] Later, for the exiled poet, Augustus, Tiberius and Livia were all gods.[2] At the very beginning of the Principate, the architect Vitruvius opened his work by recalling how Octavian's 'divine mind and spirit (*numen*) won control over the Empire of the world'. Right from the start Octavian could be presented as a god: Cicero spoke of his divine qualities, and the man who restored his property to Virgil's spokesman in the *Eclogues* was a 'god' to him. In an epigram of Domitius Marsus Augustus' mother is uncertain whether she had given birth to human being or god.[3]

Mere words can be dismissed as literary conceits. But Ovid's 'deities' were embodied in silver images. In any case, such a conceit could mean more in the ancient world than it would in Judaeo-Christian society. As I. Gradel puts it, 'The man–god divide in the pagan context could . . . be taken to represent a difference in *status* between the respective beings, rather than a distinction between their respective natures.[4] What made the difference was power, and the way it was used. Hercules may be taken as a prototype. We have already seen (Ch. 6) how the hero, already son of Jupiter and so half divine – for gods and men did not belong to separate species – earned his immortality.[5] Romulus too was the son of a god, Mars.[6] So Octavian became the son of a god and the descendant of Mars, Venus and Quirinus, and accordingly displayed *virtus* (Ch. 5). It was salubrious, according to Varro, that great men believed themselves to be of divine origin, for it inspired them to greater efforts.[7] This helps to explain why another neat dichotomy in thinking about religion at Rome, between traditional religion and the 'imperial cult', has faded, quite apart from the restructuring and redirection that Roman religion underwent in the age of Augustus, which is usually referred to as a 'restoration'. That went as far as allowing Augustus a monopoly of temple-construction, and, in the last decade of his Principate, Augustus was pervading the Roman festivals of Ovid's *Fasti*.[8] Before Augustus died there could be associations of worshippers 'in every (presumably well-off) household'. There could have been an element of fear in these developments, at least at first: Appian is writing of the Triumviral Period when he tells us that many Italian cities included Octavian among the gods.[9] Fashion, the determination not to be left behind, played a greater part. I. Gradel reports sixteen imperial temples from Italy outside Rome, of which seven are Augustan and only one, at most two, are certainly posthumous.[10]

Suetonius' claim that in Rome Augustus 'determinedly refused this honour deification during his lifetime' needed refining, and it has received that attention, notably from I. Gradel.[11] It was concrete and official for Octavian to become, as the 'adopted son' of the deified Caesar, and so himself now the offspring of a god, *Imperator Caesar divi filius*. Once he won his way to sole supremacy, homage went beyond annual celebrations of his birthday and his Actian victory.[12] His name was included in prayers, such as those of the Salian Brothers, and vows.[13] The building now known as the Pantheon was originally to have been called the Augusteum and to have his name inscribed within it.[14] Stories of his mother's impregnation by a snake could arise spontaneously among subjects astounded by the Princeps' dazzling success (Augustus' natural father was too insignificant to be the source of it), or, more probably, as we have seen (Ch. 5) be propagated. The hostile slant to the tale of Octavian's impersonation of Apollo at his Olympian

Figure 21 Gemma Augustea, c. AD 10 (akg-images Ltd. Photograph by Erich Lessing)

banquet only shows how the claims and aspirations of a Triumvir would be turned against him. His association with Jupiter, supreme among the gods, continued throughout Augustus' Principate. He ruled under Jove, Ovid associates the two in the *Metamorphoses*, and the association is intensified in the verse he wrote after his exile in AD 8, when Augustus had been in sole power for nearly four decades.[15]

The question of Augustus' *genius* has not helped to clarify the enquiry as to his lifetime status. The word was taken to represent a being separate from the man himself, a divine spark, so its cult could be hygienically distinguished from the distasteful cult of a living being. This was the line devised by L. R. Taylor and adopted by later scholars. The separation of the two now seems less convincing, and Augustus' modest stance, of allowing divine honours only in the provinces, so Suetonius and Dio seem to claim, and then in association with the cults of Rome or Julius Caesar, less acceptable. One objection to the cult of the *genius* brought forward by I. Gradel is that

a man's *genius* was worshipped in his household and by his slaves, and senators must not be made to feel that they were the Princeps' clients.[16] It was
temples and cults of the man that grew up in the towns of Italy during his
lifetime. Assuredly Augustus was informed of what had been built, altars
and temples alike; with provincial assemblies (*koina*) in Asia and Bithynia
they had been the subject of negotiation (Ch. 3); at Lugdunum (Lyon) in
Gaul the provincial cult may have been instigated in 13 BC by Nero
Drusus.[17] But individual cities were so active in their approach that the
Princeps can be removed from the equation as an initiator; the initiative, as
with the *koina*, came from below: Mytilene on Lesbos decreed that Augustus was to be informed of their games and birthday sacrifices, such as were
offered to Zeus. Their ambassadors were instructed to acknowledge the
unimportance of their offerings to those who had the power and pre-
eminence of gods; all the same the city 'would not fall short in anything that
could make him even more of a god'.[18] The constructions, the cults and the
money expended on them added warmth to his relationship with the communities involved and would win them favours in the future.[19]

At Rome in AD 6, Tiberius dedicated an altar at which the four main
priestly colleges sacrificed to Augustus, or rather to his *numen* ('divine
power'), which was no different.[20] Shocking as that might seem, in spite of
the Caesarian precedent, or even because of it, once Augustus was dead and
his direct effective power vanished, as I. Gradel points out, any offence to
conservative public opinion was diminished. In AD 14, after a funeral at
which the Roman worthies of his Forum, of whom he claimed to be the culminating example, were paraded once again,[21] Augustus was finally decreed
divine honours by the Senate, becoming Divus Augustus, and a state cult
established – with all the funding that required for the temple and priesthood – for the first time, perhaps along lines specifically laid down by Augustus himself. There was obvious interest in this development for his
successor, whose position as *Divi Augusti filius* was markedly strengthened:
history was repeating itself.[22]

The cult maintained

The cult of Augustus was religiously kept up, and his birthday, along with
those of other deified members of the imperial families that followed him,
was celebrated (in his case with the appropriate offering of a male ox) as part

of the official calendar for the troops stationed at Dura-Europus in AD 225–27, during the reign of Alexander Severus.[23] At Rome it was soon discovered that reverence for the deity could be defended by the developing law against diminishing the majesty of the Roman People (*Lex Julia maies-tatis*). In 15, a former governor of Pontus-Bithynia, who had replaced the head of a statue of Augustus with one of Tiberius, was brought to court, and acquitted only on the direction of the new Emperor. Most prosecutions on that charge would be successful: the Senate, sitting as a jury, would have to take charges seriously, even if left to itself in the absence of the Princeps (Ch. 3). For the accuser, a successful prosecution, besides bringing in the legal prize of a quarter of the condemned person's property, would demonstrate loyalty. Attached to another, lesser, charge, it would help to bring about a conviction. In AD 20 the charges brought against Cn. Calpurnius Piso, governor of Syria, were all serious – assassinating Germanicus, diminishing majesty by leaving the province and returning to it under arms, and extortion, but it was worth including the shocking and killing fact that the *numen* of Augustus had been 'violated' by Piso's removing 'all signs of honour from his memory and his portraits'.[24]

The official priests, twenty-one *Sodales Augustales* (*Claudiales* after Claudius' death in 54) and four additional members of the imperial family, were charged with keeping up the cult, and their credit depended on it; state money was being spent on their activities and on the construction of the temple. Velleius Paterculus extols Tiberius' devotion and magnificence in carrying out this project. It was completed only in 37, but on 5 October, the 'birthday' of the temple, Tiberius regularised the opening of the *Ludi Augustales* and the *magistri vici* danced there.[25] There was prestige in belonging to the priesthood, though it did not enjoy the status of the four ancient colleges. It continued to function until the mid-third century, when gold coinage of Gallienus was inscribed '*DEO AVGVSTO*'. Tacitus allows us a glimpse of Tiberius himself sacrificing to his father in 24, perhaps in his capacity as *Sodalis Augustalis*.[26]

A deified emperor was by definition dead, however, and thereby less likely to take effective action than he had been in his lifetime. Private worshippers were to concentrate on living emperors.[27] Nonetheless, they continued to pay attention to Augustus after his death. A series of statue-base inscriptions, cut or edited in Rome by a band of trumpeters and other brass players in the mid-50s AD in honour of Nero, Claudius and Agrippina, also dutifully included a dedication to Augustus originally set up in 12 BC; he guaranteed, even enhanced, the status of his family and successors.[28]

Augustus as *exemplum*

Tiberius had only to undertake to maintain the Augustan precedent. Later emperors down to Vespasian, notably Claudius and Nero, made explicit reference to Augustus in their accession speeches, pointedly opening their reigns with promises to the Senate, explicit or implicit, to adhere or return to the example of Augustus. In doing that they were, perhaps unwittingly, fulfilling Augustus' own wish to prove an example to later generations (Ch. 5). While the founder's descendants, however remote, were in power, their very portraits were modelled on his.[29] But the fact was that his successors all proved unsatisfactory, arbitrary and murderous. In the mid-first century, under Nero, it was natural to contrast Augustus as the model with the recent failings of Claudius. In a pointed contrast of Augustan rationality with Claudius' inconsequential behaviour, C. Crispus Passienus preferred, if he had the choice, to have Augustus' good opinion – and a gift from Claudius.[30] In Seneca's *Apocolocyntosis*, Augustus is naturally presented with dignity and approval as a contrast with the inept and criminal Claudius – he is allowed to speak up for himself.[31]

Vespasian himself, who knew all the emperors from Tiberius onwards, without making any specific references to Augustus that are attested in the literature, recalled him in language and political gesture. The *Lex de imperio Vespasiani*, an enabling act passed as part of the powers conferred on him at the end of 69 or a few weeks afterwards as a supplement to them, contains seven substantive clauses and Augustus is mentioned as a precedent, whenever one is relevant, for all the powers granted.[32] Even the founder's buildings were a desirable blueprint. When he came to build the Colosseum, properly known as the Flavian Amphitheatre, Vespasian discovered that it had been a project of Augustus.[33]

After Vespasian, attempts were made to put Augustus down. 'Augustus held the Latin *fasces* thirteen times as the years rolled on', wrote the poet Statius, 'but it was late when he began to serve; you [Domitian] have outstripped your ancestors, young as you are.'[34] That is, Domitian was successful at a younger age than Augustus. Technically this was true, as far as the consulship went; as for sole power, both men reached it at about the age of thirty. The strained comparison, with its criticism of Augustus, reveals him as the prevailing standard, the one to be surpassed. At the same time, the accession of Vespasian after a dangerous series of civil conflicts in 68–69 had meant that the institution of the Principate, unsatisfactory as it might be, was entrenched; individuals and whole ranks in society depended on it for their livelihood and status. The reputation of one ruler, though he was the founder, could now be reassessed.

In reality Augustus was not a perfect model, as we shall see. Nonetheless Tiberius, who must have admired his predecessor's adroitness, besides owing him his position (we can only guess at his personal feelings), used Augustus as Augustus had avoided using Caesar, as a trump card to play when his own ideas met opposition or disapproval. He called on the example of Augustus repeatedly, down to his retirement to Capri in 26. All through his Principate, Tiberius resolutely refused to attempt the invasion of Britain that Caesar had had to leave unachieved in 54 BC. What Augustus had thought of as a plan of action (*consilium*), or rather inaction, using friendly dependent monarchs to do Rome's work for her, became an injunction (*praeceptum*). The same principle emerged on the domestic front immediately after Tiberius' accession to sole power in AD 14. He was driven by pressure from the Senate to swear an oath that he would not exceed the number of praetors handed down by Augustus. The name of the deceased and revered Princeps was used to cool down senators ambitious for office who wanted to elect more than twelve praetors for the following year, as had happened in some elections not long before Augustus' death. Augustan practice is the final argument, the ace that beats all others and ends a game.[35]

Some senators were soon proving clever enough to use the same card against Tiberius. In AD 15 the Senate debated the punishment of unruly theatrical claqueurs and actors. Could actors who caused trouble be flogged? A conflict arose on traditional lines between disciplinarian praetors adopting a sternly optimate line and *popularis* tribunes, the latter predictably taking the position that they could not. Tiberius was doubtless heartily in favour of flogging, but its supporters were outmanoeuvred when it was pointed out that Augustus had not allowed the flogging of actors. The theatricals got off.[36]

A further sign of the development of Augustus as a political card might be detected in AD 20, in the senatorial decree condemning Cn. Piso the Elder. Members of the Augustan *domus* (household) are praised for their forbearance in hearing the case. Not so Agrippina the Elder: what commends her to the Senate is the number of children she has given her late husband and the good opinion that the late Princeps, her grandfather, held of her. In AD 20, after the death of her husband, Agrippina's position was already vulnerable, and Tiberius was said to disapprove of her behaviour almost from the beginning of his reign. The senatorial drafting committee, perhaps, was using the name of Augustus to cover her and enhance her prestige.[37]

The more distant commentators were from Augustus' own time, the easier it was for them to invoke him as a model: disturbing details went out of focus, recent misconduct appeared sharper. But nobody knew better than Tiberius that even after Actium, Augustus' Principate had passed through several phases, the first two of which had a distinct ideological identity. A conservative, Republican phase passed in 23 to something more radical and demagogic. After the Senate had been made to acquiesce in his rule in 19, there was a meld from which any convenient item could be drawn as required. In AD 14 Tiberius promised the regime that had been adumbrated in 28–27; Gaius Caligula and Claudius may have been less specific, calling upon the phase that had begun in 19, and which had meant little more than a *modus vivendi* in which Augustus had had his way without excessive violence. For the Alexandrian Jew Philo, who had a more distant, provincial's perspective, Tiberius was the model immediately preferable to the Emperor Gaius, whom he had had to approach on his embassy to Rome, but Philo's admiration for Augustus was manifest.[38]

Admittedly, as Augustus receded Caesar became available again as an alternative model, at any rate for specific items and for a ruler such as the historian Claudius, who was another incomer unwelcome to the Senate. The accession speech of Nero, however, as reported by Tacitus and allegedly composed by Seneca, is distinctly minimalist. The traditional functions of the Senate are to be preserved: Italian matters and those concerning the public provinces are to be dealt with by the consuls; Nero will simply look after the armies that have been entrusted to him by the Senate. It was easy for Nero's successors to speak generally of the Augustan regime, calling by implication on the phase that had begun in 19 and preceded the development of the treason law.[39]

After AD 14, Divus Augustus accordingly developed as a numismatic paradigm, illustrated under Tiberius not only by obverse legends dedicated to the deified Princeps, but by the whole series of coin obverses in bronze displaying *DIVUS AUGUSTUS PATER* in the nominative of an active divinity, sometimes with a star, as if he were still an issuing authority. Various similar, though much less copious, obverse types of Gaius and Claudius were issued in Augustus' name as his authority became less significant to the later Julio-Claudians. There was a strong revival during the civil wars of 68–69 on coins struck in Spain and probably Gaul, with both *AUGUSTUS* and *DIVUS AUGUSTUS* figuring on the obverses as an issuing authority, alongside *ROMA* and reassuring abstract qualities.[40] The first Princeps had become one of the foundations on which the future of post-Neronian Rome was to be built. Even into the Flavian period, coins with types modelled on those of his Principate continued to be struck. The echoing of his types in AD 70, the centenary of the battle of Actium, significantly had a different emphasis – the beginning of the Principate itself, which Vespasian was restoring.[41]

The so-called 'restoration' issues of Titus, Domitian, Nerva and Trajan reproduced types of those emperors' reputable predecessors, beginning with Augustus and including Tiberius. *DIVUS AUGUSTUS PATER* was prominent under Titus, perhaps because of his own debt to his father Vespasian, and commoner than that of the other personages who figured; the issues of Domitian were less plentiful, but still favoured Augustus.[42] In Nerva's case there was a tendency to assimilate the portrait of the deified Augustus to that of the failing incumbent.[43] Trajan's series was interestingly more comprehensive. It probably belongs to AD 107, when there was a melting down of old coinage.[44] The coins bear the Trajan's titles, with '*REST(ITUIT)*' ('HE [TRAJAN] RESTORED [the type]'). They celebrate Republican heroes such as Decius Mus and Horatius Cocles, Marcus Cato and Q. Metellus Scipio and their victories and civil achievements in silver *denarii*, and the emperors in *aurei*, and it was the view of H. Mattingly and E. A. Sydenham that Trajan was emphasising the glory of Rome by placing together a series of types illustrative of her development. H. Komnick notes that Caesar appears as the earliest of Trajan's *aurei*, followed by Sex. Pompeius, Augustus and other emperors. Since the counterpoint of Republic against Empire is normally signalled in these coins by *denarii vs. aurei*, silver against gold, Caesar's presence among the *denarii* too, along with Sextus Pompeius and Augustus, shows them all as transitional figures, if that is the right way to interpret the metallurgy.[45] Trajan and his mint-masters evidently saw Republican history and the shift to the Empire from a distant perspective, and in a continuum that made it possible for them to show prominent figures in the transition with equanimity, whatever their ideological position. Augustus is part of that continuum.

On the coinage of Hadrian, references to Augustus are more oblique: there are allusions to him among Hadrian's predecessors, in the form of his conception sign, the Capricorn,[46] and a *denarius* type, perhaps posthumous, where the title *IMP. CAES. AUGUSTUS* is significantly juxtaposed on the obverse with that of the current Emperor on the reverse *HADRIANUS AUG. . . . REN*, identifying the two and suggesting that Hadrian was a 'reborn' (*renatus*) Augustus. Coins in all three metals, struck from 125 onwards, present obverses with the simple legend *HADRIANUS AUG(USTUS)*. Augustus remained a numismatic ideal. There was no room for hesitancy on a coin.[47] Nor is it surprising that Hadrian restored the temple of Augustus in Tarraco (Tarragona), and at his own expense. But Hadrian went further: he asked the Senate to agree to his placing a silver shield in honour of Augustus in the House near the statues of his predecessor. On the personal level he had a seal bearing Augustus' portrait, and is said to have had a bust of him amongst his private household gods.[48] Any suggestion that his devotion had to do only with a shared and cautious foreign policy is to be resisted as unheroic and certainly misleading: Augustus spent the greater part of his reign expanding the Roman Empire. The predilection might be connected rather with Augustus' well-known good fortune, or with that particular part of it that resulted in his deification. Among others, the persistence of such reverence may be due to a natural human tendency to depend on a single saviour – religious, philosophical, scientific or political – making later generations cling loyally to the original and least imperfect 'Augustus'. Outbursts of vilification following the deaths of Tiberius, Gaius, Claudius and Nero emphasised the contrast; Vespasian was satisfactory enough, but, as we have noted, he too was intent on appearing to restore the Augustan model.

An unsatisfactory example

How imperfect a model Augustus really was, Tiberius obliquely made clear in his colloquy with the Senate in AD 14. If Augustus was a 'transformational' leader as K. Galinsky holds (see Introduction), he gave his subjects the wrong lead: he took Rome towards monarchy, removing his fellow citizens still further from the practices and rights of the Republic. Leaving aside the bloodbaths of the Triumvirate, he diminished the real powers of the Senate and began allowing his private servants, not only knights but freedmen and slaves, a role in running the state. On the first occasion after the funeral eulogy that Tiberius is seen mentioning Augustus, he used the very fact that Augustus possessed superhuman intellectual qualities (*divina mens*) to tell the Senate that running the entire Empire was not a one-man job; he was repudiating the autocracy of the past decade.

It is entertaining to see how one senator of mediocre standing coped with the difficult relationship between past and present emperors under Tiberius. In his edict on vehicle requisitioning, issued as governor of Galatia early in Tiberius' Principate, probably AD 19/20–21/22, the undistinguished ex-praetor Sex. Sotidius Strabo Libuscidianus referred to them as 'one the best of gods, the other the best of *principes*'.[49] Libuscidianus handles Augustus in the same way as Octavian handled Julius Caesar: he removes Augustus to the heavens, obviating any possibility of rivalry between the two as rulers: Tiberius can still be best Princeps. Tiberius accordingly deprecated cult for himself. A few months after he came to power he was refusing honours offered by Gytheion (Githion) in the Peloponnese; they belonged to Augustus alone.[50] We have already seen him dutifully sacrificing to the deity.

Libuscidianus' estimate was mistaken on both counts, blatantly on the first, soon on the second too. Tiberius' regime deteriorated. After AD 23 wrangling over the disputed succession led to his departure for Campania and Capri and to a series of judicial murders at Rome. His death was greeted with widespread rejoicing. Nor were any of the Julio-Claudian emperors deified except Claudius in 54, and that was because it was in Nero's interest to bear the title 'Son of the deified'. Failures of the Julio-Claudian Emperors meant that the only justification for believing in the success of the institution of the Principate itself was to believe in the merits of its founder, the first to bear the name. To condemn Augustus meant condemning the entire Principate. Contrasts with later tyrants raised Augustus' standing, but another line of argument, unjust as it might seem, could have been that he had founded the system that made those tyrannies possible: failures of the Julio-Claudian Emperors from Tiberius to Nero themselves condemned Augustus. Ultimately, Trajan came to supersede the first ruler as the moral paradigm: according to Eutropius, the Senate was accustomed to wish that a new emperor might be 'a luckier man (*felicior*) than Augustus, a better man (*melior*) than Trajan'.[51] For when it came to Trajan, scruples about the title '*Optimus Princeps*' had been laid aside: the title was formally conferred in AD 114 and used, though not in the form (*optimus principum*: best of emperors) that would have implied his overall superiority; only outstanding excellence was implicit in the phrase.[52]

Historical judgements

The two contrasting contemporary estimates of Augustus, as they purport to be, that Tacitus offers near the opening of his *Annals* at least illustrate scepticism about him after the Julio-Claudians and, as Tacitus plausibly wishes us to believe, in AD 14. The material for the comments came from oral tradition and from earlier writers, including lost memoirs, but as he constructed them they tell us more about the views of Tacitus himself (tilting unmistakeably towards the unfavourable). Ancient authors looking back on Augustus' career came to diverse conclusions, which depended on the purpose and context of their enquiries. For public orators the deified first Princeps served as a laudable, if sketchy, template: awkward detail could be airbrushed out of the picture. So with Tacitus' contemporary Pliny in his *Panegyric* on Trajan of AD 100: the very title 'Augustus' brought back its first holder – and a tacit admonition about correspondingly good conduct. After all, he and his contemporaries were looking back over a vista that included Nero and Domitian.[53]

Historians had their own perspectives and, in theory at least, as two imperial practitioners proclaimed, strict standards: Tacitus himself and Cluvius Rufus, cited by the younger Pliny.[54] Cluvius warned a Neronian general who had played an ambiguous role in the civil wars of 68–69 that he might not like what he found in Cluvius' *History* – but he knew the candour that history demanded. In the next generation, Tacitus thought that his distance from the events he was treating in the Julio-Claudian period guaranteed an impartiality that contemporaries and near-contemporaries could not afford.[55] The generation that followed the participants at Actium avoided the task of writing a history of the new age (Ch. 6).[56] Velleius Paterculus, composing his *Roman History* a decade and a half after Augustus' death, and after the alarming fate of Cremutius Cordus, was adulatory and selective.[57]

The perspective that governed what a historian said might change within a single work. Velleius Paterculus naturally had nothing but praise for the man who had brought him to the praetorship. Yet when he came to describe the accession to power of the current ruler, Tiberius, he went through a list of reforms similar to the one he had brought out when he embarked on Augustus' own Principate, documenting specific areas in which the new Princeps was able to make improvements.[58] It would be tempting to interrogate Velleius: what had gone wrong?[59] The loss of the works of Aufidius Bassus and especially the consular M. Servilius Nonianus will have deprived us of insights into the later years of Augustus' Principate, if their starting points were early enough.[60] Another minor historian, Florus, writing from a longer perspective, was to have no doubts: the frenzy of Caesar and Pompey had torn the empire apart: only the guidance and regulation of a single person could have brought it back into unity.[61] Tacitus had no illusions, but, unlike Velleius, sketchy though Velleius' scenes from history were, he explicitly rejected the task of working through Augustus' Principate: talented writers had already attempted it.[62] Consequently, he had only to make excursions into the period, and, being excused rounded consistency, did not have to make sense of it. The mid-second-century historian Appian, writing under the confident and therefore tolerant Antonines, could be cool about Octavian. Introducing his *Civil Wars* and explaining the founding of the Principate in terms of Augustus' achievements, he describes him as uniformly successful and formidable (*phoberos*). Men needed to be wary of him in war and evidently, since the adjective has no qualification, in peace as well.[63] For the third-century consul and member of the imperial Council, Cassius Dio, the reign of Augustus still had to serve as a model for the rest. That should have made for a bloodless figure, but Dio's own reading and research exposed all the ambition of the young politician, as well as abiding hypocrisy and secrecy, and led Dio, it should seem, to a negative conclusion. Yet on another view this firm believer in the efficacy of monarchy saw even the Triumvir Octavian as acting for justifiable ends and went out of his way to excuse deceit and atrocities, accepting the official version of the proscriptions. When he summed up Augustus' life he claimed that he was not naturally cruel. In the speech he put into the mouth of Augustus' wife Livia, advocating clemency for a conspirator, he simply made her admit that it was impossible to guide a city as great as Rome from 'democracy' (Dio's word for the constitution of the Republic) to monarchy and make the change without bloodshed.[64] Dio

was confronted by contradictory material and verdicts, and struggled to reconcile them, against the background of his own dispiriting and frightening
experiences.

Tacitus had already stated his own view that after eliminating the competition Augustus 'seduced' men with the enervating tranquillity he gave
them (*otio pellexit*).[65] This is the judgement of a senator who had lived
through a period in which the Principate had been at its worst for senators.
Ancient verdicts on Caesar Augustus continued to fluctuate, but M. Swan
notes how the essentially favourable opinion of Cassius Dio, conveyed in an
extensive treatment a century after Tacitus wrote, has prevailed; in the long
perspective contrasts with notorious successors such as Tiberius, Gaius
Caligula, Nero, Domitian, even Septimius Severus, certainly Elagabalus,
raised Augustus' standing; his version of the autocracy, properly managed
by those who followed him, could have succeeded better than it did.[66]

Hadrian's restoration of the temple at Tarraco is mentioned in the late
fourth-century *Historia Augusta*, which in its biographies of later emperors
abounds in laudatory references to Augustus, usually with reference to the
subject of the author's immediate memoir; he also offers direct praise of the
virtus of Trajan, the *pietas* of Antoninus, and the moderation of Augustus.[67]
There is no question of a thought-out world view here; the *Historia
Augusta* presents a conventional survey of the Principate.

Philosophers and moralists, with a longer perspective and a private literary audience, were freer than politicians. At the beginning of Nero's reign,
and to intensify the picture of Nero's merits that Seneca was drawing, ostensibly for the Emperor himself, the philosopher compared the two young
rulers, to Augustus' disadvantage: his bloodstained past was against him.[68]
So Ovid in his time had compared Romulus unfavourably with Augustus
(Ch. 6). This had become a received technique of panegyric. In fact,
Seneca's tract *On Clemency* was aimed at a senatorial and equestrian audience, with the idea of reassuring them after Nero had made away with his
rival Britannicus Caesar in 55 and friends of the victim feared for their own
lives. It is important to notice that he was not speaking in the House, where
convention, established by Tiberius, demanded the utmost respect for
Augustus. All the same, a non-political literary man of the time of Claudius
or Nero, Phaedrus, lawyer and fabulist, used Augustus to make an implied
contrast with his own age as a jurist who could find just solutions for baffled
judges of the Centumviral court.[69]

Much later, in his mid-fourth-century satire presenting a feast of gods and emperors, *The Caesars*, from Julius Caesar to Constantine, the philosopher-Emperor Julian makes Augustus enter, changing colour continually like a chameleon. Sometimes he is pale, sometimes ruddy, then dark, clouded and overcast, then again he relaxes and gives himself up to Aphrodite and the Graces, so that Silenus exclaims at the monster: 'Whatever outrage will be commit against us?' and is reassured only when Apollo promises to transform Octavian into gold with a few philosophical doctrines from Zeno the Stoic; all that had been needed was a philosopher to take the young politician in hand and turn him into the great ruler he became.[70] Julian's facile answer, based on his respect for the effectiveness of philosophy and on the belief that Octavian/Augustus' political life was sharply divided in two, between an unscrupulous Triumviral Period and a worthy Principate, will not do: Apollo's promise was flawed, and there was something to be said for Silenus' suspicions.

Undercurrents

How clearly did men see through Augustus' pretensions in all the stages of his political career to his ultimate ambition and the methods he used to fulfil it? That depended on their intellect, principles and interests, and how much information was available to them. It is the claim of R. Ridley that Augustus changed men's perceptions, and that time was on his side. But when Tacitus asks rhetorically how many on Augustus' death even remembered the Republic (meaning the unfettered working of magistrates and Senate)[71] the very question exposes the fact that a few certainly did. Admittedly, nearly half a century, two generations, had passed since the creation of the Second Triumvirate, and in a secondary sense even survivors may have preferred to forget old days except in terms of their own ancestors' achievements. Nevertheless, Tacitus goes on to offer that notoriously unfavourable report of his career. Specifically the summary exposes the claims for his entry into politics that Augustus made in the opening paragraph of the *Achievements*. Tacitus and Suetonius knew from earlier writers and oral tradition the story of how he had wrested his first consulship from the Senate.[72]

These were matters of high politics, of interest to the political classes. Disreputable stories would have spread from there further down in society, and many of them have survived to reach us, though only a fragment of the contents of graffiti and pamphlets has been transmitted. To ask when criticism began in private circles and how clearly men perceived his ultimate ambition of establishing a dynasty is hardly necessary: he was a target of vituperation throughout his life (Chs. 2 and 4). As a public figure, whatever his posture as a legislator, Augustus was vulnerable to charges of all kinds of immorality. We have learned to recognise such stories for what they are – attempts to assert control over the ruling elite – as well as pleasurable scandal-mongering based on envy, which itself conferred a sense of power on its authors.[73] They have been noticed in connexion with the young politician's struggle with Antony and his own lectures on contemporary *mores* to fellow-politicians (Chs. 1 and 3), and only a summary need be given here.

To mention the mildest charges, fornication and adultery, his best friends, probably as practised as he was, never attempted to deny them, though some said that his conquests were politically motivated. Suetonius believes without question that his wife supplied him with young women of good family to deflower, a story designed to discredit her even more than him, and the only charge against her sexual morality that might be plausible.[74] What Suetonius does not believe are the much more serious charges about Augustus' youth, when they would have been most plausible. Sex. Pompeius did not spare this charge, and Mark Antony claimed that that was how he earned his place in Caesar's will (similar accusations had been made against the young Caesar himself). The story went round that when an actor (referring to a eunuch priest) spoke the line 'D'you see the nancy playing his drum and fingering the world?', it was loudly applauded. These stories were popular because it was the passive partner whose reputation suffered. Men who played an active role, unless it was with married women, were invulnerable, certainly in law. By the mid-fourth century Augustus, as a slave to his own lust and notorious for it, could be equipped simultaneously with a dozen rent-boys and a dozen girls as his regular dinner companions.[75] The same anonymous author in mitigation credits Augustus with moderation with food, drink and even sleep (one wonders about this merit when the time saved was so ill-spent). Denigration of a figure of prime importance would not have ceased on his death, and it will have continued indefinitely, except when he was needed to draw attention by contrast to the extreme failings of his successors.[76] Even there he would not escape censure: he was responsible for promoting the tyrannical Tiberius; did he do it to benefit from the contrast with his own regime?[77]

Unmasking

To someone looking back over two millennia and able to compare the performances and achievements of more recent politicians Augustus still seems to have kept a place in the front rank. Certainly he kept up his performance to the end, under public pressure, of course. The younger Seneca elaborates:

> *The deified Augustus, to whom the gods gave more than to anyone, never stopped praying for rest for himself and to look for freedom from public life. All his talk always returned to that – how he hoped for leisure. It was with this consolation, unfulfilled but still sweet, that he would add pleasure to his work, that one day his life would be his own. In a letter addressed to the Senate, when he had undertaken that his retirement would not be lacking self-respect or out of tune with his former glory, I have found the following passage: 'But that can be brought about more clearly by deeds than by promises. On the other hand, as far as I am concerned, the realization of my happiness is still far off, so longing for that time that I most desire has brought me to anticipate some of my pleasure by enjoying it in words' . . . The man who saw everything dependent on himself alone, who meted out the destiny of individuals and peoples, was happiest thinking about the day when he would put off his greatness. He had found out how much sweat was generated by those benefits that shone through every land, how many hidden troubles they covered. He was forced to use violence, first of all against his fellow-citizens, then with his colleagues, finally with his relatives; he shed blood over land and sea.*[78]

Apart from the sentence that Seneca claims to be quoting, we cannot foist this concocted train of thought, garlanded with its pious truisms, on Augustus. Only the merest germ may be genuine, in the sense that Augustus expressed a desire to retire, carefully hedged in by conditions that made it impossible. Sincere or not, it would indeed have proved a near impossibility, until his designated successor was already impregnable to the attacks of rivals, and Augustus was too astute to miss that. His successor Tiberius also spoke in the Senate about retiring, and his remarks are taken by Tacitus for hypocrisy.[79] Tiberius meant it (he had already retired once, to Rhodes in 6 BC), and gave himself what privacy and rest he could by removing himself to Campania and then to Capri; but he remained Princeps and kept the

Princeps' necessary powers. For emperors there was none of the honourable repose (*cum dignitate otium*) that knights and senators could enjoy under the Republic.[80] Vitellius, with the Flavian forces entering Rome in 69, tried to abdicate, in vain. He had to die.[81] The first emperor to succeed in retiring, Diocletian, did so in 305, after twenty-one years in power and when he had set up a structure designed to carry the weight of empire, the Tetrarchy; even so, his return was canvassed. Augustus' life-long power stayed with him, and he could not think about the day when he could 'put off his greatness'.

Augustus, a man with much to hide, who misrepresented his political past (though not his ancestry) and made false promises about the future, is hard to know. His writing and conversation were studied (Ch. 5), and he preferred written communication, even within his household.[82] In the practice of oratory, he believed that eloquence lay in its own concealment.[83] Unsurprisingly, it was his rule in making speeches to Senate, people, or soldiery always to have a script, thus avoiding accidents, whether mere slips of the tongue committing him when he did not wish to be committed or outbursts of anger that he had intended to control (see Ch. 5).[84]

Authors made efforts to humanise the ruler. To be sure, the contemporary Nicolaus of Damascus in his opening chapters offers a childhood and youth fit for the paragon of a Victorian novel, reporting the first illnesses that alone had prevented him going on campaign with Caesar; he had read Augustus' *Autobiography*.[85] Suetonius and Dio have touching characteristics and anecdotes of incidents from Augustus' daily life, many displaying Augustus' good qualities, or crediting him with them. They tell of little foibles and simple human touches, some revealed by the man himself (see Introduction). They are of the kind that circulate among the merely curious – or more often the devoted and credulous – about their rulers, even such as Stalin, who have had journalists and film-makers to help them on their way. So we hear how short he was (1.7m., 5ft. 7ins., not much taller than the average legionary, it seems) and how he wore built-up shoes, and how comely he was, though freckled.[86] He had a sense of humour; he enjoyed a tune, dice, ballgames, fishing, games with nuts; he liked playing with small children, watching boxing, listening to story-tellers (of various kinds) and buskers.[87] In contrast to the unfriendly stories of adultery and depravity also retailed by Suetonius, Martial, who had a different perspective, writes of a purity of life that was characteristic of a Roman ('*Romana simplicitas*').[88] There were also collections of his sayings, partly surviving in the works of

Plutarch and Macrobius. Such collections are not usually made of defunct tyrants' sayings, though *Hitler's Table Talk* evidently has its fascination.[89]

Another characteristic attributed to Octavian/Augustus that exposes his humanity and, by extension, we are to believe, his sincerity, is his superstition. He believed in prodigies, worried about thunder and lightning enough to commemorate an escape from a bolt that killed one of his attendants by constructing the temple of Jupiter Tonans, kept the Etruscan diviners called *haruspices* at hand to interpret any signs that befell, consulted and even published his horoscope, and had his protecting zodiacal sign, Capricorn, deployed in art and coinage.[90] But superstition was common to most Romans and particularly to be expected in a man who plunged into danger from the beginning of his career. Very understandably for inquirers in a post-Freudian age, his own slips were significant to him, and he did not hide it: he wrote, presumably in the *Autobiography*, that he had almost been brought down by a mutiny on a day when he had put a shoe on the wrong foot.[91]

The keen gambler also looks familiar: the gambler proves his intellectual superiority to other players and his command of fate.[92] In the later Empire we have seen how it was hoped that a new emperor would turn out luckier than Augustus; Augustus himself acknowledged the importance of Fortune to his own success, and allegedly when he sent his grandson Gaius Caesar to the East he is said to have prayed for various gifts from the gods for him: Alexander's daring, Pompey's benevolence, and his own luck. There is no reason for this saying to be anything but genuine. Good Fortune was an attribute of good generals, and much to their credit. But it was also intended to display modesty, as mentioning his own daring would not have done; there was no vaunting of personal achievements in it.[93]

Despite anecdotes friendly and hostile there are still no signs of any vivid personality, even less one comparable to that of Julius Caesar. There was no poignant story that takes the hearer to the heart of the man: no tears like those of Tiberius at the sight of a wife unwillingly divorced; only hair torn out over the loss of legions and groans over the humiliating depravity of his daughter and grandchildren.[94] As Z. Yavetz has observed, the biography of Suetonius gives the impression, overall and stripped of sensational accusations, of a dull figure, simple in his taste in food, moderate with drink, unpretentious in dress and housing, conservative in outlook, the man who, in an implausible anecdote, coolly broke P. Vedius Pollio's best service to prevent the accident of a clumsy slave with one goblet resulting in the man's being 'thrown to the lampreys'.[95] One should not make much of the sphinx that he set on his signet ring and which adorned the lappets of the cuirass of the Prima Porta statue. (He inherited two identical rings from his mother and let associates use one of them.) From the ancients, in particular from the story of Oedipus, we have inherited the idea of the riddling sphinx, but the creature also symbolised hope. Nonetheless, recipients of sealed letters from Octavian during the period of the civil wars might say that they brought 'problems' (*aenigmata*).[96]

Faced with this mask, scholars from Suetonius and his sources onwards have naturally looked for clues to Augustus' thinking. If sound, they should be consistent with his behaviour. Some have to be rejected. There is an idea that Augustus touchingly revealed his mind in one of the last known pieces of writing that was intended for public consumption, the will drawn up fourteen months before he died. Its opening clause gave the reason for Tiberius' institution as heir: 'Since cruel fortune has snatched my grandsons Gaius and Lucius from me, I institute Tiberius . . .' Naturally there have been interpreters keen to see a grief-stricken Augustus casting aspersions on his new heir; that will have been the case from the time the document was read in the Senate. Certainly Augustus had written to Gaius in affectionate terms, calling him his 'utterly delightful donkey'.[97] However, the mention of living sons was obligatory if a will was not to be voided. This will of AD 14 was the last successor to many others. Gaius and Lucius, grandsons by blood as well as sons by adoption, could not be ignored, even after their deaths: they were omitted from the provisions only because they had died, not because they had been disgraced (as Agrippa Postumus had been, who was not mentioned).[98] After all Augustus had done to secure the continuity of the dynasty he will hardly have allowed himself the destructive luxury of disparaging his heir.

A better clue is provided by his motto, 'Make haste slowly.'[99] As W. Eck remarks, 'He had learned that one usually could accomplish more that way than with impetuous haste.' That is true, but it was also noted many years ago by C. E. Stevens that Augustus needed that motto and so a means of controlling his own actions and the way they were perceived by the public. It went along with the admonition of the philosopher Athenodorus, who told him to recite the alphabet before responding even verbally to provocation. Some claims made on the Princeps' behalf are not even plausible. A fourth-century source tells us that Augustus was slow to anger. Seneca on the contrary maintained that when he was young he was hotheaded; he burned with anger, and did many things that he looked back on with regret.[100] When in his latter years he urged patience on Tiberius it may have been with regret for hasty actions of his own.

Political historians are concerned with public actions. Those of Augustus show consistent deceit and the readiness for violence mentioned by Seneca and contrasted with the *innocentia* of the new young Princeps Nero. He deployed it whenever he found it necessary in the wars against the Liberators and Antony and against alleged conspirators, even in his own house. It was mitigated only when he was secure in power so that violence was less often invoked; only the possibility of it needed to be borne in mind, and that was remembered. A later and equally violent Emperor, Septimius Severus (193–211) justified his own brutality by comparing himself with Sulla, Marius – and Augustus.[101] The years from 19 to 2 BC were the apogee of Augustus' rule. After that, fresh problems, notably of the succession, were dealt with by a man of increasing age, fear and impatience, and one who knew that the Princeps could as ever get away with almost anything. The military setbacks in the Balkans and Germany put him in the hands of his designated heir Tiberius and nudged him towards more ruthless measures against subversion at home.

Versatility and ambiguity

The problem for would-be interpreters, and their bafflement, have been caused by Augustus' combination of two qualities, versatility and ambiguity: Julian's chameleon could change when necessary and adapt to his background. As H. M. Cotton and A. Yakobson note (discussing the three main political lines, Republican, monarchical and something in between, that Augustus used), an autocrat has no need to be consistent.[102] He exploited the indeterminate nature of Latin power terminology, notably the words *princeps* and *auctoritas*, to impose maximum control with minimum exposure. Augustus was not slippery only about individual concepts – he was serially slippery, changing his position without notice, and with little explanation that has come down to us. The three 'settlements' (Ch. 2) and the development of tribunician power from an instrument of government to little more than a symbol of power are prime examples.

It is worth noticing the effect even of his portrait: according to R. R. R. Smith it conveyed 'a genuinely ambiguous and ambivalent image that opened the way to an unusually wide range of receptions and variations in even the most careful, typologically precise versions'.[103] As to Augustus' personality, to begin with an instance of the first trait, his extraordinary versatility, in politics he kept to no single model. Julius Caesar would have been the obvious one, but the *popularis* and Dictator came with warnings attached. After the Triumviral Period, apart from being the deified parent of the Princeps, with a huge temple in the Forum, he served, often as not, as a model to avoid, to be mentioned in public only for special purposes (Ch. 3). Equally changeable were the different phases of his rule, two of them diametrically opposed in political colour: the 'optimate' phase of 28–23, and the *'popularis'* years of 23–19, which gave way to a long period of pragmatism, ending in an intensifying autocracy (Ch. 2). Then, not only could Augustus readily change his position, but he might adopt a single position that could be interpreted simultaneously in more than one way. The main example of that was his surrender of powers in 28–27, when everything was entrusted to the discretion of Senate and People (Ch. 2). They could act as they chose, and as they chose all remembered what had happened on earlier occasions when Octavian had been denied. So it was, in a less critical example, with the ambiguous status of Augustus' house on the Palatine, which N. Purcell uses as an instance:[104] it was both public and private property and could be interpreted as the spectator chose (Chs. 2, 3 and 5). A minor instance of ambiguity, achieved this time with a subtle use of language, can been seen in a quotation from the *Autobiography*: what he wrote about the comet that appeared after Caesar's death:[105]

> *On the very days when I was holding the games [those of Venus Genetrix, founded by Caesar] a comet was visible for the course of seven days in the northern sector of the sky . . . Ordinary people* (vulgus) *believed that the comet meant that the soul of Caesar had been received among the spirits of the immortal gods; it was on this account that that sign was set on the bust of Caesar that we later dedicated in the Forum.*

Pliny, the source of this quotation, goes on to disclose his own opinion, that the appearance of the comet had delighted Octavian for its own sake, but that is not the point here: the Princeps is distancing himself from the beliefs of ordinary folk, and claiming a concession to them in his decoration of the bust. At the same time, he is not distancing himself from the view that Caesar's soul was received into heaven; after all, that was something to which he aspired himself.[106]

Apollo's speedy transformation of the dynast in Julian's scenario prompts the idea that he was working with a lay figure, and that there is nothing to be sought behind the chameleon skin. Better, the skin and its mask *were* the vital part of the man. He was so intent on his purpose of attaining a perpetual supremacy that there was no room for anything else above the superficial level of sex, food and entertainment; it occupied him exclusively. His offending children and grandchildren became 'three sores'.[107] Perpetual control was vital, and even self-control was increasingly rarely broken. Ambiguity then is the key to interpreting Augustus' language and behaviour, so of his self-presentation, perhaps of his nature, as Cicero sometimes saw it was of Pompey's. It sets the problem, but it is also the solution. Here Augustus was the pupil of Pompey rather than of Caesar: throughout his career Pompey allowed his fellow politicians to speculate on his intentions and react to them, to his own advantage. Tacitus famously pronounced him no better a man than Caesar, but better able to hide his intentions.[108]

Ambiguity in Augustus' discourse or behaviour left him the option of interpreting it in at least two ways, with the same choice open to his fellow-citizens and Rome's subjects, according to their preconceptions and their disposition to be hopeful or not, and to future scholars, according to their preconceptions. To be sure, it will be felt that there is little that is ambiguous in his *Achievements*. The account seems pellucid and factual, for all its omissions. Even here, however, there is *suggestio falsi* – as on the conquest of Germany and on the settlement of 27 BC (Ch. 5), two vitally important areas.

Hence another conclusion that impresses itself on students of twentieth- and twenty-first-century history with unwelcome familiarity is the collusion of contemporaries with the autocrat. He offered solutions to problems that were beginning to seem insoluble and they rushed to accept them; the Princeps in turn moulded his image and his actions to the wishes of one group and another, embracing as many as possible at once. Suetonius celebrates the affection that people felt for him, discounting senatorial decrees that might have been exacted under compulsion or through awe (*verecundia*).[109]

With the help of this collusion, Augustus' endless work for himself was successful. His post (*statio*) was taken over by his unpopular successor with little disturbance from the populace, despite Tiberius' own fears of disorder at the funeral.[110] The scheme that he had devised proved irresistible whenever the Senate had to face it, as in AD 14, 37 and 41. Tacitus' comment on the situation in 14, that Augustus had seduced everyone, upper and lower classes alike, with the delights of having time to themselves, is echoed in Cassius Dio's *History of Rome* after the assassination of Gaius Caligula: the consular Cn. Sentius Saturninus accused his colleagues (and himself) of being 'victims of the delights of peace, brain-washed like slaves'.[111] This reciprocal – 'transformational' – relationship complicates, even bedevils, the study of his principate and of the Principate in general, but it was a vital element in its success.

Key words for understanding lie in the title of A. Wallace-Hadrill's subtle and influential paper on the Principate: 'Between citizen and king', in which he traces the behaviour of emperors towards their subjects as it indicated their relative status and the resemblances and differences between them and Hellenistic monarchs.[112] 'Between' is precisely the area in which Augustus operated. Something similar shows in the attitudes he strikes in his *Achievements*: he presents himself as a committed traditionalist; at the same time he is the creator of novelties, the man who performed actions more successfully than any Roman before him, or even for the first time.[113] This old story reflects the Republican conflict between a Senate that feared individual initiative and the senatorial generals after their own glory and advancement, who often claimed to be the men who achieved something for the first time. 'Between' alerts a reader to the fact that the area between one position and another was the one in which Augustus could manoeuvre most freely and where anxious subjects could place him each on the spot of his own choice, making his own Principate. That enabled Augustus, by design and self-interest, to be truly an innovator. He left a very different world from the one he entered. Fortunately, for the majority of the inhabitants of the Empire – those who benefited from peace and who, amongst the upper classes, might hope for advancement – it was a better one.

Principles

Versatility and ambiguity both raise the question of conscious hypocrisy, or perhaps rather of self-deceit, if the two can be distinguished. How conscious was the autocrat of his manipulations? It looks from his last words (at least as reported by Suetonius) as if his conduct might be subsumed under the idea that all men are players. Lying on his deathbed at Nola, Augustus asked for a mirror, had his jaws straightened and his hair combed. He asked those at the bedside to tell him whether he had carried off his part in the play of life and, if he had, asked to be sent off with applause and unanimous praise. Augustus 'performed' his death scene. His last words actually belong to comedy and the peaceful scene became paradigmatic, even mandatory, for the death of a 'good' emperor. D. Wardle has convincingly argued that Suetonius' presentation is not subversive: Augustus is shown dying with a clear conscience, reflecting on his life in Stoic and Stoicising terms, and demonstrating by his words and actions care for Empire and family. It was a death better than Alexander's.[114] Given that the scenario of Suetonius has roots in actuality, we may still ask, firstly, how good a 'performer' Augustus was at the last, and, more importantly, how much he had come to believe in his own performance. Back in Rome, Augustus' house on the Palatine had a room decorated as a stage, showing masks on the walls; it was an interesting choice.[115] But by August AD 14 he could allow himself complete belief.

Augustus, who had at least consented to the murder of Cicero in 43 BC, had the sublime effrontery to praise Cicero to his grandsons.[116] It is as if a veil had been let down between Augustus and his past, distancing it from the man he now saw himself to be and from the part he had played as Princeps. In any case, whatever had been done in the past it had been done to bring about the present or at least imminent golden age (it was hard in 14 to see how far ahead it lay), for which Augustus claimed responsibility, and which naturally depended on his life-long and his dynasty's lasting supremacy. That would have been the familiar argument of last resort, and it was acknowledged by the Senate as a body in AD 20 in its decree on Cn. Piso the Elder: 'the security (*salus*) of our Empire has been placed in the guardianship of that House'.[117]

Devious as Augustus the politician was, that does not mean that in a set of thought processes separate from his ambitions he had no strongly held beliefs, shared with many of his contemporaries. An Italian born in 63 BC, he was aware of the ills that in the general view were responsible for the Republic's slide into unviability. They included shortage of manpower due to the impoverishment and dispossession of the peasantry and, at the highest level, the reluctance of senators to pull together for the advantage of the whole, a failing he had known and exploited since his adolescence; they were unwilling, like the peasantry, even to keep their families going, it seemed. When he was safely in power Augustus gave his peers the benefit of his observations on these problems and prescribed his wormwood remedies (Ch. 3). It was acceptable (though tedious) for the man who benefited from the vision won at the top of the tree to give lectures on their behaviour to those still struggling near the base.

Then there was Augustus' genuine preoccupation with religion, shown by his emphasis on his restoration of public cults and on religious structures, concrete and institutional, erected in his own honour. This was something distinct from the superstition mentioned above: it concerned established practices of the whole Roman People, not notice taken of one individual by an unspecified higher power. The *Achievements* might be intended to reassure the Roman People that all was to be well between them and their gods, and so to secure his own position within that dispensation, but Augustus' concern with religion, how it was housed and performed, as with the detail of honours offered to himself, was also sincere and deep. The Italian Augustus was as embedded in tradition and the web of religious thinking as any other Roman of his time (more so than Julius Caesar had been); that much is shown by the complex implications of the design and ornamentation of the Altar of Peace.[118] Problems about the sincerity of Roman religious belief should not arise: it was a question of customary performance to be carried out to the satisfaction of gods and men, and if necessary manipulated, not of verbal dogma to be accepted or rejected. Due performance of ritual, military and political success, backing up immense self-belief (Augustus' idea that he had an extraordinary power in his eye comes to mind[119]), made it clear that the gods must favour him; he had every reason to believe it:[120] he was *felix*, gifted with good luck that far outstripped that of other Roman leaders, Scipio Africanus and Pompey the Great. That luck became proverbial. Some, perversely or out of ill-will, liked to dwell on another side: his ill-luck, especially with his family.[121] They were mistaken in emphasising that: as the fates of his daughter and grandchildren showed, not family but dynasty was what came first.

Endnotes

1 Ovid, *Fasti* 4, 949–54.
2 *Dei*: Ovid, *Ex Ponto* 2. 8. 1–8.
3 Octavian's 'divine' qualities: Cic. *Phil.* 5. 23. 43; Virg. *Ecl.* 1. 6–8; Domitius Marsus: E. Courtney, *The Fragmentary Latin Poets* (Oxford, 1993), 304f.
4 Distinction between men and gods: Gradel 2002, 26.
5 Val. Max. 6. 9. 15 has Caesar approaching heaven by the same route as Hercules (Livy 1.7. 15).

6 Romulus' *virtus* '*in caelum dicitur sustulisse*': Cic. *Rep.* 1. 25.

7 Divine origin of great men: Varro, *Ant. Rerum Divin.* 1 Fr. 20[†] (24), 23 ed. Cardauns.

8 Alleged dichotomy between traditional religion and imperial cult: Price 1996, 820; shift in focus: 830f. *Fasti* encapsulating Augustus' invisible presence: 838. That did not mean that there was conflict.

9 Deification: Gradel 2002, 203f. Posthumous Italian temples: 338. Sharing them from 36 BC: App. *BC* 5. 546.

10 Italian temples: Gradel 2002, 84, refining on Hänlein-Schäfer 1985, who offers an Empire-wide catalogue, and cf. 87, on known priests in Italy.

11 Abstinence: Suet. *Aug.* 52. Refining: see especially Gradel 2002.

12 Birthday: Zanker 1988, 48.

13 Augustus' honours: Salii: *RG* 10. 1; Zanker 1988, 128–35.

14 Pantheon: Dio 53. 27. 3.

15 Augustus rules under Jupiter: Hor. *Odes* 1. 12. 57; Ovid *Met.* 15, 858–60; *Fasti* 1, 650; 2, 131f.; *Tr.* 3. 1. 35–8.

16 *Genius*: Taylor 1940, 216–18, rebutted by Gradel 2002, 77–80 (Italian cults); 130–32 (senators as clients): preparation for state cult: 137; development of *genius* (of the *paterfamilias*) into state cult. Nero-Vitellius: 187.

17 Divine honours in Asia and Bithynia: Dio 51. 20. 6–8; cult at Lugdunum: Epit. Liv. 137.

18 Mytilene decree: *IGR* 4, 39 col. B, ll. 12–17, cited by C. Kelly, *The Roman Empire: A Very Short Introduction* (Oxford, 2006), 26–28.

19 Gradel 2002, 97f, is cautious on Italy, citing the Pisan decrees, EJ 68f., for the Emperor's passive role.

20 Tiberius' altar: Price 1996, 838, on *Inscr. Ital.* 13. 2, 401.

21 The funeral procession: Dio 56. 34. 1–3f, with Galinsky 1996, 206f.

22 Deification: Tac. *Ann.* 1. 10. 8. 'Divus': Gradel 2002, 69–72; state cult: 111f., accepting the general formulation of Aur.Vict. *Caes.* 1. 6; Augustus' instructions: 276–82; shock diminished: 264, also arguing that the example of Caesar's fate made it difficult to grant the title to the living Princeps.

23 *Fer. Dur.* III. 7. Naturally his birthday is also mentioned in Philocalus' *Birthdays of the Caesars* and in his *Calendar* (*CIL* 1, 255 and 272, of AD 354).

24 Piso's offences: Eck *et al.* 1996, 38–43, ll. 23–70.

25 Augustus' temple and Sodales Augustales: EJ p. 52 (*Fasti Amit.*); Vell. Pat. 2. 130. 1; Tac. *Ann.* 1. 10. 8; 6. 45. 2; Dio 56. 46. 1, with Swan 2004 *ad loc.* (bibl.). *Magistri vici* and 'birthday': Lott 2004, 172, citing John Lyd. *De Mens.* 4. 238.

26 Prosecution of Granius Marcellus: Tac. *Ann.* 1. 74. *Sodales* and their prestige: Tac. *Ann.* 3. 64. 4. End of the institution: Gradel 2002, 357–62, on Her. 7. 3. 5f. and *CIL* 6, 1984. Gallienus' coinage: *RIC* 5, 1, 131 no. 9; 133 no. 28. Tiberius' sacrifice: Tac. *Ann.* 4. 52. 2.

27 Concentration on living emperors: Gradel 2002, 339. How far 'private' cult could go in theatres and squares he explores at 226–28.

28 Wind band dedications: *AE* 1996, 246.

29 Julio-Claudian imitation of Augustan portrait style: Smith 1996, 47.

30 Benefits from Augustus and Claudius: Sen. *Ben.* 1. 15. 3–6, cited by Griffin 2003, 181.

31 Augustus contrasted with Claudius: Sen. *Apocol.* 10. 2–11. 5.

32 '*Lex de imperio Vespasiani*': EJ 364.

33 Colosseum planned by Augustus: Suet. *Vesp.* 9. 1, with Levick, *Vespasian* (London and New York, 1999), 73.

34 Domitian's superiority: Stat. *Silv.* 4. 1. 31–33.

35 Refusal to invade Britain: Tac. *Agr.* 13. 2; number of praetorships: *Ann.* 1. 14. 4.

36 Flogging actors: Tac. *Ann.* 1. 77.

37 Agrippina approved: Eck *et al.* 1996, 48, ll. 137–39; Tiberian hostility: Tac. *Ann.* 1. 69. 3–5.

38 Philo's admiration: *Leg.* 21, 147–49.

39 Tiberius' accession speech: Tac. *Ann.* 1. 11. 1; Nero's: 13. 4.

40 Tiberian obverse dedications on *sestertii* AD 34–7: *RIC* 1^2 96, nos. 56f., 62f., and 68; *DIVUS . . . PATER dupondii* and *asses* 14–37: 98f., nos. 70–83; Gaius: 108–13, notably the opening gold and silver nos. 1–6; Claudian *dupondius*: 128 no. 101; gold and silver of the Civil Wars: 197; 199f.; 210–12 nos. 81–117; Galban *denarius*: 234 no. 33 (rev.; obv. with Galba's legend).

41 Actium centenary: *RIC* 2, 6 and 61–66, nos. 384: *AETERNITAS P(opuli) R(omani)*, with Victory; 385: *ROMA ET AUGUSTUS*, with Rome offering a Victory to Vespasian; 387: *FORT(una) RED(ux)*; 397: *VICTORIA AUGUSTI*; 400: *PAX AUGUSTA*, etc.

42 *DIVUS AUGUSTUS PATER*: Titus, *aes*: *RIC* 2, 141–43, nos. 184–208; Domitian, *aes*: 211, nos. 453–56.

43 Nerva, *aes*: *RIC* 2, 222 and 232f. nos. 126–37.

44 Trajan melting worn coins: Dio 68. 15. 3^1.

45 Restoration coins: H. Mattingly, *CREBM* 3, lxxxvi–xciii, 132–44 nos. 673–706; H. Mattingly and E. A. Sydenham, *RIC* 2, 302–04, 309, nos. 800–01 (*den.*); 806f. (*den., aur.*, with Octavian); 311 no. 815f. (*aur.*); Sex. Pompeius: 310 n. 811 (*den.*); Augustus: 311 nos. 817–20 (*den.*). Caesar on *denarii CREBM* 3, 141 nos. 30, 31; *aurei*: 142 nos. 696–98; 144 no. 1a; Augustus 142 no. 699; thoroughgoing treatment in H. Komnick, *Die Restitutionszmünzen der frühen Kaiserzeit: Aspekte der Kaiserlegitimation* (Berlin, 2001); I am indebted to Dr M. T. Griffin for drawing my attention to it.

46 Representations of Capricorn in various media: Barton 1995, 48–51.

47 Hadrian: juxtaposed to Augustus: *RIC* 2, 324 and 335; 404 no. 532; *HADRIANUS AUGUSTUS*: 358–82, nos. 146–370, etc., with Capricorn at 361 no. 189.

48 Augustus' temple restored: *HA Hadr.* 12. 3. Augustus' seal: see A. R. Birley, *Hadrian, the Restless Emperor* (London and New York), 96f., rebutting the idea that Hadrian's admiration was based on Augustan foreign policy; 147. The shield: Charisius, *Gramm. Lat.* 1. 222, with Birley 201.

49 S. Mitchell, *JRS* 66 (1976) 106f.; date: *PIR*² S 790.

50 Tiberius' letter to Gytheion: EJ 102.

51 Senate's wish: Eutrop. *Breviarium* 8. 5; cf. Vict. *Caes.* 13. 2; [Epit. *De Caes.*] 13. 2. 5.

52 Trajan as Optimus Princeps: Dio 68. 23. 2.

53 Augustus as model: Pliny, *Pan.* 88. 10: '*nomine Augusti admonemur eius cui primum dicatum est*'.

54 Cluvius Rufus: see T. Cornell *et al.*, eds., *Fragments of the Roman Historians* (Oxford, forthcoming), no. 84.

55 Cluvius' candour: Pliny *Ep.* 9. 19. 4f.; Tacitus' impartiality: *Ann.* 1. 1. 3.

56 Avoidance of writing: Toher 1990.

57 Judgements on Vell. Pat.: Sumner 1970; Syme 1978 ('Mendacity'); Woodman 1975 and 1977. Cordus' death: Tac. *Ann.* 4. 34f.

58 Tiberian reforms: Vell. Pat. 2. 125, supported by Woodman 1975, 293.

59 Velleius Paterculus on Augustus: cf. 2. 89 and 124.

60 Aufidius and Nonianus: see T. Cornell *et al.*, eds, *Fragments of the Roman Historians* (Oxford, forthcoming), no. 78f.

61 Florus on Augustus: 4. 2f.

62 Tacitus' predecessors: *Ann.* 1. 1. 2.

63 'Formidable': App. *BC* 1. 23, with Gowing 1992, 57; cf. 90f.

64 Dio on Augustus's ambition: Reinhold and Swan 1990, 158 with n. 9, citing 45. 4. 3; 46. 34. 4. Bloodlessness: 173. Hypocrisy: 53. 11. 1–12. 3; 55. 6. 1; 12. 3; 56. 28.1. Secrecy: 53. 19. 3–6. Dio comparatively favourable: Gowing 1992, 91f.; proscriptions 254 on 56. 44. 2; 256f. on 47. 7. 1–3. 267 on Livia's advice: 55. 21. 4.

65 Danger of *otium*: Galinsky 1996, 138f.

66 Dio's verdict: Swan 2004, 14; he cites examples, with R. Syme the major counter-example. Perhaps with Syme in mind, Galinsky 1996, 79, considers Tacitus' influence to have been disproportionate.

67 Moderation: *HA* Claud. 2. 3.

68 Seneca on Octavian-Augustus: *De Clem.* 1. 1. 5f.; 10. 4.

69 Augustus as superior judge: Phaedrus 3. 10. 34–50, with E. Champlin, *JRS* 95 (2005) 111–15.

70 Julian, *Caesars* (*Kronia*) of *c.* 361: Octavian at 309A–D. Galinsky 1996, 9, aptly remarks that Ovid's *Met.* captures much of the Augustan spirit in its very title.

71 Remembering the Republic: Tac. *Ann.* 1. 3. 7, with Ridley 2003, 235.

72 Career summary: Tac. *Ann.* 1. 10, with Ridley 2003, 164; Suet. *Aug.* 26. 1.

73 Immorality and politics: Edwards 1993. Sense of power conferred by scandal-mongering: Osgood 2006, 265.

74 Sexual misconduct: Suet. *Aug.* 69–70. 1; Livia's role: 71. 1. Perhaps Augustus would have used the defence employed by Horace (*Sat*, 1. 2. 47–54) and available under his own adultery law, that he kept off married women. But one alleged paramour, Terentia, wife of Maecenas, was certainly married (Ch. 1).

75 Bisexual orgies: [*Epit. Vict.*] 1. 22.

76 Criticism of Augustus: Tac. *Ann.* 1. 10; 3. 28. 1f.; Sen. *De Clem.* 1. 9. 1; Suet. *Aug.* 4. 2 (Cassius Parmensis); 7. 1, 10. 4, and 16. 1f. (Antony); with Yavetz 1984, 20; Reinhold and Swan 1990, 169 n. 68.

77 Choice of Tiberius: Tac. *Ann.* 1. 10. 7.

78 Desire for rest: Sen. *Shortness of Life* 4. 2–5; see Huttner 2004, 102f.

79 Tiberius' desire for retirement hypocritical: Tac. *Ann.* 4. 9. 1.

80 See Ch. Wirszubski, 'Cicero's *cum dignitate* otium: a reconsideration', *JRS* 44 (1954), 1–14. I owe this point to Dr Herbert-Brown.

81 Vitellius' attempted abdication: Tac. *Hist.* 3. 66–8.

82 Studied communication: Suet. *Aug.* 84. 1f.

83 Eloquence: Malcovati 4.

84 Use of script: Suet. *Aug.* 84. 1; Dio 53. 2. 7, with Rich 1990 *ad loc.*; 53. 11. 1 and 4.

85 Octavius' illnesses: Nic. Dam. 15; 19–22.

86 Simplicity of manners: Suet. *Aug.* 71–73; Augustus' shortness and high-heeled shoes: Suet. *Aug.* 73; 79. 2 ('*Quinque pedum et dodrantis*').

87 Augustus the human: Southern 1998, 135–38. Pastimes: Horsfall 2003, 78 and 154 n. 23, citing Suet. *Aug.* 45. 2; 71; 74. 2; 78; 83. 1: Sense of humour: 98. 3. Playful letters: Macr. *Sat.* 2. 4.12; cf. Suet. *Aug.* 86. 2. Tender: A. Gell. *NA* 15. 7. 3. Insight: Malcovati 1969, xviii, and see the commentary of P. Cugusi, *Epistolographi Lat. Minores* (Turin, 1979) 2, 300–440.

88 *Simplicitas*: Mart. 11. 20.

89 Augustus' sayings: Plut. *Apophth. Aug,. Mor.* 207A–208A; Macr. 2. 4. H. Trevor-Roper, ed., *Hitler's Table Talk (1941–44)* (3rd edn, London, 1988).

90 Capricorn: Dwyer 1973, citing (66f.) P. Nigidius Figulus, *de Capricorno*: it was polyvalent, signifying victory and revenge; Barton 1995.

91 Superstition: Pliny *NH* 2. 24; cf. Suet. *Aug.* 90; 92. 1. Good relations with *haruspices*: Hekster and Rich 2006, 159f.

92 A gambler: Suet. *Aug.* 70. 2–4; [*Epit. Vict.*] 1. 21: *porro autem supra quam aestimari potest, dominandi cupidissimus, studiosus aleae lusor.*

93 Luck: Augustus' wish for his grandson: Plut., *Apophth., Aug.* 10, *Mor.* 207E 2. 98. 10; cf. Hor. *Odes* 4. 15. 9.

94 Tiberius' tears over Vipsania: Suet. *Tib.* 7. 3; loss of the legions: *Aug.* 23. 2; depraved posterity: 65. 4.

95 Apparent dullness of Augustus: Yavetz 1990, 30. Frugality: Suet. *Aug.* 76f. Pollio's vessels: Dio 54. 23. 2–4 (*muraenae*, moray-eels).

96 Sphinx: Suet. *Aug.* 50; Pliny, *NH* 37. 10; Zanker 1988, 271.

97 Gaius as '*asellus iucundissimus*': Gell. 15. 7. 3.

98 Wording of the will: Levick 1971. Similar language is used in the *Achievements*: 'my sons whom cruel fortune snatched from me', *RG* 14. 1. Aspersions cast on Tiberius: Tac. *Ann.* 1. 10. 13.

99 Augustus' motto: Suet. *Aug.* 25. 4; A. Gell. *NA* 10. 11. 5 ('*Speude bradeos*' in Greek, from Euripides' *Phoenissae* 599; '*Festina lente*' in Latin). That a hasty Augustus *needed* the motto was a doctrine propagated by C. E. Stevens in

tutorials. A more tranquil interpretation: Eck 2007, 58. Yavetz 1990, 33, also draws attention to Sen. *Ben.* 6. 32. 1, where, after his denunciation of his daughter in the Senate, Augustus regrets that Maecenas and Agrippa were not alive to restrain him. Athenodorus: Plut. *Apophth., Aug.* 7, *Mor.* 207C; examples of loss of control: Plut., *loc. cit.* 9, *Mor.* 207D, cf. 785D; Suet. *Aug.* 54; Dio 55. 10. 13–16 (Julia).

100 Slow to anger: [*Epit. Aur. Vict.*] 1. 21. Regret: Sen. *de Clem.* 1. 11. 1.

101 Septimius Severus: Dio 75(76). 8. 1.

102 Consistency of autocrats: Cotton and Yakobson 2002, 203–07.

103 Ambiguity of portrait: Smith 1996, 46.

104 Ambiguity of Augustus' house on the Palatine: Purcell 1996, 790.

105 Comet: Pliny, *NH* 2. 94. The *Autobiography* seems the most appropriate place for Augustus to have made this statement. Dr Herbert-Brown notes the derogatory word *vulgus* as an unlikely one for Augustus (but often used by Pliny). But Pliny does claim this as a quotation, and the period before the taking of tribunician power seems the most acceptable one for the word.

106 Augustus' hopes: Tac. *Ann.* 4. 38. 5.

107 Three sores: Suet. *Aug.* 65. 4.

108 Pompey a '*simulator*' in 58 BC: Cic. *Ad Q. fr.* 1. 3. 9; '*occultior non melior*': Tac. *Hist.* 2. 38.

109 Affection and compulsion: Suet. *Aug.* 57. 1.

110 Tiberius' fears: Tac. *Ann.* 1. 8. 6.

111 Brain-washing: Tac. *Ann.* 1. 2. 1: '*cunctos dulcedine otii pellexit*'.

112 Wallace-Hadrill 1982.

113 Traditionalism *versus* innovation: Ridley 2003, 233f., citing Hoffmann 1969.

114 Augustus' deathbed: Suet. *Aug.* 99. 1, with Hirschfeld 1883, who remarks that if Augustus had suspected what would be made of his words, he might have chosen a less ambiguous expression; Yavetz 1990, 35; Meier 1990, 69; Wardle 2007. Paradigmatic imperial death scenes: A. von Hooff in L. De Blois, P. Erdkamp, O. Hekster, G. De Kleijn and S. Mols, eds, *The Representation and Reception of Roman Imperial Power*, Proc. of 3rd Workshop of Intern. Network Impact of Empire, Rome, 20–23 March 2002 (Amsterdam, 2003); Wardle 2007, 443.

115 'Room of the masks', *The Times*, 8 March 2008, 47, with photograph.

116 Praise of Cicero: Plut. *Cic.* 49. 3.

117 Eck *et al.* 1996, 48, l.162f.

118 Ara Pacis Augustae: Torelli 1992, 27–61.

119 Power of eye: Suet. *Aug.* 79. 2.

120 Augustus' luck: Eutropius, *Brev.* 8. 5.

121 Augustus' misfortunes: Suet. *Aug.* 65.

Glossary of Ancient Terms

(Plurals in brackets)

adrogatio method of adopting an independent adult male which brings him into the power of the adopter

aes coinage in base metal (copper or *orichalcum*)

alimenta (plural) provisions, sustenance

a rationibus secretary in charge of accounts

arbitrium decision, capacity to decide

auctor promoter, originator

auctoritas respect; influence that enables a person to get others to obey, even without having the official authority to order them to do so

aureus (*aurei*), gold piece, worth 25 *denarii*

Centumviral court theoretically consisting of one hundred jurors, and presided over by a junior magistrate; it decided cases involving inheritances

centuria (*-ae*) (century) group of a (theoretically) hundred men; division of a legion or of a voting assembly, where they were ranked by wealth

cognitio judicial enquiry conducted on the initiative of the Senate or by a magistrate in virtue of his *imperium*

cognomen (*cognomina*), surname assigned to individuals for personal peculiarities or achievements (e.g. 'Strabo', 'squinting', 'Parthicus', 'victorious over the Parthians'); often hereditary and distinguishing one branch of a clan from another (e.g. Cornelii Lentuli, Cornelii Scipiones)

comes (*comites*) companion (on an expedition); origin of the title 'Count'

comitia (plural) voting assembly

congiarium (*-aria*) a gift, nominally of oil but in the imperial age of money, made occasionally by the emperor, notably on his accession, to the populace of Rome and sometimes to that of other cities

curator (*civitatis*) (*curatores*)   official given a charge, often of a community, with special reference to its financial affairs

curia   ancient division of the Roman People, thirty in number; also, the Senate House

curiate assembly (*Comitia Curiata*)   assembly of the Roman People divided into thirty *curiae*, effectively a gathering of thirty lectors each representing one division

cursus (*honorum*)   regular series (of offices held by Roman senators)

decennalia   festivities celebrating ten years of an emperor's reign

denarius (-*arii*)   silver coin, worth four sesterces, standard currency throughout the Empire

dies imperii   day on which an emperor counted himself as having come to power

diploma (-*ata*)   pair of tablets folded over, especially certificates of honourable discharge given to auxiliary troops and praetorian guardsmen

duovir (-*i*)   one of the two supreme magistrates in a Roman colony or *municipium*

dupondius (-*ii*)   two *asses*

elogium (-*a*)   epitaph

eques (*equites*)   'knight', member of the upper class who had not entered politics by standing for senatorial office; possessor of property worth 400,000 sesterces; often with financial interests in taxation, money-lending or investment in land

eques singularis (*equites singulares*)   cavalryman selected for duty as bodyguard, orderly, etc.

fanum (*fana*)   shrine

fasces   (plural) bundle of rods carried before magistrates, displaying their power to punish (consuls had twelve, praetors six, and so on)

Fasti   days on which business may be transacted; festival days; list of magistrates

fetiales   college of twenty priests whose regulations formally governed declarations of war and the striking of treaties

flamen (*flamines*)   one of a group of prestigious priests at Rome or Italian or provincial cities that had constitutions based on that of Rome

gens (*gentes*)   clan; section of Roman society bearing the same *nomen gentilicium* (-*a*), clan name *haruspex* (*-spices*)   practitioner of a form of divining (entrails, prodigies, lightning) that originated in Etruria

hostis (*-es*)   enemy; person declared by the Senate to be an enemy of the state

HS Sestertius (*-i*)   sesterce(s), unit of monetary value; the sign (=IIS) means 'two and a half times' (the *as*, a small copper coin) although after 217 BC the *sestertius* was worth four *asses*. Four sesterces made up the silver *denarius*.

imperium (*-a*)   power of command granted by assembly of Roman People; primary power of emperors (whose English title is derived from *imperator*, commander); the Roman Empire, sphere of command of the Roman People

ius Italicum   privilege granted favoured provincial cities, giving their territory the same status as Italian land and so exempting it from tax paid by provincials

Latium   privileged region near Rome; rights enjoyed by its inhabitants or similarly privileged communities, especially that of becoming a full Roman citizen after holding a magistracy in such a community

latus clavus   broad purple stripe on the tunic of senators and young men who aspired to membership of the Senate; after Augustus and Tiberius worn by permission of the emperor

legatus (*legati*),   legate (a) subordinate officer of an emperor or a proconsul, in charge of a legion or a province; *legatus iuridicus*, one concerned especially with the administration of justice; (b) ambassador

lex (*leges*)   law passed by an assembly of the people; – *annalis* law regulating the order and/or age for holding magistracies

lictor (*-es*)   attendant on a magistrate with *imperium*, often carrying their *fasces*, sometimes on other personages

ludi (*plural* of *ludus*)   games; *ludi saeculares*. Secular Games, held once a century or once every hundred and ten years

lustrum (*-a*)   purification ceremony, especially that performed by censors after completion of the census; period of five years

magister (*-tri*) *vici*   official chosen by a *vicus*

maiestas   greatness, majesty (of the Roman People or its magistrates); *minuta*, *laesa* diminished, violated (cf. *lèse-majesté*), treason

mores   customs, manners, morals

mos (*mores*)   custom, practice; *mos maiorum* traditional practice *neocory, neocorate* (*neocories*), *-ates*, Greek *neokoria* (*-ai*) wardenship of temple; title awarded to communities responsible for building and maintaining a temple, usually of the imperial cult

nomen (*nomina*) name, see *gens*

novus (*-i*) new (sometimes with unfavourable connotations); *novus homo* 'new' man (without consular or even senatorial antecedents)

numen (*numina*) divine spirit or will, godhead (literally, 'nod of the head')

officina (*-ae*) workshop, especially of the mint

optimate (*optimates*) one who favours government by the 'best' men and the supremacy of the Senate

paterfamilias (*patres-*) head of a household, with supreme authority over its members

patricius (*-ii*) patrician, member of the original ruling aristocratic families at Rome, with privileged access to priesthoods, or of one later elevated to that status

patrimonium property inherited by one emperor from another

patrocinium formal relationship between patron and client

pietas devotion

plebs common people of Rome; – *frumentaria*, those entitled to receive free grain

Pomerium sacred boundary of Rome, marking the distinction between *imperium* exercised in Rome and abroad

popularis (*-es*) favouring the people; (noun) politician who acts in the interests of the people against the wishes of the Senate

potentia power not sanctioned by law or custom; often excessive power

potestas (*-ates*) power officially granted (to carry out certain actions)

praefectus (*-i*) prefect; military officer or governor of a minor province

praenomen (*praenomina*) forename given to boys soon after birth, e.g., Publius, Lucius

procurator (*-ores*) agent in charge of estates or business affairs; if acting for the emperor (*procurator Augusti*) normally of equestrian rank and, in imperial provinces, in charge of taxation as well as estates

pro praetore acting on behalf of a praetor, and with his authority

publicanus (*-i*) tax farmer

res privata private property (of the emperors); privy purse

res publica literally 'the public thing' or 'property'; 'the Commonwealth'; or 'the Republic' as opposed to the Principate

saeculum (*-la*)   age, century, generation

sella curulis (*sellae curules*)   curule chair, a folding stool of ivory, on which consuls, praetors, and some aediles might sit as a sign of their authority

Senatus Consultum   decree of the senate

sestertius (*-tii*)   sesterce, bronze coin and unit of currency

sodales   members of a collegiate priesthood or social fraternity

spolia opima   lit. 'richest spoils', taken from a defeated enemy leader killed in hand-to-hand fighting; they were dedicated in the temple of Jupiter Feretrius

suasor   one who gives verbal support to a proposal

subsellium (*-ia*)   bench (in theatre, senate, or court)

supplicatio (*-nes*)   offering of propitiation to a deity (decreed as thanksgiving)

toga virilis   toga of manhood, garment formally assumed by Roman male citizens when they had reached puberty

tra(ns)vectio   'ride past', especially the parade of knights before the censor or Princeps

tria nomina   the 'three names', *praenomen, nomen,* and *cognomen,* making up a Roman name (such as Gaius Julius Caesar) that only Roman citizens were allowed to use

tribunus (*-i*)   tribune; – *militum* one of six junior officers in a legion or commander of an auxiliary cohort; – *plebis* magistrate of the plebs

vexillum (*-illa*)   banner of an army unit

vicennalia   festivities celebrating twenty years of an emperor's reign

vicus (*-i*)   village; in Rome, neighbourhood, street community

vigiles   nightwatchmen

vigintiviratus, vigintivirate,   set of twenty junior magistracies, divided into four groups carrying different prestige, held at the beginning of a would-be senator's career

virtus (*virtutes*)   'manliness', courage, merit

Bibliography

R. Abdy and N. Harling, 'Two important new Roman coins', *NC* 165 (2005) 175–78

F. A. Adcock, 'The interpretation of *Res Gestae Divi Augusti* 34. 1', *CQ* 45 (1951) 130–35

A. Alföldi, *Die monarchische Repräsentation im römischen Kaiserreiche* (3rd edn, Darmstadt, 1980)

G. Alföldy, 'Two Principes: Augustus and Sir Ronald Syme', *Athen.* 80 (1993) 122–31

W. Ameling, 'Augustus und Agrippa. Bemerkungen zu PKöln VI 249', *Chiron* 24 (1994) 1–28

V. Arangio-Ruiz *et al.*, eds, *Augustus: Studi in occasione del Bimillenario augusteo.* Reale Accad. Naz. Dei Lincei (Rome, 1938)

J. S. Arkenberg, 'Licinii Murenae, Terentii Varrones, and Varrones Murenae. I: a prosopographical study of three Roman families. II. The conspirator Murena', *Hist.* 42 (1993) 326–51; 471–91

K. M. T. Atkinson, 'Constitutional and legal aspects of the trials of Marcus Primus and Varro Murena', *Hist.* 9 (1960) 440–73

E. Badian, 'Crisis theories and the beginning of the Principate', in G. Wirth *et al.* eds, *Romanitas Christianitas. Untersuchungen zur Geschichte und Literatur der römischen Kaiserzeit J. Straub zum 70. Geburtstag . . . gewidmet* (Berlin and New York, 1982) 18–41

E. Badian, 'A phantom marriage law', *Philologus* 129 (1985) 82–98

B. Baldwin, 'The *acta diurna*', *Chiron* 9 (1979) 189–203

A. Barchiesi, *The Poet and the Prince. Ovid and Augustan Discourse* (Berkeley, CA, 1997)

D. Barker, '"The Golden Age is Proclaimed"? The *Carmen Saeculare* and the renaissence of the Golden Race', *CQ* NS 46 (1996) 434–46

T. D. Barnes, 'The victories of Augustus', *JRS* 64 (1974) 21–26

J. Barsby, *Ovid. Greece and Rome: New Surveys in the Classics* 12 (Oxford, 1978)

T. Barton, 'Augustus and Capricorn: Astrological polyvalency and imperial rhetoric', *JRS* 85 (1995) 33–51

S. J. Bastomsky, 'Proculeius and Augustus: a note on a friendship turned sour', *Lat.* 36 (1977) 129–31

R. A. Bauman, *The Crimen Maiestatis in the Roman Republic and Augustan Principate* (Johannesburg, 1967)

R. A. Bauman, *Impietas in Principem*. Münchener Beitr. zur Papyrusforsch. und antiken Rechtsgesch. 67 (Munich, 1974)

A. Bay, 'The Letters *SC* on Augustan Coinage', *JRS* 62 (1972) 111–22

M. Beard, 'A complex of times: no more sheep on Romulus' birthday', *PCPS* 213 (1987) 1–15

J. Bellemore, ed., *Nicolaus of Damascus Life of Augustus*, with introduction, translation and commentary (Bristol, 1984)

J. Béranger, *Recherches sur l'aspect idéologique du Principat* (Basel, 1953)

D. Van Berchem, *Les Distributions de Blé et d'Argent à la Plèbe sous l'Empire romaine* (Geneva, 1939)

A. R. Birley, 'Q. Lucretius Vespillo (cos. ord. 19)', *Chiron* 30 (2000) 711–48

E. H. Bispham, 'Pliny the Elder's Italy', in E. H. Bispham *et al.*, eds, *Vita Vigilia Est'*, ICST Suppl. Papers 100 (London, 2007) 41–68

J. Bleicken, *Zwischen Republik und Prinzipat: zum Charakter des Zweiten Triumvirats*. Abh. der Akad. der Wiss. in Göttingen, phil.-hist. Kl. 3. 185 (1990)

J. Bleicken, *Augustus, eine Biographie* (Berlin, 2000)

W. M. Bloomer, *Valerius Maximus and the Rhetoric of the new Nobility* (Chapel Hill, NC, and London, 1992)

A. Bonanno, *Portraits and Other Heads in Roman Historical Relief up to the Age of Septimius Severus*. BAR Suppl. 6 (Oxford, 1976)

A. B. Bosworth, 'Asinius Pollio and Augustus', *Hist.* 21 (1972) 441–73

A. B. Bosworth, 'Augustus, the "Res Gestae" and Hellenistic theories of Apotheosis', *JRS* 89 (1999) 1–18

G. W. Bowersock, 'Augustus and the East: the problem of the succession', in Millar and Segal 1984, 169–88

G. W. Bowersock, 'The Pontificate of Augustus', in Raaflaub and Toher 1990, 380–94

A. K. Bowman, E. Champlin and A. Lintott, eds, *The Augustan Empire, 43 BC–AD 69, CAH* 10 (1996)

A. J. Boyle, *Ovid and the Monuments: A Poet's Rome*. Ramus Monographs 4 (Bendigo, Vic., 2003)

T. C. Brennan, 'Triumphus in Monte Albano', in R. W. Wallace and E. M. Harris, eds, *Transitions to Empire: Essays in Greco-Roman History, 360–146 BC, in Honor of E. Badian*. Oklahoma Series in Classical Culture 21 (Norman, OK and London, 1996) 315–37

P. A. Brunt, 'The Lex Valeria Cornelia', *JRS* 51 (1961) 71–84

P. A. Brunt, 'Augustan Imperialism', *JRS* 53 (1963) 170–76 (= *RIT* 96–109)

P. A. Brunt, Italian Manpower *225 BC–AD 14* (Oxford, 1971)

P. A. Brunt, 'Lex de Imperio Vespasiani', *JRS* 67 (1977) 91–116

P. A. Brunt, 'The role of the Senate in the Augustan regime', *CQ* 34 (1984) 423–44

P. A. Brunt and J. M. Moore, eds, *Res Gestae Divi Augusti. The Achievements of the Divine Augustus*, with introduction and commentary (Oxford, 1967, corr. repr. 1970)

E. Buchner, *Die Sonnenuhr des Augustus* (Mainz, 1982)

H. E. Butler and M. Cary, *C. Suetonii Tranquilli* Divus Iulius, ed. with Introduction and Commentary (Oxford, 1927)

F. Cairns, 'Propertius and the Battle of Actium', in Woodman and West 1984, 129–68

L. Canali, 'Il "manifesto" del regime augusteo', *Rivista di Cultura Classica e Medioevale* 15, 2 (1973) 151–75.

L. Canfora, *Julius Caesar: the People's Dictator* (tr. by M. Hill and K. Windle from *Giulio Cesare: Il Dittatore Democratico*, Roma-Bari, 1999) (Edinburgh University Press, 2007)

P. Cartledge, 'The second thoughts of Augustus on the Res Publica in 28/7 B.C.', *Hermathena* 119 (1975) 30–40

P. Ceauşescu, 'Das programmatische Edikt des Augustus (Suet. *Aug.* 28, 2) – eine missverstandene Stelle', *Rhein. Mus.* NF 124 (1981) 348–53

C. Cichorius, *Römische Studien: hist., epigr., literat. aus vier Jahrhundert Roms* (Leipzig, 1922)

M. E. Clark, 'Spes in the early imperial Cult: "The hope of Augustus"', *Numen* 30 (1983) 80–105

K. Clarke, 'In search of the author of Strabo's geography', *JRS* 87 (1997) 92–110

A. E. Cooley, *Res Gestae Divi Augusti: Text, Translation, and Commentary* (Cambridge, 2009)

M. Corbier, 'Male power and legitimacy through women: The *domus Augusta* under the Julio-Claudians', in R. Hawley and B. Levick, eds, *Women in Antiquity: New Assessments* (London, 1995) 178–93

T. J. Cornell *et al.*, eds, *The fragments of the Roman Historians* (Oxford, 2011)

H. M. Cotton and A. Yakobson, '*Arcanum imperii*: the powers of Augustus', in G. Clark and T. Rajak, *Philosophy and Power in the Graeco-Roman World. Essays in Honour of Miriam Griffin* (Oxford, 2002) 193–209

M. H. Crawford, *Roman Republican Coinage* (2 vols, Cambridge, 1974)

J. A. Crook, *Consilium Principis: Imperial Councils and Counsellors from Augustus to Diocletian* (Cambridge, 1955)

J. A. Crook, 'Political history, 30 BC to AD 14', and 'Augustus: power: authority, achievement', in *CAH* 10^2 (1996) 70–112 and 113–46

P. J. Cuff, 'The settlement of 23 BC: a note', *Riv. Fil.* 101 (1973) 466–77

L. J. Daly, 'The report of Varro Murena's death (Dio 54. 3. 5). Its mistranslation and his assassination', *Klio* 65 (1983) 245–61

L. J. Daly, 'Augustus and the murder of Varro Murena (*cos.* 23 BC)', *Klio* 66 (1984) 157–69

L. De Biasi and A. M. Ferrero, *Gli atti compiuti e i frammenti delle opere di Cesare Augusto Imperatore* (Turin, 2003) (*n.v.*)

S. Delle Donne, 'I *grammata* di Marco Antonio e Cassio Dione 52, 42, 8', in Traina *et al.* 2006, 39–127

H. Dessau, 'Livius und Augustus', *Hermes* 41 (1906) 142–51 (= Schmitthenner 1969, 1–11)

M. H. Dettenhofer, *Herrschaft und Widerstand im augusteischen Principat: Die Konkurrenz zwischen* res publica *und* domus Augusta. Historia Einzelschriften 140 (Stuttgart, 2000)

T. Drew-Bear and J. Scheid, 'La copie des *Res Gestae* d'Antioche de Pisidie', *ZPE* 154 (2005) 217–60

I. M. Le M. DuQuesnay, 'Horace and Maecenas: the propaganda value of *Sermones* 1', in Woodman and West 1984, 19–58

E. Dwyer, 'Augustus and the Capricorn', *MDAI(R)* 80 (1973) 59–67

W. Eck, 'Senatorial self-representation: developments in the Augustan Period', in Millar and Segal 1984, 129–68

W. Eck, *The Age of Augustus*, tr. by D. L. Schneider of *Augustus und seine Zeit*, (Munich, 1998), with new material by S. A. Takács (Oxford, 2003; 2nd edn, 2007)

W. Eck, L. Ruscu, C. Ciongradi, R. Ardevan, C. Roman and C. Găzdac, eds, *Das Senatus consultum de Cn. Pisone patre*. Vestigia 48 (Munich, 1996) (*SCdPp*)

W. Eder, 'Augustus and the power of tradition: the Augustan Principate as binding link between Republic and Empire', in Raaflaub and Toher 1990, 71–122

C. Edwards, *The Politics of Immorality in ancient Rome* (Cambridge, 1993)

A. Eich, 'Die Idealtypen "Propaganda" und "Repräsentation" als heueristische Mittel bei der Bestimmung gesellschaftlicher Konvergenzen und Divergenzen von moderne und römischer Keiserzeit, in G. Weber and M. Zimmermann, eds, *Propaganda – Selbstdarstellung – Repräsentation im röm. Kaiserreich des 1Jhs, n. Chr.* Hist. Einzelschr. 164 (Stuttgart, 2003) 41–84

J. Elsner, 'Cult and Sculpture: Sacrifice in the *Ara Pacis Augustae*", *JRS* 81 (1991) 50–61

W. Ensslin, 'Zu den *Res Gestae Divi Augusti*', *RM* NF 81 (1932) 335–65

V. Fadinger, *Die Begründung des Prinzipats. Quellenkritische und staatsrechtliche Untersuchungen zu Cassius Dio und der Parallel Überlieferung* (Berlin, 1969)

D. Favro, *The Urban Image of Augustan Rome* (Cambridge, 1996)

D. C. Feeney, '"*Si licet et fas est*": Ovid's *Fasti* and the problem of free speech under the Principate', in Powell 1992, 1–25

D. C. Feeney, *Caesar's Calendar: Ancient Time and the Beginnings of History*. Sather Classical Lectures 65 (Berkeley, CA, Los Angeles, CA, and London, 2007)

J.-L. Ferrary, 'A propos des pouvoirs d'Auguste', *CCG* 12 (2001) 101–54

H. I. Flower, *The Art of Forgetting: Disgrace and Oblivion in Roman Political Culture*. Studies in the History of Greece and Rome (Chapel Hill, NC, 2006)

P. Frisch, 'Zu den Elogien des Augustusforums', *ZPE* 39 (1980) 91–8

E. Gabba, *Appiano e la Storia delle Guerre civili* (Florence, 1956)

G. K. Galinsky, 'The Cipus episode in Ovid's *Metamorphoses* (15.565–621)', *TAPA* 98 (1967) 181–91

G. K. Galinsky, *Ovid's* Metamorphoses*: An Introduction to the Basic Aspects* (Berkeley, CA and Los Angeles, CA, 1975)

K. Galinsky, *Augustan Culture: an Interpretative Introduction* (Princeton, NJ, 1996)

H. Galsterer, 'A man, a book, and a method: Sir Ronald Syme's *Roman Revolution* after fifty years', in Raaflaub and Toher 1990, 1–20

C. Geertz, 'Ideology as a cultural system', in D. E. Apter, ed., *Ideology and Discontent* (New York, 1964) 47–76

J. Ginsburg, *Representing Agrippina: Constructions of Female Power in the Early Roman Empire*. Amer. Phil. Assoc., Amer. Class. Stud. 50 (Oxford, New York, 2006)

A. Giovannini, 'Les pouvoirs d'Auguste de 27 à 23 av. J.-C. Une relecture de l'ordonnance de Kymè de l'an 27 (IK 5, N° 17)', *ZPE* 124 (1999) 95–106

A. Giovannini, ed., *La Révolution romaine après Ronald Syme. Bilans et perspectives.* Entretiens Hardt 46 (Geneva, 2000)

K. M. Girardet, 'Per continuos annos decem (res gestae divi Augusti 7, 1). Zur Frage nach den Endtermin des Triumvirats', *Chiron* 25 (1995) 147–61

K. M. Girardet, 'Das Edikt des Imperator Caesar in Suetonius Augustusvita 28.2: politisches Programme und Publikationszeit', *ZPE* 131 (2000) 231–43 ['Edikt']

K. M. Girardet, 'Imperium «maius»: politische und verfassungsrechtliche Aspekt. Versuch einer Klärung', in Giovannini 2000, 167–236 ['*Imperium maius*']

J. González, 'The first oath *pro salute Augusti* found in Baetica', *ZPE* 72 (1988) 113–27

A. M. Gowing, *The Triumviral Narratives of Appian and Cassius Dio* (Ann Arbor, MI, 1992) ['*Narratives*']

A. M. Gowing, 'Lepidus, the proscriptions and the *Laudatio Turiae*', *Hist.* 41 (1992) 283–96 ['Lepidus']

I. Gradel, *Emperor Worship and Roman Religion* (Oxford, 2002)

E. W. Gray, 'The crisis in Rome at the beginning of 32', *Proc. Afr. Class. Assoc.* 13 (1975) 15–29

A. P. Gregory, "Powerful images": responses to portraits and the political uses of images in Rome', *JRA* 7 (1994) 80–99

J. Griffin, 'Augustan poetry and the life of luxury' *JRS* 66 (1976) 87–105

J. Griffin, 'Propertius and Antony', *JRS* 67 (1977) 17–26

J. Griffin, 'Augustus and the poets: "Caesar qui cogere posset"', in Millar and Segal 1984, 189–218

M. T. Griffin, '*Urbs Roma, Plebs* and *Princeps*', in L. Alexander, ed., *Images of Empire*. Journ. for Stud. of Old Testament, Suppl. 122 (Sheffield, 1991) 19–46

M. T. Griffin, 'Clementia after Caesar', in F. Cairns and E. Fantham, eds, *Caesar against Liberty? Perspectives on his Autocracy*. Papers of the Langord Latin Seminar 11, ARCA 43 (2003) 157–82

P. Grimal, 'Enée à Rome et le triomphe d'Octave', *REA* 53 (1951) 51–61

M. Gronewald, 'Eine neues Fragment der Laudatio Funebris des Augustus auf Agrippa', *ZPE* 52 (1983) 61f.

E. Gruen, 'The Imperial Policy of Augustus', in Raaflaub and Toher 1990, 395–416

E. Gruen, 'Expansion of the Empire' in *CAH* 10², (1996), 147–97

F. Van Haeperen, *Le Collège pontifical (3ème s. a. C.-4ème s. p.C.)*. Inst. hist. Belge de Rome, Études de Phil., d'Arch. et d'Hist. anc. 39 (Brussels-Rome, 2002)

J. P. Hallett, 'Perusine *glandes* and the changing image of Augustus', *AJAH* 2 (1977) 151–71

M. Hammond, 'The sincerity of Augustus', *HSCP* 69 (1965) 139–62

H. Hänlein-Schaefer, H., *Veneratio Augusti: Eine Studie zu den Tempeln des ersten römischen Kaisers* (Rome, 1985)

P. R. Hardie, *Vergil's* Aeneid*: Cosmos and Imperium* (Oxford, 1986)

J. Harries, *Cicero and the Jurists: from Citizens' Law to the Lawful State* (London, 2006)

S. J. Harrison, 'Augustus, the poets, and the *spolia opima*', *CQ* 39 (1989) 408–14

S. J. Harrison, 'The sword-belt of Pallas: moral symbolism and political ideology (*Aen.* 10. 495–505), in Stahl 1998, 223–42

L. Haselberger, Urbem Adornare: *Die Stadt Rom und ihre Gestaltumwandlung unter Augustus. Rome's Urban Metamorphosis under Augustus.* JRA Suppl. 64 (English tr. of the main text by A. Thein, Portsmouth, RI, 2007)

U. Hausmann, 'Zur Typologie und Ideologie des Augustusporträts', *ANRW* 2. 12. 2 (1981) 513–98

O. J. Hekster, 'Hercules, Omphale, and Octavian's Counter-propaganda', *Babesch* 79 (2004), 158–66 ['Omphale']

O. J. Hekster, 'The constraints of tradition: depictions of Hercules in Augustus' reign', in L. Ruscu *et al.*, eds, *Orbis Antiquus: Studia in Honorem I. Pisonis* (Cluj-Napoca, 2004) 235–41 ['Constraints']

O. J. Hekster, 'Captured in the gaze of power', in O. J. Hekster and R. Fowler, eds, *Imaginary Kings: Royal Images in the Ancient Near East, Greece and Rome.* Oriens et Occidens 11 (Stuttgart, 2005) 157–76

O. J. Hekster and J. Rich, 'Octavian and the thunderbolt: the Temple of Apollo Palatinus and Roman traditions of temple building', *CQ* 56 (2006) 149–68

E. A. Hemelrijk, 'Octavian and the introduction of public statues for women in Rome', *Athen.* 93 (2005) 311–17

G. Herbert-Brown, *Ovid and the* Fasti*: A Historical Study* (Oxford, 1994)

G. Herbert-Brown, ed., *Ovid's* Fasti. *Historical Readings at its Bimillennium* (Oxford, 2002)

P. Herrmann, *Der römische Kaisereid.* Hypomnemata 20 (Göttingen, 1968)

P. Herz, 'Kaiserfeste der Prinzipatszeit', *ANRW* 2. 16. 2 (1978) 1135–200

P. J. Heslin, 'Augustus, Domitian and the so-called Horologium Augusti', *JRS* 97 (2007) 1–20

A. Heuss, 'Zeitgeschichte als Ideologie. Bemerkungen zu Komposition und Gedankenführung der Res Gestae Divi Augusti', in E. Lefèvre, ed., *Monumentum Chiloniense. Studien zur augusteischen Zeit.* Kieler Festschrift für E. Burck zum 70. Geburtsdag (Amsterdam, 1975) 55–95 (= *Gesammelte Schriften* 2 (Stuttgart, 1995), 1319–59)

F. Hinard, *Les Proscriptions de la Rome républicaine. CÉFR* (Rome, 1985)

O. Hirschfeld, 'Augustus und sein Mimus vitae', *WS* 5 (1883) 116–19

W. Hoffmann, 'Der Wiedersprach von Tradition and Gegenwart im Tatenbericht des Augustus', *Gymnasium* 76 (1969) 17–33

A. J. Holladay, 'The election of magistrates in the early Principate', *Lat.* 37 (1978) 872–93

N. Horsfall, 'Some problems in the "Laudatio Turiae"', *BICS* 30 (1983) 85–98

N. Horsfall, *The Culture of the Roman* Plebs (London, 2003)

U. Hüttner: *Recusatio Imperii: Ein politisches Ritual zwischen Ethik und Taktik.* Spudasmata 93 (Hildesheim, etc., 2004)

H. U. Instinsky, 'Consensus universorum', *Hermes* 75 (1940) 265–78

S. A. Jameson, 'Chronology of the campaigns of Aelius Gallus and C. Petronius', *JRS* 58 (1968) 71–84

S. A. Jameson, '22 or 23', *Hist.* 18 (1969) 204–29

A. H. M. Jones, 'Imperial and senatorial jurisdiction in the early Principate', *Hist.* 3 (1954/5) 464–88 (= *Studies* 1960, 69–98)

A. H. M. Jones, *Studies in Roman Government and Law* (Oxford, 1960)

A. H. M. Jones, *Augustus* (London, 1970)

C. P. Jones, *Plutarch and Rome* (Oxford, 1971)

E. A. Judge, '"Respublica restituta": a modern illusion?', in J. A. S. Evans, ed., *Polis and Imperium: Studies in Honour of E. T. Salmon* (Toronto, 1974) 279–311

D. F. Kennedy, Review of Woodman and West 1984, *LCM* 9.10 (1984) 157–60

D. F. Kennedy, '"Augustan" and "Anti-Augustan". Reflections on Terms of Reference', in Powell 1992, 26–58

L. Keppie, *The Making of the Roman Army from Republic to Empire* (London, 1984)

D. Kienast, *Augustus: Prinzeps und Monarch* (Darmstadt, 1982)

D. Kienast, 'Augustus und Caesar', *Chiron* 31 (2001) 1–26

L. Koenen, 'Die "laudatio funebris" des Augustus für Agrippa auf einem neuen Papyrus (P. Colon. inv. nr. 4701)', *ZPE* 5 (1970) 217–83; 'Summum Fastigium: Zu der Laudatio Funebris des Augustus', 6 (1970) 239–43

W. Kolbe, 'Der zweite Triumvirat', *Hermes* 49 (1914) 273–95 (= Schmitthenner 1969, 12–37)

K. Kraft, 'S(enatus) C(onsulto)', *JNG* 12 (1962) 7–49 (= Schmitthenner 1969, 336–403)

K. Kraft, 'Der Sinn des Mausoleums des Augustus', *Hist.* 16 (1967) 189–206

D. Krömer, 'Textkritisches zu Augustus und Tiberius (*Res gestae* c. 34-Tac. *Ann.* 6, 30, 3)', *ZPE* 28 (1978) 127–43

A. Kuttner, *Dynasty and Empire in the Age of Augustus: The Case of the Boscoreale Cups* (Berkeley, CA, Los Angeles, CA, and London, 1995)

W. K. Lacey, 'Octavian in the Senate, January 27 BC', *JRS* 64 (1974) 176–94

W. K. Lacey, 'Augustus and the Senate: 23 BC', *Antichthon* 19 (1985) 57–68

W. K. Lacey, *Augustus and the Principate. The Evolution of the System.* ARCA Class. and Med. Texts, Papers and Monogr. 35 (Leeds, 1996)

U. Laffi, 'Poteri triumvirali e organi repubblicani', in A. Gara and D. Foraboschi, eds, *Il Triumvirato Costituente alla fine della Repubblica Romana. Scritti in Onore di Mario Attilio Levi*. Bibl. Athen. 20 (Como, 1993) 37–65

A. La Penna, *La Lirica civile di Orazio e l'ideologia del Principato* (Turin, 1963)

H. Last, 'On the "tribunicia potestas" of Augustus', *Rendiconti del Ist. Lombardo di Scienze e Lett.* 84 (Milan, 1951) 93–110

B. Levick, 'Imperial control of the elections under the early Principate: Commendatio, Suffragatio, and "Nominatio"', *Hist.* 16 (1967) 207–30

B. Levick, 'Tiberius' retirement to Rhodes in 6 BC', *Lat.* 31 (1972) 779–813.

B. Levick, 'Primus, Murena, and *Fides*', *Greece and Rome* 22 (1975), 156–63 ('Primus')

B. Levick, *Tiberius the Politician* (London, 1976; repr. with add. 1999)

B. Levick, 'The fall of Julia the Younger', *Lat.* 35 (1976) 301–39

B. Levick, 'Concordia at Rome', in R. A. G. Carson and C. M. Kraay, eds, *Scripta Nummaria Romana: Essays Presented to Humphrey Sutherland* (London, 1978) 217–33

B. Levick, 'Propaganda and the imperial coinage', *Antichthon* 16 (1982) 104–16

B. Levick, *Claudius* (London, 1990)

B. Levick, 'Augustan imperialism and the year 19 BC', in A. F. Basson and W. J. Dominik, eds, *Literature, Art, History: Studies on Classical Antiquity and Tradition in Honour of W. J. Henderson* (Frankfurt, 2003) 306–22

J. Linderski, 'Rome, Aphrodisias and the *Res Gestae*: the *Genera Militiae* and the status of Octavian', *JRS* 74 (1984) 74–80

J. Linderski, 'Julia in Regium', *ZPE* 72 (1988) 181–200

J. Linderski, 'Mommsen and Syme: law and power in the Principate of Augustus', in Raaflaub and Toher 1990, 42–53

J. A. Lobur, Consensus, Concordia, *and the Formation of Roman Imperial Ideology* (New York and London, 2007)

R. S. Lorsch Wildfang, 'The propaganda of omens: six dreams involving Augustus', in R. S. Lorsch Wildfang and J. Isager, eds, *Divination and Portents in the Roman World* Odense Univ. Class. Stud. 21 (Odense, 2000) 43–55

J. B. Lott, *The Neighbourhoods of Augustan Rome* (Cambridge, 2004)

T. J. Luce, 'Livy, Augustus, and the Forum Augustum', in Raaflaub and Toher 1990, 123–38

S. Lundström, *Ovids Metamorphosen und die Politik des Kaisers* (Uppsala, 1980)

R. O. A. M. Lyne, *Horace Behind the Public Poetry* (New Haven, CT, and London, 1995)

M. McDonnell, *Roman Manliness: Virtus and the Roman Republic* (Cambridge and New York, 2006)

A. G. McKay, '*Non enarrabile textum?* The shield of Aeneas and the triple triumph of 29 BC (*Aeneid* 8.630–728)', in Stahl 1998, 199–222

J. C. McKeown, 'Fabula proposito nulla tegenda meo', in Woodman and West 1984, 169–87

N. K. Mackie, '*Res publica restituta*. A Roman myth', in C. Deroux, ed., *Studies in Latin Literature and Roman History* 4 (Brussels, 1986) 303–40

N. K. Mackie, 'Ovid and the birth of maiestas', in Powell 1992, 83–97

A. Magdelain, *Auctoritas Principis* (Paris, 1947)

E. Malcovati, ed., *Imperatoris Caesaris Augusti Operum Fragmenta* Corp. Script. Latin. Paravianum (5th edn, Turin, 1969)

J.-Y. Maleuvre, 'Les *Odes romaines* d'Horace, ou un chef d'oeuvre ignoré de la cacozélie (presque) invisible', *Rev. belge de Phil. et d'Hist.* 73 (1995) 53–72

D. Mantovani, '*Leges et iura P(opuli) R(omani) Restituit.* Principe e Diritto in un Aureo do Ottaviano', *Ath.* 96 (2008) 5–51

B. Manuwald, *Cassius Dio und Augustus: Philologische Untersuchungen des Geschichtswerkes.* Palingenesia 14 (Wiesbaden, 1979)

Chr. Marek, 'Die Expedition des Aelius Gallus nach Arabien im Jahre 25 v. Chr.', *Chiron* 23 (1993) 121–36

C. Meier, 'C. Caesar Divi filius and the Formation of the Alternative in Rome', in Raaflaub and Toher 1990, 54–70

F. G. B. Millar, 'The Fiscus in the first two centuries', *JRS* 53 (1963) 29–42

F. G. B. Millar, *A Study of Cassius Dio* (Oxford, 1964)

F. G. B. Millar, 'Two Augustan notes', *CR* 18 (1968) 263–6

F. G. B. Millar, 'Triumvirate and Principate', *JRS* 63 (1973) 50–61

F. G. B. Millar, *The Emperor in the Roman World* (London, 1977, rev. 1991)

F. G. B. Millar, '"Senatorial" provinces: an institutionalized Ghost', *Anc. World* 20 (1989) 1–5

F. G. B. Millar and E. Segal, eds, *Caesar Augustus: Seven Aspects* (Oxford, 1984, 2nd edn, 1990)

K. Milnor, *Gender, Domesticity and the Age of Augustus: Inventing Private Life* (New York, 2005)

A. Momigliano, review of Syme 1939, *JRS* 30 (1940) 75–80

L. Morgan, 'The autopsy of C. Asinius Pollio', *JRS* 90 (2000) 51–69

A. Murdoch, *Rome's Greatest Defeat: Massacre in the Teutoburg Forest* (Stroud, 2006)

W. M. Murray and P. M. Petsas, *Octavian's Campsite Memorial for the Actian War.* *TAPA* 79. 4 (Philadelphia, PA, 1989)

C. Nappa, *Reading after Actium: Vergil's* Georgics, *Octavian, and Rome* (Ann Arbor, MI, 2005)

R. F. Newbold, 'Social tension at Rome in the early years of Tiberius' reign', *Athen.* NS 52 (1974) 110–43

C. Nicolet, 'Le Cens senatorial sous la République et sous Auguste', *JRS* 66 (1976) 20–38

C. Nicolet, *Space, Geography, and Politics in the Early Roman Empire* Jerome Lectures 19 (Ann Arbor, MI, 1990)

R. Nisbet, 'Horace's *Epodes* and history', in Woodman and West 1984, 1–18

E. Noè, *Commento storico a Cassio Dione LIII.* Bibl. di Athen. 22 (Como, 1994)

C. F. Noreña, 'The communication of the Emperor's virtues', *JRS* 91 (2001) 146–62

J. Osgood, *Caesar's Legacy: Civil War and the Emergence of the Roman Empire* (Cambridge, 2006)

S. E. Ostrow, 'The *Augustales* in the Augustan scheme', in Raaflaub and Toher 1990, 364–79

R. E. A. Palmer, 'Octavian's first attempt to restore the constitution (36 BC)', *Athen.* 56 (1978) 315–28

A. Parry, 'The two voices of Vergil's Aeneid', *Arion* 2.4 (1963) 66–80

C. Pelling, 'The Triumviral Period', in *CAH²* 10 (1996) 1–70

C. R. Phillips, 'Rethinking Augustan poetry', *Lat.* 42 (1983) 780–818

D. A. Phillips, 'The conspiracy of Egnatius Rufus and the election of suffect consuls under Augustus', *Hist.* 46 (1997) 103–12

J. B. Pighi, *De ludis saecularibus populi Romani Quiritium libri sex* (2nd edn, Amsterdam, 1965)

J. Pollini, 'Man or God: divine assimilation and imitation in the late Republic and early Principate', in Raaflaub and Toher 1990, 334–63

A. Powell, ed., *Roman Poetry and Propaganda in the Age of Augustus* (London, 1992)

A. Powell, 'The *Aeneid* and the embarrassments of Augustus', in Powell 1992, 141–74 ['*Aeneid*']

A. Powell and K. Welch, eds, *Sextus Pompeius* (Swansea, 2002)

A. von Premerstein, *Vom Werden und Wesen des Prinzipats. Abh. Der Bayer. Akad. Der Wiss., Phil.-hist. Abt.*, NF 15 (Munich, 1937)

S. R. F. Price, 'The place of religion: Rome in the early empire', *CAH²* 10 (1996) 812–47

N. Purcell, 'Rome and its development under Augustus and his successors', *CAH²* 10 (1996) 782–811

M. C. J. Putnam, 'Horace, *Carm.* 2. 9: Augustus and the ambiguities of encomium', in Raaflaub and Toher 1990, 212–38

M. C. J. Putnam, *Virgil's Epic Designs: Ekphrasis in the Aeneid* (New Haven, CI and London, 1998)

K. A. Raaflaub and M. Toher, eds, *Between Republic and Empire: Interpretations of Augustus and his Principate* (Berkeley, CA, 1990)

K. A. Raaflaub and L. J. Samons II, 'Opposition to Augustus', in Raaflaub and Toher 1990, 417–54

E. S. Ramage, *The Nature and Purpose of Augustus' 'Res Gestae'*, Hist. Einzelschr. 54 (Stuttgart, 1987)

E. S. Ramage, 'The date of Augustus' Res Gestae', *Chiron* 18 (1988) 71–82

J. T. Ramsey, 'Mark Antony's judiciary reform and its revival under the triumvirs', *JRS* 95 (2005) 1–37

J. T. Ramsey and A. L. Licht, *The Comet of 44 BC and Caesar's Funeral Games.* Amer. Phil. Assoc., Amer. Class. Stud. 39 (Atlanta, GA, 1997)

E. D. Rawson, '*Discrimina ordinum* in the *Lex Julia theatralis*', *PBSR* 55 (1987) 83–114

J. A. Rea, *Legendary Rome: Myth, Monuments, and Memory on the Palatine and Capitoline* (London, 2007)

P. Rehak, in J. G. Younger, ed., *Imperium and Cosmos: Augustus and the Northern Campus Martius* (Madison, WI, 2006)

M. Reinhold and P. M. Swan, 'Cassius Dio's assessment of Augustus', in Raaflaub and Toher 1990, 156–73

J. W. Rich, 'Agrippa and the nobles: a note on Dio, 54. 29. 6', *LCM* 5 (1980) 217–21

J. W. Rich, *Cassius Dio, the Augustan Settlement (Roman History 53–55.9)* ed. with translation and commentary (Warminster, 1990)

J. W. Rich, 'Dio on Augustus', in A. Cameron, ed., *History as Text. The Writing of Ancient History* (Chapel Hill, NC, 1990) 87–110

J. W. Rich, 'Augustus and the *spolia opima*', *Chiron* 26 (1996) 85–127

J. W. Rich, 'Augustus' Parthian honours, the temple of Mars Ultor, and the Arch in the Forum Romanum', *PBSR* 66 (1998) 71–128

J. W. Rich and J. H. C. Williams, '*Leges et ivra P. R. Restitvit*: A new Aureus of Octavian and the Settlement of 28–27 BC', *NC* 159 (1999) 169–213

R. T. Ridley, *The Emperor's Retrospect. Augustus'* res gestae *in Epigraphy, Historiography and Commentary*. Studia Hellenistica 39 (Leuven-Dudley, MA, 2003)

J.-M. Roddaz, 'Un Thème de la "Propagande" augustéenne: L'image populaire d'Agrippa', *MÉFRA* 92 (1980) 947–56

J.-M. Roddaz, *Marcus Agrippa*, BÉFAR 253 (Rome, 1984)

G. D. Rowe, *Princes and Political Cultures: The New Tiberian Senatorial Decrees* (Ann Arbor, MI, 2002)

G. D. Rowe, review of Ridley 2003, *JRS* 97 (2007) 273f.

M. Royo, Domus imperatoriae: *Topographie, formation et imaginaire des palais impéri-aux du Palatin (IIe siècle av. J.-C. – Ier siècle ap.J.-C.)* BÉFAR 303 (Rome, 1999)

S. Rutledge, *Imperial Inquisitions. Prosecutors and Informants from Tiberius to Domitian* (London and New York, 2001)

M. Santirocco, 'Horace and Augustan ideology', *Arethusa* 28 (1995) 225–43

P. Sattler, 'Julia und Tiberius: Beiträge zur römischen Innenpolitik zwischen den Jahren 12 vor und 2 n. Chr.', *Studien aus dem Gebiet der alten Geschichte* (Wiesbaden, 1962) 1–36 (= Schmitthenner 1969, 486–530) ['Julia']

P. Sattler, *Augustus und der Senat: Untersuchungen zur römischen Innenpolitik zwis-chen 30 und 17 v. Chr.* (Göttingen, 1969) ['Senat']

J. Scheid, *Les Frères arvales, Recrutement et origine sociale sous les empereurs julio-claudiens*. Bibl. de l'École des hautes Études, Sect. des Science rel. 77 (Paris, 1975)

W. Schmitthenner, 'Augustus' spanischer Feldzug und der Kampf um den Prinzipat', *Hist.* 11 (1962) 29–85 (= Schmitthenner 1969, 404–85)

W. Schmitthenner, ed., *Augustus*. Wege der Forschung 128 (Darmstadt, 1969)

W. Schmitthenner, *Oktavian und das Testament Caesars, eine Untersuchung zu den politischen Anfängen des Augustus.* Zetemata 4 (Munich, 1952, 2nd edn, 1973)

B. Schnegg-Kohler, *Die augusteischen Säkularspiele* (Munich, 2002)

L. Schumacher, 'Oktavian und das Testament Caesars', *ZSS* 116 (1999) 49–70

S. von Schnurbein, 'Augustus in Germany and the new "Town" at Waldgirmes', *JRA* 16 (2003) 93–107

K. Scott, 'The identification of Augustus with Romulus-Quirinus', *TAPA* 56 (1925) 82–105

R. Seager, 'Horace and Augustus: poetry and politics', in N. Rudd, *Horace 2000: A Celebration. Essays for the Millenium* (London, 1993) 23–40

B. Severy, *Augustus and the Family at the Birth of the Roman Empire* (New York and London, 2000)

N. Shumate, 'Gender and nationalism in Horace's "Roman" odes (*Odes* 3.2, 3.5, 3.6)', *Helios* 32. 1 (2005) 81–107

E. Simon, *Ara Pacis Augustae* (Tübingen, 1967)

C. J. Simpson, 'The date of the dedication of the temple of Mars Ultor', *JRS* 67 (1977) 91–94

C. J. Simpson, 'Agrippa's rejection of a triumph in 19 BC', *LCM* 16. 9 (1991) 137f.

C. J. Simpson, '"*Reddita omnis provincia*": Ratification by the people in January, 27 B.C.', in C. Deroux, ed., *Studies in Latin Literature and Roman History* 7 (Brussels 1994) 297–309

C. J. Simpson, 'Imp. Caesar Divi filius: his second imperatorial acclamation and the evolution of an allegedly "exorbitant" name', *Athen.* NS 86 (1998) 419–37

C. J. Simpson, 'Why March? Hereditary Julian *Pontifices Maximi* and the Date of Julius Caesar's Assassination', *Lat.* 66 (2007) 327–35

R. R. R. Smith, 'Typology and diversity in the portraits of Augustus', *JRA* 9 (1996) 30–47

P. Southern, *Augustus* (London and New York, 1998)

H.-P. Stahl, *Propertius' 'Love' and 'War': Individual and State under Augustus* (Berkeley, CA, 1985)

H.-P. Stahl, ed., '*Vergil's Aeneid: Augustan Epic and Political Context* (London, 1998)

T. Stevenson, 'Roman coins and refusals of the title *Pater patriae*', *NC* 167 (2007) 119–42

D. L. Stockton, 'Primus and Murena', *Hist.* 14 (1965) 18–40

M. Strothmann, *Augustus – Vater der res publica. Zur Funktion der drei Begriffe restitutio – saeculum – pater patriae im augusteischen Principat* (Stuttgart, 2000)

W. Suerbaum, 'Merkwürdige Geburtstage', *Chiron* 10 (1980) 327–55

G. Sumi, 'Civil war, women and spectacle in the Triumviral Period', *The Anc. World* 35 (2004) 196–206

G. V. Sumner, 'The truth about Velleius Paterculus: Prolegomena', *HSCP* 74 (1970) 257–97

G. V. Sumner, 'Varrones Murenae', *HSCP* 82 (1978) 187–95

C. H. V. Sutherland, *Coinage in Roman Imperial Policy* (London, 1951)

C. H. V. Sutherland, *The Emperor and the Coinage. Julio-Claudian Studies* (London, 1976)

M. Swan, 'The consular fasti of 23 BC and the conspiracy of Varro Murena', HSCP 71 (1967) 235–47

P. M. Swan, *The Augustan Succcession. An Historical Commentary on Cassius Dio's Roman History Books 55–56 (9 B.C.–A.D. 14)*. Amer. Phil. Assoc., Amer. Class. Stud. 47 (Oxford and New York, 2004)

R. Syme, *The Roman Revolution* (Oxford, 1939)

R. Syme, Review of H. Siber, *Das Führeramt des Augustus* (Leipzig, 1940) in *JRS* 36 (1946) 149–58 = *RP* 1, 181–96

R. Syme, *Tacitus* (2 vols, Oxford, 1958) [*Tac.*]

R. Syme, 'Imperator Caesar: a study in imperial nomenclature', *Hist.* 7 (1958), 172–88 = *Roman Papers* 1 (Oxford, 1979), 361–7 ['Imperator']

R. Syme, *History in Ovid* (Oxford, 1978) [*Ovid*]

R. Syme, 'Mendacity in Velleius', *AJP* 99 (1978) 45–63 = *RP* 3 (1984) 1090–104 ['Mendacity']

R. Syme, 'Problems about Janus', *AJP* 100 (1979) 188–212 = *RP* 3 (1984) 1179–97

R. Syme, 'History and language at Rome', *Diogenes* 85 (1974) 1–11 = *RP* 3 (1984) 953–61

R. Syme, *The Augustan Aristocracy* (Oxford, 1986)

R. Syme, 'Neglected children on the *Ara Pacis*', *AJA* 88 (1984) 583–9 (= *RP* 4 (1988) 418–30) ['Children']

R. Syme, 'Janus and Parthia in Horace', in J. Diggle *et al.*, *Studies in Latin Literature and its Tradition in Honour of C. O. Brink. PCPS*, Suppl. Vol. 15 (1989) 13–24 (= *RP* 6 (1991) 441–50)

R. J. A. Talbert, *The Senate of Imperial Rome* (Princeton, NJ, 1984)

R. J. A. Talbert, 'The Senate', in *CAH* 10² (Cambridge, 1996) 324–36

L. R. Taylor, 'New light on the history of the Secular Games', *AJP* 55 (1934) 100–20

L. R. Taylor, *The Divinity of the Roman Emperor*, TAPA Philological Monogr. 1 (Middletown, CO, 1941)

R. F. Thomas, *Virgil and the Augustan Reception* (Cambridge, 2001)

M. Toher, 'The date of Nicolaus' "*Bíos Kaísaros*"', *GRBS* 26 (1985) 199–206

M. Toher, 'Augustus and the evolution of Roman historiography', in Raaflaub and Toher 1990, 139–54

M. Torelli, *Typology and Structure of Roman Historical Reliefs*. Jerome Lectures 14 (Ann Arbor, MI, 1992)

M. Torelli, 'Roman Art, 43 BC to AD 69', in *CAH* ² 10 (1996) 930–58

G. Townend, 'Literature and Society', in *CAH* ² 10 (1996) 905–29

G. Traina, with B. Tisé and P. Buongiorno, eds, *Studi sull'età di Marco Antonio*. Rudiae 18 (Lecce, 2006)

H. Tränkle, 'Zu Cremutius Cordus Fr. 4 Peter', *Mus. Helv.* 37 (1980) 231–41

S. M. Treggiari, 'Social Status and Social Legislation', in $CAH^2$10 (1996) 873–904

F. De Visscher, 'Les Pouvoirs d'Octavien en 32 av. J.-C.', *Nouvelles Et. de Droit romain public et privé* (Milan, 1949) 1–26 (= [German] Schmitthenner 1969, 199–229)

S. Walker, 'The moral museum: Augustus and the City of Rome', in J. Coulston and H. Dodge, eds, *Ancient Rome: the Architecture of the Eternal City*. O. U.'School of Archaeology Mon. 54 (Oxford, 2000) 61–75

A. Wallace-Hadrill, 'Family and inheritance in the Augustan marriage laws', *PCPS* 207 (1981) 58–80

A. Wallace-Hadrill, 'The Golden Age and sin in Augustan ideology', *Past and Present* 95 (1982) 19–36 ['Sin']

A. Wallace-Hadrill, 'Civilis Princeps: between citizen and king', *JRS* 72 (1982) 32–48 ['Civilis']

A. Wallace-Hadrill, *Suetonius: the Scholar and his Caesars* (London, 1983)

A. Wallace-Hadrill, 'Image and authority in the coinage of Augustus', *JRS* 76 (1986) 76–87

A. Wallace-Hadrill, 'Time for Augustus: Ovid, Augustus, and the Fasti', in Whitby *et al.* 1987, 221–30

A. Wallace-Hadrill, 'The imperial court', in CAH 10^2 (1996) 283–308

P. Wallmann, 'Zur Zusammensetzung und Haltung des Senats im Jahre 32 v. Chr.', *Hist.* 25 (1976) 305–12

P. Wallmann, *Triumviri rei publicae constituendae. Untersuchungen zur politischen Propaganda im Zweiten Triumvirat (43–30 v. Chr.)*. Europ. Hochschulschriften 3. Geschichte u. ihre Hilfswissenschaften 383 (Frankfurt, 1989)

D. Wardle, 'Agrippa's refusal of a triumph in 19 BC', *Antichthon* 28 (1994) 58–64

D. Wardle, '"The Sainted Julius": Valerius Maximus and the Dictator', *CP* 92 (1997) 323–45

D. Wardle, 'Valerius Maximus on the *Domus Augusta*, Augustus, and Tiberius', *CQ* 50 (2000) 479–93

D. Wardle, 'Unimpeachable sponsors of imperial autocracy, or Augustus' Dream Team (Suetonius *Divus Augustus* 94.8–9 and Dio Cassius 45. 2. 2–4)', *Antichthon* 39 (2005) 29–47 ['Sponsors']

D. Wardle, 'Suetonius and Augustus' "programmatic edict"', *Rhein. Mus.* NF 148 (2005) 181–201 ['Edict']

D. Wardle, 'A perfect send-off: Suetonius and the dying art of Augustus (Suetonius, *Aug.* 99)', *Mnem.* 60 (2007) 443–63

T. H. Watkins, *L. Munatius Plancus. Serving and Surviving in the Roman Revolution*. Illinois Class. Stud., Suppl. 7 (Atlanta, GA, 1997)

L. Watson, '*Epode* 9, or The art of falsehood', in Whitby *et al.* 1987, 119–29

W. Weber, *Princeps. Studien zur Geschichte des Augustus*. 1 (Stuttgart, 1936)

E. J. Weinrib, 'The family connections of M. Livius Drusus Libo', *HSCP* 72 (1968) 247–78

S. Weinstock, *Divus Julius* (Oxford, 1971)

T. S. Welch, *The Elegiac Cityscape: Propertius and the Meaning of Roman Monuments* (Columbus, OH, 2005)

K.-W. Welwei, 'Augustus als *vindex libertatis*. Freiheitsideologie und Propaganda im frühen Prinzipat', in M. Meier and M. Strothmann, Res publica *und* imperium: *Kleine Schriften zur römischen Geschichte* (Stuttgart, 2004) 217–29

D. West, 'The end and the meaning (*Aen.* 12. 791–842)', in Stahl 1998, 303–18

M. Whitby, P. Hardie and M. Whitby, Homo Viator*: Classical Essays for John Bramble* (Bristol, 1987)

P. White, *Promised Verse: Poetry in the Society of Augustan Rome* (Cambridge, 1993)

P. White, 'Julius Caesar and the publication of Acta in late Republican Rome', *Chiron* 27 (1997) 73–84

T. Wiedemann, 'The political background to Ovid's *Tristia* 2', *CQ* NS 25 (1975) 264–71

U. Wilcken, 'Der angeblich Staatstreich Octavians im Jahre 32 v. Chr.', *Sitzungsber. der Preussisch. Akad. der Wissenschaft.* Phil.-hist. Kl. 90 (1925) 10, 66–87 (= Schmitthenner 1969, 38–97)

G. Williams, *Change and Decline: Roman Literature in the Early Empire.* Sather Class. Lect. 45 (Berkeley, CA, 1978)

G. W. Williams, 'Did Maecenas "Fall from favor"? Augustan Literary Patronage', in Raaflaub and Toher 1990, 258–75

T. P. Wiseman, *New Men in the Roman Senate* (Oxford, 1971)

T. P. Wiseman, 'Cybele, Virgil and Augustus', in Woodman and West 1984, 117–28

E. K. H. Wistrand. *The So-called 'Laudatio Turiae'. Introduction, Text, Commentary.* Stud. Gr. et Lat. Goth. 34. Acta Univ. Goth. (Gothenburg, 1976)

A. J. Woodman, *Velleius Paterculus: The Tiberian Narrative (2.94–131)* and the *Caesarian and Augustan Narrative (2.41–93).* Cambridge Classical Texts and Commentaries 19 and 25 (Cambridge, 1977 and 1983)

A. J. Woodman and D. West, eds, *Poetry and Politics in the Age of Augustus* (Cambridge, 1984) 178–84

A. Wright, 'Velleius Paterculus and L. Munatius Plancus', *CP* 97 (2002) 178–84

M. Wyke, 'Augustan Cleopatras: female power and poetic authority', in Powell 1992, 98–140

L. Yarrow, *Historiography at the end of the Republic: Provincial Perspectives on Roman Rule* (New York, 2006)

Z. Yavetz, 'The *Res Gestae* and Augustus' public image', in Millar and Segal 1984, 1–36

Z. Yavetz, 'The personality of Augustus: reflections on Syme's *Roman Revolution*', in Raaflaub and Toher 1990, 21–41

K. L. Zachos, 'Nikopolis', *JRA* 16 (2003) 93–107

P. Zanker, *The Power of Images in the Age of Augustus*, tr. A. Shapiro. Jerome Lectures 16 (Ann Arbor, MI, 1988)

G. Zecchini, 'Il cognomen "Augustus"', *Acta class. Univ. Scientiarum Debreceniensis* 32 (1996) 129–35

Index of Peoples and Places

Index of Persons Human and Divine

Romans, except emperors and their close kin and eminent literary men, are registered under their gentile names. B. = brother, d. daughter, m. mother, n. nephew, s. son, u. uncle, w. wife; *cos.* = consul.

General Index

See also Glossary of Ancient Terms